Dynamic HTML
Weekend Crash Course™

Dave Taylor

Hungry Minds™

Best-Selling Books • Digital Downloads • e-Books • Answer Networks • e-Newsletters • Branded Web Sites • e-Learning

Cleveland, OH • Indianapolis, IN • New York, NY

Dynamic HTML Weekend Crash Course™
Published by
Hungry Minds, Inc.
909 Third Avenue
New York, NY 10022
www.hungryminds.com

Library of Congress Control Number: 2001092905
ISBN: 0-7645-4890-5
Printed in the United States of America
10 9 8 7 6 5 4 3 2 1
1B/SZ/RQ/QR/IN
Distributed in the United States by
Hungry Minds, Inc.
Distributed by CDG Books Canada Inc. for Canada; by Transworld Publishers Limited in the United Kingdom; by IDG Norge Books for Norway; by IDG Sweden Books for Sweden; by IDG Books Australia Publishing Corporation Pty. Ltd. for Australia and New Zealand; by TransQuest Publishers Pte Ltd. for Singapore, Malaysia, Thailand, Indonesia, and Hong Kong; by Gotop Information Inc. for Taiwan; by ICG Muse, Inc. for Japan; by Intersoft for South Africa; by Eyrolles for France; by International Thomson Publishing for Germany, Austria, and Switzerland; by Distribuidora Cuspide for Argentina; by LR International for Brazil; by Galileo Libros for Chile; by Ediciones ZETA S.C.R. Ltda. for Peru; by WS Computer Publishing Corporation, Inc., for the Philippines; by Contemporanea de Ediciones for Venezuela; by Express Computer Distributors for the Caribbean and West Indies; by Micronesia Media Distributor, Inc. for Micronesia; by Chips Computadoras S.A. de C.V. for Mexico; by Editorial Norma de Panama S.A. for Panama; by American Bookshops for Finland.

For general information on Hungry Minds' products and services please contact our Customer Care department within the U.S. at 800-762-2974, outside the U.S. at 317-572-3993 or fax 317-572-4002.

For sales inquiries and reseller information, including discounts, premium and bulk quantity sales, and foreign-language translations, please contact our Customer Care department at 800-434-3422, fax 317-572-4002 or write to Hungry Minds, Inc., Attn: Customer Care Department, 10475 Crosspoint Boulevard, Indianapolis, IN 46256.

For information on licensing foreign or domestic rights, please contact our Sub-Rights Customer Care department at 212-884-5000.

For information on using Hungry Minds' products and services in the classroom or for ordering examination copies, please contact our Educational Sales department at 800-434-2086 or fax 317-572-4005.

For press review copies, author interviews, or other publicity information, please contact our Public Relations department at 317-572-3168 or fax 317-572-4168.

For authorization to photocopy items for corporate, personal, or educational use, please contact Copyright Clearance Center, 222 Rosewood Drive, Danvers, MA 01923, or fax 978-750-4470.

 **Hungry Minds**™ is a trademark of Hungry Minds, Inc.

About the Author

Dave Taylor has been involved with the development of the Internet and Web for more than 20 years. The author of the international bestseller *Creating Cool HTML 4 Web Pages* (published by Hungry Minds, Inc.), he's also written three other books of note: *Teach Yourself Unix in 24 Hours* (published by Sams.Net), *The eAuction Insider* (published by Osborne/McGraw-Hill), and *Global Software* (published by Springer-Verlag). Dave also worked as a research scientist at Hewlett-Packard's Palo Alto R&D Laboratory and founded three different startups: The Internet Mall, iTrack.com, and Growing Ventures, Inc. He has a bachelor's degree in Computer Science, a master's degree in Educational Computing, and is working on a distance-learning MBA. Although he's frequently busy toiling over a complex Web-site solution, advising entrepreneurs on startup strategies, and answering his overflowing e-mailbox, Dave much prefers to play with his two delightful kids and wonderful wife.

Credits

Acquisitions Editor
Carol Sheehan

Project Editor
Sharon Nash

Technical Editor
Michele Davis

Copy Editor
Bill Barton

Editorial Assistant
Cordelia Heaney

Editorial Manager
Colleen Totz

Senior Vice President, Technical Publishing
Richard Swadley

Vice President and Publisher
Joseph B. Wikert

Project Coordinator
Maridee Ennis

Graphics and Production Specialists
Joyce Haughey
Betty Schulte
Brian Torwelle
Erin Zeltner

Quality Control Technicians
John Greenough
Andy Hollandbeck
Marianne Santy

Proofreading and Indexing
TECHBOOKS Production Services

I dedicate this book to my lovely wife, Linda,
and my two darling children, Ashley and Gareth.
We make quite a team.

Preface

Thanks for picking up this book! I know how confusing a visit to a bookstore can be — and even if you opt for a Web bookstore, figuring out which of the hundreds of different technical books really meet your needs is still bewildering. If you really want to learn how to build cool sites and add exciting and compelling dynamic content to your existing pages, the good news is that you picked up the right book.

I've been building Web sites both professionally and as a hobby for many years, and I'm well aware of how hard figuring out the alphabet-soup terms of modern Web development often is. Whether you're just reorganizing the site for your local community organization or rethinking the underlying technologies powering your corporate behemoth, the same questions come up again and again. Should you use Cascading Style Sheets? Should you add JavaScript? Should you build the site to a specific Web browser or technology?

I address all these topics in depth as I take you through the two core topics that make up Dynamic HTML: Cascading Style Sheets, and JavaScript. I cover a lot more, too, but those two subjects are the heart and soul of this book.

It's Up to Date

A number of different books are available that purport to cover Dynamic HTML in some fashion or other, but seeing how much they cover CSS (if at all) and how much they cover JavaScript is often enlightening. Now, of the remaining few books, how many also ensure that their scripts and styles work with Netscape 6 and Internet Explorer 6, the latest and most standards-compliant browsers available?

One of the best reasons to use this book (instead of one of those other books) as your guide to learning about Dynamic HTML is that it's completely up to date.

Who Should Read This Book

If you want to learn about Dynamic HTML without having to wade through a reference work that exhaustively lists every property of every element of every object of everything associated with the document object model, then this book is the one for you.

If you want to get down to the nitty-gritty but still find lots of explanation — covering not only *what* you need to do but *why* — this book is for you.

If you want examples of the sort that I explain in detail — rather than those that someone glibly presents without giving you much chance to learn how to build your own solutions — then this book, again, is that one you want.

If you want to *enjoy* learning about a new and cutting-edge Web technology, this book — written by a popular author (ahem!) with a great sense of humor — is definitely for you. (I know I have a great sense of humor because my mom told me for years that I *had* no sense of humor. *Sorry, Mom!*)

If you want to find a CD-ROM full of cut-and-paste JavaScript that you can drop onto your site without using any brain cells in the process, well, this book is for you, too — but you really do want to use that gray matter to learn how to build your own solutions, too!

If you're a student, teacher, or anyone else in an educational setting, you're sure to find this book particularly good. I cover the material in straightforward sections with quiz questions at the end of each chapter — and you get an accompanying CD-ROM that includes all examples and other material to boot. (What a bargain!)

What's In the Book

Dynamic HTML Weekend Crash Course covers two major topics in great depth: Cascading Style Sheets and JavaScript. CSS enable you to quickly turn dull and pedestrian Web pages — even entire sites — into gorgeous online material with remarkably little effort. JavaScript adds the *dynamic* to Dynamic HTML, offering a wide range of interactive fundamentals within a modern and sophisticated programming language that borrows the best of Java, C, and Perl — while adding many of its own elements. Better yet, JavaScript is easy to learn and fun to use. You can start with small, simple scripts and slowly work your way up to quite complex solutions.

I do expect you to have a basic knowledge of HyperText Markup Language (HTML), including the knowledge of how to create your own Web pages on your computer and test them in your favorite browser. If you're not sure about HTML, I recommend my book *Creating Cool HTML 4 Web Pages* as a breezy and highly informative introduction to the topic.

 **One important note: I'm writing this book for people who use the most recent Web browser available. If you don't use at least Microsoft Internet Explorer 5.5 or Netscape 6, you need to upgrade. IE5.5 is available on this book's CD-ROM, and you can download N6 from the Netscape Web site at (www.netscape.com/).**

What really doesn't matter to me is what kind of computer you use. I'm just about completely noncommittal in this regard, switching from Mac to Windows to Unix on a daily basis. The book reflects a similar lack of bias, although you can see that the screen shots all come from my Macintosh. Why? First, the Mac is my primary computer, but second, the 5.5 version of Microsoft Internet Explorer for the Macintosh is the best browser available today. What's frustrating is how different it is from IE5.5 for Windows. But I talk about that in Session 4.

Organization and Presentation

I organize this book into 30 sessions, each requiring approximately 30 minutes. They divide up as follows:

- **Friday evening.** Sessions 1 through 4. Reading time: 2 hours.
- **Saturday morning.** Sessions 5 through 10. Reading time: 3 hours.
- **Saturday afternoon.** Sessions 11 through 16. Reading time: 3 hours.
- **Saturday evening.** Sessions 17 through 20. Reading time: 2 hours.
- **Sunday morning.** Sessions 21 through 26. Reading time: 3 hours.
- **Sunday afternoon.** Sessions 27 through 30. Reading time: 2 hours.

At the end of each session, I present you with questions to check your progress.

As you quickly see, I sprinkle the text with the following icons to catch your attention and help you quickly find the information you seek:

The "minutes to go" icons mark your progress in the session. They come in 30-, 20-, and 10-minute varieties. (I also use a Done icon to tell you that the session is complete, except for a Review and the Quiz.)

30 Min.
To Go

The Tip icons offer suggestions on style and mention shortcuts that can save programming effort.

The Note icons highlight incidental or technical information that clarifies and expands the discussion.

The CD-ROM icon refers to material that I furnish on the book's CD. Use it to find electronic versions of programs and software elements that I mention in the text. Just about everything on the CD-ROM I also duplicate on the book's Web site (www.intuitive.com/dhtml/), in case you lose the disc or are borrowing this book from the library.

The Online Dimension

In the dynamic world of Web development, actually *writing a book* about Dynamic HTML is almost an exercise in futility. Everything changes so fast that you should probably have David Bowie's "Changes" playing in the background just to remind you of that reality. Fortunately, the experts at Hungry Minds have fast publishing down to a science, and this book's gone from words on my computer to pages in your hand in record time.

Nonetheless, things change.

To keep you up to date with Dynamic HTML and the developments in this area, I created a Web site just for readers, and I encourage you to visit it during your *Weekend Crash Course*.

The official Web site for this book is www.intuitive.com/dhtml/.

In addition, I truly enjoy receiving e-mail from readers, whether kudos or brickbats, so please feel free to contact me at the following address if you're so inclined: taylor@intuitive.com.

I hope you find that this book meets your needs and is enjoyable to boot!

Acknowledgments

A number of different people have helped me as I've written this book and developed all the many examples herein. Gideon Shaanan more than once helped me rethink a problem and illuminate the solution. Jon Stephens, frequent contributor to Builder.com's Builder Buzz, solved a puzzle I had, and Jeff Dumo of Design Reactor offered some good advice regarding cascading-menu solutions. Carol Sheehan and Sharon Nash, my editorial partners at Hungry Minds, have been a delight to work with and are jointly responsible for the speed and quality of this manuscript. You're also benefiting from the painstaking editorial heavy lifting work of Bill Barton and the terrific work that Michele Davis, the Technical Editor, contributed in testing each example and URL before publication.

Finally, I also want to acknowledge the wonderful support of my wife Linda, who's learned to accept my never-ending late-night writing sessions and act quite interested in my latest DHTML examples and developments, however obscure.

My Platform: In case you're interested in the proverbial "man behind the curtain," I wrote the first half of this book on my Mac G4 tower system, using Microsoft Office, with BBEdit as my development editor and GraphicConverter and Photoshop trading off as graphical development systems. The second half I wrote on my PowerBook system while on summer vacation at the scenic Lake of the Ozarks in central Missouri. ("You call this a summer vacation?") Through the wonder of modern telecommunications, I experienced nary a hiccup with the relocation and change in hardware. Go Mac!

Contents at a Glance

Contents

☑ **Friday**

☐ Saturday

☐ Sunday

PART

I

Friday
Evening

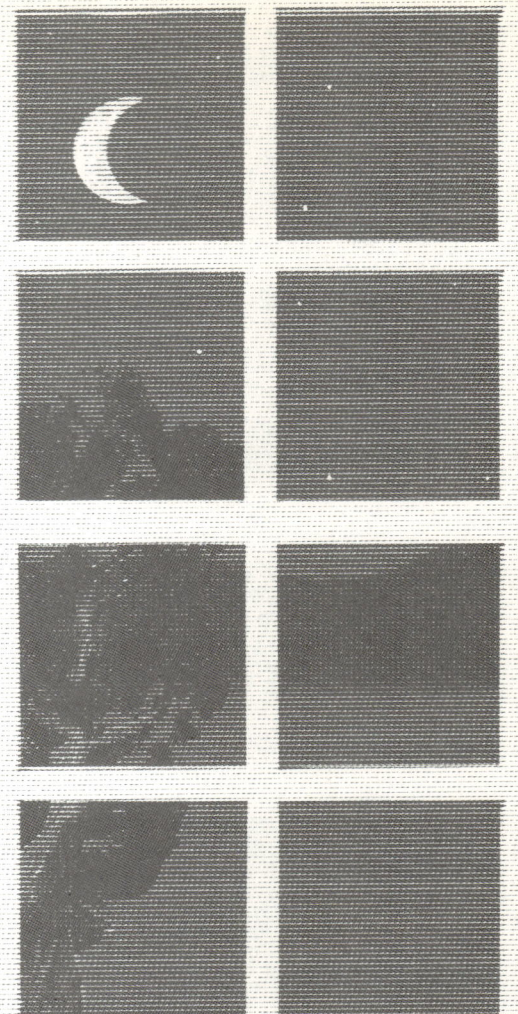

SESSION

1

DHTML and How It Relates to HTML

Session Checklist

✔ Form versus content

✔ Why use style sheets?

✔ XML and alphabet soup

✔ Scripting with JavaScript/Visual Basic Script

**30 Min.
To Go**

Hello and welcome aboard! You've had a tough week at work, and as you settle down to drive home on Friday afternoon, you remember — with a sinking feeling — that Monday morning, bright and early, you must demonstrate your expertise in the mysterious area of Dynamic HTML. If so, you've come to the right place! If not, this is still going to be a great way for you to learn DHTML.

In fact, even if you're already an expert on some flavor of Dynamic HTML, this book can help you learn more and understand how all the pieces of DHTML fit together.

A Philosophy of Design

I want to start by stating my philosophy of advanced Web page design to ensure that you understand the underpinnings of this book: I believe that having an attractive and functional Web site is almost always more important than having a graphical interaction tour-de-force. If I must pick between something amazing, sexy, and eye-popping yet doesn't work for 75 percent of the people who come to the site and something more pedestrian and less inter-active that works for 95 percent of the visitors, I choose the latter every time.

Having said that, my goal with this Weekend Crash Course is to explain how you can add sophisticated layout and formatting to Web pages in such a way that they still function gracefully on older, less capable browsers. That way, you get the best of both worlds: If your visitors are using the latest version of browser with all the plug-in bells-and-whistles, they get an exciting interactive experience. If they're a bit earlier in the evolution of browser applications (say, for example, that they're using WebTV), they still find a functional site that enables them to get around and find the material that they seek.

I think that explaining this philosophy up front is very important, because too many of the sophisticated sites I see on the Web are completely broken for browsers, rendering material incorrectly, and OS configurations other than the one or two that the designer used during the development process. I've even visited sites run by savvy Internet companies — sites that purport to be developer resources — that are just blank pages if I don't have exactly the configuration of browser they require. And to me, that's just bad design and bad coding.

One more thing before you bend your head and brace yourself against the buffeting winds of knowledge: This book has an official Web site (at www.intuitive.com/dhtml/) that includes updates and a discussion area, so if you get stumped at any point, please don't hesitate to drop by and see what's going on.

Form versus Content

In the beginning of the Web, the hypertext markup language (HTML) was a crude, primitive mechanism that essentially served one purpose: It enabled text-only display units to link documents together through what was known as *hypertext*. (Old timers called these units *terminals*, and they were the state of the art back then. See Figure 1-1.)

Hypertext is a term that Ted Nelson originally coined in his great '70s-retro computing book *Computer Lib*. It's well worth reading if you can find a copy.

Figure 1-1   Ah, the good old days. A real "terminal."

TiM

Ted Berners-Lee worked at CERN, the high-energy particle physics laboratory in Switzerland. He was trying to invent a way for physicists to explore a collection of related documents without leaving their document-reader programs. His invention was, of course, the first generation of hypertext markup language (HTML), along with a program to display HTML documents, including the all-important capability of enabling you to pop from document to document with a keystroke. He also invented the hypertext transport protocol (*http*) server that can deliver these documents on-demand to users on the network.

The next step in the evolution of the Web was at the National Center for Supercomputer Applications at the University of Illinois, Urbana-Champaign. At NCSA, a group of bright folk, notably including Marc Andresson, decided to add some extensions to the text-only HTML language to incorporate graphics (through the IMG tag). They also built a new browser that worked on both Windows and Mac systems. They called the browser *Mosaic* (or, more formally, NCSA Mosaic). They also rewrote and beefed up the http server, but that's another story.

Mosaic was a critical step in the evolution of the World Wide Web as we know it today. I'd argue, in fact, that it was *the* most important step, because for the first time, reading multiple-media documents via the Net became possible with a freely distributed application. And boy did it distribute! NCSA Mosaic exploded onto the Internet, and before long, thousands of different Web sites were online. The Web even became so clogged with new sites that people such as Jerry Yang and David Filo (then graduate students at Stanford) were famously side-tracked from their studies to build a database of bookmarks that they eventually called Yahoo! (You've probably heard of it.)

The unfortunate evolution of HTML

Somewhere along the way, however, as HTML evolved from HTML to HTML+, to HTML 1.1, to HTML 3.2, to HTML 4.0, and HTML 4.01, the original vision of Tim Berners-Lee — and even that of the NCSA gang — got lost. In the beginning, the markup language, modeled after a super-complex markup language known as SGML, was intended only to denote the function or purpose of the elements in a document, leaving presentation issues to the browser itself.

SGML is the Standard Generalized Markup Language, also known as *ISO 88791*, and the U.S. Department of Defense created it to enable multiple people to edit huge tomes, thousands of pages long. Ready for an instant headache? Find out more about SGML at www.arbortext.com/wp.html.

Indeed, as I wrote the first edition of my book *Creating Cool Web Pages with HTML* (published by Hungry Minds) way back in 1995, I remember telling readers, as developers, to make their mantra "It's up to the browser" whenever specific format questions arose. Wonder whether H1 is bigger than H2? It's up to the browser. Want to force 14-point Arial for a paragraph? Can't do it in HTML.

But, of course, you *can* do it, and the more that designers and developers worked with the HTML language, the more that they pushed it into "form" and presentation issues and pulled away from "content" areas. A quick example: The intent of the <CITE> tag is to indicate academic citations in documents, but HTML books don't even mention it any more.

The irony is that, by trying to be all things to all people, HTML ultimately fails as a solution. Its incapability to offer a very high level of layout control spawned the Cascading Style Sheets and JavaScript that now comprise the core of DHTML. HTML's incapability to completely denote the functionality of elements is what forced the creation of *XML*, the e*X*tensible *M*arkup *L*anguage, and its mutant offspring *XHTML (eXtensible HTML, really XML + HTML)*, an uncomfortable hybrid of the two.

More than anything, Dynamic HTML is a new environment, layered atop HTML, that offers better control over the presentation of information on a Web page: control over the fonts, the colors, the layout of material on-screen, and every other aspect of what appears for a user. Just as important, Dynamic HTML adds the ingredient of time to the stew: By using DHTML/JavaScript, you can script events that occur after certain things occur with the user, such as a mouse-over-graphic event or an on-the-fly validation of field values on a fill-in form.

Being part of the continued evolution of the Web through the added capabilities of Dynamic HTML is exciting, but it can become confusing, too. You find a lot of new capabilities and a variety of different ways to accomplish any given effect. Worse, backward-compatible and other approaches to DHTML send a very distinct "Go away!" message to people who don't use the requisite browser and OS configuration.

Why Use Style Sheets?

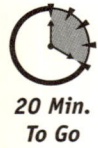

**20 Min.
To Go**

If you're reading this book, you're probably comfortable with at least some level of raw HTML markup. You can most likely view source code in your browser and get a rough idea of what's going on from just about any Web page. If so, you know that the FONT tag, for example, enables you specify typefaces and sizes and that you can coerce the omnipotent TABLE tag into just about any task, including offering an easy mechanism for indenting paragraphs and much more.

I agree. You can unquestionably accomplish many nice layout effects by using straight HTML 4.0 markup tags with some effort and ingenuity. But I promise you that, after you learn more about Cascading Style Sheets, the formatting half of DHTML, you will never once look back. The situation's kind of like saying, "I can circle the Indianapolis 500 track on my bicycle, so why do I need one of those fancy race cars?"

Having said that, I agree, however, that style sheets are a totally different way to approach page design for Web sites. And even at its least intrusive (as STYLE attributes on existing tags), integrating these style specifications into your development process can still prove quite awkward. That's why page-wide and even site-wide style sheets are such a tremendous aid to the developer. Imagine — you need only to code "H1 is 14-point Arial bold, blue, with a green background" once in a master style sheet file. Then you simply reference this style specification for all pages on your site, whether it includes 10 or 10,000.

If you've worked with Microsoft Word or a similar sophisticated document-layout program, you already know what I'm talking about. The irony, of course, is that you may have no idea that MS Word is a "sophisticated document-layout program" because you may never have used any of the style capabilities of the program. But they're available, and the more complex the project is, the more valuable predefined, specific styles prove.

An interesting example: I'm writing this book in Microsoft Word on my Macintosh, and I'm using a predefined style sheet (well, Word people call it a *template*) that the publisher sent me. The template not only includes roughly 45 different specific styles that I can access with a single keystroke but even includes custom menu bars that provide icons that I can click for all these styles, too. By using a style sheet approach, Hungry Minds can ensure that all chapters display identical formatting and layout, just as using style sheets on your Web site can ensure that all pages display an identical format and layout. As an added historical note, style sheets for the Web came out of Microsoft's efforts with Internet Explorer, which shouldn't surprise anyone, given the robust style templates available in Microsoft Word.

You soon see that using style sheets is straightforward and easy. And doing so revolutionizes the way that you think about Web development.

XML and Alphabet Soup

Although the style sheet contingent was getting increasingly excited about control over the presentation of information on Web pages, another group in the background was grumbling about the divergence from the *content* emphasis of Web markup. I mention, for example, the obsolete CITE tag in the section "The unfortunate evolution of HTML," just a little earlier in this chapter. A lot of people began to see the value of using content-description tags that were completely presentation and formatting free.

Imagine, for example, that your Web page lists all the CDs in your music collection, including track information. You can code the page as a *definition list*, perhaps as follows:

```
<DL>
<DT><B>Fagin, Donald</B></DT>
<DD>"The Nightfly"
<OL>
<LI>I.G.Y</LI>
<LI>Green Flower Street</LI>
<LI>Ruby Baby</LI>
<LI>Maxine</LI>
<LI>New Frontier</LI>
<LI>The Nightfly</LI>
<LI>The Goodbye Look</LI>
<LI>Walk Between the Raindrops</LI>
</OL>
</DD>
</DL>
```

This code gives you an okay but not particularly scintillating presentation, as shown in Figure 1-2.

Now imagine that your friend says, "Hey! If you've gone to the trouble of listing all your CDs and tracks, why don't I write a quick database that enables you to search by track name?"

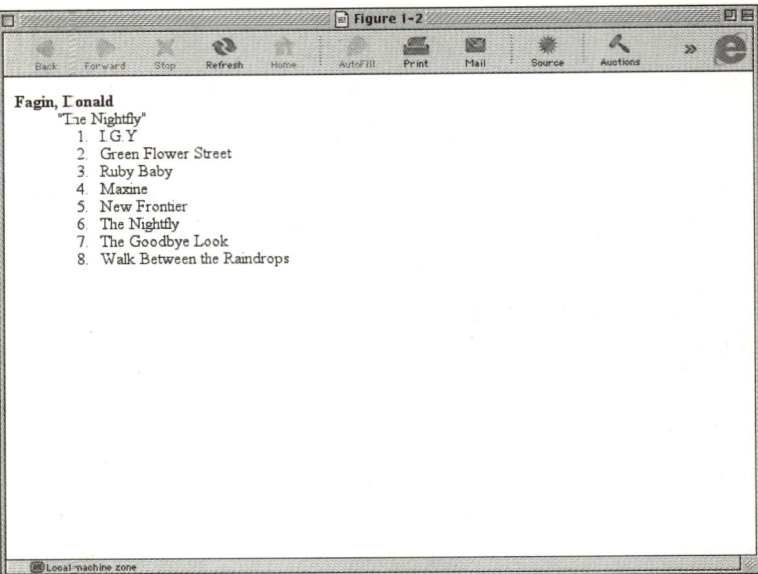

**Figure 1-2**   _Content — but with just HTML, it's unattractive and pretty useless._

Organizing information by type with XML

Sounds cool, doesn't it? The problem is that creating such a database is almost impossible, because your list provides no actual information about _what_ each element on the page represents. For example, what _is_ "Green Flower Street" in the above list? Instead, imagine something similar to the following code, which identifies the type of each element in our CD description:

```
<LIBRARY>
 <CDITEM TITLE="The Nightfly" ARTIST="Fagin, Donald"
  RELEASED="1992">
 <TRACK ORDER="1">I.G.Y</TRACK>
 <TRACK ORDER="2">Green Flower Street</TRACK>
 <TRACK ORDER="3">Ruby Baby</TRACK>
 <TRACK ORDER="4">Maxine</TRACK>
 <TRACK ORDER="5">New Frontier</TRACK>
 <TRACK ORDER="6">The Nightfly</TRACK>
 <TRACK ORDER="7">The Goodbye Look</TRACK>
 <TRACK ORDER="8">Walk Between the Raindrops </TRACK>
 </CDITEM>
 </LIBRARY>
```

Now you have something that you can access through a search engine or indexing system and the information in this CD listing is also easier for a visitor to figure out, because you clearly identify each element.

The Document Type Definition

Before you rush off and start inventing your own markup tags, XML has a second part to it that makes it work, and that's the *Document Type Definition*, or *DTD*. The DTD is where you define each of your tags and indicate their possible values, attributes and whether these values are necessary or optional.

The following example shows how you may write the DTD for the CD catalog that I describe in the preceding two sections:

```
<!DOCTYPE LIBRARY [
  <!ELEMENT LIBRARY (CDITEM*)>
  <!ELEMENT CDITEM (TRACK*)>
  <!ATTLIST CDITEM
       TITLE     CDATA    #REQUIRED
       ARTIST    CDATA    #REQUIRED
       RELEASED  CDATA    #REQUIRED
  >
  <!ELEMENT  TRACK   (#PCDATA)>
  <!ATTLIST  TRACK
     ORDER        CDATA    #REQUIRED
  >
]>
```

I don't want to spend too much time talking about XML other than to simply demonstrate how it focuses directly on identifying the *purpose* of each element of a Web page. The history that has lead to the creation of XML is directly opposite the evolutionary pressure of HTML, which has moved more and more toward the *presentation* of the information, leaving <CITE> and its functional brethren behind in the primordial ooze.

The good news is that, as you become more adept at using DHTML and its style sheets for layout and presentation, you're naturally moving towards a more XML-compatible world anyway.

10 Min. To Go

Scripting by Using JavaScript/Visual Basic Script

I now want to go back in time a few years before leaving this first lesson. The year is 1998–1999, and two companies are aggressively competing to produce the Web browser of choice: Microsoft and Netscape. Netscape has the edge, because it's developed the first truly great browser (Navigator), and Marc Andreessen (who was part of the original NCSA Mosaic team) heads the development team. Microsoft, on the other hand, has tremendous engineering resources, limitless reach in the computing world, and a very aggressive management team that's willing to do just about *anything* to win, and their Internet Explorer browser is by far the most popular on the Web today.

To compete, each company innovates in different, frustratingly incompatible ways. Netscape adds sophisticated HTML tags such as FONT that enable better control of formatting in Navigator, and Microsoft responds by including a style-sheet capability in its Internet Explorer browser. Netscape creates a scripting language that Java inspires and calls it JavaScript, but Microsoft ignores it, instead repurposing its Visual Basic language to offer similar capabilities. And on and on it went for years, to the point where the very phrase Dynamic HTML now means different things to Microsoft and Netscape designers.

To remove any trace of suspense, Microsoft won. Netscape continues to build and ship Navigator as part of its Communicator suite of Web and Internet applications, but the Netscape ship is sinking as a greater and greater majority of Web users embrace Internet Explorer as the browser of choice.

The moral of this story is . . .

What's interesting about this tale is that Web developers had a remarkable level of influence on the evolution of these browsers over time. And although Microsoft introduced style sheets, Netscape was forced to include support for them. Similarly, Microsoft secretly hoped that Visual Basic would win the scripting war, but instead, JavaScript won, so Microsoft was forced to include JavaScript support in its browsers. *javascript / ECMA standard*

How can anyone force a company such as Microsoft to do anything, you ask? By the sheer force of the Web tidal wave: For every page written using Visual Basic scripting, a thousand came online using JavaScript. To compete, Microsoft needed to extend its capabilities appropriately.

Enough history. Suffice to say, if you're curious why JavaScript is the scripting language of choice for DHTML, it's because Netscape won the scripting war. Don't feel too bad for the team at Redmond, however: They won the style-sheet war with CSS.

Done!

REVIEW

This first lesson focuses on establishing the foundation and history of Dynamic HTML, ensuring that you understand how it fits into the greater world of Web and Internet development. I also try to acknowledge some of the lesser-known personalities who helped us get to this point in Internet history — doing so, I hope, without putting you to sleep.

QUIZ YOURSELF

1. What core concept does "graceful degradation" describe, and why is it important? (See "A Philosophy of Design.")
2. What was the crucial capability that Tim Berners-Lee implemented and Ted Nelson named that led to the growth of the World Wide Web? (See "Form versus Content.")
3. What was the original vision of HTML that was lost as designers became more involved with the evolution of the markup language? What new development has resurrected the vision? (See "Form versus Content.")
4. What happened to the <CITE> tag, and what does it signify? (See "The unfortunate evolution of HTML.")
5. Name at least two good reasons why using style sheets is a smart way to code the pages of a Web site. (See "Why Use Style Sheets.")
6. Fill in the blanks: _____ invented JavaScript, and _____ invented Web style sheets. (See "Scripting by Using JavaScript/Visual Basic Script" and "Why Use Style Sheets.")
7. Bonus question: What's the ground speed of an unladen swallow?

30 Minute Crash Course on HTML 4.01

Session Checklist

✔ HTML Basics

✔ Fonts and Text

✔ Tables

✔ HTML 4.01 Extensions

**30 Min.
To Go**

I f you're reading this book, you probably already know HTML — certainly enough that you're comfortable using the View Source capability of your favorite Web browser as you visit interesting sites.

Nonetheless, I think that spending 30 minutes of your weekend crash course going over the hypertext markup language can prove very helpful at this point. This chapter, therefore, reviews the basics and highlights of some of the improvements that you find in the very latest version of HTML, Version 4.01.

As you read along, keep in mind the problems that HTML developers face in trying to increase their control over the layout of Web pages while remaining within the constraints of what's ultimately a primitive and coarse markup language.

HTML Basics

I'm starting right at the beginning. Web pages are text files that contain markup language instructions denoted by open and close angle brackets: < >. You have two types of HTML instructions:

- **Standalone tags:** These tags don't need a closing tag; thus they "stand alone." An example of a standalone tag is the <BR> tag, which forces a line break.
- **Paired tags:** These tags require a closing tag. An example of a paired tag is the <B> tag, which sets text in bold. To specify bold text, you use <B>text to set in bold</B>. All closing tags of paired tags repeat the opening tag but add a forward slash between the open angle bracket and the tag itself.

You also find paired tags that double as standalone tags because of lazy HTML programming practices. Most notable among such tags is the <P> paragraph break tag. According to the HTML standard, <P> is a paired tag, but 99 percent of Web sites simply use it as a standalone tag to force a blank line between paragraphs of text.

Basic text layout

The preceding section describes two of the core HTML tags that help Web designers build pages of information: <BR> and <P>, which offer a line and paragraph break respectively. Toss in a few more HTML tags, and you have the basics of text layout, as you can see in Table 2-1.

Table 2-1 *Basic HTML Tags*

Opening Tag	Closing Tag	What It Does
<P>	</P>*	Creates paragraph break.
 		Creates line break.
<BLOCKQUOTE>	</BLOCKQUOTE>	Forces horizontal indentation around contents.
<HR>		Creates horizontal rule.
<PRE>	</PRE>	Creates preformatted text.

* You rarely use the </P> in HTML coding.

Dozens of different HTML tags exist, and just about every HTML tag can include specific attributes, usually in a NAME="value" format. The tag <HR SIZE="2" WIDTH="300">, for example, indicates that the browser is to display a two-pixel high horizontal rule that's exactly 300 pixels wide.

Lists

The HTML language includes a variety of simple list formats, as the following list describes:

- Unordered (or bullet) lists, which use <UL> and <LI> tags
- Ordered (or numbered) lists, which use <OL> and <LI> tags
- Definition lists, which use <DL>, <DT> and <DD> tags.

These lists are interesting because they use a set of different tags working together. Table 2-2 shows the HTML tags necessary for encoding the various types of lists.

Table 2-2   *Basic List HTML Tags*

Opening Tag	Closing Tag	What It Does
<UL>	</UL>	Unordered or bullet list
<OL>	</OL>	Ordered or numbered list
<LI>	</LI>	List item member
<DL>	</DL>	Definition list
<DD>	</DD>	Definition list data
<DT>	</DT>	Definition list term

Here's an example that shows all these HTML working together on a page:

```
This is an example of some HTML that<BR>
includes a variety of different list formats.<P>
First, a bullet list:
<UL><LI>"Bullet to Beijing"</LI>
<LI>"Bullet Ballet"</LI>
<LI>"Bullet Code"</LI></UL>
Then a numbered list:
<OL><LI>"Air Force One"</LI>
<LI>"Two Against the World"</LI>
<LI>"Three Kings"</LI></OL>
And, finally, a definition list, which, you may recall, presents two
elements for each definition (think of it as a glossary and you can see
what's going on):
<DL><DT>best boy</DT>
<DD>the person on the film set who keeps the timecards of the crew
members, among other tasks.</DD>
<DT>boom</DT>
<DD>a long pole allowing overhead microphones on the set</DD>
<DT>cue</DT>
<DD>the signal for an actor to begin their lines or action</DD>
</DL>
```

In a Web browser, the HTML listing looks similar to what you see in Figure 2-1. Notice the additional line spacing and the lack of consistency across formats and lists.

You can find all the examples in the book on the included CDROM, so do make sure that you access all these examples on your computer to see exactly how they look on your own setup.

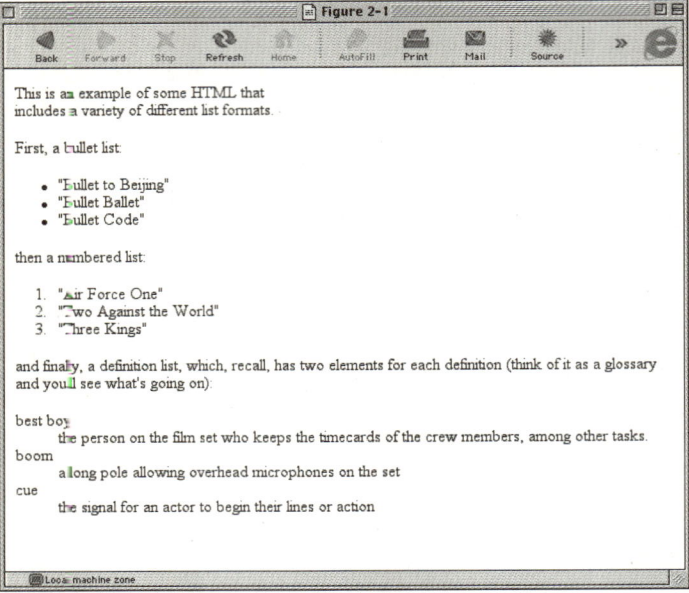

Figure 2-1   *Simple lists in HTML.*

In addition to these HTML tags, two other critical tags make the Web much more interesting than a page layout tool: *anchor tags* (A) for hypertext references and the *image tag* (IMG) for graphics. As you see in Table 2-3, each tag has a couple different attributes.

Table 2-3   *Anchor and Image Tags*

Tag	Attribute	What It Does
<A		Anchor/hypermedia tag. Has the associated closing tag </A>.
	HREF=	Pointer to hypertext reference.
	NAME=	Internal anchor name (reference with HREF='#*name*').
	TARGET=	Redirects resultant page to specified browser window or area.
<IMG		Graphics inclusion tag. Has no associated closing tag.
	SRC=	Source for the graphics file to include.
	ALT=	Alternative text to display if graphic can't appear.
	HEIGHT=	Height of graphic, in pixels.
	WIDTH=	Width of graphic, in pixels.
	ALIGN=	Either alignment of graphic on page or alignment of material subsequent to the graphic.

Tag	Attribute	What It Does
	BORDER=	Size of border around graphic (usually set to zero for linked graphics).
	HSPACE=	Additional horizontal space to include on left and right of graphic.
	VSPACE=	Additional vertical space to include above and below graphic.
	NAME=	Reference name of graphic box for scripting.
	ID=	Alternative to NAME, similar functionality.

**20 Min.
To Go**

Here's another, very simple example that demonstrates both these tags:

```
<A HREF="http://www.hungryminds.com/">Learn
more about Hungry Minds</A>
<BR>
<A HREF="http://www.hungryminds.com/"><IMG
  SRC="http://www.hungryminds.com/images/homepage/logo.gif"
  BORDER="0" ALT="Hungry Minds Logo"></A>
```

Figure 2-2 shows how this example appears in a Web browser. Notice that both the text link and the graphic take you to the Hungry Minds Web site if you click either one.

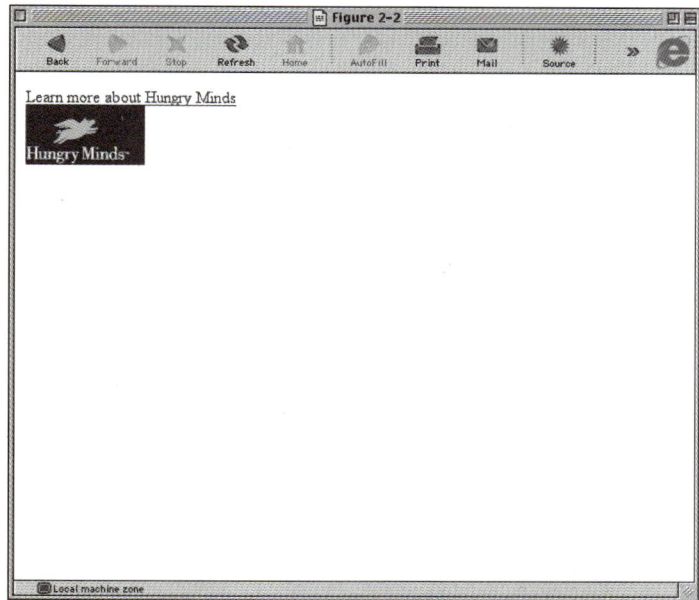

Figure 2-2   *Anchor tags and image tags both function as anchors.*

You use a variety of other HTML tags to create correctly formed HTML pages, including `<HTML>`, `<HEAD>`, `<BODY>`, `<TITLE>` and `<META>`. You can find out more about these tags (and much more) by previewing my book *Creating Cool HTML 4 Web Pages,* Second Edition, on the CD-ROM that comes with this book.

To quickly demonstrate these tags, here's a rewrite of the preceding listing:

```
<HTML>
<HEAD>
<TITLE>Sample text and graphical links</TITLE>
<META NAME="description" CONTENTS="Example of text and graphical HTML
links from the book DHTML Weekend Crash Course">
</HEAD>
<BODY>
<A HREF="http://www.hungryminds.com/">Learn
more about Hungry Minds</A>
<BR>
<A HREF="http://www.hungryminds.com/"><IMG
  SRC="http://www.hungryminds.com/images/homepage/logo.gif"
  BORDER="0" ALT="Hungry Minds Logo"></A>
</BODY>
</HTML>
```

In a browser, this example lays out almost exactly as shown in Figure 2-2, which you can experimentally verify by looking at Listing 2.2a on the CD-ROM.

Fonts

The most interesting part of HTML in terms of this book is the font and character formatting and presentation controls that the HTML language includes. You have two basic sets of font formats: the various font style tags and the FONT tag itself. Although these formats combine to offer a fair amount of control over the presentation of textual material on a Web page, they're weak and don't offer sufficient control for most advanced Web designers.

Font styles

In the early days of the Web, developers used tags such as <STRONG> and <BIG> to change the presentation format of text. The problem was that these tags offered almost no control over how elements appeared in a Web browser. (Remember the mantra that I talk about earlier? *It's up to the browser* to figure out how to format elements.) Indeed, some Web browsers showed the text that <STRONG> marked as bold, and others showed it as italicized.

The simplest styles currently in use are bold, italics, underline, and nonproportional type, the tags for which are shown in Table 2-4.

Table 2-4 *Font Styles*

Opening Tag	Closing Tag	What It Does
<B>	</B>	Bold text
<I>	</I>	Italics

Opening Tag	Closing Tag	What It Does
<U>	</U>	Underline
<TT>	</TT>	Nonproportional (monospace) text

The FONT tag

— use css > font tag instead

Introduced in HTML 3.2, the FONT tag demonstrates quite clearly the challenge of trying to give designers control over more sophisticated text appearance elements while still fitting into the limitations of the HTML language.

This tag has three attributes: FACE, SIZE, and COLOR. These attributes enable designers to specify typefaces by name, the size of the text to present, and the color. Sounds useful, but they're not as wonderful as you may hope. In particular, the SIZE attribute is odd because it enables you to specify typeface size on a 1–7 scale, but the scale doesn't correspond directly to any other typeface measure such as points or pixels.

**10 Min.
To Go**

Following is an example of all three attributes at work:

```
<FONT FACE="Arial,Helvetica" SIZE="5" COLOR="blue"><B>big blue bold
text</B></FONT>
```

css {font-family: Arial, Helvetica;}

Notice that, whenever HTML tags have attributes, the closing tag doesn't need to repeat the attributes — a great timesaver.

You can see in this one-line example how HTML tags work together to enable you to achieve specific results: In this example, the phrase big blue bold text is to appear in a large (size=5) Arial face (or Helvetica, if Arial isn't available to the browser) and in bold, too.

The FACE attribute, however, presents a problem: You need to match the exact typeface name, and that's not always easy to do. If you want Times Roman on a Macintosh, for example, you need to specify Times, but on a Windows machine, it's probably Times Roman PS. And on a Unix system? Who knows . . .? The practical ramification of this peculiarity is that you end up creating specifications such as the following example:

```
<FONT FACE="Times Roman PS, Times, Palatino, Helvetica">
```

And you *still* can't guarantee that you ~~certain to~~ *will* end up with the typeface that you want. Later in the book, in Session 7, you see how Cascading Style Sheets enable you to neatly avoid this problem altogether, while giving you more control over your use of typefaces at the same time.

Tables

First introduced officially in HTML 3.2, tables are perhaps the most complex and misused of HTML tags. At their most basic, tables are a combination of three different tags working together, *a la* the definition list that I show you in the section "Lists," earlier in this chapter. To fully understand tables, you must realize that a table consists of rows, each of which contains a set of columnar data cells.

The HTML for the most basic table may look as follows:

[handwritten: x-large]

[handwritten: css { font-size: x-large; }]

```
<TABLE BORDER="1">
<TR><TD><FONT SIZE="5">Folding Table</FONT></TD>
<TD>Item: F031854A002</TD></TR>
<TR><TD><FONT SIZE="5">Typewriter Table</FONT></TD>
<TD>Item: F0328210001P</TD></TR>
</TABLE>
```

This table is shown in Figure 2-3. Notice how the table is rectilinear, although the cells contain different amounts of information, and also check out what the SIZE="5" attribute does to the text in the first column.

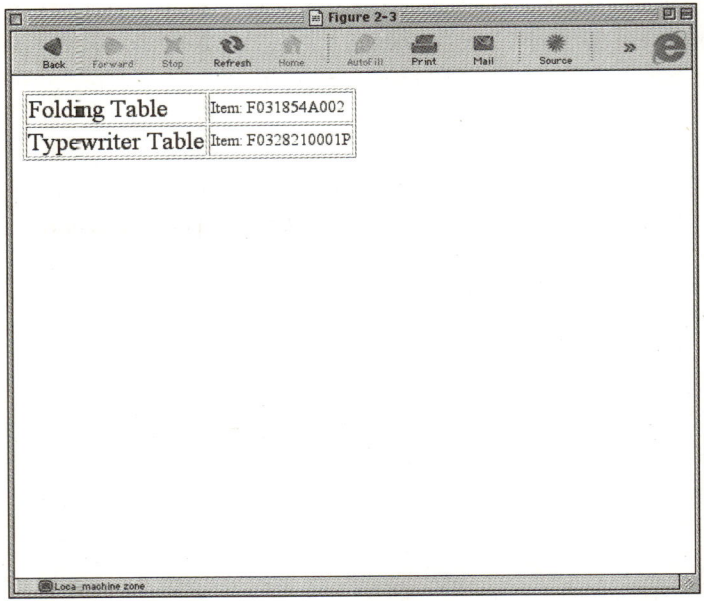

Figure 2-3 *Basic table formatting.*

In fact, the TABLE tag alone uses at least a dozen different attributes, including those highlighted in Table 2-5.

Table 2-5 *Attributes of the TABLE Tag*

Tag	Attribute	What It Does	*[handwritten: css]*
<TABLE		Table tag	
	BORDER=	Outside border size, in pixels	*[handwritten: border-size; top-size]*
	CELLSPACING=	Space between data cells and rows in table	*[handwritten: cell-spacing]*
	CELLPADDING=	Space within a cell, around the contents	*[handwritten: padding;]*

Tag	Attribute	What It Does
	WIDTH=	Width of table relative to window
	FRAME=	Fine-tuned frame format elements (HTML 4.0)
	RULES=	Fine-tuned frame rule lines (HTML 4.0)
	ALIGN=	Alignment of table relative to page
	HSPACE=	Additional horizontal space requested
	VSPACE=	Additional vertical space requested
	COLS=	Specify columns in table (HTML 4.0)

Almost as many attributes can appear in the TH (table data cell column header) and TD (table data cell) tags, and you also see a special TH variant on the TD tag that automatically centers the cell contents and enables bold for text therein. (In this case, TH is the tag for a table header.)

Chapter 9 of *Creating Cool HTML 4 Web Pages,* **which I include on the CD-ROM that comes with this book, explains all these TABLE tags and attributes in great detail.**

HTML 4.01 Extensions

The change from HTML 3.2 to HTML 4.0 introduced and standardized a variety of different tags and capabilities that provide the cornerstones of Dynamic HTML, including a formal definition of JavaScript compatibility and Cascading Style Sheets.

Perhaps surprisingly, the standardization committee — the World Wide Web Consortium, or W3C — didn't take long to add some additional HTML elements (in the 4.01 version of HTML) that one can only presume were accidentally omitted when HTML 4.0 was cast in stone. In addition, the HTML 4.01 specification fixes various errors and gaffes in the HTML 4.0 specification.

Insert and delete tags

Demonstrating that you still can't find any agreement on what HTML should encompass and how it should work, HTML 4.01 includes two new tags INS and DEL, development tools that enable you to denote who made specific changes to HTML text. You use them as the following example shows:

```
Richard's Boat Parts is <DEL CITE="edit1.html"
DATETIME="2001-08-03T13:15:34PST">a pretty
good</DEL><INS CITE="edit1.html"
DATETIME="2001-08-03T13:15:53PST">the very
best</INS> boat supply shop in Redondo
Beach, California.
```

What happened here is hard to see in the HTML, but the intent is to show a pretty good as deleted text (probably in a strikethrough format) and to highlight the very best as new text. Perhaps moving the cursor over the deletion/insertion causes a small explanatory window to pop up, displaying the date and time of the edit and a link to the specified explanatory HTML page edit1.html. (I'd show you with a figure, but Web browsers don't yet support these tags.)

Other HTML 4.01 additions

HTML 4.01 provides some other additions to the HTML specification, such as the ­ code to create a soft hyphen, but frankly, they're not meaningful for most Web developers, and don't affect my approach to Dynamic HTML development in this book. I'm simply going to point you to the official HTML 4.01 specification for details, which you can find online at www.w3.org/TR/html4/.

The two most important additions to modern HTML for our purposes are the DIV and SPAN tags, which I describe — in depth — later in the book.

Done!

REVIEW

This session is a whirlwind reintroduction to the hypertext markup language, from the rudiments of the original HTML to the latest advances in HTML 4.01. As you know, angle brackets surround all HTML tags by and paired tags close with an additional / character following the open angle bracket and before the tag itself. You express attributes in NAME=value pairs and surround the value of well-formed attributes with quote marks, as in WIDTH="30".

QUIZ YOURSELF

1. Which of the following HTML tags is rare to see?
, <LI>, </P> or <B> (See "Basic text layout.")

2. What changes occur in the browser if you add <HEAD> and <BODY> tags? (See "Lists.")

3. What's the greatest limitation of the FACE attribute to the FONT tag? (See "The FONT Tag.")

4. One of the following four tags isn't part of the TABLE tag set. Which one? <TABLE>, <ROW>, <TR>, or <TD> (See "Tables.")

5. What was the main reason the W3C standards group issued the 4.01 standard so soon after the HTML 4.0 standard was released? (See "HTML 4.01 Extensions.")

</P> essential for xhtml

<html> <head> <body> <title> required for well formed xhtml
~ <!DOCTYPE>

<font-family>

30 Minute Crash Course on JavaScript

Session Checklist

✔ Variables

✔ Expressions and conditionals

✔ Looping mechanisms

✔ Subroutines, built-in and user-defined

**30 Min.
To Go**

The first wave of Web browser development came in the mid-1990s, as the team at Netscape Corporation released the first version of Netscape Navigator. It offered support for the relatively primitive version of HTML that was available back then. With little more than bullet lists, paragraph breaks, and crude tables (an experimental addition at the time), people were still doing remarkable things and creating valuable Web sites for the online community.

In the second major wave of Web browser development in the late 1990s, the Netscape team recognized that, even with lots of evolution, HTML wasn't going to prove sufficient to meet the needs of designers and developers. A scripting language was a logical addition, and the innovation that Netscape added was JavaScript.

A little-known bit of trivia is that the original name for Netscape Corporation was Mosaic Communications, named after the original Mosaic Web browser from the University of Illinois. The regents of UIUC didn't like an independent company naming itself after a UI trademark, so Mosaic Communications became Netscape. You can see a tiny bit of this original name left over: Go to www.mcom.com/ **and see where you end up!**

Why JavaScript instead of an existing, known language? Because simultaneous to this second wave of browser development, another company, Sun Microsystems, was beginning to promote a platform-neutral programming language that it called *Java*. The Java programming language gave developers the capability to write software applications that simultaneously work on Macs, PCs, Unix boxes, and more. Netscape faced just one catch: how to distribute these applications? The solution was to incorporate the Java runtime environment into the Web browser itself, and that was an important addition.

Microsoft didn't like someone else telling it what scripting language to include in its browser, so the early versions of Internet Explorer included support for Visual Basic Script, the company's alternative choice. The problem was that no Web sites used VB Script, while everyone was using JavaScript. Eventually, Microsoft succumbed and the tale ends with JavaScript receiving a universal blessing as the standard and incorporation (albeit, loosely) into the HTML 4.0 specification.

To correct a common point of confusion, JavaScript and Java aren't the same. In fact, Java is what's known as an *object-oriented programming language*, and it's not for the faint of heart. JavaScript, however, which shares only some minimal syntax structure in common with Java, is a simple scripting language that you can add to your Web pages quickly and easily.

This chapter gives you a quick overview of the basic structure and format of the JavaScript language. Don't panic, however — as I said, JavaScript isn't a heavy-duty programming language, and you needn't anticipate something that requires thousands of lines of obscure punctuation marks and hieroglyphics! Quite the opposite, in fact: JavaScript is small, elegant, and very powerful, as you soon see.

Variables

The building block of all scripting is *variables*, the named containers that store specific information and enable you both to manipulate and display it whenever you want. If you remember your algebra, where x=y+4, you're already familiar with variables, because that's what the *x* and *y* are in that equation. If you imagine the two variables as boxes that can take on any value, the equation describes a relationship between them. If *y* is 10, *x* is 14.

JavaScript features three primary types of variables that you need to know: *numeric*, *string*, and *Boolean*. Numeric variables are just like the *x* and *y* of the preceding paragraph and can store either an integer value (123) or a floating-point value (4.4353). String variables store a sequence of letters, digits, or punctuation. By using a string variable, you can say name = "Dave Taylor" and it has the effect of putting the letters D, a, v, and e (and so on) into the container name. By contrast, Booleans can have only one of two possible values: true or false.

Examples of different values

The most complex of the variable types, numeric variable can hold values that are positive or negative and can have a fractional portion or not. Table 3-1 summarizes the different numeric values.

Table 3-1   *Acceptable Numeric Values in JavaScript*

Value	What It is
123	Positive integer
−14	Negative integer
14.43	Positive floating point value
−0.5	Negative floating point value with fractional part

You express the values of string variables by surrounding them with quotes. Usually, you use the double-quote character, but JavaScript is forgiving, and you can use the single-quote to surround the value, too, if you want. Either of the following two values are acceptable for a string in JavaScript:

```
"An exploration of inner space"
'test, test, and test again.'
```

The third type of variable is a Boolean, and it can take on either a positive `true` or negative `false` value. You use it for conditional tests and *flags* (variables that track the status of a sequence of code), as they're known.

 **Booleans are named after George Boole, a famous British logician.**

You can embed some special characters in strings by using a backslash notation that's identical to what you use in both C and Java, as shown in Table 3-2.

Table 3-2   *Common Backslash Values in JavaScript Strings*

Value	What It Does
\\	The backslash character
\n	A ~~carriage return~~ *line feed*
\r	A ~~line feed~~ *carriage return*
\b	A backspace
\t	A tab
\'	A single quote (as in "It\'s what I want.")
\"	A double quote

Defining and assigning variables

To use a variable, you need to define it beforehand, which is easily done by using the `var` statement. To demonstrate, the following examples show the definition of a couple variables:

```
var name;
var monthly_wage;
```

One cool thing about variable definitions is that you can actually make an initial value assignment at the same time! You can modify the preceding examples as follows:

```
var name = "Sean Connery";
var monthly_wage = 3500;
```

Notice something else on all these lines: They all end with a semicolon. Every statement in JavaScript must end in a semicolon.

I keep saying that you must define every variable by using a `var` statement, but that's entirely not true. JavaScript is a loosely typed programming language, so you can implicitly define variables simply by using them in your script. I highly recommend, however, that you define them.

After you define variables, of course, you want to assign values to them. This procedure, too, is easy, as the following example shows:

```
var x, y = 3;
x = y + 4;
```

This example results in the variable x containing the value 7 and the variable y containing the value 3.

20 Min.
To Go

Expressions and Conditionals

Much more interesting than assignment statements are *expressions*, which are the real building blocks of JavaScript. Expressions can evaluate to a Boolean (as in "if this condition is true, then . . . .") or can evaluate to a string or numeric expression. Table 3-3 takes a look at each of these expressions.

Table 3-3   *Three types of expressions in JavaScript*

Expression	What It Evaluates To
x + y > z	Evaluates to a Boolean: either *true* or *false*.
x+(2*y)-3	Evaluates to a numeric value, the sum of these two variables.
name + " (given name)"	Appends the specified string to the end of the value of the string name.

To understand how each of the expressions works in Table 3-3, I need to assign values to the variables in question. Here's how they may look:

```
var x, y, z, name;
x = 20;
y = -5;
z = 4.5;
name = "Ashley Taylor";
```

The first expression shown in Table 3-3 is evaluating whether x + y is greater than z. x = 20 and y = -5, so x + y = 15. z = 4.5, so yes, x + y is greater than z. An interesting thing to notice here is that JavaScript can implicitly coerce numeric variables from one type of number to another, so it can compare the integer value 15 to the floating-point value 4.5 correctly.

In the second expression, you're back to algebra. (Just when you though you were safe!) Because x = 20 and y = -5, 20 + (2 × -5) − 3 reduces to 20 + -10 − 3, which ends up as 7. JavaScript uses a standard operator precedence to evaluate mathematical expressions, so it evaluates parenthetical expressions first and does multiplication and division before addition or subtraction.

In the third expression, you get a peek at one of the many powerful string-manipulation features of JavaScript: the + between two string values is the *concatenation function*. It's similar to the strcat() function in C (if you're familiar with that programming language). What I think is most interesting about the concatenation function in JavaScript is that, because the language is so loosely typed (that is, variables can flip from integer to floating point, to strings and back with minimal effort), you can do things in JavaScript that you definitely can't do in any other programming language, such as is shown in the following example:

```
oddstring = name + ", and x = " + x;
```

The numeric value x automatically converts into the equivalent string value before JavaScript concatenates it to the other values. If name is "Ashley Taylor" and x is 20, the resultant value of oddstring is "Ashley Taylor, and x = 20".

You have a ton of helpful shortcuts for expressions, including the common ++ and -- notation from C to increment or decrement a variable, respectively, and += and -= to add the right-hand-side of the expression to the existing value on the left (or subtract). Here's a quick example:

```
salary = 20;
salary++;           // now salary is 21
salary--;           // salary is back to 20
salary += 10;       // salary is 30: this is identical
// to salary = salary + 10;
salary -= (5+5);    // salary is back to 20
```

 **Comments in JavaScript begin with a double-forward-slash and continue to the end of the line.**

One area where programming languages diverge is with the notation for equality testing, and JavaScript does its own thing here, too. Unlike Perl, C, or Pascal, for example, JavaScript uses == as an equality test for numeric or string values and != for inequality tests. A few quick examples (and remember that all these evaluate to a Boolean value of *true* or *false*) are as follows:

```
salary = 20;          newsalary = 20;
name = "Ashley";      newname = "Gareth";

val = (salary == newsalary); // false true
val = (name == newname);      // false
val = (name == name);    // true
val = (name < salary);     // false [see note]
val = (name != newname);     // true
val = (salary < newsalary+1);  // true
```

I hope that these examples are straightforward and that you can see how I reach the different values that I cite in the comments. The only weird one here is the middle one: Comparing the string value name with the numeric value salary forces salary to convert to its string equivalent 20 and then compares the two strings. JavaScript considers a string as lesser than another if it appears earlier in a so-called dictionary sort. As a result, *2* (the first character of the string "20") appears earlier in a dictionary than *A* (the first letter of "Ashley") so the test to determine whether *A* is less than *2* (in essence) proves false.

A sneaky shorthand that many JavaScript programmers use is the comma operator, which enables you to put multiple statements on the same line without using semicolons. By using this notation, you can write the first line of the preceding code listing as `salary = 20, newsalary = 20;`.

Looping Mechanisms

I know that the information that I present in the preceding (and following) sections is a lot to absorb (this whirlwind introduction to JavaScript. If you're finding you're starting to get a headache, I recommend that you consider either saying "No worries, mate" and go straight to the next chapter, coming back here as you find JavaScript structures that don't make sense, or taking a few hours off of our crash course to check out *JavaScript Weekend Crash Course* (Steven W. Disbrow, Hungry Minds, ISBN: 0-7645-4804-2).

I hope that you're still with me!

Although writing programs without any sort of looping or conditional execution is theoretically possible, doing so is a complete nightmare, requiring you to type and type and type till the cows came home. Instead, JavaScript offers a typical lineup of looping and control structures, as shown in Table 3-4.

Table 3-4 *Common JavaScript Looping Mechanisms*

Looping Mechanism	What It Does
if (*expr*) *statement*	Conditionally executes statement or statement block
else *statement*	If you tie it with the `if` statement, this executes statement if expr is false.
switch (*expr*)	Acts as a case statement, a series of `if`/`else` tests
while (*expr*) *statement*	Loops, continually executing statement until expr is false
do *statement* while (*expr*)	Same as `while`, but guarantees one time through loop
for (*expr1;expr2;expr3*) *statement*	Loops, continually executing statement until expr2 is false: expr1 is the initializing expression prior to looping, and expr3 is done after each loop but before expr2 evaluates.

Some of these are pretty straightforward. Writing `if (a < 10) a = 10;`, for example, indicates that you want JavaScript to evaluate the conditional expression `a < 10`: If it's *true*, the subsequent statement, `a = 10`, executes. If the conditional is *false*, the value of a remains untouched.

A more complex conditional statement may look as follows:

```
if (name == "Ashley")       salary = 20;
else if (name == "Gareth")  salary = 10;
else                        salary = 15;
```

In this case, you're testing the value of variable name multiple times. If the value is `"Ashley"`, `salary` sets to 20. If it's Gareth, `salary` is 10. And for everyone else, `salary` is 15.

Switch statements

Another way to write the set of conditional statements that I present in the preceding section is to use the nifty `switch` statement, which saves typing and looks cleaner, too, as shown in the following example:

```
switch (name) {
  case "Ashley":   salary = 20;   break;
  case "Gareth":   salary = 10;   break;
       default:    salary = 15;   break;
}
```

Is this sequence easier to understand than the earlier sequence of `if/else` statements?

Anywhere that you can place a single statement, you can also place a block of statements by wrapping all of them in curly brackets. You can see that in the preceding example using the `switch` **statement, and you see it appear again shortly in this session.**

Notice that you can have dozens of different case values and that they can consist of any constant value — that is, using anything similar to the following examples is okay:

```
case 3:
case 4+5*3:
case "test":
case "number" + " ":
```

They're all constant (unvarying) values, but you can't use variables as `case` statement expressions, so both the following examples are illegal:

```
case name:
case x + 30:
```

If you need to use statements similar to the last two, you need to jump back to the `if/else` structure that I describe in the preceding section.

While loops

The control structures that I describe in the preceding sections enable you to conditionally execute one of a set of statements. The while loop serves a very different purpose, however, in that it enables you to execute the same set of statements multiple times. Here's a typical usage:

```
var countdown = 10, salary = 10;
while (countdown > 0) {
    salary += salary;
    countdown--;
}
```

The code starts out by defining two variables. It initializes countdown with a value of 10 and also initializes salary as 10. Then the while loop controls how many times the subsequent block of statements (remember the meaning of the curly brackets?) executes. Within each iteration of the loop, salary adds to itself and then the countdown variable decrements by one. After ten times through this loop, the while condition evaluates to *false*, and it's done.

After the loop finishes, what is the value of salary?

Sometimes you want to have a loop where the statements always evaluate once, even if the condition is immediately false. Using a control structure such as while (*expr*) doesn't work, because the expression is false and the statements are skipped. You could ostensibly use an iteration counter such as you see in the following example:

```
var timesthrough = 0;
while (timesthrough == 0 && expr) {
    statements
    timesthrough++;
}
```

But frankly, what this example shows is pretty awkward. Instead, a more graceful solution is to use the do/while loop instead, as in the following example:

```
do {
    statements
} while (expr);
```

Only a slight variation on the tune, the do-while loop is a great control structure to have in your utility kit!

For loops

Don't let the complex appearance of a for loop turn you off; it's the most useful looping mechanism in JavaScript. A for loop consists of three components: an initializer, a conditional, and a loop increment, as you see in the following example:

```
for (var j = 0; j < 10; j++) {
  salary += salary;
}
```

The preceding setup is 100 percent identical to the following example:

```
var j = 0;
while (j < 10) {
  salary += salary;
  j++;
}
```

The for loop is just a delightfully succinct way to express this sort of sequence.

 **Did you notice that the variable definition (var) slipped into the for loop initializer? Neat, eh?**

Subroutines, Built-in and User-Defined

Many programs have sequences of statements that appear over and over again. Smart programmers turn those into subroutines, named functions that you can invoke anywhere in your JavaScript. A simple function may look like the following example:

```
function swap(a, b) {
  var hold = b; a;
  a = b; b = hold;
}
```

This function enables you easily swap the values of any two variables, which you can reference in your JavaScript with swap(name, address);.

Subroutines can also return values by using the return statement. Here's a subroutine that returns the square of the given value:

```
function square(x) {
  return (x * x);
}
```

A statement such as y = square(20); results in y having the value of 400 (20 squared).

Built-in functions

The really good news is that hundreds of different functions are built in to the JavaScript language so that most of your user-defined subroutines end up implementing your algorithms instead of doing the real dirty work of string or number manipulation.

Because JavaScript is a roughly object-oriented programming language, you invoke many functions by essentially appending their names to a given variable. As an example, you obtain the length of the string variable name by using the following code:

```
name.length
```

So you can use this attribute in a conditional as follows:

```
if (name.length > 50)
```

Frankly, I find this notation kind of funky and weird. I'm used to a structure that's much more like that of the Perl length(name) function, but JavaScript ain't Perl, and you ain't in Kansas anymore!

JavaScript uses way more built-in functions that I can squeeze into this book, but Table 3-5 highlights some that are of particular value to DHTML developers.

Table 3-5 *Some Great JavaScript Functions for DHTML Developers*

Function	What It Does
back()	Returns to the previous URL
close()	Closes the specified window
confirm()	Confirms an action with an OK/CANCEL answer.
open()	Creates and opens a new window
submit()	Submits the specified form, as if you'd clicked the Submit button

How can you use these functions? How about as in the following example:

```
if (confirm("Are you sure that you want to close this window?"))
  close();
```

This code causes a dialog box to pop up reading, Are you sure that you want to close this window? along with two buttons: OK and Cancel. If you choose OK the confirm() function returns *true* and the close() statement executes. (The window closes.) If you choose Cancel, confirm() returns *false* and it skips the close() statement.

REVIEW

This 30-minute session covers a lot of ground, giving you a quick and easy overview of the JavaScript programming language. JavaScript is a cornerstone of Dynamic HTML, and later in the book, I spend quite a bit of time showing you how to use and exploit JavaScript so that your pages jump through hoops for you.

Starting with an overview of variables, numeric, string, and Boolean, I move to a discussion of how to assign specific values to variables, including a discussion of the JavaScript string concatenation construct. Next is an overview of conditional expressions and the if/else construct, which I follow with a discussion of the two variants of the while loop and the confusing but useful for loop. Finally, I provide a discussion of how to define your own functions in JavaScript and a brief list of some of the most useful JavaScript functions for DHTML developers, wrapping up the chapter.

QUIZ YOURSELF

1. What fundamental problem forced Microsoft into adding support for JavaScript to Internet Explorer? (See introductory paragraphs.)

2. Three types of variables are in JavaScript, but one of them can have two different types of values. All things considered, what are the *four* types of values that you can place in a JavaScript variable? (See "Examples of different values.")

3. Which of the following is a correct assignment statement and which is a correct conditional comparison of two numeric values? a = 3, a == 3, a := 3, a ?= 3, a.value = 3 (See "Defining and assigning variables" and "Expressions and Conditionals.")

4. Write a string assignment where you give the variable oddstring a value that contains both a single and double-quoted passage. (See "Expressions and Conditionals.")

5. What character sequence denotes a comment in JavaScript? (See "Expressions and Conditionals.")

6. Write the for loop equivalent to the following JavaScript. (This one is a bit tricky!)

```
a = 3, b = 5;
while (a + b < 10) {
    do_something();
    a += 2;
    b -= 1;
}
```

(See "For loops.")

The Compatibility Bugaboo

Session Checklist

✔ Netscape's Dynamic HTML

✔ Microsoft's Dynamic HTML

✔ Setting Expectations

**30 Min.
To Go**

Before you get too far into this weekend crash course, I must warn you that this material is known as *Dynamic* HTML for a reason: It's always changing. Every Web browser version supports a different subset of the complete set of possible standards and capabilities. Even the same browser and browser version number can display quite different capabilities on different operating system platforms. Microsoft Internet Explorer 5.5 on the PC, for example, is surprisingly different from Microsoft Internet Explorer 5.5 on the Macintosh.

Figure 4-1 shows a great Web-feature compatibility table from Webreview.com. It gives you an idea of how much difference you can find between browsers.

See this chart yourself at www.webreview.com/browsers/browsers.shtml.

Correctly and accurately identifying the browser within your own Dynamic HTML pages also involves problems. If I explore different developer sites using Netscape 6, the latest version of the Netscape Web browser (which is quite divergent from Netscape Navigator 4, but that's a different story), some sites tell me that I'm using Netscape 5 (which was never released); some say I'm using Netscape 6; and others can't figure it out. Similarly, some sites report that Internet Explorer 6 is really version 4 of the browser!

For the purposes of this book, I've decided that the most important thing is to prepare you for the future of the Web and not stay mired in the past, trying to attain the impossible goal of complete compatibility across all previous versions of all browsers on all operating-system platforms. So I tested all examples against the latest Microsoft browsers (Internet Explorer 5.5 and 6.0) and the latest Netscape browser (Netscape 6).

Figure 4-1   *Browser compatibility chart from Webreview.com.*

Platform	Browser	java	frames	tables	plug-ins	jscript	CSS	gif89	dhtml	1-frames	XML
Win	MS IE 5.5	JDK 1.1[1]	y	y[2]	y	1.5 ECMA[3]	CSS2[4]	y	y[5]	y	p[6]
Win	MS IE 5.0	y	y	y	y	1.3 ECMA	CSS2	y	y	y	p
Win	MS IE 4.0	y	y	y	y	1.2 ECMA	CSS1	y	y	y	n
Win	MS IE 3.0	y	y	y	y	1.0 (k)	p	y	n	y	n
Win	MS IE 2.0	n	n	y	n	n	n	n	n	n	n
Mac	MS IE 5.0	JDK 1.1 [21]	y	y	y	1.3 ECMA	CSS2[20]	y	y[18]	y	p[19]
Mac	MS IE 4.0	y	y	y	y	1.2 ECMA	CSS1	y	y	y	n
Mac	MS IE 3.0	y	y	y	y	1.0 (k)	p	y	n	y	n
Mac	MS IE 2.0	n	y	y	y	n	n	n	n	n	n
UNIX	MS IE 4.01	y	y	y	y	1.2 ECMA	CSS1	y	y	y	n
Platform	Browser	java	frames	tables	plug-ins	jscript	CSS	gif89	dhtml	1-frames	XML
Win	NN 6	JDK 1.3[7]	y	y[2]	y	1.5 ECMA[8]	CSS2[9]	y	y[10]	y[11]	p[12]
Win	NN 4.7/4.5	JDK 1.1	y	y	y	1.3 ECMA	CSS1	y	y	n	n
Win	NN 4	y	y	y	y	1.2	CSS1	y	y	n	n
Win	NN 3.0	y	y	y	y	1.1	n	y	n	n	n
Win	NN 2.0	y	y	y	y	1.0	n	y	n	n	n

Wherever possible, the book's code works on older and divergent browsers. Some of the differences between these browsers, however, are so dramatic — as I discuss shortly regarding the <LAYER> tag — that to make all the examples compatible with all possible browsers would double the length of this book, as well as make the examples many times more complex.

If maximal compatibility is critical to you, well, you've got your work cut out for you. Some scripts are available at the Web archive sites that I highlight in Session 30 that claim a high level of compatibility. The price that you pay, however, is that most don't work for Netscape 6. Yet Netscape 6 is more compliant to the World Wide Web Consortium standards than any other browser currently available, so it represents the future of the Web.

A classic place where compatibility is a problem is with uninitialized properties or variables. Suppose that you have a Web page with an onLoad event handler such as that of the following example:

```
<BODY onLoad="alert("The value of x is currently" + x);
```

The results of this statement are undefined: Most browsers automatically initialize new variables (x, in this case) to zero, but none carry any guarantee to do so.

A more insidious example results if you define a new DIV object that contains, say, a pop-up menu. Assume that you use the correct CSS to specify that it's an absolutely positioned object, and you remember to specify the width and height of the object, but you forget to indicate *where* it's to appear on the page. So where does it appear? On some browsers, an unplaced object automatically goes at 0,0 (the top-left corner), but on many other browsers, the placement seems random. As I developed some of the examples for this book, I was constantly stymied by these differences across different browsers.

Furthermore, you need to understand the history of Web technology, which means that you should recognize that Microsoft prefers ActiveX over Java and VB Script over

JavaScript — even though Java and JavaScript not only are the de-facto standards of the Web, but also are standards that the key national and international standards bodies endorse.

> **Actually, the standardized version of JavaScript is known as ECMAScript, because the European ECMA consortium developed the standard and specification. ECMAScript is, however, based so heavily on JavaScript that distinguishing between the two is almost impossible.**

The greatest irony is that no Dynamic HTML standard actually exists at all. Netscape and Microsoft simply began talking about their collections of layer, style, and scripting capabilities as DHTML, and the term stuck. That's one reason why, if you look at different DHTML books in the bookstore, you find that some cover Cascading Style Sheets, some cover JavaScript, and quite few cover both topics.

> **If you want to learn more about compatibility and standards, a terrific place to explore is the Web Standards Group, at** www.webstandards.org/.

Netscape's Dynamic HTML

20 Min. To Go

Netscape didn't invent so-called Dynamic HTML, but the company was at the forefront of the development of a sophisticated scripting language that offered significant new capabilities for Web developers. Unfortunately, Netscape took a wrong turn during the development of its browser, and Netscape Navigator 4 is an orphan child in the world of Web standards.

The main culprit in Navigator 4 is the <LAYER> tag. It's somewhat similar to the DIV tag, but only Netscape's browser supports it. In fact, not even Netscape 6 supports it. But Netscape 4 doesn't support the DIV tag, so one of the biggest challenges for a Web developer is this conundrum: Develop for Netscape 4? Develop for Netscape 6? Or develop for both?

To adequately develop DHTML solutions that work with both generations of Netscape browsers requires quite complex HTML style Every DIV tag must have a parallel LAYER tag. You see code such as the following example:

```
<if browser == "Netscape" && version == "4">
LAYER tag information
<else>
DIV tag information
```

A lot of people are using Netscape 4.x (usually 4.7) on the Web, but the numbers are dropping every week. Current figures, according to Webreview.com, are as shown in Table 4-1.

Table 4-1   *Popularity of Different Web Browsers, by Version Number*

Browser Version	Market Share (%)
MS IE 5.x	24.9
MS IE 4.x	44.7

Continued

Table 4-1   *Continued*

Browser Version	Market Share (%)
MS IE 3.*x*	3.6
NN 4.*x*	22.0
NN 3.*x*	2.3

Figures from Webreview.com

Slice things a different way, and Microsoft Internet Explorer (MS IE) is still the most popular. Busy Web site Internet.com reports that 77.6 percent of all its visitors use Internet Explorer 5.*x* and 9.5 percent use Internet Explorer 4.*x*, while only 8.3 percent use Netscape Navigator (NN) 4.

You can see these stats for yourself — up-to-date — at
`http://browserwatch.internet.com/stats/icstats.html.`

You find different statistics for just about every site on the Net, but although Netscape 4.*x* continues to play a diminishing role on the Web, whether Netscape 6 can gain traction and become an important browser is still unclear.

If you do want to ensure that you're backward compatible with previous versions of the Netscape browser, your best bet is to read through the materials available at its DevEdge developers Web site. Focus particularly on information about the <LAYER> HTML tag.

DevEdge is online at `http://developer.netscape.com/.`

Microsoft's Dynamic HTML

**10 Min.
To Go**

On the other hand, although Microsoft innovations led to the Cascading Style Sheet standard, the folk at Redmond have a really difficult time accepting that they aren't the inventors of every Web technology. High-tech companies talk about *NIH*, the *not-invented-here* syndrome, where a company must re-invent everything to ensure that it's a unique property of that company. Microsoft definitely suffers from NIH in this regard.

The earlier stats show the popularity of Internet Explorer 4, years after its release, although IE 4 offers miserable support for JavaScript. (Microsoft was still aggressively promoting VB Script at the time and all but ignored the Netscape-invented alternative and subsequent standard.)

The bad news is that Internet Explorer 4 exhibits other shortcomings that make it a difficult browser to develop code for. Not only is its implementation of JavaScript weak, but much of the style-sheet innovation that produced CSS levels 1 and 2 are absent from IE4, too.

But you don't find all this information out on the Microsoft developer's Web site: The Microsoft Developer Network (MSDN) provides far more material on ActiveX than it does about Java and on VB Script than ECMAScript or JavaScript. As a developer, you must be leery of this tendency, because as soon as you develop IE-exclusive sites you program yourself into a corner. Besides, Internet Explorer 6 more fully conforms to the W3C document object model, so it ends up even *more* like Netscape 6 than were earlier versions of IE.

And indeed, that's the point of standardization — so that you don't need to write about how to ensure compatibility across the most recent releases of browsers but can instead focus on backward compatibility. *C'est la vie.*

Setting Expectations

Frankly, my approach to all the compatibility issues is to make sure that my pages and scripts work with Internet Explorer 5.5, add compatibility for Netscape 6, validate again with Internet Explorer 6.0, and then ensure that everything gracefully degrades in earlier browsers. Many of the features that break in earlier browsers are trivial, such as anchor "hover" properties that the browser ignores, so the compatibility hiccups are usually not a big problem. For more serious limitations such as pop-up menus that don't pop up, a good idea is to develop an alternative navigational scheme anyway (such as a text list of navigational choices at the bottom of the page) that solves the problem.

That's the graceful degradation philosophy in a nutshell. If the user has an advanced browser, he gets an advanced level of interaction (you may even say a *dynamic* interaction!), and if he has an older browser, things work, but they're just less exciting.

One important audience to keep in mind is people with disabilities. Well-designed Web sites that support visually impaired surfers, for example, can earn you considerable kudos in this large community. Although DHTML can make your pages a delightfully interactive experience, making it accessible to the *entire* Web community is the best solution.

In the same spirit, I intend to try to set your expectations as you go through this book. All the examples I've tested against the three most current browsers: Internet Explorer 5.5 (Mac), Internet Explorer 6.0 (Windows) and Netscape 6. If you use an older browser, you may find that some of the screenshots don't match your own results, and if you use a *really* old browser, you find that most of these code samples probably don't produce much of anything other than plain old HTML. The solution? Upgrade your browser. To develop state-of-the-art Web sites, you need state-of-the-art tools, and the most important tool is your Web browser.

I include the popular 5.5 release of Internet Explorer on the CD-ROM, but Netscape prefers that you download its software instead. Go to www.netscape.com/ **and click the** download link**. Then get a cup of tea; the process takes quite a while. . . .**

Done!

REVIEW

This session focuses on the origins and effect of incompatible browsers to Web designers. Between the dozens of Web browsers available and the many versions of each — as well as the different operating systems — your user may have any of hundreds of possible configurations. The recommended solution here is to start by developing for Internet Explorer 5.5, the most popular browser on the Net, and then ensure that your code works for Netscape 6, the most standards-compatible browser on the Web. Whether you go farther with your compatibility efforts is most likely to prove a function of your project and target audience. You find no easy answers, and all developers look forward to a day when more compatibility exists between user environments.

QUIZ YOURSELF

1. What does the official standard for Dynamic HTML specify? (See introductory paragraphs.)
2. What happened to Netscape 5? (See introductory paragraphs.)
3. What's notable about the <LAYER> tag? (See "Netscape's Dynamic HTML.")
4. What's the easiest way to avoid seeing uninitialized variables in your own Dynamic HTML development tripping you up? (See introductory paragraphs.)
5. Based on reading the Microsoft Developers Network tutorials and Web reference material, you can safely conclude that Microsoft prefers _____ over Java and _____ over JavaScript. (See introductory paragraphs.)

MAD SCIENTIST WORKSHOP

6. If you have any interest in learning about alternatives to the Big Two browsers, you're in good company if you check out the Opera Web browser or iCab for the Macintosh. Their official sites are at www.opera.com/ and www.icab.de/, respectively.

PART

I

Friday Evening

1. Is "graceful degradation" a good thing or a bad thing?

2. Which of the tags `<BIG>` or `<B>` represent the original intent of the HTML developers?

3. Microsoft/Netscape invented Web style sheets, and Microsoft/Netscape invented JavaScript. Circle the correct company name for each of those two statements.

4. True/False: JavaScript is a subset of the Java programming language.

5. True/False: Neither `</P>` nor `</BR>` are valid tags in HTML 4.01.

6. The `FACE` attribute of the `<FONT>` tag enables you to specify a series of typefaces to try to match for a range of text on a Web page. So why do developers still dislike it?

7. True/False: You use the `<LI>` tag only to produce bullets for a bullet list.

8. The HTML 4.0 specification had some problems. What did the consortium that's responsible for HTML specifications do about them?

9. For that matter, what's the name of the Web-standards consortium?

10. True/False: All JavaScript statements can optionally end with an exclamation mark to force execution.

11. True/False: Single quotes and double quotes are considered interchangeable in JavaScript.

12. What's the correct way to add three to the variable counter in JavaScript?

13. Write the correct JavaScript that assigns the variable `hisQuote` the value
    `"It's exactly as you predicted, Dr. Frankenstein!"` (include the
    opening and closing double quotes).

14. How do you add comments in JavaScript?

15. Write the equivalent `while()` loop sequence for the following:

    ```
    for (var i=0; i<10; i++) {
    write("another line is output");
    }
    ```

16. Write the `if-then-else` equivalent of the following shorthand:

    ```
    x = status==1? 4 : 5
    ```

17. What fundamental problem causes vendors to ignore the DHTML standard
    specification?

18. Netscape 4.x uses a special HTML tag to create layers instead of the `<DIV>`
    tag with absolute positioning. What is it?

19. True/False: The following line of JavaScript is illegal:

    ```
    a = 3; b = 4; c = 5; if (e) f = 33;
    ```

20. Microsoft has its own view of the world. It prefers developers to use
    ActiveX instead of _____ and VB Script instead of _____.

☑ Friday

☑ **Saturday**

☐ Sunday

Part II — Saturday Morning

Session 5
The CSS Language

Session 6
Basic CSS Usage

Session 7
Nifty Font Tricks

Session 8
Additional CSS Text Control

Session 9
CSS Lists

Session 10
Backgrounds and Colors

Part III — Saturday Afternoon

Session 11
Margins and Borders

Session 12
Positioning Content with CSS

Session 13
Visibility, the CSS Solution

Session 14
Layering Content: 3D Web Pages

Session 15
Putting It All Together: Drop-Down Menus

Session 16
Cool CSS Tricks

Part IV — Saturday Evening

Session 17
The Document Object Model

Session 18
Writing and Debugging JavaScript

Session 19
Testing Browser Compatibility

Session 20
Creating a Cross-Platform JavaScript Library

PART

II

Saturday Morning

The CSS Language

Session Checklist

✔ Overview of CSS

✔ Units and colors

✔ Where it goes on your page

✔ CSS isn't HTML

✔ CSS versus JavaScript Style Sheets

**30 Min.
To Go**

Sleep well, I hope? Not too many strange dreams about curly brackets and angle braces chasing you around a strange and peculiar browser environment? Today, I'm really going to jump into the heart of Dynamic HTML, starting with Cascading Style Sheets. Later, I switch to JavaScript, the other core component of DHTML.

As I discuss earlier, Cascading Style Sheets were an innovation added to HTML and Web page layout to enable considerably finer control over the layout and presentation of material on Web pages. Undoubtedly based on templates (which are style sheets, of course) in Microsoft Word, they're a great addition to your Web design skill set because they offer a range of formatting capabilities otherwise unavailable on Web pages.

Why are they *Cascading* Style Sheets? Not because of any beautiful waterfall in the middle of a forest in Washington state, but simply because style definitions cascade down from farthest to closest definition. You see what I mean in this session.

A simple example may be a paragraph of text that you want to indent one inch from the left margin and double-space. You can certainly do so in any word-processing and page-layout program worth its salt, but how do you accomplish this task in HTML? Perhaps a zero-border table with an empty one-inch left column can accomplish the desired indentation, but what about the line spacing? By using CSS, it's super-simple, as the following example shows:

```
<P STYLE="margin-left: 1in; line-height: 200%">
I could not help laughing at the ease with which he
explained his process of deduction. "When I hear
```

```
you give your reasons," I remarked, "the thing
always appears to me to be so ridiculously simple
that I could easily do it myself, though at each
success've instance of your reasoning I am
baffled until you explain your process. And yet
I believe that my eyes are as good as yours."
</P>
```

This code snippet includes a couple things that you want to notice, not the least of which is that the <P> tag is, in fact, a paired tag! You probably never knew that it has a closing tag, because the vast majority of HTML programmers use it without ever closing it. Just as important, the tag uses a new attribute, STYLE, that enables the designer to apply specific styles to a character, line, paragraph, or whatever other container is appropriate. In this case, we're setting the left margin with left-margin: 1in; and changing the line spacing with line-height: 200%.

Most of the examples in this book are from the Project Gutenberg public-domain version of Arthur Conan Doyle's immortal *Adventures of Sherlock Holmes*, specifically one of my favorite Holmes stories: "A Scandal In Bohemia." You can learn more about Project Gutenberg at www.gutenberg. org/, **and you can also read these stories on the CD-ROM that this book includes. Enjoy!**

The style in the code listing specifies a left margin of one inch and a line height that's 200 percent (that is, twice) the default size for the typeface to display. You can see the results of this simple formatting in Figure 5-1.

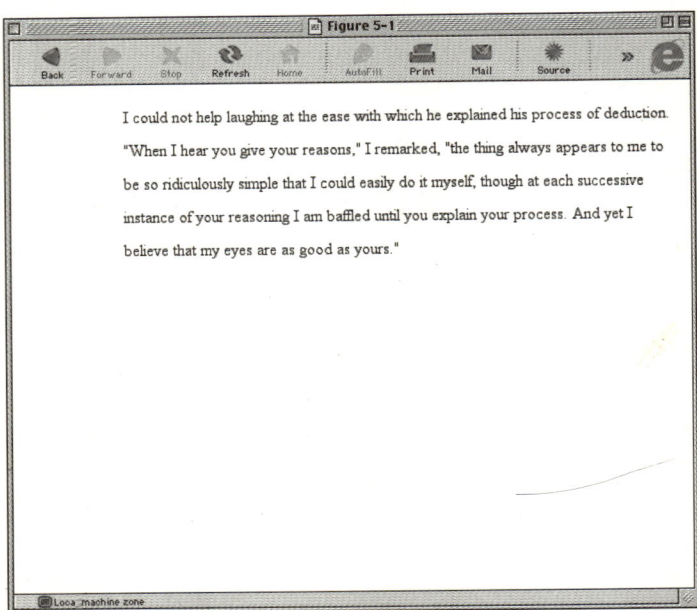

Figure 5-1   Simple in-line style modifications to a paragraph of text.

I need to quickly mention two additional tags here, too, as they became part of HTML simply to make possible these local STYLE definitions without affecting the overall layout of material. They're SPAN and DIV. To explain these tags a different way, the DIV tag forces a break before and after its material, quite similarly to the <P> tag, but the SPAN tag doesn't affect the flow of information other than the styles that you specify in the tag itself.

To be exact, the DIV **container adds a blank line above and below the material that it surrounds, whereas you can use** SPAN **in the middle of a line without any ill effect.**

The difference between the SPAN and DIV tags is really more in intent rather than definition because both are used as neutral containers for information. In general usage, you use SPAN for character and line-oriented formatting, while you use DIV as a larger (document) container. Here's a quick example of the effective use of both:

```
<DIV STYLE="font: blue">
<SPAN STYLE="font: green">"Quite so,"</SPAN>
he answered, lighting a cigarette, and throwing
himself down into an armchair.
<SPAN CLASS="holmes">"You see, but you do not
observe. The distinction is clear. For example,
you have frequently seen the steps which lead
up from the hall to this room."</SPAN>
</DIV>
```

Without any change in the location of characters on the page, the DIV enables me to specify a range of paragraphs or whatever that all display blue text, unless I specify otherwise. Within this container, quotes from Holmes appear in green, first with a SPAN that explicitly states font: green and then with a SPAN that uses a CLASS attribute (which then refers to a larger style definition).

This part of the chapter is a good spot to come back to the *cascading* part of CSS: In this case, the entire document may set text in black (either by using an explicit style definition or simply with a <BODY TEXT=black> HTML tag), but the DIV container specifies that, within its range, text is set in blue. And then, within that range, the SPAN sets text in green. Think of these elements as nesting boxes: The biggest box is the document; then comes the DIV; and then, within the DIV box come a couple SPAN boxes.

Enough introduction! Time to jump right in with an overview of the Cascading Style Sheet language and how it fits into your HTML documents.

Overview of CSS

Using the STYLE attribute on an HTML tag is a nice and succinct way to start exploring style sheets, but it's somewhat of an anomalous usage in a sense, because the formal CSS style definition actually looks as follows:

```
selector { declaration block }
```

A specific example of the elements of a CSS statement can appear as follows:

```
P { margin: 20pt; border: 5px; font-size: 18pt;
    color: blue; }
```

This section of code specifies that every paragraph in the document gets a 20-point margin at the top, bottom, and to both left and right; a five-pixel border; and appears in 18-point blue type. The great thing, of course, is that you need to define this style only *once* and it then affects all subsequent paragraph tags on the page, unless you specify otherwise.

Including CSS styles

You have a variety of ways to include CSS styles on a Web page, too, as you see in a few minutes, but one of the two most common methods is to imply the selector and just specify the declaration block by using the STYLE attribute, as follows:

```
<P STYLE="color: green">some text</P>
```

You can also set a CSS style definition as an HTML block by using the STYLE tag, as follows:

```
<STYLE TYPE="text/css">
P { color: green; }
</STYLE>
```

Both the preceding two code samples show the same typeface color change that you specify. The difference between them is that the former affects only a single paragraph, whereas the latter redefines the <P> tag to include green text throughout the page.

Language considerations

**20 Min.
To Go**

If you're familiar with the American English bias of HTML, discovering that you also define CSS styles by using the same spelling and character set probably comes as no surprise to you. Whether you want to write a Web page in Chinese, Danish, Hebrew or French, you must write your CSS styles in American English. The only exception to this rule are unique identifiers that you create yourself, such as a CLASS definition, but even in that case, you must stick within 8-bit ASCII characters (also known as *Latin-1*).

As a general rule of thumb, if you can't display it on an HTML page without some special sequence such as a character entity (e.g., < or ©), you can't use it in a CSS definition either.

You write *señor*, for example, in HTML as señor, which is your clue that you can't use it within your CSS definitions.

Here's an example of how CSS may integrate two languages, albeit awkwardly:

```
P.arbeitserfahrung { margin: 1in }
```

This line indicates that, each time the <P> tag (which, of course, is a mnemonic for the English word *paragraph* and not the German word *absatz*) is of class *arbeitserfahrung* (*experience*, in English), you need to apply a one-inch margin to it.

Units and Colors

CSS supports a variety of different units of measurement and color specifications. You see a number of them in the examples in preceding sections of this chapter, but I define them all for reference in Table 5-1.

Table 5-1 *CSS Units of Measure*

Measure	Definition	Comment
in	inches	This measure can prove problematic with layout, although people commonly use it. To understand why, try to figure out what 1in becomes if you're simultaneously looking at a page on a computer monitor and projecting it on a screen through an LCD projector.
cm	centimeter	Same problem as inches, of course — just a different measurement.
mm	millimeter	Ditto.
pt	points	A traditional typographic unit. You have 72 points to an inch. You see these measurements a lot because that's the mystery value whenever you talk about a typeface as 18 point (which you describe in CSS as 18pt). For display use, this measure poses the exact same problem as all the preceding measures, as you may expect.
pc	pica	Yet another measure, 1 pica = 12 points = ⅙ inch, so you have 6 picas to an inch. This measure presents the same problem as all the other physical-unit measures.
em	em-height	This measure is relative to the size of the current typeface in use; it's the height of the character box within which you render each character. If you want to make a particular character 50 percent larger than the text surrounding it, you can use <SPAN STYLE="font-size: 150em">bigger</SPAN> than this.
px	pixel	The size of a specific dot of information on-screen, this measure works great for screen displays, but you must redefine it for printers to avoid startling and unexpected results. (Consider: A typical screen is 72-75 dpi, so each pixel is ¹⁄₇₂nd of an inch. On a typical modern printer, however, output renders at 300 dpi, so each pixel is ¹⁄₃₀₀th of an inch. Most browsers sidestep this by multiplying out, so 10px is actually 40px as rendered for printing.)

An amazing number of different units of measure are available in CSS, but you commonly use only two or three: inches, points, and pixels. As is commonly the case on a language that an international committee defines, every possibility is accounted for, even if they don't make much sense. (Why even have centimeters and millimeters?)

A lot of books try to jam every possible value of every possible field into the text, making them 1,000+ pages. Because you want to learn DHTML in a single weekend, I'm skipping that wacky practice and focusing on only the most common and most useful choices. I include some formal specification documents on the CD-ROM if you're dying to know all the possible values for everything!

Color specifications

If you're coming from the world of HTML, you're familiar with one primary mechanism for specifying colors: *hexadecimal RGB notation*. The good news is that CSS style definitions support exactly the same notation. The bad news, however, is that you also have four other ways to specify a color, as shown in Table 5-2.

Table 5-2   *Color Specification Options in CSS*

Specifier	Example	Comment
#RRGGBB	#009900	This notation is the color specification that you've been using for a long time if you're an HTML coder; it's a two-hexadecimal-digit red, green, and blue value, where 00 is the least of a color and FF is the most. It offers more than 16 million possible colors.
#RGB	#090	An interesting variant on the regular #RRGGBB scheme, this specification duplicates each of the values to create a six-digit color. The #090 value, therefore, is identical to #009900. It offers more than 4,000 different possible colors, although if you stick with the so-called Internet-safe color palette, you need only 216 (#0, #3, #6, #9, #C, #F, times three).
rgb(r%,g% b%)	rgb(0%,100%,50%)	An unusual notation, where you specify integer color values for each of the red, green, and blue components. It offers exactly one million possible colors.

Specifier	Example	Comment
rgb(rr,gg,bb)	rgb(128,0,128)	Similar to the previous notation, this specification enables you to use integer color values, but the value can range from 0 to 255. If you do the decimal to hexadecimal math, you find that the two-digit hex notation #RRGGBB offers exactly the same number of choices — just in a different way. It offers more than 16 million possible colors.
Colorname	blue	The CSS standard defines 16 colors by name, and they're the 16 colors of the original VGA palette: aqua, black, blue, fuchsia, gray, green, lime, maroon, navy, olive, purple, red, silver, teal, white, and yellow. Some browsers can recognize more color names, but the specification includes only these 16.

One important thing to point out is that, whenever you specify a value, you also need to specify a unit of measure, and you must append that the unit of measure to the numeric value without any spaces. Using 15 pt is wrong, while 15pt is correct.

In addition, a number of CSS elements enable you to specify the URL of a Web site or other material. If you use any of these elements, you're strongly recommended to make all your URLs absolute. Don't use ../part2.css or any other shorthand; always use a complete specifier, starting with http:// ...

 The CSS specification talks about URIs rather than URLs. They're essentially the same thing, but *URI* stands for *Uniform Resource Identifier*, whereas *URL* is *Uniform Resource Locator*.

10 Min.
To Go

Where It Goes on Your Page

Before getting too involved with the CSS specification, learning where this stuff goes on a Web page is pretty helpful, isn't it? In the section "Including CSS styles" earlier in this chapter, you see an example of adding a STYLE attribute and another example of using a DIV or SPAN container to apply the STYLE attribute to a specific sequence of HTML, but you have even more options!

You have three basic ways to include CSS styles on your Web page: inline, in the HEAD section, or in a referenced file. The following sections describe each method.

Inline CSS

This method is the most obvious of the possibilities and is the one that I use in earlier examples: add a STYLE attribute to just about any HTML tag and, magically, you apply the style to the contents of that tag in all CSS-compliant browsers.

**Didja catch that last disclaimer? Yep, I said, "in all CSS-compliant browsers."
Try as they may, Web developers can't force every person on the planet to
upgrade to a 100-percent CSS-compliant Web browser. Although most modern
browsers support at least the most valuable parts of the CSS language, excep-
tions do exist. Please jump back to Chapter 4 to explore this subject further.**

The two most common tags where I see added STYLE attributes are the <P> tag and the
<A> tag. The following listing demonstrates both:

```
<P STYLE="font-size: 18pt; line-height: 30pt;
    background: #9F9; text-align: center">
<A HREF="http://www.gutenberg.org/"
    STYLE="background: yellow; color: black;">
The Project Gutenberg</A> Etext of<BR>
The Adventures of Sherlock Holmes<BR>
#15 in our series by Arthur Conan Doyle
</P>
```

The preceding HTML typifies inline CSS, with a paragraph that specifies 18-point text
with a 30-point leading, a light-green background, and centered text. The single hypertext
reference puts the text in black (rather than the default blue) and the background of the
link in yellow. Figure 5-2 shows the results in a Web browser.

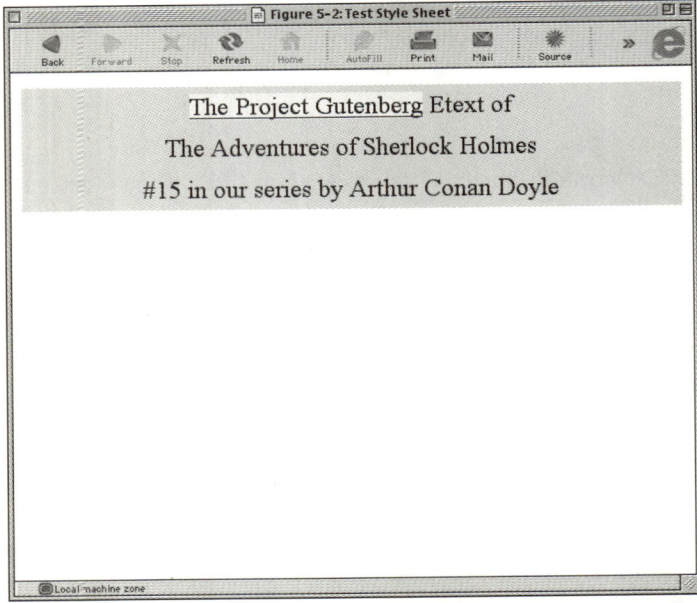

Figure 5-2   Inline CSS example offers easy color changes.

The STYLE element

The second approach to including CSS in your Web page is considerably more efficient than having it inline, embedded who-knows-where in your HTML documents. It uses an HTML tag that you probably haven't used before — STYLE — and enables you to drop full CSS specifications therein, as the following example demonstrates:

```
<HEAD>
<TITLE>The Rockin' Style Element at Work!</TITLE>
<STYLE TYPE="text/css">
P     { background: blue; color: white;
        padding: 4pt; }
H1    { color: #339; text-align: center;
        background: yellow; }
BODY { color: #060; background: #CFC;
        margin-left: 5em; margin-right: 5em;
        font-weight: 700; }
.ACT { background: #66F; }
</STYLE>
</HEAD>
```

Subsequent to this definition, you can then list pure HTML, knowing that the CSS specified at the beginning affects the definition of the different tags.

The following straightforward HTML, for example, produces some rather delightful results if you view it in a browser:

```
<H1>A Scandal In Bohemia</H1>
<I>continued...</I>
<P>
"The man who wrote it was presumably well to do,"
I remarked, endeavoring to imitate my companion's
processes. "Such paper
could not be bought under half a crown a packet.
It is peculiarly strong and stiff."</P>
<P>
"Peculiar--that is the very word," said Holmes.
"It is not an
English paper at all. Hold it up to the light."</P>
<P CLASS="ACT">
I did so, and saw a large "E" with a small "g,"
a "P," and a
large "G" with a small "t" woven into the
texture of the paper.</P>
```

Other than the single reference to the class "ACT" in the last paragraph tag, this example is the type of HTML you were writing after you first learned how to organize text so that it'd appear reasonably coherent on a Web page. Surprise! Look in Figure 5-3 at how this example formats with the CSS definitions.

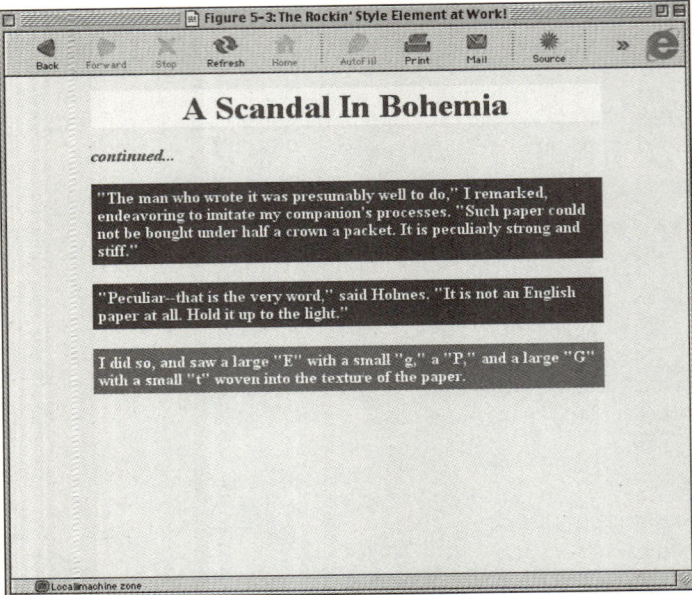

Figure 5-3   Remarkable results for CSS and plain old HTML!

The LINK element

If you can take the CSS elements out of the STYLE attribute and drop them into a STYLE block, why not share a single STYLE block across all the Web pages on your site? That's exactly what the LINK element enables you to do, as the following example shows:

```
<LINK TYPE="text/css"
  HREF="http://www.intuitive.com/stylesheet.css">
```

Add this code to the beginning of every page on the Web site, and a single set of CSS definitions now control the appearance of the entire site. This approach is really the ideal one to using CSS on a site, because it not only offers complete consistency across the site, but it also makes updating and modifying the site a breeze.

Imagine that you just finished a 238-page online employee handbook for your company, and your boss pops her head in, saying, "Sorry, but we've decided that all the text needs to be in Palatino, not Arial, and that we want 1½ spacing throughout. Is that a hassle?" If you didn't use a shared style sheet, you can kiss that long weekend in Maui goodbye right about now, but if you were smart enough to do things the right way, it's only 30 seconds work and then "Hello, beautiful white sand beaches!"

CSS Isn't HTML

This statement — that CSS isn't HTML — may seem an obvious point, but I do want to highlight that CSS isn't a formal part of the HTML language specification at all and that a browser that's completely and 100-percent compliant with even the very latest version of HTML may experience a very broken CSS implementation.

I'm not so worried about Internet Explorer or Netscape Navigator, but think more about the mini-Web browsers showing up on smaller devices, such as PocketPC systems, from Microsoft, or the latest Web-enabled cellular telephone.

These particular examples face other presentation issues, but I predict that small, custom Web browsers are going to become pervasive in the technologically overzealous Western nations and that they're likely to have varying CSS support.

Do you really care whether the Web browser built in to your 2006 model-year refrigerator supports every possible style sheet attribute? Well, maybe you do! Certainly, if you're going to rely on CSS support in newer browsers, you may want to think carefully before betting the family farm.

On the bright side, CSS *isn't* HTML, so you're free of the shackles of a primitive and limiting mechanism for specifying layout and presentation of material on a Web page. The awkward and oft-torturous HTML required for sophisticated layout with tables and one-pixel GIFs were the two killer design strategies for Web pages in the late 1990s for good reason: No better solutions were available.

Now you have a much better layout solution! Although the Cascading Style Sheet language is a bit peculiar and very unlike HTML, CSS is very powerful and, as you see as you progress through this book, it offers all sorts of way-cool capabilities that HTML designers can only dream about if they're trapped in the straight HTML world.

 How different are the two languages? Well, even down to the most fundamental name/value pairs: In HTML, it's `NAME="value"` and, in CSS, it's `NAME: value`. Can't anyone ever agree in these crazy committees?

CSS versus JavaScript Style Sheets

Just as you thought it was safe to finish reading this session, I'm springing something completely new on you, aren't I? Yes, you may now encounter a completely different type of Style Sheet called *JavaScript Style Sheets*. Now, before you pop that Prozac or call that Web design consultant, I can assure you that, in fact, JSS are incredibly similar to CSS. Really.

JSS came from the people at Netscape who, having finally gotten the rest of the world to agree that JavaScript 1.2 was a cool scripting language, decided that it'd be doubly cool to reinvent Cascading Style Sheets to more explicitly support JavaScript syntax. Seems an unhelpful move to me, but — hey! — I'm just the writer, right?

Anyway, JSS is Netscape Navigator-only, and it's quite similar to CSS, although not exactly the same. Most notably, the majority of CSS attributes lose the hyphen after they become JSS, as Table 5-3 highlights.

Table 5-3   *A Few Highlights of CSS:JSS Correspondence*

CSS	JSS Equivalent
font-size	fontSize
line-height	lineHeight

Continued

Table 5-3   Continued

CSS	JSS Equivalent
text-align	textAlign
background-image	backgroundImage

One important difference is that JSS uses the familiar equals sign (=) for name/value pairs, so font-size: 12pt works for CSS, but fontSize="12pt" is the JSS equivalent.

 So why use JSS? I can cite very few compelling reasons. At best, if you're developing for a pure Netscape environment, JSS offer a couple of capabilities that may push you over to this alternative, but the downside of becoming less portable should make the decision a careful one.

Here's a brief example of JSS at work:

```
<STYLE TYPE="text/javascript">
    tags.P.fontSize="16pt";
</STYLE>
```

Looks pretty familiar, but remember, it works *only* on a Netscape browser.

For the remainder of this book, I don't reference JavaScript Style Sheets at all.

Done!

REVIEW

This session is the first of two that give you the foundation of Cascading Style Sheets; this one focuses on where you add CSS specifications to your Web pages and Web site and talks about the specific measurements and color specifications that are available. In addition, I cover the core differences between CSS and HTML and also briefly touch on the aberrant stepchild, JavaScript Style Sheets, which are likely to have come and gone as you continue through the crash course. Most important, this session demonstrates the value of centralized styles and how simple changes to a single CSS definition can easily trickle throughout dozens, hundreds, or even thousands of Web pages.

QUIZ YOURSELF

1. Why are Cascading Style Sheets called "Cascading"? (See introductory paragraphs.)
2. What's the difference between DIV and SPAN? (See introductory paragraphs.)
3. In what situations do you use a CLASS CSS style? (See "Language considerations.")
4. Which of the following are legal CSS class identifiers? *Añejo, frosch, aeroporto, soupcor* (See "Language considerations.")
5. What's the essential problem with inches, centimeters, and so on, and CSS styles? (See "Units and Colors.")
6. Where in the sequence <HTML><HEAD></HEAD><BODY></BODY></HTML> do you correctly put the STYLE element? (See "Where It Goes on Your Page.")

Basic CSS Usage

Session Checklist

✔ Working with CSS
✔ Selectors
✔ CLASS versus ID

**30 Min.
To Go**

ast session focused on the foundations of the Cascading Style Sheet language, including highlighting some weaknesses and peculiarities. This session expands on that foundation and prepares you to jump right in and start adding CSS styles to your own Web pages, starting with the very next chapter.

As a result, I'm going to cheat; this 30-minute lesson should take you only 28 minutes! Ready? Go to it!

Working with CSS

To fully understand the rules of CSS, your best course is to start trying to think of CSS as a programming language unto itself. What makes using CSS tricky, however, is that your Web browser won't give any indication if it encounters any problems in your style specification; instead, it simply ignores the problem. No helpful error messages appear on-screen: no `colon expected` or `Did you mean 'font-width:' in line 35`? You save yourself lots of grief, therefore, if you learn right off to be careful and methodical with your CSS definitions.

The first rule of working with CSS, then, is that Web browsers display results but never indicate errors.

The spotty history of CSS support

Given the popularity of Cascading Style Sheets, you'd think that the groups developing Web browsers would be eager to be the first to state that they're 100-percent compliant with the specification. The sad reality is otherwise: Each development team uses a subset of CSS that it supports, and none includes absolutely everything.

This situation is also true across platforms, as I discuss in Session 4. Features that may be available in Internet Explorer 5.0 for Windows aren't necessarily available in Internet Explorer 5.0 for the Macintosh. This situation isn't too surprising really. Between incorporating plug-ins, adding complete JavaScript support, and including new HTML tags and oodles of other features (such built-in auction-tracking capabilities), these development teams have had quite a job just keeping up. No wonder they haven't had time to standardize across platforms.

But the situation isn't all gloom and doom, however, because the vast majority of style definitions that I discuss in this book work exactly as you want them to in most modern browsers.

Nonetheless, CSS rule two is that no Web browser works with every element of the CSS specification.

Hiding your STYLE

One remarkable feature of HTML is that it's silent in encountering errors, which can become a problem, as I explain earlier in this section on working with CSS. But it can also prove a boon. Specifically, Web browsers silently ignore anything that they don't understand. Misspell BLOCKQUOTE as BLOKQOTE and your browser just ignores it: no error, no problem — just no formatting or layout change occurs.

The same holds true of attributes in an HTML tag, so the following example is perfectly valid and usable HTML:

```
<IMG SRC="pic2.jpg" CUTE="yes" SINGLE="yes">
```

This tag is functionally identical to an HTML tag that doesn't include the CUTE or SINGLE attributes, but you can't find a browser that complains about it, so they can be included knowing that the IMG tag will be interpreted as if they were omitted.

So why is this characteristic of silently ignoring unknown HTML a good thing? Because after you start adding CSS to your Web pages, you need to consider what happens to people who use non-CSS-enabled browsers (Lynx, WebTV, etc). Adding a STYLE attribute to an existing tag is completely safe; the browser just ignores them, as it ignores the CUTE and SINGLE attributes in the preceding example.

More challenging is to create a style block in the head of a page that a browser ignores. Fortunately, you can subvert HTML comments to accomplish this task quite transparently. So you don't want to create a sequence such as the following:

```
<STYLE TYPE="text/css">
 B { color: blue; }
</STYLE>
```

Instead, the safer and more portable way to specify this sequence is to wrap the style in comments, as in the following example:

```
<STYLE TYPE="text/css">
<!--
B { color: blue; }
-->
</STYLE>
```

I usually skip the comments in the listings in this book in the interest of squeezing more in, but good form dictates that you use the sequence shown here.

Some HTML tags can't receive styles

I also need to mention that you can't add the STYLE attribute to a couple HTML tags at all — in particular, the following:

-
- <FRAMESET>
- <FRAME>

What may surprise you, however, is that you can change the styles associated with every other HTML tag, although you can't apply all types of CSS styles to all tags.

That makes sense if you think about it: You can't add a margin specification or additional line spacing to an italic tag.

Again, you know that it's not working if . . . well, it doesn't work.

**20 Min.
To Go**

CSS supports two kinds of comments

Earlier, you saw that // denotes a comment in your CSS that runs through until the end of the line, as in the following example:

```
B { color: blue; }    // We really like bold to be blue.
```

This double-slash comment notation comes from JavaScript, as you learned in Session 3.

You can also add a multiline comment by using a completely different type of comment notation, this one coming from the C programming language, as the following example shows:

```
/* This is the notation that you need for a multiline comment.
   Added by: Dave Taylor
   Date: 3 August
   Justification: S43/9, from client
*/
```

These comments can appear anywhere in a CSS segment, even within a declaration block, as shown in the following example:

```
B { color: blue; /* blue is cool */  margin: 3em; }
```

Use lots of comments in your more complex CSS segments, particularly if you use separate style sheets that you share among multiple pages on your site. A few minutes that you can spend documenting your style definitions is worth hours of puzzling things out later if someone requests modifications.

Selectors

All CSS specifications consist of two parts, a selector and a declaration block, as in the following example:

```
selector    { declaration block }
```

The most common selector is an existing HTML tag, as in the following example (which would be wrapped in <STYLE> and </STYLE> tags or in its own CSS include file, recall):

```
BODY { font: blue; }
```

This tag specifies that all text on the page is set in blue type (a feat that you can also accomplish by using the HTML sequence <BODY TEXT=blue>, but as you shortly see, CSS is infinitely more powerful and flexible than HTML tags).

The declaration block, which you surround with curly brackets ({}), always appears in the form of *name*: *value*, with semicolons separating multiple definitions. The language that can go in declaration blocks is the subject of much of this book, actually, and hundreds of capabilities enable you to use thousands of different combinations and results.

I show in Figure 5-1, in Chapter 5, how to use the STYLE attribute with the P tag to specify a left margin and additional leading. To apply this style to *all P tags*, you can instead define it as follows:

```
P   { margin-left: 1in; line-height: 200% }
```

The capability to simultaneously affect the presentation of all occurrences of a particular HTML tag is one of the biggest benefits of CSS.

One nice shorthand, too, is that you can specify a style definition for a number of HTML tags simultaneously simply by separating them with commas as you list them, as in the following example:

```
B, I, U, TT { color: green; }
```

This line automatically turns all bold, italic, underlined, or monospace (TT) type sequences green.

The preceding example demonstrates the most common sort of CSS selector — a type selector — but a bunch of different selectors actually are possible. These different selectors offer you considerable flexibility in formatting not only Web pages, but also entire sites.

Class selectors

As you write Web documents, you may want to apply a consistent set of formatting attributes to all material of a particular type. In CSS, this set of attributes is a *class*, and a *class selector* is one that you preface with a period, as in the following example:

```
.prod { font: blue; margin-left: 1in; margin-right: 1in; border: 1px solid
blue }
```

This selector indicates that any material that you denote as CLASS="prod" appears in blue type with a one-inch left and right margin and inside a one-pixel, solid-blue border.

If I were writing a screenplay, here's how I might use the prod class definition:

```
<P>
<B>ELDER HARITH</B><BR>
He for whom nothing is written may write himself a clan. Salaam.
<P>
<B>LAWRENCE</B><BR>
Salaams.
<P CLASS="prod">He strides a hesitant pace or two and
smiles bashfully. For once it is he who is waiting for a lead.</P>
<B>ELDER HARITH</B><BR>
They are good for riding. Try!
<P>
<B>LAWRENCE</B><BR>
Yes.<BR>
(he turns and picks up his camel saddle,
turns back to them. Strongly.)<BR>
Great honour!
```

 **This example is pretty awkward HTML, other than the class specifier, I admit.**

One interesting thing to notice in this example is that mixing <P> tags with closing tags and those without is perfectly acceptable (although not fabulous form). Really, all <P> tags in your HTML should end with </P>, but that's just not too common on the Web.

The .prod class specifier is a generic class specifier and matches any tag that indicates that it's part of that particular class. So I can also use it in <H2 CLASS="prod"> and <TD CLASS="prod">.

If you'd rather specify a class in association with a specific tag, CSS supports that capability, too, as the following example shows:

```
P.prod { font: blue; margin-left: 1in; margin-right: 1in; border: 1px
solid blue }
```

With this definition, <H2 CLASS="prod"> refers to an undefined style specifier (the prod class is only defined for the P tag) and the class, therefore, is ignored for presentation and formatting.

To put a couple of these class styles together, here's how a few lines of a CSS definition may look:

```
P.fx   { margin: 1in; }
H1.fx { margin: 2in; border: 4px solid blue }
H2.fx { margin: 2in; border: 1px solid blue }
```

I hope that you can follow what's happening here! If not, I suggest you take a few minutes to read through Session 5 again.

Other specialized selectors

CSS supports a couple other selectors, but the odds are very good that you're unlikely ever to use them, and in any case, your browser probably doesn't implement them correctly anyway. Nonetheless, for completeness sake, the following sections offer a very fast overview.

Descendant selectors

A *descendant selector* is quite a bit more sophisticated than the type selector, shown at beginning of this section, and it looks as follows:

```
P B { font-weight: 900; color: blue; }
```

This line specifies that you're applying these formatting instructions — a double-bold font weight and a blue color — to all B tags but only those that appear within a P container. If you have a B tag that doesn't appear within the scope of a P tag, these specifications don't affect it.

 **Font weights in CSS range from 100 (the lightest) to 900 (the heaviest), with 400 as regular type and 700 as bold type. A weight of 900 is essentially double-bold, or *heavy*, in typeface jargon.**

Following's an example of how to use a descendant selector:

```
<STYLE TYPE="text/css">
 P B { font-weight: 900; color: blue; }
</STYLE>
"Peculiar--that is the very word," said Holmes.
"It is not an <B>English paper</B> at all.
Hold it up to the light."
<P>
I did so, and saw a large "E" with a small
"g," a "P," and a large "G" with a small "t"
woven <B>into the texture of the paper.</B>
</P>
"What do you make of that?" asked Holmes.
```

Figure 6-1 shows the results of this CSS snippet as you view it in a Web browser.

Remarkably, you can go three, four, five, or more levels deep by using this kind of descendant selector (imagine: "P B TT I" says that it should only be applied to I tags within TT tags, within B tags, within P containers!), but I'm unclear why you'd want to ever get that much of a headache.

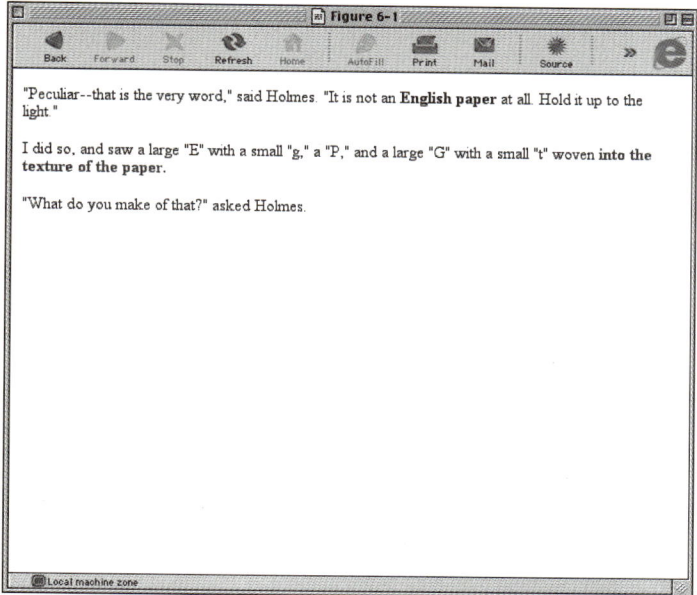

Figure 6-1　*Descendant Selectors enable you to apply styles in context.*

Attribute selectors

An *attribute selector* enables you to specify the formatting of a specific attribute of a tag, as the following example demonstrates:

```
A[link] { color: blue; }
```

This example specifies that the unvisited link color of A (anchor) tags appear in blue. The attributes can also contain values for the browser to test against, as in the following line:

```
A[link="http://www.intuitive.com/"] { font-weight: bold; }
```

This line specifies that if an unvisited link points to the specified URL, that link is to appear in bold text.

ID selectors

Very similar to class selectors, *ID selectors* enable you to associate a specific style with what are typically unique elements on a Web page. An ID selector begins with a # and looks as follows:

```
#firstline { font-size: 150%; margin-left: 5em; }
```

And you reference it in an HTML tag as follows:

```
<P ID="firstline">Material to have the special formatting applied...</P>
```

Read on in the following section for more information about class versus ID in CSS.

 **A couple of additional selector possibilities exist, but I've never seen them in use and surmise that you're unlikely to either. If you really want to get into the guts of the CSS definition and find out about these selectors, I recommend** www.w3c.org/ **on the Web as a good starting point.**

Class versus ID

You can associate a set of style attributes with a given section of a Web page or even across elements of a Web site in a bunch of ways, as I describe in the preceding sections. You probably assume that, as the standardization group began to debate different solutions for addressing this need, they agreed to include every possibility.

But, perhaps surprisingly, they didn't. One possibility that intrigued me as I first started reading about style sheets years ago was the idea that I could literally define my own HTML tags. What a cool idea! I'd use H0 for super-important headers, and IP for indented paragraphs, NOTE for notes, TIP for tips, and so on. Fortunately for the rest of the world, CSS and Web browsers don't support that capability!

That's what CLASS and ID styles are for instead. In many ways, the two are interchangeable on your Web page, and both enable you to associate styles with an arbitrary set of different HTML tags as necessary. You define them, for example, as follows:

```
.myclass { margin: 3em; }
#myid { margin: 4em; }
```

And you use them as follows:

```
<P CLASS="myclass">material with a 3em margin added.</P>
<P ID="myid">and some material with a 4em margin.</P>
```

The important nuance between these two is that a CLASS is for use to denote a recurring style, whereas you use an ID for a single element on a Web page. Think of an old illuminated manuscript, where the first letter of the first word of the first paragraph of each chapter was beautifully illustrated with ornate details and the rest of the text was plain and ordinary by comparison. Now imagine that this same illuminated manuscript used Note boxes as this book does. The former would be an ID element, whereas the latter, which could appear anywhere from zero to dozens of times in a chapter, would be a CLASS element.

Also worth pointing out is that fact that you can reference both CLASS and ID elements — and even reference more than one CLASS — in a single HTML tag, as the following example shows:

```
<P CLASS="note" CLASS="illustrated" ID="firstnote">This is the first note
and it should be illustrated, too, if we can believe the class names</P>
```

I haven't found the ID value too useful in my Web development, but CLASS is a handy way to pretend that you can define your own HTML tags. Instead of using <NOTE></NOTE> as a way to wrap special notes on a page, <P CLASS="NOTE"></P> is a pretty reasonable alternative.

Actually, the classic CSS solution to this situation is to use the DIV or SPAN tags, as appropriate: <SPAN CLASS="note"> gives me an HTML element that's relative to the styles that I define for the 'note' class.

Done!

REVIEW

This session completes your overview of Cascading Style Sheets, which I start in the preceding session. Here, I focus on some of the key rules of working with CSS, including the various comment formats and the good and bad of how Web browsers ignore markup that they don't understand. The main topic of this session, however, is the many different selectors that are available in CSS definitions, which offer you great control over what styles affect what markup on your page. The most common selectors are HTML tags, but you can add your own CLASS and ID styles, as necessary, and you can also use contextual and attribute selectors for complete control. Finally, I look at the differences between CLASS and ID and explore when they're appropriate in your design work.

QUIZ YOURSELF

1. You're best off thinking of CSS as what to help you remember syntax rules? (See "Working with CSS.")

2. What's the worst thing about how Web browsers ignore errors? The best? (See "Hiding your STYLE.")

3. All the following lines are wrong. Fix them.

```
.joe { font-family: cursive; /* joe always curses }
.mike { color: green; // mike's always been envious of joe }
.sue { margin: 5 in; /* she's marginal, at best */ }
.nikki { padding: 4em } // no comment.
```

(See "CSS supports two kinds of comments.")

4. Match the selector with the example:

```
BODY { color: blue; }          ID
.NOTE { margin: 2in; }         Descendant
P I { color: green; }          Type
A[link] { padding: 1in; }      Class
#ILLUM { font-weight: 800; }   Attribute
```

(See "Selectors.")

5. Typically, you use CLASS styles for _____ whereas you use ID styles for _____. (See "Class versus ID.")

Nifty Font Tricks

Session Checklist

✔ Setting fonts

✔ Tweaking font sizes

✔ Setting font styles

✔ Font name issues

**30 Min.
To Go**

The last few sessions focused on giving you the foundations of working with Cascading Style Sheets, and I hope that you're now eager to get started actually getting your hands dirty (or your HTML dirty!) with actual CSS styles, because this session begins the fun part of the book. Starting with this session, you learn all about the CSS language, what you can — and should — do on your pages and have lots to try.

In fact, I strongly suggest that you ensure that, for the rest of the sessions today and tomorrow, you have a computer in front of you, with this book right by the monitor and your fingers flashing across the keyboard trying everything out.

Of course, all the examples in this session are also on the CD-ROM, but I think you're likely to find that taking a sample Web page of your own and starting to experiment with styles therein is considerably more exciting than just using the CD examples.

I'm a very hands-on learner myself, so my setup looks as follows: On my Macintosh, I keep either BBEdit or SimpleText open on an HTML document and a Web browser (usually Microsoft Internet Explorer) showing me the same document with all the formatting as it appears on the Web. My PC equivalent setup is either HomeSite or NotePad for the HTML document and a Web browser there (again, probably IE), too. With these programs open, typing some sample CSS, JavaScript, or HTML into the editor, saving it to disk, and then reloading the page in the Web browser to see what happens is quite simple.

Not only are the examples in this session on the CD-ROM, but trial versions of BBEdit and HomeSite (along with lots of other goodies!) are also on the disk. If you haven't popped it into your computer yet, now's a good time to take a few minutes to check it out!

Most of the CSS styles that I explore in this session (and subsequently) you can put either in a style declaration (the <STYLE></STYLE> block) or add as a STYLE attribute to an individual HTML tag. To keep the source listings as simple as possible, I mostly use the inline STYLE attribute so that I can contrast different styles on a single page, but please feel free to place them in a style declaration instead if you prefer. The first few examples I present both ways to help clarify this difference.

Ready? Go!

Setting Fonts

Among the easiest and most powerful presentation elements that CSS offers control over are *fonts*. More correctly, these elements are *typefaces*, but as is true of so many modern programming languages, CSS suffers from just a bit of confusion about the difference between the two.

Typefaces are a general design of text, so Times is a typeface. A *font*, by contrast, is a specific example of a typeface. So although *Times* is a typeface, *Times 14-point bold* is a font. (I grew up steeped in this stuff, because my Dad was a typeface designer for many years.)

As you know, you don't have much control over type presentation on a Web page other than by using the rather clunky FONT tag with its three attributes; FACE, SIZE, and COLOR. The SIZE is probably the worst of these three, because it enables you to specify only a size ranging from 1 to 7, with 1 the smallest and 7 the largest. But who knows what size SIZE=1 really represents for any given user?

The FONT NAME attribute (which, of course, is really a TYPEFACE NAME, but I'm not going there!) is similar to one of the CSS font attributes, and it's a good place to start.

HTML and CSS, as a general rule, enable you to specify a particular style, format, or presentation element, and then the Web browser either renders it on-screen or fails and ignores it. The FONT NAME attribute is rather unique, however, because it enables you to list a series of possible values, and the Web browser then tries to match them, one by one, left to right, until it either succeeds or fails and defaults to the current typeface in use.

The tag and attribute usually looks as follows:

```
<FONT NAME="Arial,Palatino,Helvetica">
The rain in Spain falls mainly on the plain.
</FONT>
```

A browser interprets this example as requesting Arial as the typeface to use for the passage, and if that font isn't available on the computer, it tries Palatino. If Palatino isn't available, it attempts to use Helvetica; finally, if all of these options fail, it uses instead the default typeface (as users configure in their Web-browser preferences).

The CSS equivalent of this statement is as follows:

```
<P STYLE="font-family: Arial, Palatino, Helvetica">
The rain in Spain falls mainly on the plain. (inline STYLE attribute)
</P>
```

The style block version of this example looks quite similar, although I'm going to define a CSS CLASS so that I can avoid automatically changing all paragraphs on the page, as follows:

```
<STYLE TYPE="text/css">
P.arial {font-family: Arial, Palatino, Helvetica; }
</STYLE>
<P CLASS="arial">
The rain in Spain falls mainly on the plain. (CLASS=arial)
</P>
```

I combine both of these examples for Figure 7-1 so that you can see that they display identical results if you view them in a Web browser.

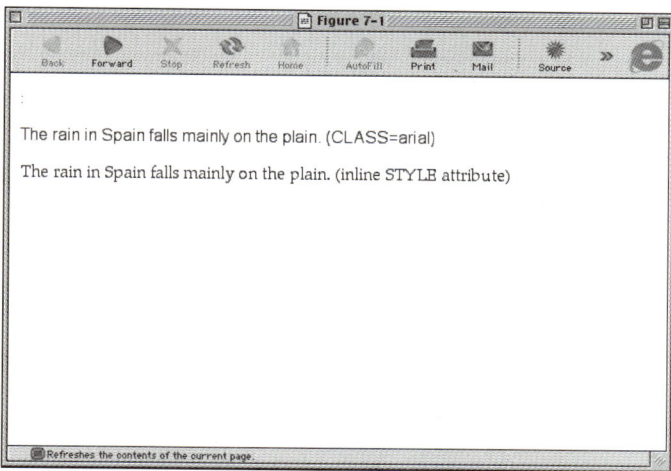

Figure 7-1   *A list of named typefaces in CSS.*

To make this situation a bit more interesting, look what happens if I add a couple non-sensical typeface names to the list in the following example:

```
<P STYLE="font-family: puddlejump, helvetica, dogbowl">
It was a dark and stormy night, but 222 1/2 Baker Street remained
peaceful.
</P>
```

If you're expecting the results to be identical to what you'd see if you used only font-family: helvetica, you're absolutely correct. Try typing the preceding snippet on your computer to see what happens!

One rule worth mentioning is that, if the typeface names have spaces, you must surround them with quote marks in the list — for example, "Times Roman PS", Arial. Some people suggest using quote marks around all typeface names in these sort of lists, but I recommend only that you pay attention to single versus double quotes: If you're using a STYLE attribute that requires double quotes, use single quotes for the typeface names or, if they don't contain spaces, simply omit the quote marks from the names themselves for simplicity.

Notice that typeface names are case insensitive, so Arial, arial, and ARIAL all specify the same typeface. I recommend that you pick a standard naming convention and try to stick with it for simplicity. (I like just using a first-letter uppercase version, because it's a formal name.)

This approach to listing typefaces by name seems quite easy and straightforward until you remember that thousands of different typefaces are available and that the same typeface can use different names on different computer systems. Then this approach suddenly starts to seem a wee bit more tricky. . . .

I discuss some of the problems inherent with differing typeface names shortly, but for now, Table 7-1 shows a list of some of the most common Mac and PC typefaces.

Table 7-1 *Common Mac and PC Typeface Names*

Typeface Name	Platform
Arial	Mac/PC
Bookman	PC
Chicago	Mac
Courier	Mac/PC
Geneva	Mac
Gill Sans	PC
Helvetica	Mac
Lucida	PC
Palatino	Mac
Times	Mac/PC

Some of these typefaces are available on more platforms because application programs install the typefaces as you install them on the computer — most notably, the Arial family, which installs automatically with Microsoft Internet Explorer. Originally, Arial was a Windows typeface, and you were unlikely to find it on a Macintosh system.

If you want to emulate the <TT> HTML tag, you can do so by adding the following line to your CSS:

```
<SPAN STYLE="font-family: Courier">monospace element</SPAN>
```

Or you can get fancy and specify a CSS CLASS of monospace, as in the following example:

```
<STYLE TYPE="text/css">
.monospace { font-family: Courier; font-size: 90%; >
</STYLE>
```

This example results in an appearance more like that of the <TT>, tag because it also slightly shrinks down the type, too. It's more visually appealing.

Tweaking Font Sizes

**20 Min.
To Go**

Now that you can specify typefaces by name, you need to know how to specify the size of a particular passage of text or style overall. Recall that the <SPAN> tag is the perfect container for an inline STYLE attribute, so that's what I use in the following example:

```
<P STYLE="font-size: 16pt">
"Wedlock suits you," he remarked. "I think, Watson, that you have put on
<SPAN STYLE="font-size: 22pt">seven and a half pounds</SPAN> since I saw
you."
</P>
<P STYLE="font-size: 16pt; color: blue">
"<SPAN STYLE="font-size: 22pt">Seven</SPAN>!" I answered.
</P>
<P STYLE="font-size: 16pt">
"Indeed, I should have thought a little more. Just a trifle more, I fancy,
Watson...
</P>
```

The results of this formatting appear are as shown in Figure 7-2.

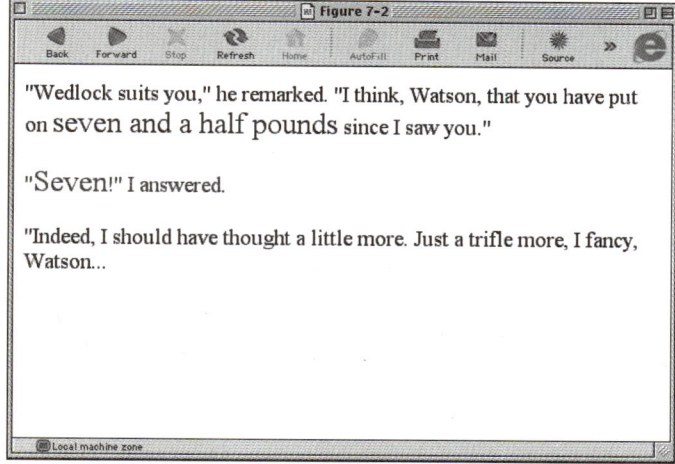

Figure 7-2 *Typeface sizes are inherited if not specified.*

You want to notice a number of things in this example, not the least of which is the all-important CSS *inheritance* concept (the "Cascading" part), which the protestation by Watson in the second line neatly demonstrates. The <P> tag style specifies the typeface as 16 point for all text within its container and also specifies that it appears in blue. Within the <P> container, however, the SPAN tag overrides the size specification with its own (22pt) setting, but because it doesn't specify a type color, it inherits the blue color from the <P> container. The next paragraph, however, in its own container, *doesn't* inherit the blue attribute that only applied to the second paragraph container. This point is very important!

The second thing to notice here is that this HTML code is really begging for either an overall redefinition of the paragraph tag as 16-point type or at least a CSS CLASS of paragraph that displays this attribute. These two improvements to the coding style simplify things considerably, as the following example shows:

```
<STYLE TYPE="text/css">
P { font-size: 16pt; }
P.story { font-size: 16pt }
</STYLE>
```

You may prefer one or the other, but either way, my druthers are always to minimize the amount of typing necessary to produce the desired effect.

The FONT SIZE attribute offers seven possible typeface sizes, with quite a jump between them. By contrast, the CSS specification offers hundreds of possible sizes, and only the capabilities of the Web browser and its underlying operating system to render the specified size really limits the possibilities.

Here's a fun example of what you can produce with the font-size: specification:

```
<P STYLE="font-size: 14pt">
Slowly
<SPAN STYLE="font-size: 16pt">we</SPAN>
<SPAN STYLE="font-size: 18pt">come,</SPAN>
<SPAN STYLE="font-size: 20pt">step</SPAN>
<SPAN STYLE="font-size: 22pt">by</SPAN>
<SPAN STYLE="font-size: 24pt">step,</SPAN>
<SPAN STYLE="font-size: 26pt">until</SPAN>
<SPAN STYLE="font-size: 28pt">*poof*</SPAN>
<SPAN STYLE="font-size: 30pt">we're</SPAN>
<SPAN STYLE="font-size: 40pt">here!</SPAN>
</P>
```

Can you guess what this example looks like in a Web browser? (Figure 7-3 shows you how it appears on-screen.) Notice that, by using the FONT SIZE tag, you can never accomplish this effect, because only seven possible font sizes are available, with the smallest considerably smaller than 14 point and the largest approximately 36 point.

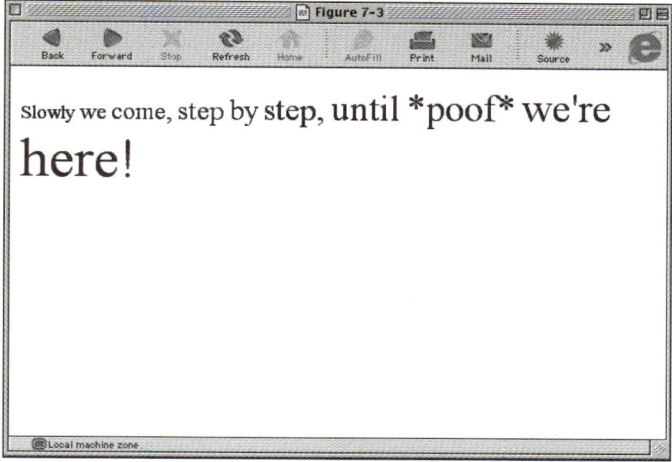

Figure 7-3 *Font size, stepping up and up by using the handy* SPAN *tag.*

You can also reference a variety of relative and absolute sizes by name if you're not comfortable with point sizes, as shown in the following list:

- xx-small
- x-small
- small
- medium
- large
- x-large
- xx-large
- smaller (a relative size, comparing it to the surrounding text)
- larger (also a relative size, comparing it to the surrounding text)

Finally, you can also specify a font size as a percentage relative to the surrounding text — that is, if you want to set a word 50 percent larger than the rest of the text in a sentence, you can format it as follows:

```
"This is indeed a mystery,"
<SPAN STYLE="font-size: 150%">I remarked.</SPAN>
"What do you imagine that it means?"
```

This method is a pretty smart way to alter font sizes, actually, because you don't need to keep track of the specific sizes in use at this point in the document. It's similar to using the <BIG> HTML tag (which no one ever uses, but that's another story).

Setting Font Styles

With the formal incorporation of CSS into the HTML specification in HTML 4.0, the standards group stamped the death knell on the forehead of a number of typeface-related formatting tags. That the FONT tag is now *deprecated*, as they call it, shouldn't surprise you, but the B, I, U and TT tags are also on their way out, too, for exactly the same reason: Style sheets enable you to specify these attributes and many more.

A number of different font styles are accessible through CSS styles, but what I find most interesting is that the generic concept of "bold" now extends to give you considerably more control over the *weight* of the type appearing on-screen.

No, you don't measure the *weight* of a font in ounces but rather in thickness. A thick, wide typeface that you use in a heading (such as the "Setting Font Styles" heading of this section) you describe as heavier, or having a greater weight, than regular text, which itself is heavier than that of a thin or narrow typeface.

10 Min. To Go

Bold and Italics

I'm going to approach these two styles — bold and italics — backwards, okay? You specify the *italics* style characteristic as a value of the font-style attribute, as the following example shows:

```
"Precisely. And the man who wrote the note is a German.
Do you note the peculiar construction of the
sentence—
<SPAN STYLE="font-style:italic;">
'This account of you we have from all
quarters received.'</SPAN>
A Frenchman or Russian could
not have written that. It is the German who is
so uncourteous to his verbs."
```

The other possible values for font-style are normal and oblique. The first is the default font presentation style on a Web page without any modification, whereas oblique is a slanted typeface — and usually one that you slant through a computational transformation (which contrasts with an italic font, which is explicitly designed to appear at a specific angle).

Current browsers display italic and oblique type identically, although print devices may differentiate between the two. Usually, a programmatically obliqued typeface slants at up to a 15-percent angle, while a good italic font displays a 10-percent angle. To make this situation more complex, this difference in the slant angle holds true only for sans-serif typefaces, because italicized serif faces are often a completely different design.

By contrast, no font-style: bold option is available; things are a wee bit more complex in the world of CSS. The CSS attribute that you need to use is font-weight, and the possible values are as the following list describes:

- bold
- bolder

- lighter
- normal

In addition, you can specify the weight of the font that you want, ranging from 100 (the lightest) to 900 (the heaviest). Roughly speaking, 100 to 200 is extra light; 300 to 400 is light; 500 is normal type; 600 to 700 is bold; and 800 to 900 is extra bold or "heavy."

Here's an example that combines a number of styles and weights:

```
<BODY STYLE="font-size: 22pt; // big enough to see!">
<P STYLE="font-weight: 100;">
"I think that I had better go, Holmes."</P>
<P STYLE="font-weight: 500; font-style: oblique;">
"Not a bit, Doctor. Stay where you are.
<SPAN STYLE="font-style: italic;">
I am lost without my
Boswell.</SPAN>
And this promises to be interesting. It would be a pity
to miss it."</P>
<P STYLE="font-weight: 900;">
"But your client--"</P>
<P STYLE="font-weight: bolder;">
"Never mind him. I may want your help, and so may he. Here he
comes. Sit down in that armchair, Doctor, and give us your best
attention."</P>
</BODY>
```

The result of this example is as shown in Figure 7-4. Notice the nifty trick in the <BODY> tag, which uses a CSS comment to clarify why I chose such a large typeface.

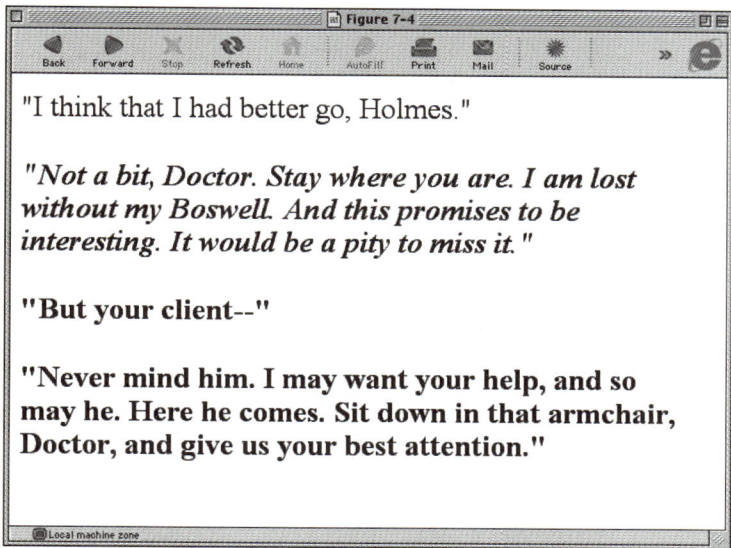

Figure 7-4   *Various weights and a comparison of italic and oblique type.*

As you may expect, oblique and italic look identical on-screen, but also notice that, although you have nine different possible weight values, in practical use, the weight range from 100 to 500 appears as normal text and the weight range from 600 to 900 appears bold.

Small caps

Another neat visual effect that you can use in your CSS style specification is *small caps*. In a nutshell, it transforms all the text to capital letters but also steps them down a little bit in size. You commonly see this effect in use on acronyms in print to retain a pleasing visual appearance. The following example shows how to use small caps in your CSS:

```
"Not a bit, Doctor. Stay where you are.
<SPAN STYLE="font-variant: small-caps;">
I am lost without my Boswell</SPAN>
```

The CSS specification defines a number of other variants, but the current versions of Web browsers don't implemented them.

Color

The third attribute of the HTML <FONT> tag is COLOR, and in the world of CSS, you easily specify this attribute as color: value;, where you can express the value in any of the many color notations that I specify in Session 5. You use either color names for simple colors (white, black, blue) or six-digit RGB hexadecimal notations exactly as you use them in the FONT tag itself.

So, for a quick translation, check out the following HTML example:

```
<FONT FACE="Palatino,Gill Sans" SIZE=2 COLOR="blue">
```

You express this same example in CSS as follows:

```
STYLE="font-family: Palatino, 'Gill Sans'; font-size: 12pt;
       color: blue;"
```

Notice that, because I surround the entire STYLE definition in double quotes, I switch to single quotes for the typeface name, Gill Sans.

Font Name Issues

Flip back for a moment to Table 7-1. If someone quizzed you and gave you the chance to earn oodles of money, could you identify the differences between Helvetica and Arial? Both are sans-serif typefaces and look almost identical. The only difference is that Arial is a little bit narrower.

A *serif* is a small "foot" on a letter. Look very closely at letters in the preceding paragraph of text, and you see little feet, or serifs. By contrast, the typeface that this book uses for section headings doesn't have these little feet, so it's known as a *sans-serif* typeface.

The problem with differentiating typeface names is a big one, and if you start to consider Windows versus Macintosh versus Unix typeface names, you can quickly see why the CSS designers came up with an alternative: the font family.

Font families

I tell you about serif versus sans-serif typefaces in the preceding section, so I'm just going to jump right in now and list all five font families that the CSS standard defines, as shown in Table 7-2.

Table 7-2   *The Five CSS Font Families*

Family Name	Representative Typefaces
Serif	Times
Sans-serif	Arial, Helvetica
Monospace	Courier
Cursive	Zapf-Chancery, Vivaldi
Fantasy	A decorative face, such as Comic Sans

This method of referencing typefaces by their family name is really a great way to avoid needing to guess typeface names. Here's an improved redefinition of the <TT> tag as an example:

```
<STYLE TYPE="text/css">
.monospace { font-family: monospace; font-size: 90%; >
</STYLE>
```

CSS font shorthand

One more tip and I give you a few minutes' break before the next session. This one, you're sure to like, however: Instead of all these different *font-this* and *font-that* attributes, you can use some shorthand and compress a lot of different font characteristics into a single font: style.

Here's a complex example:

```
H1 { font-weight: bold; font-size: 22pt; line-height: 30pt; font-family:
Courier, monospace; }
```

A simpler way to specify this set of font characteristics is as follows:

```
H1 { font: bold 22/30pt Courier, monospace }
```

Notice that you can mix typeface names and font families in the same font-family statement. This practice is a very good one for CSS and one that I encourage you to learn.

Done!

REVIEW

This session is a whirlwind tour of the many ways that you can control the presentation of type on your Web page by using CSS styles. Starting with a comparison of the FONT tag and exploring how its attributes map to CSS styles, I also talk about the challenge of specifying typefaces by name and how the font-family neatly solves this problem. Then, in a dizzying progression, I cover font sizes, font styles, font weights, font variants, and font colors. The session wraps up with a demonstration of the font: shorthand mechanism in CSS that enables you to specify a variety of attributes with minimal typing.

QUIZ YOURSELF

1. Name the five HTML font-related tags that CSS font styles deprecated (made obsolete). (See "Setting Fonts.")

2. Match the HTML tag and the CSS equivalent:

I	Font-weight: bold;
B	Font-style: italics;
TT	Font-family: monospace;

    (See "Setting Fonts.")

3. What's wrong with the following two lines?

    ```
    font-family: Courier New, Times Roman PS;
    <P CLASS=jeckle and hyde>go to janus</P>
    ```

    (See "Setting Fonts.")

4. Why is specifying font-size: 125% a better strategy than font-size: 20pt, assuming that the surrounding text is 16 point? (See "Tweaking Font Sizes.")

5. What common T-shirt size isn't also a font-size reference value? (See "Tweaking Font Sizes.")

6. What font variant do you commonly use in publishing if you're including all-uppercase acronyms in text? (See "Small caps.")

Additional CSS Text Control

Session Checklist

✔ Kerning

✔ Leading

✔ Justifying Text

✔ Text Decorations

**30 Min.
To Go**

I n the last session, I focus on the many ways that you can affect the typeface that you use for displaying your CSS Web content. This session is primarily going to explore the other half of text presentation on a page: *spacing*. (I'm tempted to say "Space, the final frontier," but I'm trying to fight my urge to reveal my Trekkie background!)

Cascading Style Sheets were the result of pressure from the design community on the HTML development groups and reflect the need for a considerably higher level of control over presentation and layout elements on a Web page. Particularly in considering printed materials, good designers obsess over even the most minute of details. A good example is that, in high-quality text layout systems, a double lowercase *f* is literally a different letter in the typeface, not simply two lowercase *f*s that you hook together.

Pairs of characters that a font character set includes are known as *ligatures* and usually offer a considerably improved visual appearance.

A more classic example of a ligature is a lowercase *fi* sequence. A poor type-layout program ends up distorting the ascender of the *f* (the topmost part) by merging it with the dot of the *i*. The *fi* ligature, however, offers a more visually appealing result for just this situation.

The underlying issue in character positioning is known *kerning*, and it refers to the amount of space between individual letters in a word.

Kerning

The vast majority of typeface designs give every single letter in its own rectangular box. In fact, that's also how all graphics on a Web page work, regardless of how irregular they may appear to the end user. This setup works fine in character layout if you're not too particular, but if you look at the spacing between letters and ask whether it's visually the same, as opposed to mathematically consistent from letter box to letter box, it's a different story.

Consider the letter spacing — the kerning — in the following word:

VALVESTOP

Anything look odd about this word? Compare the kerning between the *V* and the *A* at the beginning of the word and the spacing between the *E* and the *S* in the middle of the word. In fact, *VES* has a very visually pleasing default spacing, while many of the other letters appear weirdly and inconsistently spaced.

Sophisticated page layout and document design systems such as Quark Xpress are of great value, specifically because they make fine-tuning intercharacter spacing (to tighten things up and make text look considerably more attractive) easy for designers.

Furthermore, special types of character spacing that are available are also useful to have in your design toolbox, including abnormally squished letters (typically called *compressed* or *narrow* in the type-design world) and abnormally stretched-out letters (*wide* or *expanded*).

To accomplish these nifty kerning tricks in your CSS styles, use the `letter-spacing` attribute. To increase the spacing, use a positive value, and to decrease the spacing, use a negative value.

Consider the following CSS style listing:

```
<BODY STYLE="font-size: 36pt; font-family: arial;
 font-weight: 900;">
<CENTER>
<SPAN STYLE="letter-spacing: -4px;">
The Adventures of Sherlock Holmes</SPAN>
<BR>
The Red-Headed League
```

In this first snippet, I'm decreasing (tightening) the kerning between letters by four pixels, which is a lot, but it works because the default font size on the page is 36 points. The words `The Adventures of Sherlock Holmes` should appear a bit scrunched together, particularly if you compare them to the default letter spacing that I use for `The Red-Headed League` immediately after it.

 **Many of the popular Windows-based Web browsers have a hard time with inter-letter and inter-word spacing adjustments in CSS, so you probably won't see the same spacing on your screen that you see in the figure below.**

Figure 8-1 shows what this sequence produces, but before you get to see it, I'm slipping another bit of `letter-spacing` into the code, too, to demonstrate how someone who really obsesses over the appearance of a word may use `letter-spacing` to really fine-tune the kerning of a word; just check out the following example:

```
<SPAN STYLE="letter-spacing: -9px">V</SPAN><SPAN
STYLE="letter-spacing: -5px">A</SPAN><SPAN
STYLE="letter-spacing: -8px">L</SPAN><SPAN
STYLE="letter-spacing: -4px">V</SPAN>E
  versus  
VALVE
```

Figure 8-1 shows both of these interesting letter-spacing effects.

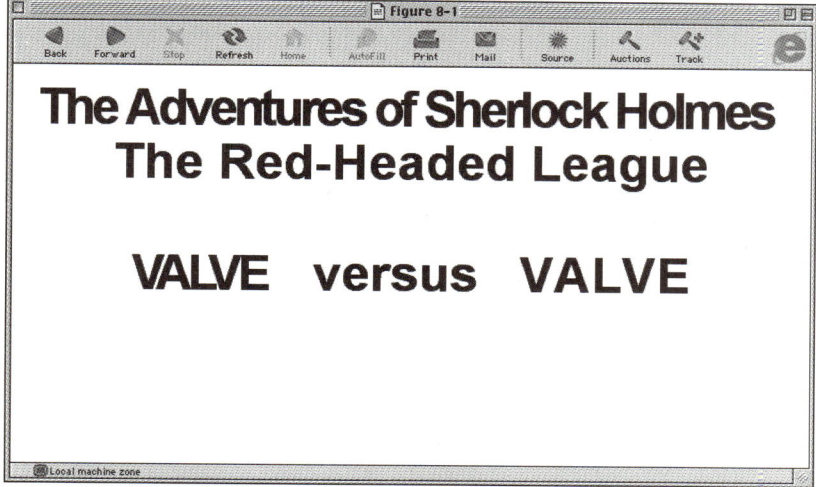

Figure 8-1 *You get fine kerning control by using the CSS* letter-spacing *attribute.*

Realistically, most CSS developers don't do too much with kerning, but at times, knowing that you have very fine control over this particular spacing issue is helpful.

Interword Spacing

Another characteristic of type presentation that you can control with CSS attributes is the spacing between words. I see this feature as less useful than intercharacter spacing, but I'm going to give you a quick peek at how to use it. Take a look at the following example:

```
<BODY STYLE="font-size: 18pt; font-family: arial;">
"I am Mr. Holmes," answered my companion, looking at
her with a questioning and rather startled gaze.
<P STYLE="word-spacing: 20px;">
"Indeed! My mistress told me that you were likely to
call. She left this morning with her husband by the
5:15 train from Charing Cross for the Continent."
</P>
```

The new style attribute is word-spacing: and, as does letter-spacing: it can take either a positive value (as demonstrated here, with the addition of 20 pixels of space between each word) or a negative value. Remember, with a negative value, you can have words actually atop each other, which will adversely impact the readability of your text, but might be perfect for the legal jargon on the bottom of the page!

Leading

You can tweak the spacing between characters and the spacing between words; deducing, therefore, that you can adjust the spacing between lines, too, is only logical. You can, and you've already seen the CSS attribute at work in Session 5: `line-height`.

For most CSS attributes, the units are immediately obvious, but `line-height` offers a unique measurement unit of its own, in addition to em, px, in, mm, percentages, and so on. If you specify a numeric value without a unit qualifier, the browser interprets it as a multiple of the current leading, or line height. This feature is cool, because it enables you to easily double-space text by using `line-height: 2;`, which is quite straightforward. Even better, the browser interprets `line-height: 1.5;` correctly, too, offering a leading halfway between single spacing and double spacing.

Here's a listing that builds on the word-spacing sample and demonstrates both capabilities:

```
<BODY STYLE="font-size: 18pt; font-family: arial;">
"I am Mr. Holmes," answered my companion, looking at
her with a questioning and rather startled gaze.
<P STYLE="word-spacing: 20px; line-height: 1.5;">
"Indeed  My mistress told me that you were likely to
call. She left this morning with her husband by the
5:15 train from Charing Cross for the Continent."
</P>
```

Figure 8-2 shows the result of viewing this set of CSS styles in Internet Explorer.

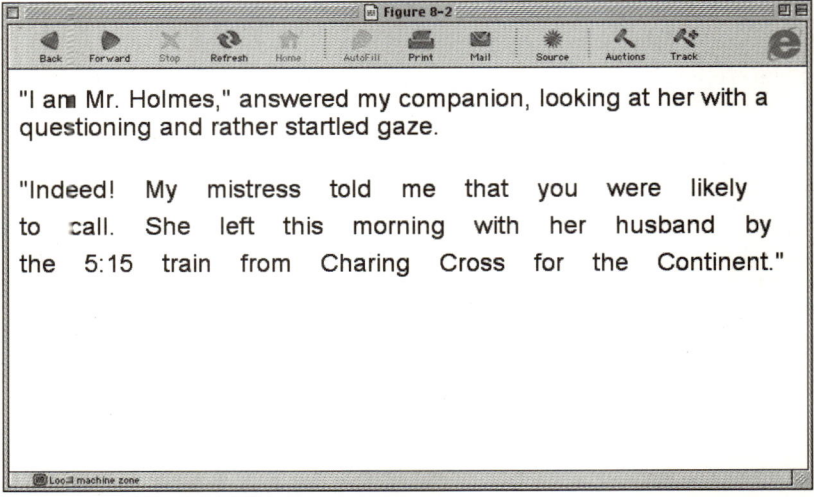

Figure 8-2   *Setting word and line spacing by using CSS attributes.*

As you can see, you can most politely describe the word spacing as "interesting," but the line spacing is unquestionably quite useful. Indeed, setting a default style for my Web sites of `line-height: 110%`, which adds an additional 10 percent leading to the default interline spacing, is most tempting as an easy way to improve the overall readability of my content. If you use it thoughtfully, leading can significantly increase legibility.

All these spacing adjustments are two-edged swords: On one hand, they offer you tremendous control over the layout of characters, words, and lines on the page, but on the other hand, you can abuse this control and produce pages that are awkward and unreadable.

As an aside, remember that, if you use the `font:` attribute in your CSS, you can very easily specify line spacing as you specify font size by putting a / between the two values, as in the following example:

```
BODY { font: Arial 14pt/21pt; }
```

This line specifies that 14 point Arial is the default typeface for the Web page and that the default line spacing is 21 points (which, if you do the math, is 150 percent, or 1.5, normal line spacing).

Justifying Text

20 Min.
To Go

The first wave of HTML development had minimal text justification, and only later was the `<CENTER>` tag added to the HTML specification. `<CENTER>` works well enough, but it doesn't help you either right-align text or justify a paragraph of text so that the left and right margins both line up attractively. Expanding `<CENTER>` to include an alignment attribute is clearly a direct path to migraine headaches. (Can you imagine how confusing `<CENTER ALIGN=right>` may appear?). So the HTML developers came up with the `ALIGN` attribute to the paragraph tag. As it's formalized in HTML 4.0, you can assign the paragraph alignment attribute `LEFT`, `CENTER`, `RIGHT`, or `JUSTIFY` as its four possible values, with `LEFT` as the default.

Using the `<P>` tag doesn't make much sense, however, because many times, you want to center nonparagraph material. As an example, see whether you think that the following code block really makes any sense:

```
<P ALIGN="center">
<h2>Holmes Visits Moriarty</h2>
</P>
```

It's better HTML than using the `<CENTER>` tag, which is now long out of favor, but I really don't think of level-two headers as an element of a paragraph container.

Worse, both `<CENTER>` and the `ALIGN` attribute of the P tag are deprecated; fortunately, CSS enables you to sidestep these obsolete HTML elements and instead add it to your style definitions.

The CSS attribute in question is text-align, and unsurprisingly, the possible values are as follows:

- left
- right
- center
- justify

Take a look at the following example, and you can see how these attributes all work together:

```
<P STYLE="text-align: justify;">
"You had my note?" he asked with a deep harsh voice
and a strongly marked German accent. "I told you that
I would call." He looked from one to the other of us,
as if uncertain which to address.
</P>
<P STYLE="text-align: right;">
"Pray take a seat," said Holmes. "This is my friend
and colleague, Dr. Watson, who is occasionally good
enough to help me in my cases. Whom have I the honor
to address?"
</P>
<P STYLE="text-align: center;">
"You may address me as the Count Von Kramm, a
Bohemian nobleman. I understand that this gentleman,
your friend, is a man of honor and discretion, whom I
may trust with a matter of the most extreme importance.
If not, I should much prefer to communicate with you alone."
</P>
<P STYLE="text-align: left;">
I rose to go, but Holmes caught me by the wrist and
pushed me back into my chair. "It is both, or none,"
said he. "You may say before this gentleman anything
which you may say to me."
</P>
```

Figure 8-3 shows the results of viewing this material in a Web browser.

Notice the difference in readability between the four paragraphs. On a computer screen, where you can adjust the kerning and interword spacing only coarsely, the left-only justification of the last paragraph is visibly easiest to read. In printed material, however, sophisticated layout programs can do a much better job of distributing necessary extra spacing to justify both the left and right margins.

Page-layout programs have another edge on justifying text attractively: They can automatically hyphenate long words as necessary. Web browser can't do that — yet — although HTML 4.0 added the ­ *soft hyphen* character entity and suggested its use as an on-demand hyphen to embed in long words.

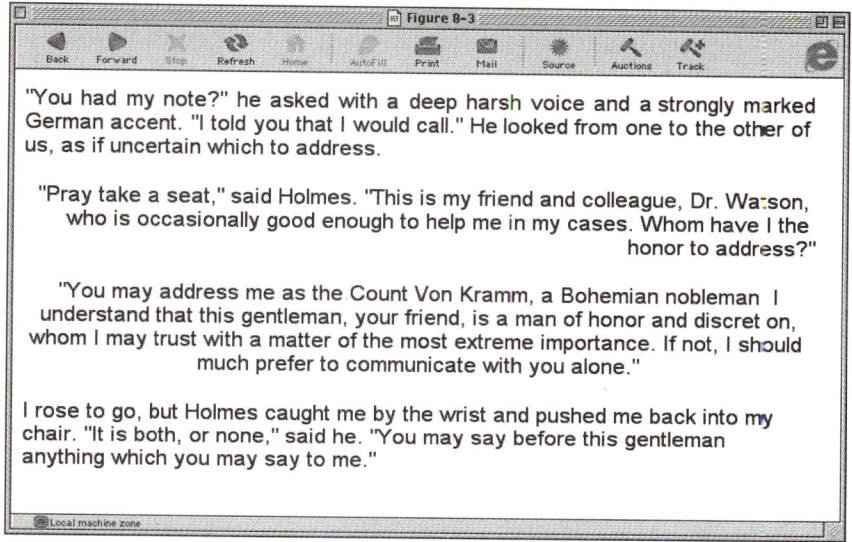

Figure 8-3　*Various text-alignment options.*

Vertical Text Alignment

Two more deprecated HTML tags that CSS replaces with attributes that offer a finer layout control are SUP and SUB — superscript and subscript elements, respectively. With these two HTML attributes, it's just as well they're replaced, because every single time that I've ever used a superscript, I've needed to tweak things additionally to get the effect that I want, as in the following example:

```
LaunchLine.com<SUP><FONT SIZE="-2">tm</FONT></SUP>
```

This example is clearly awkward HTML at best.

Instead, CSS offers the more interesting vertical-align attribute, which encompasses the five possible values that I list in Table 8-1.

Table 8-1　*CSS Vertical Alignment Values*

Value	Explanation
top	Top of element aligns with top of highest element in line.
middle	Middle of element aligns with middle of line.
bottom	Bottom of element aligns with bottom of lowest element in line.
text-top	Top of element aligns with top of highest text element in line.
text-bottom	Bottom of element aligns with bottom of lowest text element in line.

Continued

Table 8-1 *Continued*

Value	Explanation
super	Superscript shorthand.
sub	Subscript shorthand.

In addition, you can also specify a percentage variation from the parent text's baseline, but more likely than not, the values that I list in Table 8-1 cover all your needs.

Now that you're armed with this new CSS attribute and your growing knowledge of CSS, I give you the following example as a nice CSS CLASS definition for trademark symbols:

```
.tm { vertical-align: top; font-size: 33%; font-weight: bold; }
```

Now you can replace the earlier ugly HTML sequence with the following more elegant and visually attractive version:

```
LaunchLine.com<SPAN CLASS="tm">TM</SPAN>
```

Text Decorations

I know that I said that this session was focusing completely on spacing issues, but I'd like to highlight a couple additional text characteristics — capabilities that I'm sure you can appreciate.

The first of these is text-decoration, which doesn't enable you to add festive bows and ribbons on your letters, as its name may suggest, but rather enables you to specify any combination of the following decorative styles:

- underline
- overline
- line-through
- blink

If you look at that list and think, "Hey, those all look like HTML formatting tags!" you're 75 percent correct. You can specify underlines by using the HTML <U> tag; line-through is the equivalent of the <STRIKE> tag; and blink is the equivalent of the <BLINK> tag. You have no way to achieve an overline effect in HTML.

More important, however, <U>, <STRIKE>, and <BLINK> are all deprecated HTML in the latest specification in favor of the equivalent CSS styles that I show here.

So why is this deprecated stuff such a big deal? Because as the Web evolves, expect to see newer browsers that don't support deprecated elements at all, which eventually makes your legacy pages that use FONT, STRIKE, **and so on instantly obsolete. Plus CSS is far cooler, in my opinion!**

Text decorations can help produce some very interesting visual effects. Consider the following sequence and its results in Figure 8-4:

```
<P STYLE="text-decoration: overline underline;
 text-align: center;">
The Five Orange Pips
</P>
```

Notice here that I'm specifying two different text decorations in the same style element: I want both and over- and underline. The results are quite attractive.

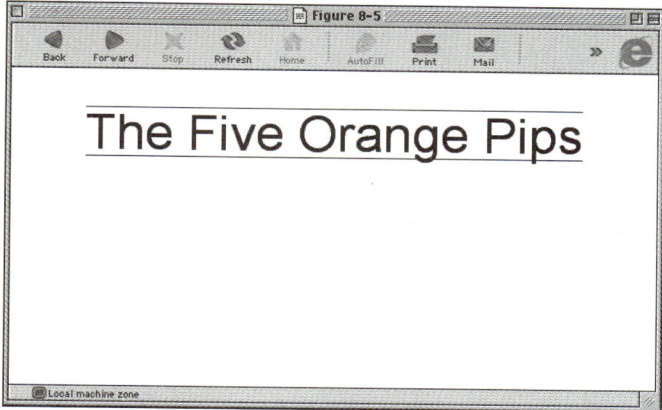

Figure 8-4 *Text decorations add visual pizzazz!*

A compatibility warning: Most smart Web browser programmers have long since disabled support for the `blink` attribute because it's horribly annoying, and most versions of Netscape Navigator don't support the `overline` attribute.

**10 Min.
To Go**

Text Transformation

When Bill Watterson was writing the popular comic strip *Calvin and Hobbes*, I used to read it avidly. I particularly looked forward to the strips where Calvin used his transmogrification gun, turning both Hobbes and himself into weird monsters or twisted animals.

Text transformation in CSS isn't quite that capable, alas, but it enables you to apply some useful transformations to elements, as shown in Table 8-2.

Table 8-2 *Text Transformation Values*

Value	Meaning
`capitalize`	Displays the first letter of each word as caps and all others as lowercase.
`uppercase`	Displays all letters as uppercase.
`lowercase`	Displays all letters as lowercase.

The most important thing to realize if you're using the `text-transform:` CSS style is that it doesn't affect the actual letters in the source HTML file — just the presentation of the information in a Web browser.

Consider the following sequence:

```
<STYLE TYPE="text/css">
.tm { vertical-align: top; font-size: 33%;
     font-weight: bold; text-transform: uppercase; }
H1  { text-transform: capitalize; background: #CCC;
     padding: 10; text-align: center; }
</STYLE>
</HEAD>
<BODY STYLE="font-size: 36pt; font-family: arial;">
<H1>the Adventures of Sherlock Holmes<SPAN CLASS="tm">tm</SPAN></H1>
```

Look at the output, as shown in Figure 8-5, and then look closely at what's uppercase and what's lowercase in the actual listing.

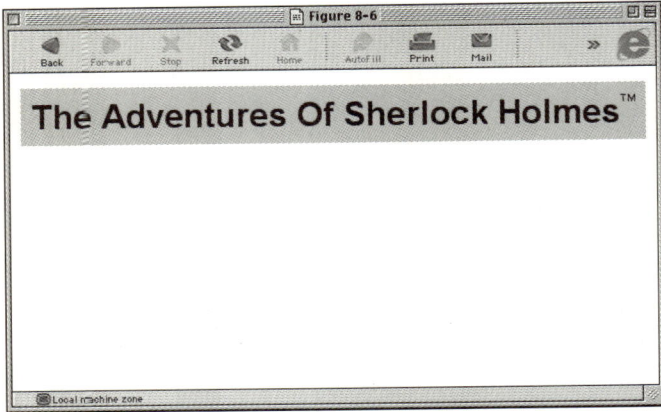

Figure 8-5   *Text transformations help build considerably improved headers.*

The text in the listing puts the and of in lowercase, but the capitalize attribute of the H1 style definition forces them to uppercase, exactly as the uppercase transform forces the TM to uppercase, although the letters tm in the SPAN element are lowercase.

Done!

REVIEW

This session focuses on spacing and transformation styles within the CSS language and also demonstrates a number of HTML tags that are deprecated and their new, improved CSS style equivalents. I cover kerning (character spacing), word spacing, and leading (line spacing) in depth and then examine CSS support for text justification within paragraphs and vertical alignment of elements within a given line. The session wraps up with text decorations and text transformations, both of which combine to offer considerable control over the presentation of information on the final page.

QUIZ YOURSELF

1. Write down the deprecated HTML tag after each of the following CSS style attributes:
   ```
   text-decoration: underline;
   text-decoration: line-through;
   text-align: right;
   vertical-align: super;
   ```
   (See "Justifying Text.")

2. Name both HTML equivalents that `text-align: center;` neatly replaces. (See "Justifying Text.")

3. Define kerning and leading. (See "Kerning" and "Leading.")

4. Explain when increasing interword spacing can prove helpful. (See "Interword spacing.")

5. What are the percentile equivalent ways of writing the CSS style attributes `line-height: 1.25` and `line-height: 1.5`? (See "Leading.")

6. Use the `<SPAN>` tag and STYLE attribute to write the necessary code to produce the formula for water on a Web page. (The formula is H_2O.) (See "Text Transformation.")

CSS Lists

Session Checklist

✔ Bullet lists

✔ Building your own bullet

✔ Counting on numbered lists

✔ Hanging indents by using `text-indent`

**30 Min.
To Go**

This session covers ways that you can use CSS to spruce up the lists on your Web page. Lists aren't fundamentally a thrilling topic, but how often they crop up in site design and information presentation is really rather surprising. In fact, I'm constantly using definition lists because of the easy combination of automatic indentation and vertical spacing that they offer.

Additionally, you spend some time looking at some of the many ways that you can specify a numbering scheme for an ordered, or numbered, list.

Before you pull out your red pen and your HTML books, however, I quickly need to add that the <UL>, <OL>, and <DL> list types aren't deprecated in favor of CSS styles. Instead, styles offer a more sophisticated way to specify the presentation of list information and can neatly work in conjunction with their HTML equivalents. Having said that, I must add that one attribute to these HTML tags is deprecated: TYPE=, either specifying a numeric presentation scheme or the shape of the bullets for an unordered list.

Bullet Lists

The simplest of lists for a Web page are *unordered*, or *bullet* lists, and by using CSS, you can control which of three built-in bullets that you use for a particular list. A subtlety of Web browsers is that most automatically change the bullet, basing what they show on the indent level of the list, as you can see in the following simple listing:

```
<UL><LI>indent level one, and perhaps the single most
important point that we'll make in this nested
```

```
bullet list.<UL><LI>level two
<UL><LI>level three</UL><LI>level two
</UL><LI>back to level one</UL>
```

Look at Figure 9-1 to see what I mean: Without any modifications to the HTML, the Web browser uses three different kinds of bullets, basing its choices on the indentation level, with the first level using a filled-in black circle, the second a hollow circle, and the third level a filled-in square.

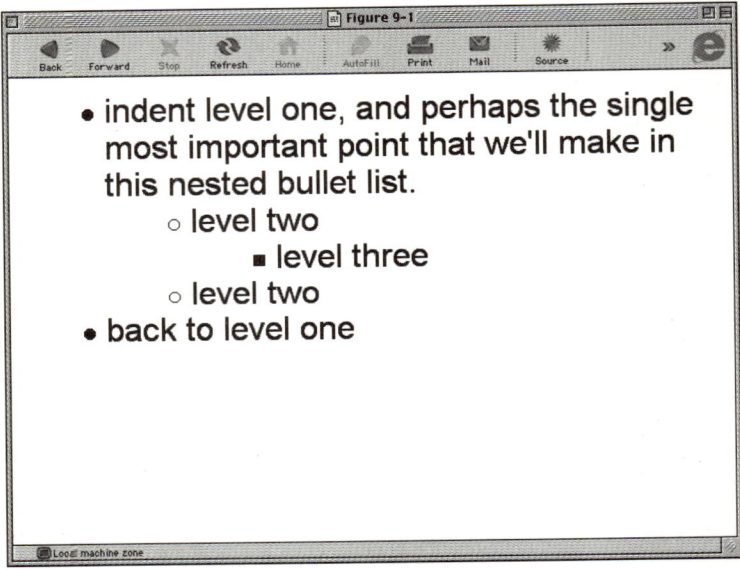

Figure 9-1   *Default bullets that a Web browser produces based on nesting-level.*

Instead, however, suppose that you want to use CSS to force all bullets to appear as filled-in circles. My first attempt to do so looks as follows:

```
<STYLE TYPE="text/css">
UL { list-style-type: disc; }
</STYLE>
<UL><LI>indent level one, and perhaps the single most
important point that we'll make in this nested
bullet list.<UL><LI>level two
<UL><LI>level three</UL><LI>level two
</UL><LI>back to level one</UL>
```

The HTML doesn't change a bit, but the addition of the style definition of the <UL> tag as a disc changes all three levels of bullet to the shape that you want.

You can accomplish the same result here in a different way: You can redefine the <LI> style instead, but this method produces a potential collision with ordered lists, which also use the <LI> tag.

Figure 9-2 shows the result of the new style definition. Notice in both figures how the additional text on the first bullet indents to align away from the bullet itself.

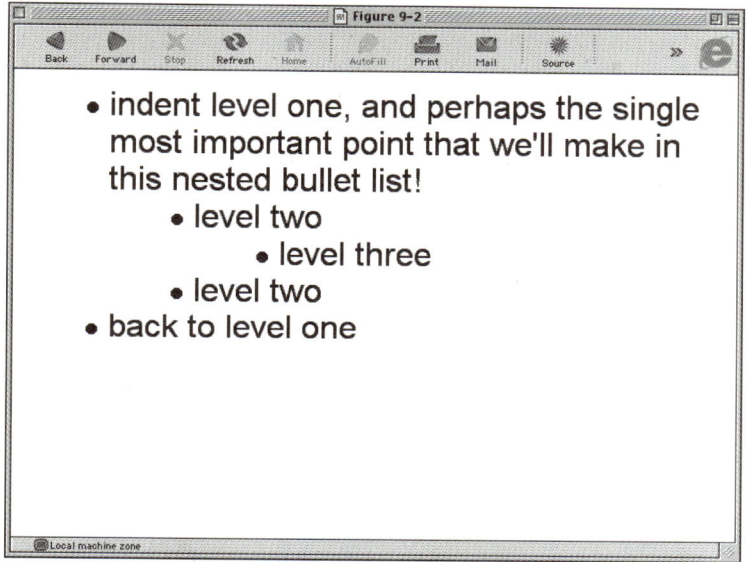

Figure 9-2 *Redefine <UL> once and all the bullet lists change.*

Table 9-1 shows the three possible bullet-related values for list-style-type.

Table 9-1 *Possible Bullet-Related Values for List-Style-Type*

Value	Appearance
disc	●
circle	○
square	■

You have a remarkable number of different possibilities for list-style-type if you're using numbered lists, but I get to that subject shortly!

**20 Min.
To Go**

Building your own bullet

The set of CSS style options that I show you in the preceding sections for altering your bullet lists are rather dull and nothing that makes a designer do handstands or backflips. One new feature of unordered lists is the capability for you to specify your own bullets. Way cool!

This capability addresses a long-time limitation in HTML, one that most designers circumvent by using a zero-border table. Without CSS capabilities, a bullet list that uses the graphic mydiamond.gif probably looks as follows:

```
<TABLE BORDER="0" CELLPADDING="2" CELLSPACING="0">
<TR><TD VALIGN="top"><IMG SRC="mydiamond.gif"></TD>
  <TD>Create attention-grabbing Web pages</TD></TR>
<TR><TD VALIGN="top"><IMG SRC="mydiamond.gif"></TD>
  <TD>Integrate new image map tools</TD></TR>
<TR><TD VALIGN="top"><IMG SRC="mydiamond.gif"></TD>
  <TD>Attract visitors through smart online marketing</TD></TR>
</TABLE>
```

It's quite functional, but a lot of HTML is necessary to produce a simple three-element bullet list. Worse, it's difficult to maintain and edit.

That's where the CSS `list-style-image` attribute is of tremendous value. Here's exactly the same list, which I simplify dramatically by using CSS:

```
<UL STYLE="list-style-image: url(mydiamond.gif);">
<LI>Create attention-grabbing Web pages
<LI>Integrate new image map tools
<LI>Attract visitors through smart online marketing
</UL>
```

Have a look at Figure 9-3 to see the results of this additional style definition.

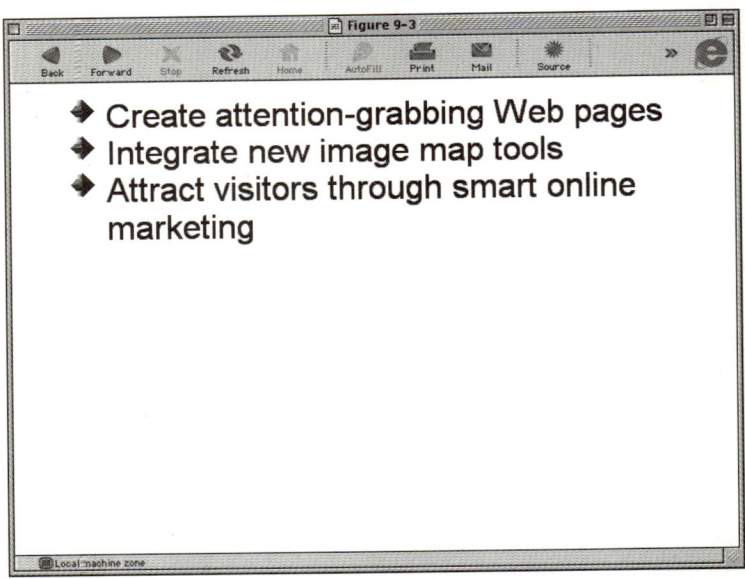

Figure 9-3   *A bullet list displaying my own custom bullet.*

This change in bullet style CSS is the first CSS element that you've encountered that includes a pointer to another Web element. Notice that you don't need to surround the URL with quote marks, as it correctly appears with an IMG tag, but instead, you identify it as if it's an argument to a function that you call url().

 **Although CSS supports relative URLs as shown here, many CSS experts recommend that you fully qualify every reference, that is, make sure it always begins with the** http: **sequence.**

Unfortunately, the latest versions of Netscape 6 don't yet support the `list-style-image` CSS attribute, so if you really, really want to get this effect, you may end up using the TABLE sequence just a little while longer after all, as shown at the beginning of this section.

Controlling the position of the bullet

Earlier, in reference to the very first figure of this session, I suggested that you observe how the text on continuation lines aligns under the first character of the bullet *text* rather than the bullet itself. Surprisingly, if you want slightly different results, you can fine-tune this particular characteristic by using the `list-style-position` attribute.

The `list-style-position` attribute includes two possible values: `inside` and `outside`. The default is `outside`, which displays the bullet graphic (either built-in or a specified graphical element) separate from the overall alignment of the text.

Here's a simple example that demonstrates both these possibilities:

```
<UL STYLE="list-style-image: url(mydiamond.gif);">
<LI>
"Good-night, Mister Sherlock Holmes."
<LI STYLE="list-style-position: inside;">
There were several people on the pavement at the time,
but the greeting appeared to come from a slim youth
in an ulster who had hurried by.
<LI STYLE="list-style-position: outside;">
"I've heard that voice before," said Holmes, staring
down the dimly lit street. "Now, I wonder who the deuce
that could have been."
</UL>
```

You can see the difference between the two different styles in Figure 9-4. Notice that the default style position is `outside`.

The same `list-style-position` also enables you to affect the placement of the numeric values on an ordered list.

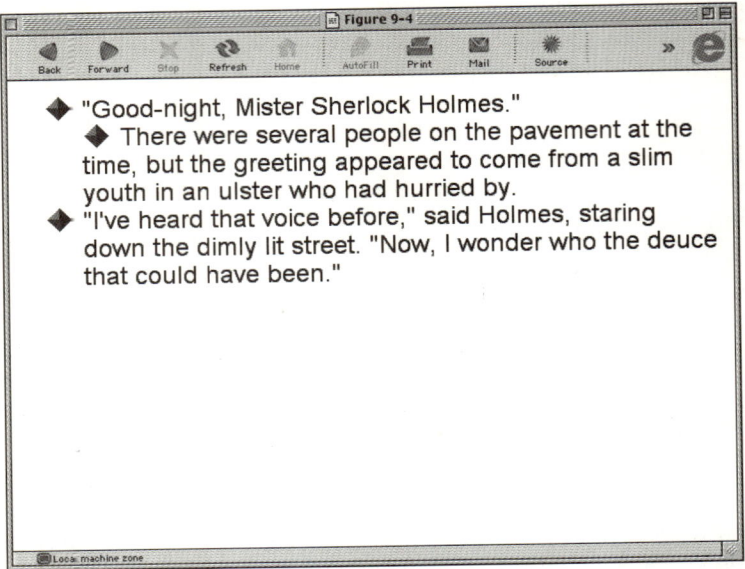

Figure 9-4   *The* `list-style-position` *attribute enables you to fine-tune where bullets appear in a list.*

Counting on Numbered Lists

If I think about the many lists I've created for different Web sites, I realize that just about all of them are unordered, or bullet, lists. Sometimes, however, the capability to automatically number a set of choices is very helpful, and that's where ordered lists — <OL> — come in handy.

You can use two CSS styles to tune the appearance of your ordered lists: `list-style-type` and `list-style-position`. I've already explored both to some extent, but you need to see how you can use the `list-style-type` style with ordered lists.

Table 9-2 enumerates the many possible values for `list-style-type`.

Table 9-2   *The Many, Many Possible Values of* `list-style-type`

Name	Explanation	Implemented?
decimal	The default: 1, 2, 3, . .	👍
decimal-leading-zero	The same as decimal, but with leading zeroes: 01, 02, . . .	👎
lower-roman	Lowercase roman numerals: i, ii, iii, iv, v, vi, . . .	👍

Name	Explanation	Implemented?
upper-roman	Uppercase roman numerals: I, II, III, IV, V, VI, . . .	👍
lower-greek	Counts using Greek letters: alpha, beta, gamma, delta, . . .	👎
lower-alpha	Lowercase alphabetic: a, b, c, d, e, . . .	👍
lower-latin	Lowercase alphabetic — identical to lower-alpha	👎
upper-alpha	Uppercase alphabetic: A, B, C, D, E, . . .	👍
upper-latin	Uppercase alphabetic — identical to upper-alpha	👎
hebrew	Counts using Hebrew numbering	👎
armenian	Counts using Armenian numbering	👎
georgian	Counts using Georgian numbering	👎
cjk-ideographic	Counts using ideographic numbers	👎
hiragana	Counts using Japanese *hiragana* system	👎
katakana	Counts using Japanese *katakana* system	👎
hiragana-iroha	Counts using Japanese *hiragana-iroha* system	👎
katakana-iroha	Counts using Japanese *katakana-iroha* system	👎

Based on the many possibilities, you can apparently have lots of fun with different counting options, but unfortunately, only a few of these values are implemented, as the table indicates. If you're expert with the HTML TYPE attribute to the `<OL>` tag, you recognize all the implemented values; they're exactly the same as the implemented values for the `list-style-type` tag.

So why are so many elements in the CSS standard not implemented? Two reasons: First, you're on the cutting edge here, exploring the CSS 2.0 specification rather than the older CSS 1.0 spec, and second, most of the standards I've encountered contain elements that are never implemented. HTML 4.01 is the same, for example, with some of the site navigation elements added to aid disabled people consistently ignored by Web developers.

**10 Min.
To Go**

List-Style Shortcuts

Just as you can use the `font:` attribute as a convenient shortcut for specifying a variety of font- and typeface-related style attributes, so can you use the `list-style` attribute to make fine-tuning the presentation of your lists a breeze.

I can best demonstrate this shorthand by showing you the following snippet:

```
UL { list-style: disc outside url(diamond.gif); }
```

This example is functionally identical to the following example:

```
UL { list-style: disc; list-style-position: outside;
     list-style-image: url(diamond.gif); }
```

Hanging Indents by Using text-indent

I know that this last CSS style isn't part of the `list-style` set, per se, but it's closely related to the `list-style-position` attribute. The `text-indent` attribute can take two possible values: either a specific length (in whatever unit of measure that you prefer) or a percentage value that's against the size of the container that it affects, both of which appear in the following example:

```
<P STYLE="text-indent: 20%">
"You will excuse this mask," continued our strange
visitor. "The august person who employs me wishes
his agent to be unknown to you, and I may confess at
once that the title by which I have just called myself
is not exactly my own."</P>
<P>
"I was aware of it," said Holmes drily.</P>
<P STYLE="text-indent: 1in;">
"The circumstances are of great delicacy, and every
precaution has to be taken to quench what might
grow to be an immense scandal and seriously compromise
```

```
one of the reigning families of Europe. To speak plainly,
the matter implicates the great House
of Ormstein, hereditary kings of Bohemia."</P>
<P>
"I was also aware of that," murmured Holmes, settling
himself down in his armchair and closing his eyes.
```

Figure 9-5 shows how `text-indent` affects the layout of the material.

The results are a bit confusing, but if you really like the traditional text-layout rule of always indenting the first line of each paragraph of material, you can now do so by using the following example:

```
<STYLE TYPE="text/css">
P { text-indent: 10%; }
</STYLE>
```

Now every paragraph of text on the page displays a small leading indent.

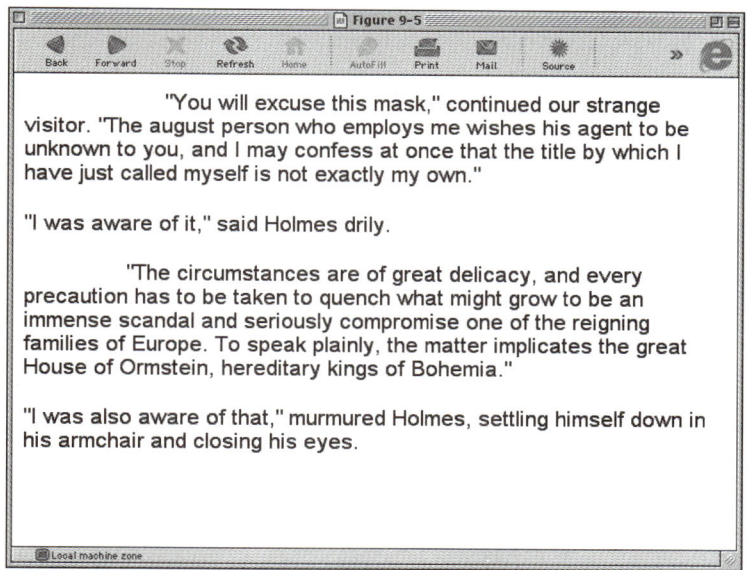

Figure 9-5   *A demonstration of the text-indent attribute.*

Overriding Global Attribute Settings

One thing that I've skipped up to now that's actually quite important is how you can use the *cascading* part of Cascading Style Sheets to your advantage for particular layout effects.

As an example, say that I'm using a shared global style sheet that defines a 10-percent indentation for any paragraph of text on a site that I'm building. Seems a great idea, but my client informs me that, as a special case, she wants unindented paragraphs on some pages any time that text immediately follows a header.

The most straightforward way to code this effect is to apply the global paragraph definition and then override it in the requisite unintended paragraphs, as follows:

```
<P STYLE="text-indent: 0;">
```

But this concept of setting a global style and then overriding it locally is more general than just the `text-indent` attribute. Just about every attribute I've shown you in CSS offers a `none` option that resets the format for that particular characteristic of presentation to the default for the Web browser. As an example, this allows you to create the following style definition:

```
LI { list-style-image: url(bigfoot.gif); }
```

And then, later, in a specific fragment of code where you want to avoid the weird image of `bigfoot.gif` and just have a regular old bullet, you can set things up as follows:

```
<UL>
<LI STYLE="list-style-image: none;">
```

The capability to override global settings is one of the best reasons to try to always generalize your style definitions so that you can put them either at the top of the document or, better, in a separate style sheet.

As another example, imagine that my client decides that she wants to switch the indent scheme of the paragraphs so that they display two types: indented and not indented. Suppose that I'd originally written the page to use a default paragraph style of indented and a secondary class of `flush left`, as follows:

```
P { text-indent: 10%; }     // by default, paragraphs are indented
P.fl { text-indent: 0; }     // the 'fl' paragraphs are flush left
```

Then making the change that my client is requesting becomes a breeze, as you see in the following example:

```
P { text-indent: 0; }     // redundant since it's the default
P.fl { text-indent: 10%; }     // fl redefined to have an indent after all
```

If this CSS sequence is in a central shared style sheet, the entire update may take less than 60 seconds!

Done!

REVIEW

This session primarily focuses on list elements, list styles, and how to mold and sculpt your CSS styles and HTML to get a wide variety of different list appearances. I also discuss two important subjects along the way: URL references in CSS styles and global styles with local overrides as a common design philosophy. I also explore the way-cool capability to specify any graphic as a bullet, and the session wraps up with a discussion of the `text-indent` capability and how you can use it on your Web site.

QUIZ YOURSELF

1. Which of the following aren't built-in bullet shapes?

    ```
    circle, square, triangle, disc, dodecahedron, bullet, dash
    ```
    (See "Bullet Lists.")

2. What's the old-style HTML equivalent of the following sequence?

    ```
    <UL STYLE="list-style-image: url(bluedot.gif);">
    <LI>The first point
    <LI>and the second point
    </UL>
    ```
    (See "Building your own bullet.")

3. What CSS attribute can you use to make the text on multiline unordered list entries line up with the left edge of the bullet rather than the first character of text in the first line? (See "Controlling the position of the bullet.")

4. Which of the following aren't defined `list-style-type` values?

    ```
    hebrew, arabic, armenian, romanian, klingon,
    katakana, lower-greek, high-german
    ```
    (See "Counting on Numbered Lists.")

5. Write out the equivalent `list-style` shortcuts for the following two list classes:

    ```
    UL.disco  { list-style: disc; list-style-position: insice;
       color: blue; }
    OL.level2 { list-style: lower-roman;
       list-style-position: outside; }
    ```
    (See "List-Style Shortcuts.")

6. What do you think may happen with the following CSS styles?

    ```
    text-indent: 100%
    text-indent: 125%
    text-indent: -10%
    ```

    Pop open an edit window and try 'em out to see whether you're right!
    (See "Overriding Global Attribute Settings.")

Backgrounds and Colors

Session Checklist

✔ Color

✔ Background colors

✔ Background images

✔ Positioning background images

**30 Min.
To Go**

U
p to this point, the different presentation styles that I've focused on enable you to change the layout of textual elements on your page, but everything's in a remarkably monochromatic universe. This session changes all that by exploring the amazingly flexible world of color in CSS.

As a reminder right off, you can specify color five different ways in CSS, but herein, I'm going to focus on the hexadecimal RGB notation that you're already familiar with from your HTML work — that is, white is #FFFFFF, black is #000000, and so on. I may use the helpful three-digit shorthand that CSS supports (where white is #FFF, black is #000, and so on) or reference a color by its name (white, yellow), but the six-digit hex form is the notation that I'm most familiar with, too.

Time to get started!

Color

The color: CSS attribute is perhaps the most basic of CSS color style attributes, and it's already snuck into a number of examples earlier in the book. The color attribute is what controls this style, and you need to observe that it isn't "text-color" or "font-color" that you use but a more general color specification for the container.

In fact, color sets the display color for all possible elements in the container. If you use it on an HR tag, the horizontal line appears in the color you specify. If you use it on a bullet list, in theory, the bullets also come out in the color that you request.

To test the color attribute out, check out the following example:

```
<STYLE TYPE="text/css">
HR { color: #F00; }
UL { color: #009; }
</STYLE>
<H3 STYLE="text-align: center;">More Adventures of Mr. Holmes</H3>
<HR>
Please choose from the following adventures:
<UL>
<LI>A Case of Identity
<LI>The Boscombe Valley Mystery
<LI>The Five Orange Pips
<LI>The Man with the Twisted Lip
</UL>
```

Figure 10-1 shows the results.

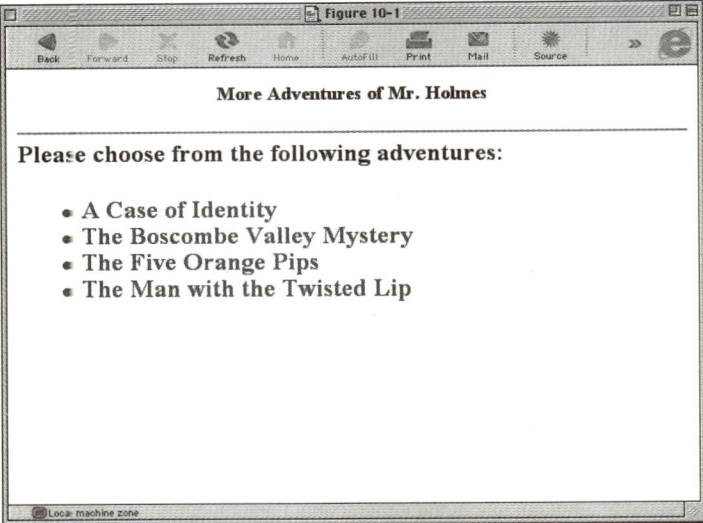

Figure 10-1   *Color adds pizzazz to the presentation of information.*

And very nice results they are — not only is the bullet list (including the bullets!) blue, but the horizontal rule is a bright red, too.

Colored bullets

The completely blue bullet list in the example above leads to the obvious conclusion that, with a bit more CSS tweaking, you can get a bullet list with blue bullets and regular black text, too, as in the following example:

```
<UL>
<LI><SPAN STYLE="color: black;">A Case of Identity</SPAN>
```

```
<LI><SPAN STYLE="color: black;">The Boscombe Valley
Mystery</SPAN>
<LI><SPAN STYLE="color: black;">The Five Orange
Pips</SPAN>
<LI><SPAN STYLE="color: black;">The Man with the Twisted Lip</SPAN>
</UL>
```

The HTML is a bit awkward here, but the results are most pleasing, as shown in Figure 10-2.

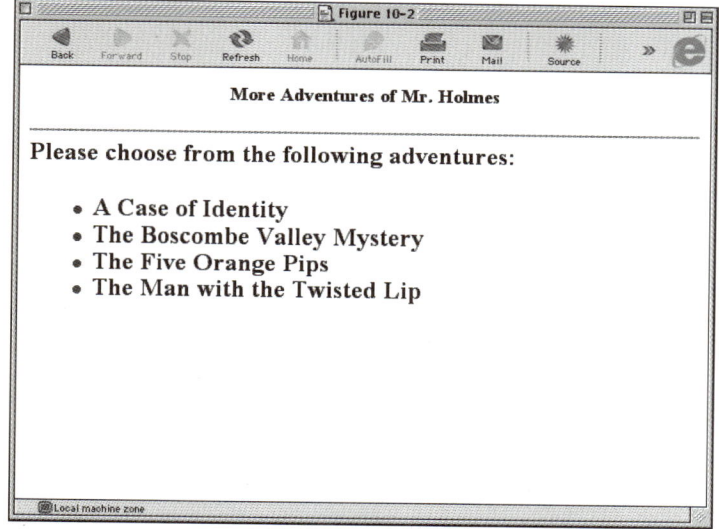

Figure 10-2   *This time, you get colored bullets and black text.*

To fully understand what's going on with colors in your CSS, this session is a great one for you to make sure that you can reference the CD-ROM examples on your own computer.

Colored bullets are a good example of the nature of *inheritance* in CSS. I talk about inheritance elsewhere in this book, but it's such an important concept that reiterating it here is quite helpful: A Web page is a series of nested containers, with the BODY as the top-level presentation container; then (in this example) the UL defines the next-level container and then each LI and, finally, the SPAN. To understand what color the text within the SPAN is, simply work outward (SPAN → LI → UL → BODY) until you find a specification. If you don't find one, the document default, as the user configures it, is what a browser uses.

Oh, before I leave this topic, a much more graceful way to achieve a colored bullet on a bullet list is by using the list-style-image attribute and designating the blue bullet as a separate GIF image. Although this solution references a separate graphics file, a solid unicolor bullet graphic is usually no more than a few dozen bytes in size. The value of simplifying your bullet lists by sidestepping the SPAN elements more than makes up for the extra download time for the graphic to appear, at least in my experience.

Background Colors

**20 Min.
To Go**

The color attribute affects the color of material in its container, which may seem a bit abstract. After you also change the background color of the container, however, all suddenly becomes quite clear.

The CSS attribute that enables you to change the background color is background-color. Armed with this new attribute, I'm going to tweak the following bullet list example to more clearly denote the different levels of container nesting:

```
<STYLE TYPE="text/css">
HR { color: #F00; }
UL { color: #009; background-color: #99F; }
</STYLE>
<BODY STYLE="background-color: #F99;">
<H3 STYLE="text-align: center;">More Adventures of Mr. Holmes</H3>
<HR>
Please choose from the following adventures:
<UL>
<LI><SPAN STYLE="background-color: yellow;">A Case of Identity</SPAN>
<LI><SPAN STYLE="background-color: yellow;">The Boscombe Valley
Mystery</SPAN>
<LI><SPAN STYLE="background-color: yellow;">The Five Orange
Pips</SPAN>
<LI><SPAN STYLE="background-color: yellow;">The Man with the Twisted
Lip</SPAN>
</UL>
```

A quick look at the rather peculiar results in Figure 10-3 now makes clear which container overrides which other container. The yellow bullet text is within the blue (#99F) UL list box, which is itself within the pink (#F99) of the background container.

In Figure 10-3, the light-red background is the background color of the entire page, as set in the STYLE attribute of the BODY tag (color #F99, which is identical to #FF9999, light red). The UL container has its own background of light blue (#99F), which you specify in the UL style definition at the very top of the HTML sequence. Finally, the SPAN on each LI element specifies a yellow background, which affects only the background of the words actually output.

I know, I know — here in this book, the figure actually just looks like different gray levels. Please check this particularly colorful example on the CD-ROM.

A really useful place where background colors can prove particularly effective is as part of a redefinition of the header tag. Check out the following example:

```
<STYLE TYPE="text/css">
H1 { background-color: #009; color: white;
     text-align: center; font-weight: bolder; }
</STYLE>
```

This example produces H1 elements that consist of centered white text, bold, against a dark-blue background. And it produces them automatically for every occurrence.

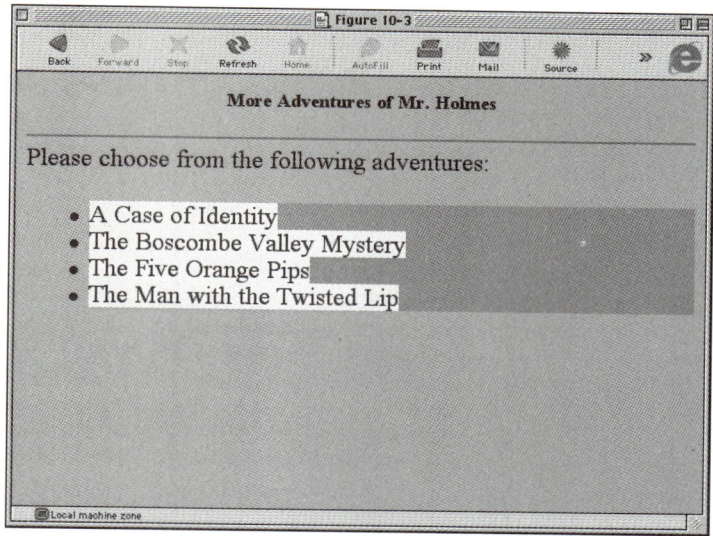

Figure 10-3 *Now you see some strange colored boxes, showing how the container nesting works.*

Just as font: **is a shorthand method for setting a variety of font-related attributes, CSS also supports the** background: **shorthand for setting any of** background-color, background-image, background-repeat, background-attachment, **and** background-position. **Conveniently, you can use** background: **to set just the color, which is why the examples throughout this book specify** background: blue, **for example, instead of** background-color: blue.

You can also create paragraphs of text with colored backgrounds, but the space between paragraphs that the <P> (or DIV) tag automatically adds doesn't turn out as you may hope, as the following example demonstrates:

```
<P STYLE="background: yellow;">
"What can it mean?" I gasped.
</P><P STYLE="background: yellow;">
"It means that it is all over," Holmes answered. "And perhaps,
after all, it is for the best. Take your pistol, and we will
enter Dr. Roylott's room."
</P><P STYLE="background: yellow;">
With a grave face he lit the lamp and led the way down the
corridor. Twice he struck at the chamber door without any reply
from within. Then he turned the handle and entered, I at his
heels, with the cocked pistol in my hand.
</P>
```

A quick glance at Figure 10-4 shows what I mean.

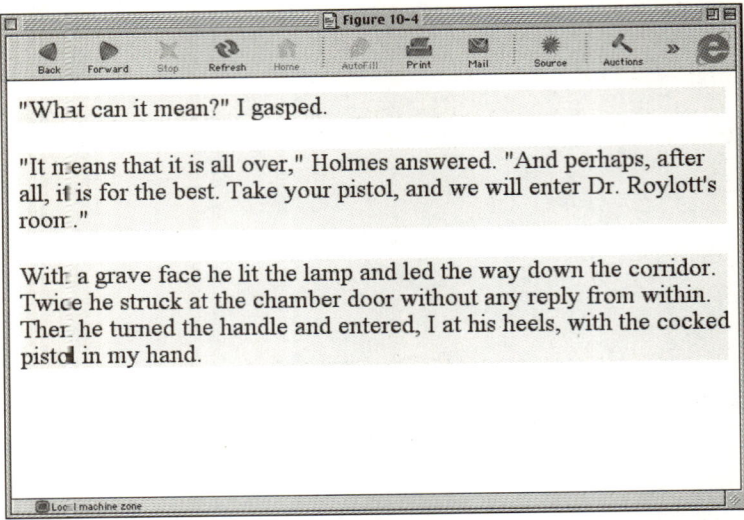

Figure 10-4   Paragraphs gain the background color but in a limited way.

The way to avoid this situation where the space between the paragraphs isn't the same color as the background of the paragraphs themselves, if you really want a colored passage, is to use the <TABLE> tag and skip the CSS background color entirely, surprisingly enough, as in the following example:

```
<TABLE BORDER=0 BGCOLOR="yellow"><TR><TD>
"What can it mean?" I gasped.
<P>
"It means that it is all over," Holmes answered. "And perhaps,
after all, it is for the best. Take your pistol, and we will
enter Dr. Roylott's room."
<P>
With a grave face he lit the lamp and led the way down the
corridor. Twice he struck at the chamber door without any reply
from within. Then he turned the handle and entered, I at his
heels, with the cocked pistol in my hand.
</TD></TR></TABLE>
```

This passage is a good example of why knowing your way around HTML, in addition to learning all about CSS and other approaches to presentation and formatting, is invaluable. In a nutshell, the more tools that you have at your disposal, the more likely you can build exactly what you want.

Background Images

Two different CSS attributes work together to enable you not only to add background images to your Web pages (which is old hat, after all), but also to enable you to add background images to *any container on the page*.

You read that correctly. You can have a background graphic on a paragraph, a header, or even a bullet item. The key attribute is `background-image:`, and the value is the URL of the graphic that you want to appear.

Take the couple of paragraphs from the Holmes story that I use in the preceding section and see how adding some background images can take a dull page and make it startling, as in the following example:

```
<BODY STYLE="font: 24pt bold;
 background-image: url(background1.jpg);">

<P STYLE="background: yellow url(background2.jpg);
   color: white;">
"What can it mean?" I gasped.
</P><P STYLE="background: yellow url(background3.jpg);
   color: yellow;">
"It means that it is all over," Holmes answered. "And perhaps,
after all, it is for the best. Take your pistol, and we will
enter Dr. Roylott's room."
</P><P STYLE="background: yellow url(background4.jpg);">
With a grave face he lit the lamp and led the way down the
corridor. Twice he struck at the chamber door without any reply
from within. Then he turned the handle and entered, I at his
heels, with the cocked pistol in my hand.
</P>
```

The results are going to look unexciting here in the book, as you can see in Figure 10-5, but if you view this sequence from the CD-ROM, I promise you that it looks way-cool!

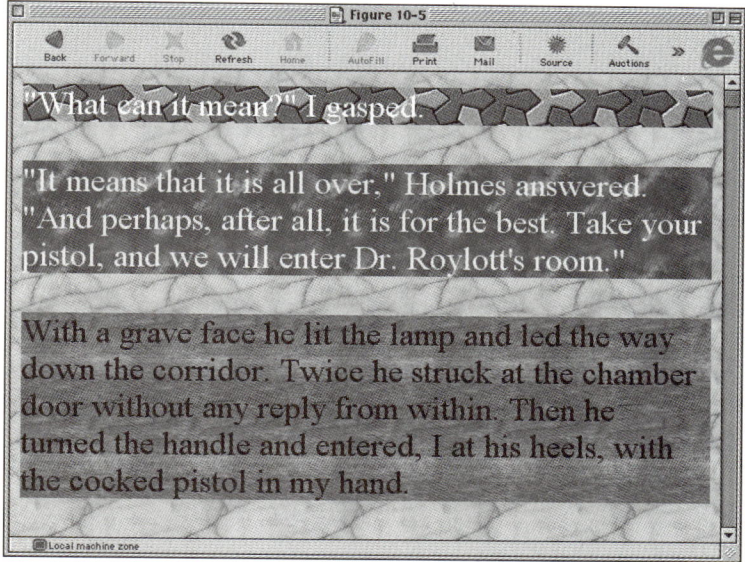

Figure 10-5 *Background images can turn a dull page into something amazing!*

Of course, *amazing* can prove either good or bad. As you can clearly see, even here in the book, the overuse of background graphics is actually somewhat annoying, and it certainly makes the text difficult to read (particularly against the first pattern). In general, however, the capability to add background images to individual containers on your page is a remarkable capability and one well worth exploring, albeit in moderation!

**10 Min.
To Go**

Background-repeat

A second CSS attribute that I need to talk about is `background-repeat`. If you've worked with background images on Web pages, you're already familiar with the frustrating limitation that you can't control the tiling of background images on a page. As a result, if you want to place, say, a spiral notebook edge down the left side, you end up needing to create a graphic that's actually as wide as the widest possible user window that you expect, although the graphic may actually run only 10 to 20 pixels tall. Why? Because otherwise, the spiral not only appears on the left side (from vertical tiling), but also down the middle of the page (from horizontal tiling of the background graphic).

By using the CSS `background-repeat` attribute, however, you can sidestep this problem (*finally!*). The greater level of control demonstrated by the following possible values for this attribute show why:

- `repeat`
- `repeat-x`
- `repeat-y`
- `no-repeat`

For the spiral notebook background, as an example, simply specify the following value:

```
background-repeat: repeat-y;
```

If you use this example, the background graphic doesn't tile horizontally at all. This improved level of control frees you up to create the smallest possible graphic necessary, which also results in the added benefit of making your page load faster, too.

Needless to say, the control capabilities apply to background images in any container on the page.

Positioning Background Images

The `background-repeat` attribute enables you to control the horizontal and vertical tiling of your background graphic, whether across the entire page or within a specific CSS container. You may also want greater control over the positioning of the graphic itself, however, although it's in the background. An example that comes to mind is a *watermark* on a page — perhaps one that reads DRAFT or CONFIDENTIAL.

To control the positioning of the background image, the necessary CSS attribute is `background-position:`, and its possible values are rather tricky to understand.

You have seven possible values for `background-position`: a percentage, a length, top, bottom, left, right, or center. The latter five are fairly self-explanatory, so I'm going to focus on the first two possibilities in the following sections.

Percentage values for background-position

You have two possibilities for percentage values — either you're using a single percentage value to specify the horizontal and vertical *origin* of the graphical element in the container or, if you specify two values, you're specifying the horizontal and then the vertical origin.

Check out the following example:

```
P { background-image: url(background3.jpg);
    background-repeat: no-repeat;
    background-position: 50%; }
```

This snippet produces paragraphs with the background image `background3.jpg` centered in the paragraph container with no tiling.

 **A better way to center the graphic is to use the** `center` **value, as in** `background-position: center`.

The results with the wrong background look most peculiar, but imagine if you have a page with a starry sky background, and individual containers with nonrepeating planetary elements that have their text contents superimposed atop. Could be tricky to build, but great to see.

Numeric values for background-position

Similar to specifying the one- or two-value possibilities for percentages, as I describe in the preceding section, specifying a single numeric value for `background-position` results in a browser using that value as the X-axis and Y-axis offset from the top-left corner of the parent container. Specify two values and a browser interprets the first as the X-axis and the second as the Y-axis.

Take the following example:

```
P { background-image: url(background3.jpg);
    background-repeat: repeat-y;
    background-position: 25 0; }
```

This example makes the background image appear 25 pixels to the right of the left margin (the default origin being the top-left corner of the container) but along the very top of the container.

You can use this example as an easy way to drop a spiral-notebook graphical element down the left side of a specific container without needing to constantly tweak the graphic itself to get the exact placement that you want for your particular visual look. Simply change 25 to 23, for example, and you slide it two pixels closer to the left edge.

Another example that's fun is the following one, where `lensflare.jpg` is a small element that looks like the flare you'd see in a camera lens from direct sunlight:

```
<P STYLE="background: #339 url(lensflare.jpg)
    top right no-repeat; color: white;">
With a grave face he lit the lamp and led the way
down the corridor. Twice he struck at the chamber
door without any reply from within. Then he turned
the handle and entered, I at his heels, with the
cocked pistol in my hand.
</P>
```

Figure 10-6 shows the results, although the effect is pretty subtle as shown here in the book. Again, look at this example on the CD-ROM (and resize your window a few times, too) to really understand what's occurring.

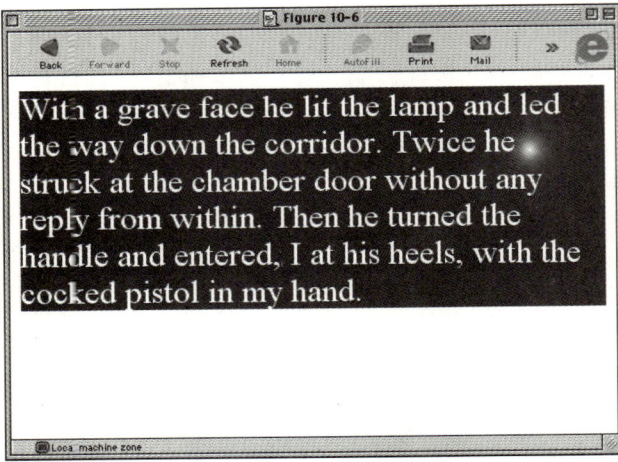

Figure 10-6 *A floating background graphic element (the lens flare) appears within a paragraph container.*

In a similar way, you can easily define a container that looks like a sticky note as follows:

```
<STYLE TYPE="text/css">
P.stickynote { background: #FF6 url(torncorner.jpg)
  bottom right no-repeat }
</STYLE>
```

The `torncorner.jpg` image looks like a curled paper corner and displays a background that matches the #FF6 background of the container.

Fixing the background in place

One more background attribute to know is `background-attachment:`, which enables you to fix a background graphic in place so that, as you scroll the page vertically or horizontally, the background graphic stays fixed.

The two possible values for `background-attachment` are `fixed` or `scroll`. The default is `scroll`.

You don't find too many times that you need this capability, but it's good to have in your toolkit nevertheless.

Done!

REVIEW

This session focuses on foreground and background colors for CSS containers and then spends lots of time exploring the five different CSS attributes associated with background images. By using these five you can achieve a remarkable number of different effects, particularly for smaller containers such as paragraphs or table data cells.

QUIZ YOURSELF

1. What's the problem that lurks in the following sequence?

    ```
    <STYLE TYPE="text/css">
    BODY { background: blue; }
    P { color: #00F; }
    </STYLE>
    ```

    (See "Colors.")

2. What's the difference between `background: green;` and `background-color: green`? (See "Background Colors.")

3. Explain why you want both a background color and a background image in specifying background images on your page? (See "Positioning Background Images.")

4. What problem was the reason I switched from CSS to an HTML table earlier in this session? (See "Background Colors.")

5. What does the following produce?

    ```
    <P STYLE="background: black; color: white;">
    Some information worth
    <SPAN STYLE="background-image: url(mars.jpg);">highlighting
    on this page</SPAN> and some material that's just dull and plain.
    </P>
    ```

    (See "Background Images.")

6. Name a type of background image that you'd tile only vertically and another background image that you'd want to tile only horizontally. (See "Background Images.")

P A R T

II

Saturday Morning

1. True/False: Cascading Style Sheets are named after the Cascade River in Washington.

2. <DIV> tags are more like which of the following: <P>, <BLOCKQUOTE>, <TT>?

3. <SPAN> tags are more like which of the following: <P>, <BLOCKQUOTE>, <TT>?

4. For a style that you're planning on applying to a number of different containers, is using a CLASS or ID specifier better?

5. True/False: 1 em = $1/24$ inch.

6. True/False: 12 points = 17 cm.

7. What common problem with Web pages does the tendency of Web browsers to ignore unknown tags without warning exacerbate?

8. Which of the following are legal CSS ID identifiers: *Añejo, frösch, aeroporto, soupçon*?

9. Fix the following two lines of CSS, if necessary, to make them correct:

   ```
   .jane { font-family: cursive; /* jane always curses }
   .larry { color: green; // larry's always been envious of jane }
   ```

10. Fix the following lines of CSS, if necessary, to make them correct:

    ```
    .tasha { margin: 5 in; /* she's marginal, at best */ }
    .coolJ { padding: 4em } // no comment.
    ```

11. Is the following line of CSS correct?

    ```
    UL LI { background-color: yellow; line-height: 1pt }
    ```

12. A CSS ID tag is recognizable by what leading character?

13. A CSS CLASS tag is recognizable by what leading character?

14. Is the following a valid CSS statement?

    ```
    P P { font-weight: bold; }
    ```

15. The CSS selector `A[link]` is an example of what type of selector?

16. The CSS font capability has deprecated (made obsolete) quite a few different HTML tags. Name at least four of them.

17. A unique style you want to apply to a single element on a page you can best represent as a _____ selector in CSS.

18. Which of the following best matches the `<TT>` HTML tag?

    ```
    font-weight: bold;
    font-style: italics
    font-family: monospace;
    ```

19. True/False: the following line is a valid CSS statement:

    ```
    font-family: Courier New, Times Roman PS
    ```

20. If you're using a 16-point type for the content on your page and want a headline that's 25 percent larger type, what are the two most straightforward ways that you can specify the larger size?

PART

III

Saturday Afternoon

Margins and Borders

Session Checklist

✔ Boxes and containers

✔ Margins

✔ Borders

✔ Padding

**30 Min.
To Go**

By this point, I hope that you're comfortable with my convention of referring to the space that a Web-page element occupies as a *container*, because this session is going to focus on the concept of containers and how they affect your Web design in the CSS world.

So jump right in!

Boxes and Containers

If you've been working with HTML for a while, you already think about the containers that comprise a page. Whether a container is an overt one such as a data cell in a table or the semi-obvious container of a paragraph or block quote — or even the subtle container of a hypertext reference or italicized passage — you construct all your Web pages from containers within containers within containers.

In regular HTML, this concept isn't really that important because, for the most part, you can't do anything with the containers or even really affect their layout much, other than perhaps by using CELLSPACING and WIDTH on a table, or MARGIN attributes in a BODY tag.

Cascading Style Sheets are a different story, however, and just about every HTML tag turns out to be a container — and you can resize and modify them all as you desire!

What don't I include in this list of resizable containers? HEAD, TITLE, **and** META **tags and similar elements that relate to the elements of a Web page that don't directly appear in the browser window.**

In the last session, you saw an interesting example of cascading background colors on a CSS-enhanced Web page. What may not have been obvious in that example is that the regions that were colored were the containers on the page and that they can nest quite deeply on a typical page.

As a simple example, consider the following HTML block:

```
<BODY>
<TABLE>
<TR>
<TD>
<P>
This is an <I>example</I> to explore.
</P>
</TD>
</TR>
</TABLE>
</BODY>
```

How many different containers do you count in that example?

I count six. They're easier to see if I indent things to suggest the containers at work, as in the following version:

```
<BODY>
    <TABLE>
        <TR>
            <TD>
                <P>
                    This is an
                    <I>
                        example
                    </I>
                    to explore.
                </P>
            </TD>
        </TR>
    </TABLE>
</BODY>
```

If you imagine each level of container having its own attributes, you can see where the *cascading* part of Cascading Style Sheets can really force you to keep track of everything happening on your page and not just the closest enclosing tag values.

In the CSS world containers are said to *nest*, such that the <I></I> container nests within the <P></P> container, the <TD></TD> container, and so on. Furthermore, the <I></I> container is the *child* of the <P></P> container. You also sometimes state this relationship by calling the <P></P> container the *parent* of the <I></I> container.

 **Unix is much more into all these ancestral names, with orphans, zombie children, parent processes, and much more. But I'm going to avoid talking about Unix in this book, okay?**

The Different Parts of a Container

To make this situation a bit more complex, a couple elements of each container are worth exploring further, as shown in Figure 11-1:

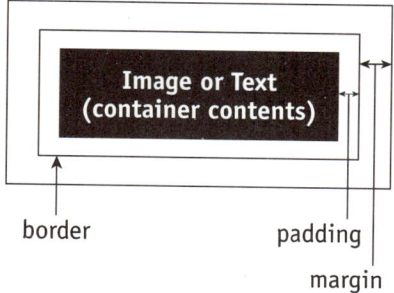

Figure 11-1 *Margins, padding, and borders on a CSS container.*

As you can see in Figure 11-1, an invisible buffer zone, or a *padding*, surrounds every element on a Web page. That buffer zone is identical in concept to the CELLPADDING attribute of a table data cell. On the very edge of the padding is a *border*, which is almost always invisible, and the space between the border and the rest of the contents of the page is the *margin* of the element, which I discuss in the following section.

Margins

The most common element of a container that people change is the *margin*. In a way, that process is analogous to setting the margin in your document before typing in a report, but it's considerably more powerful.

20 Min. To Go

You set and alter margins in CSS by using the margin: attribute, which is actually a shorthand way to access margin-left, margin-right, margin-top, and margin-bottom. You can give each of these attributes a different value — either a numeric measure (in, cm, em, and so on) or a percentage value. Because you almost always change all four margins at the same time, the margin: attribute is a convenient shorthand.

The following example shows how these values can affect layout:

```
<BODY STYLE="margin: 1cm; ">
<P STYLE="margin: 1cm;">
"I am about to be married."
</P><P STYLE="margin: 1cm;">
<B>"So I have heard."</B>
</P>
<P STYLE="margin-right: 3cm;">
"To Clotilde Lothman von Saxe-Meningen, second daughter
of the King of Scandinavia. You may know the strict
principles of her family. She is herself the very soul
of delicacy. A shadow of a doubt as to my conduct would
bring the matter to an end."
</P><P>
```

```
"And Irene Adler?"
</P><P STYLE="margin-left: 25%">
"Threatens to send them the photograph. And she will
do it. I know that she will do it. You do not know her,
but she has a soul of steel. She has the face of the
most beautiful of women, and the mind of the most
resolute of men. Rather than I should marry another
woman, there are no lengths to which she would not
go--none."
</P>
</BODY>
```

Figure 11-2 shows how you can give the different paragraphs dramatically different spacing and layout simply by changing the `margin:` settings. Notice that, by setting a default margin of 1cm in the `<BODY>` tag, I force more white space around the entire contents of the page, to which each paragraph container (other than `"And Irene Adler?"`) adds its additional margin spacing. Most important, remember that margins affect top and bottom spacing in addition to left and right spacing.

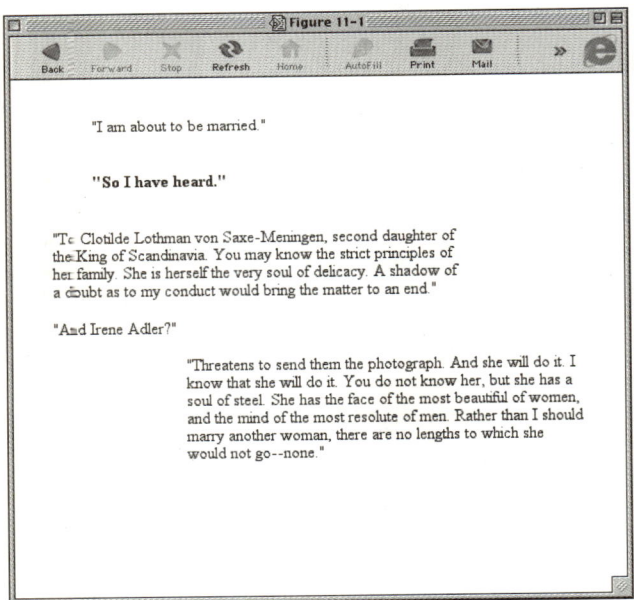

Figure 11-2 *Margin spacing dramatically changes the appearance of text.*

To really get an idea of how much things can change, I'm going to change the spacing of the bold paragraph container, paragraph number two, to a negative value, as follows:

```
<P STYLE="margin: -1cm;">
<B>"So I have heard."</B>
</P>
```

Now consider how different Figure 11-3 becomes. You must look hard for the bold paragraph because the new `margin:` setting buries it underneath other text.

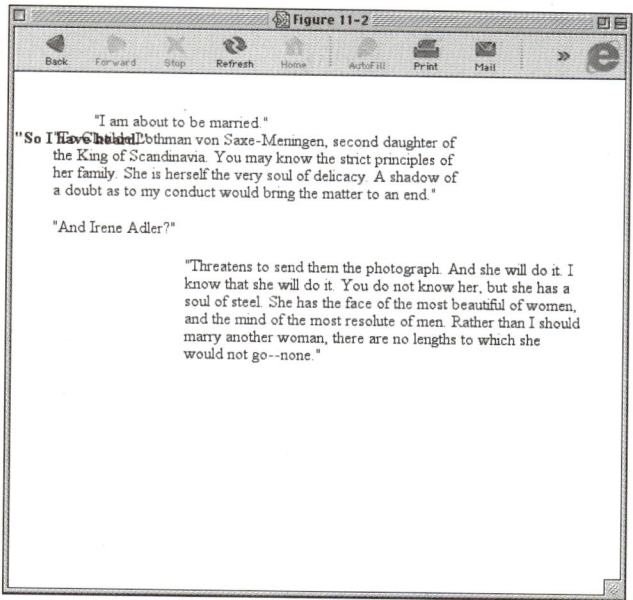

Figure 11-3 *Negative margin spacing produces some, uh, interesting results.*

Strange and weird, isn't it? This time is as good as any to point out that, if you want to explore negative margins, you must prepare yourself for unusual results as you develop the exact spacing that you want!

The margin: shorthand is the most complex of the shorthand attributes that you've seen so far: If you specify a single value, it applies to all four sides. Specify two values, and the first becomes the top and bottom while the second becomes the left and right. Specify three values, and you specify the top, left and right, and bottom margins, respectively. Specify four values, and you specify each of the four possible sides: top, right, bottom, and left. Why they're not in a consistent order, I don't understand!

So that you don't think that margins only create mass confusion on your page, try to visualize the result of the following set of styles:

```
<STYLE TYPE="text/css">
BODY { margin: 1cm; }
P    { margin-left: 1cm; }
H1   { margin-left: -5mm; }
H2   { margin-left: -5mm; }
</STYLE>
```

If you're imagining an attractive indented paragraph format with headers that outdent, you're right!

Did you notice the margin-left **attribute that I slipped into that last example? If you don't want to use the** margin: **shorthand, you can specify any of (or all) the four margin values for a container by using** margin-left, margin-right, margin-top, **and** margin-bottom.

Borders

The best way to understand the different containers is to draw a box around them all — literally. As you see in Figure 11-1, earlier in this session, every container includes three elements: an external margin, a border, and an internal padding.

The *border* is the most obvious visual element, so I'm going to switch now and explore some of the CSS border capabilities and then take a look at container padding. What the latter does then becomes quite obvious.

A number of different CSS attributes enable you to define the characteristics of a container border: `border-width`, `border-style`, and `border-color`. To demonstrate, I'm going to add the following style to the very top of the HTML that I use for Figure 11-2:

```
<STYLE TYPE="text/css">
BODY { margin: 1cm;
       border-width: 4px; border-style: solid;
       border-color: #999; }
</STYLE>
```

Figure 11-4 shows what this addition does: It draws an attractive four-pixel-wide gray box around the contents of this page of information.

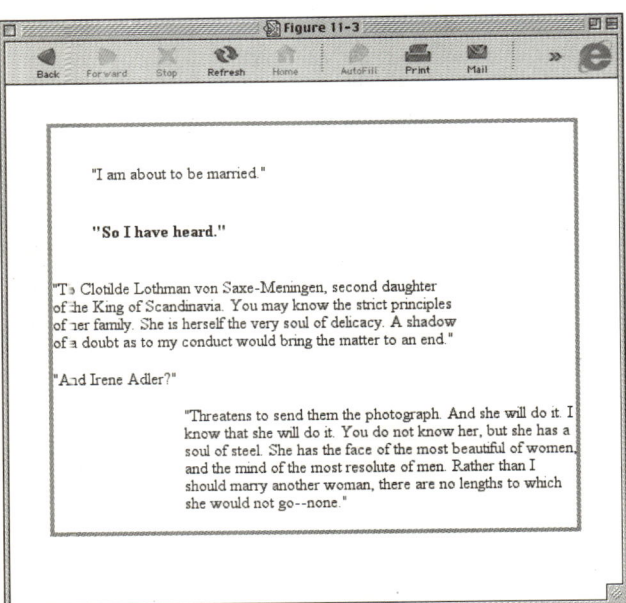

Figure 11-4 *A basic* BODY *border makes the page considerably more interesting visually.*

The `border-width` attribute can take a measure, as you see here, or you can simply specify `thin`, `medium`, or `thick`. The `border-color` attribute can also take any of the usual color specifications, depending on your personal preference.

Multiple value options

Both `border-width` and `border-color` can take more than one value if you want finer control over your presentation, so you can achieve a left-margin-only border by using the following example:

```
border-width: 0 0 0 3px;
```

And the code for a margin where the top and bottom are blue, while the left is yellow and the right border is green, looks as follows:

```
border-color: blue green blue yellow;
```

As you see with the multiple-value `margin` attribute in the section "Margins" earlier, these two also interpret values as top, right, bottom, and left. If you specify only two values, the attribute interprets them as top/bottom and then left/right, and if you specify three values, it interprets them as top, left/right, bottom.

Just as you can sidestep the order of parameters to the `margin` style by using `margin-left`, `margin-right`, and so on, you can also specify sides by using `border-width` or `border-color`.

Here's another way to specify a three-pixel-wide left border:

```
border-left-width: 3px;
```

And here's another way to specify the rainbow border:

```
border-bottom-color: blue;
border-top-color: blue;
border-right-color: green;
border-left-color: yellow;
```

Frankly, if I'm going to specify different widths for different sides of a border element, I use the explicit side name to avoid confusion.

 **To add to the potential confusion, you have a shorthand for each of the sides of the border, too. Use `border-left:` and you can specify width, color, and style all at once: `border-left: 3px solid black`**

One more element to consider before I get to the fun `border-style` values is `border-collapse`. The `border-collapse` CSS attribute takes two possible values: `collapse` or `separate`. This attribute comes into play only if two borders would otherwise touch each other on the page. If you specify `collapse`, the two borders merge and become one border (the size of the larger of the two, usually), whereas if you specify `separate`, they both show up as well, even if the result is essentially a double-wide border.

Border-style values

The most interesting of the border attributes is `border-style`, because a number of way-cool values are available to the page designer. See Table 11-1 for a list.

**10 Min.
To Go**

Table 11-1 *The Many Values of* `border-style`

Border Style Name	Explanation
none	No border (overrides parent border style).
hidden	Hidden border (again, overrides parent border style).
dotted	A dotted line.
dashed	A dashed line.
solid	A solid line, no shading.
double	A double solid line.
groove	Drawn as if it's carved into the screen.
ridge	Like groove but with an outward rather than inward cut appearance.
inset	Appears to push the contents of the container "into" the screen.
outset	Like inset but pushes contents "outward."

These different values become quite apparent in the following example:

```
<STYLE TYPE="text/css">
BODY { margin: 1cm;
       border-width: 10px; border-style: groove;
       border-color: #999999; padding: 5px; }
</STYLE>
<BODY>
<P STYLE="border: 10px inset;">
"I am about to be married."
</P><P STYLE="border: 10px dashed;">
<B>"So I have heard."</B>
</P><P STYLE="border: 10px outset;">
"To Clotilde Lothman von Saxe-Meningen, second daughter
of the King of Scandinavia. You may know the strict
principles of her family. She is herself the very soul
of delicacy. A shadow of a doubt as to my conduct would
bring the matter to an end."
</P><P STYLE="border: 10px double;">
"And Irene Adler?"
</P><P STYLE="border: 10px dotted;">
"Threatens to send them the photograph. And she will do
it. I know that she will do it. You do not know her, but
she has a soul of steel. She has the face of the most
beautiful of women, and the mind of the most resolute of
men. Rather than I should marry another woman, there are
no lengths to which she would not go--none."
</P>
</BODY>
```

Take a look at Figure 11-5 and you see how this example renders in Internet Explorer. Quite a busy page all of a sudden, isn't it?

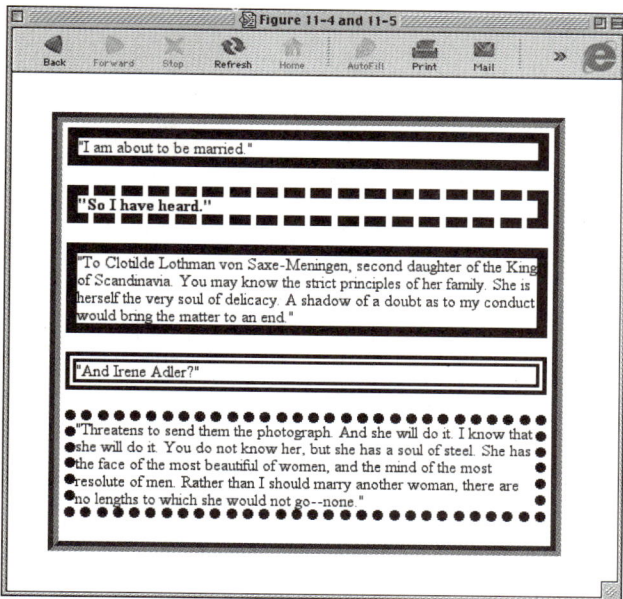

Figure 11-5 *Borders within borders in Microsoft Internet Explorer.*

One important thing to notice about Figure 11-5 is that, although Internet Explorer 5.5 doesn't appear to implement the inset and outset border styles, it actually does, but it just doesn't know how to render them visible if they're black. Figure 11-7 shows inset and outset borders in IE, because I specify different colors for them.

Figure 11-6 reveals that the old standby Netscape 4.7 actually does a better job in this case, implementing both inset and outset correctly in the default black. Notice, however, the difference in interpretation of the width of the internal paragraph borders and that Navigator can't render either the dashed or dotted border styles.

In Session four, I talk about the cross-platform and cross-browser issues associated with CSS. You may want to pop back and read it again if you're surprised by the difference in CSS support between these two browsers on my reference Macintosh system. You'll have similar results on your PC.

In a bit of foreshadowing worthy of Alfred Hitchcock (if he'd coded in CSS!), I slipped in a border-padding addition in the preceding example, with padding: 5px;.

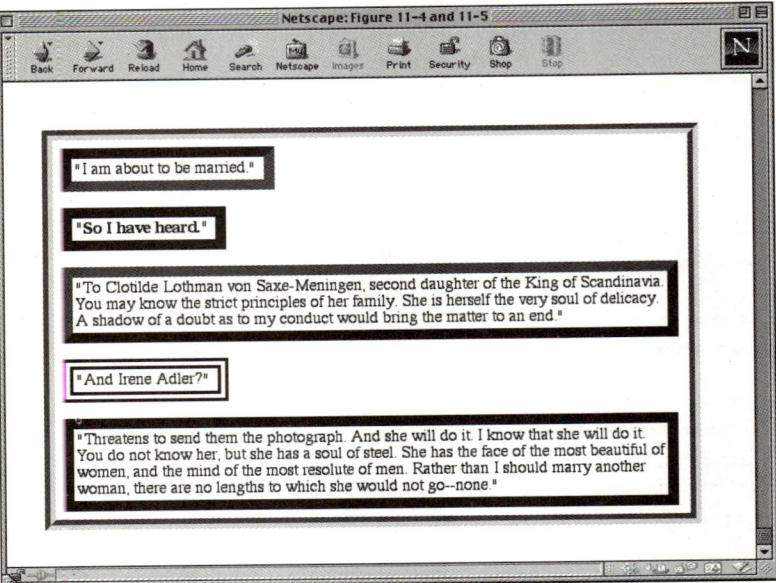

Figure 11-6   Different border options in black in Netscape Navigator.

Padding

The last topic to consider in dealing with containers is the *padding*, which affects the space between the border and the contents of the container. In the last example in the preceding section, I added `padding: 5px;` to ensure that the outermost border and the borders of each paragraph container don't touch but instead maintain a fixed pixel space around them.

The following example gives you one more variation on the Holmes snippet, with padding added to the many different containers to help you clearly see the difference. Watch for the negative padding to see what happens!

```
<STYLE TYPE="text/css">
BODY { margin: 1cm;
       border-width: 10px; border-style: groove;
       border-color: #999999; padding: 5px; }
</STYLE>
<BODY>
<P STYLE="border: 10px inset blue; padding: 5px; ">
"I am about to be married."
</P><P STYLE="border: 10px dashed green; padding: 1em;">
<B>"So I have heard."</B>
</P><P STYLE="border: 10px outset yellow; padding: -10px;">
"To Clotilde Lothman von Saxe-Meningen, second daughter of
the King of Scandinavia. You may know the strict principles
of her family. She is herself the very soul of delicacy.
A shadow of a doubt as to my conduct would bring the matter
to an end."
```

```
</P><P STYLE="border: 10px double red; padding: 2%;">
"And Irene Adler?"
</P><P STYLE="border: 10px dotted; padding: 1mm;
 border-top-color: blue; border-left-color: red;
 border-bottom-color: yellow; border-right-color: cyan;
 border-top-width: 4px;">
"Threatens to send them the photograph. And she will do it.
I know that she will do it. You do not know her, but she
has a soul of steel. She has the face of the most beautiful
of women, and the mind of the most resolute of men. Rather
than I should marry another woman, there are no lengths
to which she would not go--none."
</P>
```

The results are as shown in Figure 11-7.

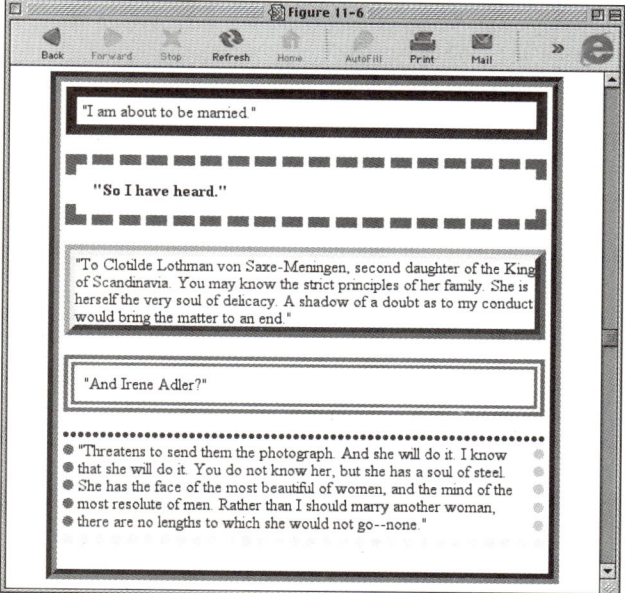

Figure 11-7 *Padding dramatically changes the feel of container borders.*

 **Figure 11-7 is a figure that you definitely must view on your own computer screen to see how it's delightfully colorful!**

Notice particularly the complex border specification of the very last paragraph and its results on-screen. It's quite festive! And did you catch that the browser interprets a negative padding as a zero-padding request? That's quite fortunate, in my opinion, otherwise we'd doubtless have some pretty peculiar and unreadable results.

Done!

REVIEW

This session focuses on three interrelated elements of CSS containers: *margins, padding,* and *borders.* Containers are really critical to your understanding and exploiting of CSS styles for your page layout, and a few simple border, margin, and padding specifications can dramatically improve the appearance of a Web page. Different Web browsers interpret containers differently, however, so cross-platform testing is critical if you're doing any complex layout.

QUIZ YOURSELF

1. What's the difference between the padding and margin of a container? (See "The different parts of a container.")

2. Is the margin most like the CELLSPACING or CELLPADDING attribute of an HTML table? (See "Margins.")

3. What's the relationship between a parent and child container, and why is that relationship important? (See "Boxes and Containers.")

4. What's wrong with the following code?
   ```
   <STYLE TYPE="text/css">
   BODY { margin-left: 3px; margin-sides: 10px; }
   </STYLE>
   ```
   (See "Margins.")

5. What do you think may happen if you try the following code:
   ```
   STYLE="padding: 100%;"
   ```
   Try it and see the results!
   (See "Padding.")

6. What color is the left side of the resultant border in the following specification?
   ```
   STYLE="border-color: blue black yellow green;"
   ```
   (See "Borders.")

7. A more elegant way to write the four-color specification that I show in the preceding example is available to you. What is it? (See "Borders.")

Positioning Content with CSS

Session Checklist

✔ Container dimensions

✔ Positioning

✔ Clipping containers

T he last session explored how borders, margins, and padding offer you lots of control over the presentation of individual containers of information on a Web page through CSS. In this session, you explore how to size and control additional characteristics of containers, including how other material flows around the contents of the container.

Container Dimensions

Two key CSS attributes enable you to control the dimensions of each container of information on your Web page: `width:` and `height:`. The following example shows how you can use them:

```
<P STYLE="width: 50%; margin-left: 25%;
   border: 1px solid; padding: 2px;">
The stout gentleman half rose from his chair and gave
a bob of greeting, with a quick little questioning
glance from his small fat-encircled eyes.
</P>
<P>
"Try the settee," said Holmes, relapsing into his
armchair and putting his fingertips together, as was
his custom when in judicial moods. "I know, my dear
Watson, that you share my love of all that is bizarre
and outside the conventions and humdrum routine of
```

```
everyday life. You have shown your relish for it by
the enthusiasm which has prompted you to chronicle,
and, if you will excuse my saying so, somewhat to
embellish so many of my own little adventures."
</P>
```

Most of the CSS attributes in the first paragraph I explain in the preceding session, but here's a review: I'm specifying here that the first container (paragraph) is 50 percent of the width of the parent container (the BODY), with a left margin that's 25 percent of the width of the parent container (effectively centering the material). A one-pixel, solid-black border is drawn around the contents of the container, with a two-pixel padding. The results are as shown in Figure 12-1.

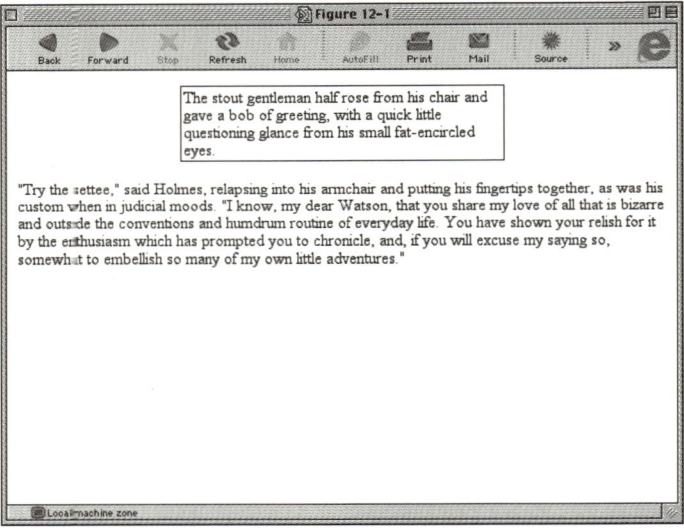

Figure 12-1　*Width can profoundly affect the appearance of material on a Web page.*

The value of the width: attribute is obvious, but the value of height: is a bit subtler.

Setting the container height

By default, you automatically create containers at the minimum height necessary to contain all the information therein. The default behavior if you have more material than fits in the specified container size is to spill out of the container. You can use the overflow attribute (which I talk about in the section "Clipping Containers" later in this session) to duplicate some of the Internet Explorer-only IFRAME HTML tag characteristics, but I'm just going to let it spill over for now. As a result, specifying a height that's insufficient for the contents of a container can give you bizarre results, as Figure 12-2 demonstrates.

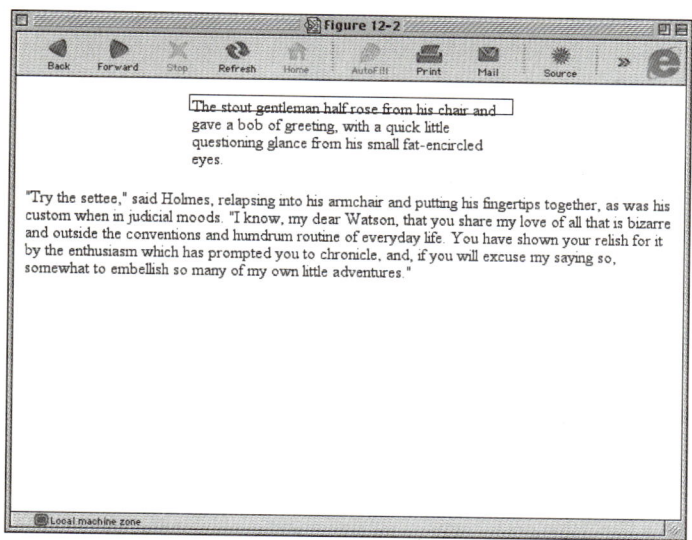

Figure 12-2 *Don't specify a height that's too little to contain the text.*

The only change in HTML between what you see in Figure 12-1 and 12-2 is that I add `height: 1em;` to the STYLE attribute of the first paragraph for the second figure, as shown in the following example:

```
<P STYLE="width: 50%; margin-left: 25%; height: 1em;
    border: 1px solid; padding: 2px;">
```

Explore this example on your computer by resizing your browser window; watch what happens as it gets very narrow and very wide.

20 Min. To Go

Text and container flow

To really understand why the `height:` attribute is actually useful, you need to look at the `float:` attribute, which enables you to align a container relative to the rest of the content on the page.

The best way to understand how the `float:` attribute works is to recognize that it's exactly the same as the ALIGN attribute of the <TABLE> tag. Within a <TABLE> tag, you can specify ALIGN=left or ALIGN=right, and the subsequent material flows around the table on the side other than the one that you specify. To phrase it differently, left alignment causes the table to align against the left margin, with the subsequent text flowing to its right.

The `float:` attribute works in exactly the same way, as the following example shows:

```
<P STYLE="width: 50%; margin: 10px; background-color: #FDF;
    float: left; border: 1px solid; padding: 2px;">
```

```
The stout gentleman half rose from his chair and gave a bob
of greeting, with a quick little questioning glance from
his small fat-encircled eyes.
</P>
<P>
"Try the settee," said Holmes, relapsing into his armchair and
putting his fingertips together, as was his custom when in
judicial moods. "I know, my dear Watson, that you share my love
of all that is bizarre and outside the conventions and humdrum
routine of everyday life. You have shown your relish for it by
the enthusiasm which has prompted you to chronicle, and, if you
will excuse my saying so, somewhat to embellish so
many of my own little adventures."
</P>
```

Notice that, in addition to specifying `float: left;` in the STYLE attribute, I also add a 10-pixel margin around all four sides of the container border and spruce things up with a light-red background.

Technically, `#FDF` results in a light purple – red + blue = purple — but your color may vary, as mine does! If you really want purple, try `#C9F` instead.

Figure 12-3 shows the attractive results and should certainly inspire you regarding ways to improve long passages of text!

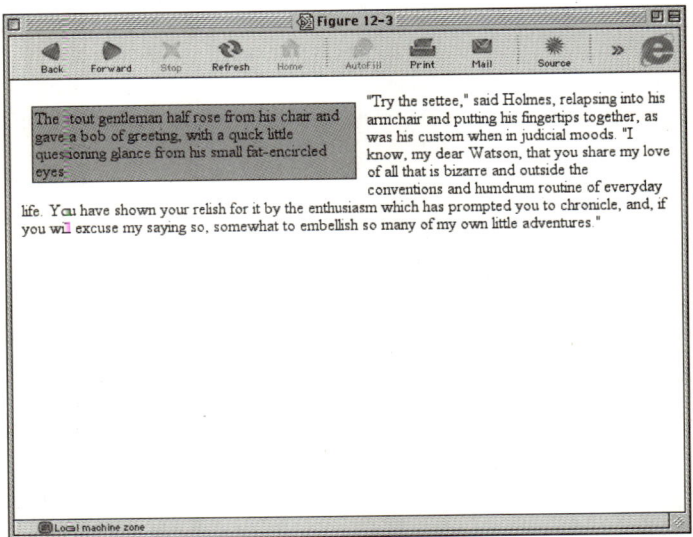

Figure 12-3   *Float and container tweaks produce a delightful result.*

The float: CSS attribute can take three possible values: left, right, or none, where you use the last to override the parent float: value if you specify one.

Remember that this attribute affects *any container, even one that has child containers,* so you can use this layout technique with a parent container that includes multiple paragraphs of text, graphics, hyperlinks, or whatever, and it still acts as a single unit for any CSS presentation specifications that you apply at the parent container level.

Positioning

The idea that containers can hold child containers and that you can alter the appearance of the parent through CSS is a cornerstone of advanced DHTML Web design. It's also why accurately and precisely positioning the container is so important. In the CSS world, you have four different container-positioning options: absolute, relative, fixed, and static.

The good news is that one of these — static — is the default, so you're already familiar with it. In static positioning, the container lays out as usual, with preceding material appearing on-screen before the container and subsequent material appearing after the container.

Absolute positioning

Absolute positioning offers a way to specify, pixel by pixel, *exactly* where the container appears on-screen. You set this positioning through a combination of three CSS attributes. The most obvious is position: with the value absolute, but you also need to specify some combination of the top:, left:, right:, and bottom: values, all of which are relative to the edges of the parent container.

Those last few words are so critical, I want to repeat them again: *all of which are relative to the edges of the parent container — not* relative to the Web page itself. If you specify top: and left:, for example, they're relative to the top-left corner of the parent container.

Here's an example of how you may use absolute positioning to change the appearance of our working passage from Doyle's "The Red-Headed League":

```
<P STYLE="width: 50%; margin: 10px; color: red;
    position: absolute; top: -6px; left: -6px;
    border: 1px solid; padding: 2px;">
The stout gentleman half rose from his chair and gave a bob of
greeting, with a quick little questioning glance from his small
fat-encircled eyes.
</P>
<P>
"Try the settee," said Holmes, relapsing into his armchair and
putting his fingertips together, as was his custom when in
```

```
judicia moods. "I know, my dear Watson, that you share my love
of all that is bizarre and outside the conventions and humdrum
routine of everyday life. You have shown your relish for it by
the enthusiasm which has prompted you to chronicle, and, if you
will excuse my saying so, somewhat to embellish so many of my own
little adventures."
</P>
```

Figure 12-4 shows the results.

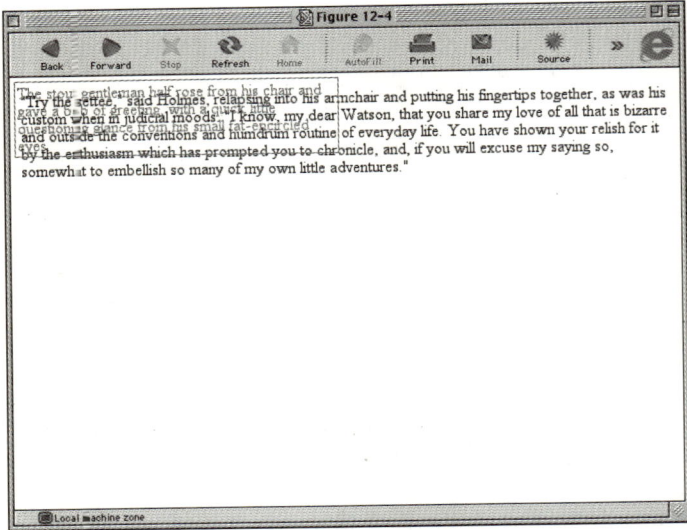

Figure 12-4   *Absolute positioning often layers containers atop each other.*

I don't know about you, but Figure 12-4 gives me a bit of a headache! The good news is that you have a couple different ways to address the overlapping container problem. The fastest solution is to simply restore the background color so that you simply can't see the text of the second paragraph, which the following example accomplishes:

```
<P STYLE="width: 50%; margin: 10px; background-color: #C9F;
    position: absolute; top: -6px; left: -6px;
    border: 1px solid; padding: 2px;">
```

This result is as shown in Figure 12-5, which is considerably easier on the eye.

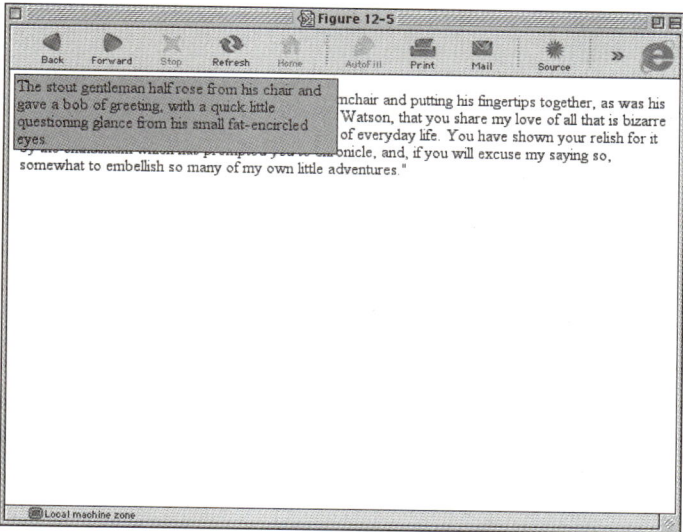

Figure 12-5   *Specifying a background color hides the overlapping text problem.*

It's not a completely satisfying solution, however, because you still face the issue of the missing text. In this particular example, the best solution is to use the `float: left` CSS attribute. Experiment with it yourself and you'll see what I mean!

 **Imagine, however, if you could just click the purple box and make it vanish. . . . That's what activating your DHTML with JavaScript enables you to do later in the book. Stay tuned.**

10 Min.
To Go

Relative positioning

Absolute positioning is absolute only within the parent container, and most DHTML designers prefer *relative positioning*, which they consider part of the normal flow of the document for layout. Taking the example in the preceding section and switching from absolute to relative solves the overlap problem but in a somewhat inelegant manner (leaving a big empty space to the right of the purple box), as follows:

```
<P STYLE="width: 50%; margin: 10px; background-color: #C9F;
    position: relative; top: -6px; left: -6px;
    border: 1px solid; padding: 2px;">
```

Figure 12-6 shows the result.

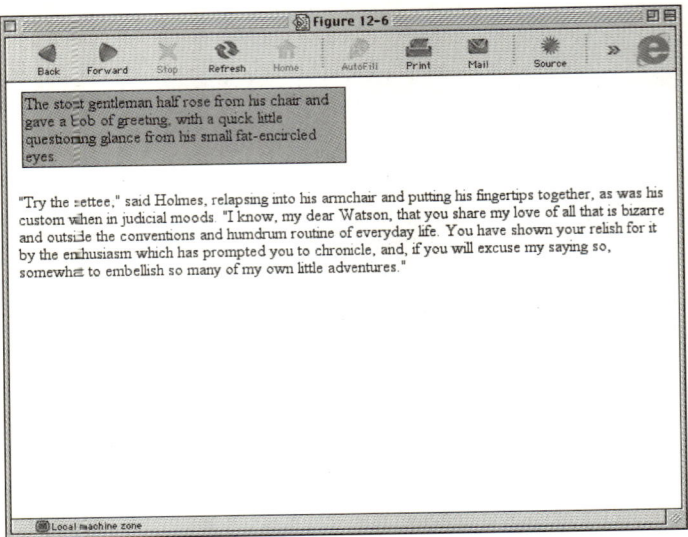

Figure 12-6   *Relative positioning makes the container part of the regular document flow.*

In this case, `float: left` produces a more attractive result.

So what's the point?

To see why the positioning of elements can prove so useful, I need to change the perspective a bit. Instead of merely providing you with a tool to create big containers of information, relative positioning can actually become your best friend for the purpose of exerting fine control over the positioning of inline elements.

In Session 8, you learned about the `vertical-align` CSS attribute as a way to change the relative location of an element such as the trademark symbol in a line of text. Relative positioning offers far greater control over positioning of this nature, and that's its greatest value, as the following example shows:

```
<STYLE TYPE="text/css">
.tm { position: relative;  top: -2.2em; left: -2em;
      font: 8pt bold; border: 1px red groove; padding: 1px;
      background-color: #009; color: white; }
</STYLE>
</HEAD>
<BODY>

<P STYLE="font: 36pt bold Courier;">
This book has been brought to you by
Hungry Minds, Inc.
<A HREF="trademark-info.html" TARGET="new" CLASS="tm">tm</A>--
formerly IDG Books Worldwide, Inc.
</P>
```

Here I create a new class, `.tm`, that creates a small blue box with white `tm` lettering inside that's actually a hyperlink to the trademark information on the site. By using the `top` and `left` attributes, I can carefully tune exactly where the box appears on the layout, pixel by pixel.

Figure 12-7 shows how it looks on a line of very large text.

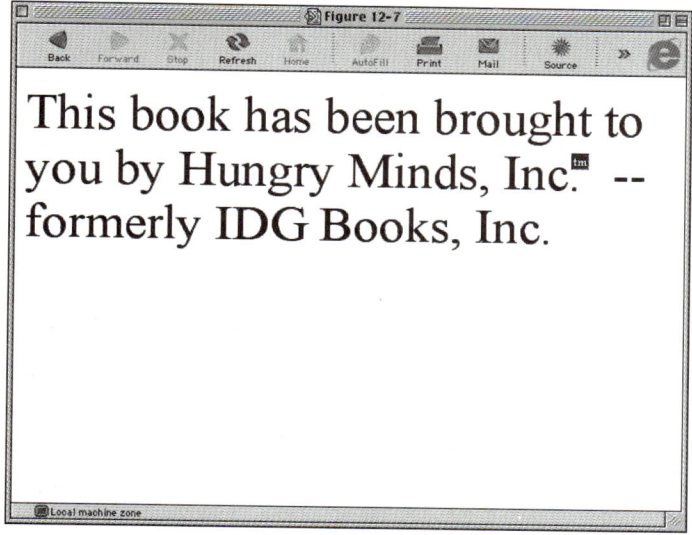

Figure 12-7 *Relative positioning is great for setting up inline elements.*

Fixed positioning

You have one more possible positioning value, and that's *fixed*. This position is essentially the same as absolute with one spiffy difference: Fixed containers *don't scroll as the rest of the page scrolls*.

So, finally, you have another way to get around the hidden text problem: Simply let the user scroll to reveal the otherwise hidden text. Probably not the most user-friendly solution, but it works!

Here's a nifty, fixed header that shows up in the listing for Figure 12-8, which appears exclusively on the CD-ROM that comes with this book. Before you jump up and try this on your computer, fair warning: Windows browsers don't support fixed positioning yet.

```
<P STYLE="position: fixed; width=75%;
   top: -25px; left: 12%; background-color: #CFC;
   font: 18pt bold Arial; padding: 8px;
   border: 3px dashed #090; text-align: center;">
ADVENTURE II. THE RED-HEADED LEAGUE
</P>
```

To see how Figure 12-8 works, you need to access it on the book's CD-ROM; the preceding header proves to represent a fixed position block. Make sure that you resize your window and scroll down to see what happens!

Clipping Containers

The capability to size and position containers with a high degree of precision is useful, but if the contents are larger than the container parameters, browsers ignore the dimensions that you specify. Two CSS attributes offer control over what happens if the contents of a container are larger than the size that you specify.

The first is overflow, and it offers three possible values: hidden, visible, and scroll. For hidden or scroll to work, you must define a clipping region, too, using the clip CSS attribute. You define the clipping region as a rectangle. Think of it as a stencil cut-out superimposed atop the region, with its top left and bottom right vertices defined. If the material can be seen "through" the cut-out, it's displayed. If not, the material is hidden.

Now for the bad news.

Very few of the browsers available as of this writing support either overflow or clip as the CSS specification defines them. Worse, the Cascading Style Sheet 2.0 spec defines the rectangular region associated with the clip attribute as rect(top, right, bottom, left), but Microsoft Internet Explorer, in its flaky implementation of clip, expects a rectangular definition of rect(top, left, width, height).

I encourage you to experiment with a combination of size, overflow, and clip values to see whether you obtain results that are a reasonable solution for your specific design needs.

Done!

REVIEW

This session explores the many ways that you can affect the size and appearance of individual containers on a Web page. It also considers ways to define what occurs if the contents of a container are more than can fit in the specified parameters. In such as case, you learn that, just as with the HTML 4.01 specification versus the reality of browser implementations, the current breed of browsers don't conform to the entire CSS 2.0 specification. More useful is this session's examination of the combination of float: width, height, and relative.

QUIZ YOURSELF

1. What does the following HTML sequence produce?

```
<P STYLE="width: 0px; height: 0px;
overflow: hidden;">Hello World!</P>
```

(See "Setting the container height.")

2. Write the CSS equivalent to the following HTML:

```
<TABLE BORDER=0 CELLPADDING=5 ALIGN=right>
  <TR><TD><FONT FACE="Arial"><B>The Beginning...</B>
  of the end</TD></TR>
</TABLE>
```

   (See "Container Dimensions.")

3. What's the difference between relative and absolute positioning? (See "Positioning.")

4. For that matter, what's the difference between absolute and fixed positioning? (See "Positioning.")

5. What is a good use for fixed positioning, and what HTML tag offers a somewhat similar capability? (See "Positioning.")

6. One characteristic of absolute positioning makes it remarkably similar to relative positioning. What is it? (See "Positioning.")

Visibility, the CSS Solution

Session Checklist

✔ Visibility enables you to hide containers

✔ Display controls visibility and flow

✔ Pop-up elements

**30 Min.
To Go**

U p till now, you've looked at only half the DHTML picture with Cascading Style Sheets. Dynamic HTML is actually a combination of both CSS and JavaScript, and this session is the first one in which JavaScript moves forward from the sidelines.

By this point in your Weekend Crash Course, you probably understand that a container bounds every logical element that appears on a Web page and that these containers are almost invariably invisible. Whether you're using a <B> attribute, a paragraph, or an explicit DIV or SPAN tag, everything lives in a box. And that's the key to what you're going to explore herein.

Visibility Enables You to Hide Containers

Examples in preceding sessions demonstrated how you can assign containers a wide variety of layout attributes and can even make them float above other containers by setting position changes. Something that you may find remarkable is that every container also has a visibility: attribute, too — one that controls whether its contents appear on-screen or remain hidden to the viewer.

Jump straight in to the following example to see how this visibility: attribute works:

```
As he spoke there was the sharp sound of horses'
hoofs and grating wheels against the curb, followed
by a sharp pull at the bell. Holmes whistled.
<P STYLE="visibility: hidden;" ID="holmes1">
"A pair, by the sound," said he. "Yes," he continued,
glancing out of the window. "A nice little brougham
and a pair of beauties. A hundred and fifty guineas
apiece. There's money in
this case, Watson, if there is nothing else."
```

```
</P>
<P>
"I think that I had better go, Holmes."
<P>
"Not a bit, Doctor. Stay where you are. I am lost
without my Boswell. And this promises to be interesting.
It would be a pity to miss it."
```

Figure 13-1 shows the results.

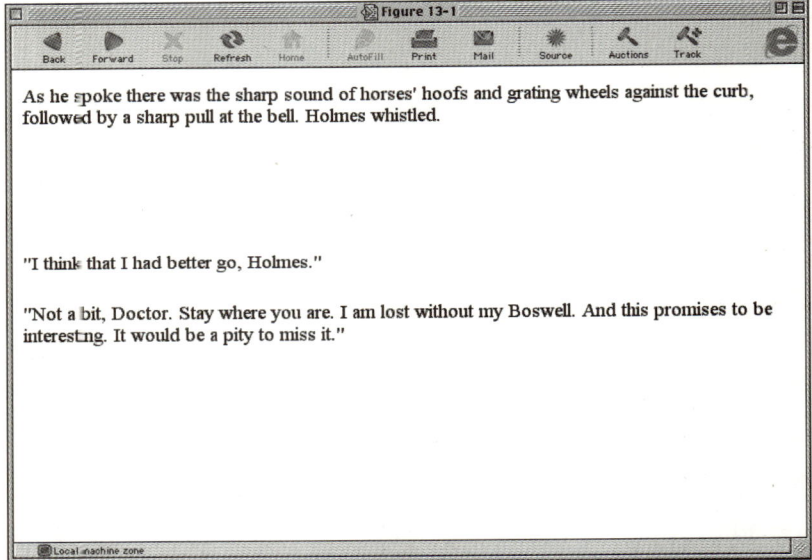

Figure 13-1   *You still must allocate space even for hidden containers.*

The most important thing to notice about Figure 13-1 is that the paragraph of information that's hidden still has its space allocated in the layout of the page. And to work with the `visibility` of a container, it needs you to specify a unique ID (in this case, `"holmes1"`).

To go further, you need to jump ahead into the world of JavaScript. . . .

Controlling Visibility by Using JavaScript

The `visibility:` attribute isn't of much use unless you can make it visible on demand. To accomplish any event-based scripting on a Web page requires JavaScript, the official scripting language of HTML 4.0 and CSS 2.0.

Don't panic, however, as this session offers you a chance to dip your toe into the waters of JavaScript event programming. The second half of the book then goes into great detail about JavaScript and how to use it to activate your pages.

For now, just accept that the Web browser uses a *document object model* (*DOM*) and that every container and element on the page is accessible through an appropriate reference to that element in the DOM. Again, you learn more about the DOM later in this crash course.

To switch the value of the visibility: attribute from hidden to visible, you need to reference the paragraph by ID through the circuitous route of the DOM itself, as follows:

```
document.all.holmes1.style.visibility="visible";
```

I'd better explain.

You're already familiar with the idea that a series of nested containers surrounds a given element on your Web page, right? Simply imagine that you now want a method of referring uniquely to any of the elements in any of the containers, and you see that this "dot" notation (e.g., separating elements with a period) makes sense. In fact, by using a unique ID value, all you really have in the preceding line is the following:

```
document.all.holmes1
```

This line uniquely refers to the container (paragraph) that you designate as holmes1 on the Web page.

After you initially specify a unique element, you can access a wide variety of different attributes of that container by further utilizing the dot notation. To get to visibility:, you must use the .style element and then specify the exact name of the attribute that you want. Conceptually, it's as follows:

**20 Min.
To Go**

```
unique container descriptor.style.visibility
```

After you specify the visibility: attribute of the style of the holmes1 paragraph, you can change its value by using a simple assignment statement in JavaScript, as follows:

```
document.all.holmes1.style.visibility = "visible";
```

I hope that makes a bit more sense now.

 **If you can't get the examples in this session to work, perhaps your Web browser is using an older document model. If that's the case, try using document.holmes.visibility = "visible"; instead.**

JavaScript is all event based, so to test this snippet of code, I'm going to associate the reassignment of visible to a simple event that occurs on all Web pages: OnLoad. After you specify this event in the <BODY> tag of a page, it enables you to easily specify JavaScript to execute as soon as the Web browser receives every element of the page from the network.

Inline JavaScript looks a little bit different from inline CSS because you don't have a single attribute that you always use, a la STYLE. Instead, you list the desired event, with the associated JavaScript code on the right-hand side of the statement.

The <BODY> tag of our page may look as follows:

```
<BODY OnLoad="document.all.holmes1.style.visibility='visible';">
```

 **By convention, you write JavaScript events in mixed upper- and lowercase letters, as you can see, even if all your other HTML is all uppercase.**

Following's a complete listing of the source for Figure 13-2:

```
<BODY OnLoad="document.all.holmes1.style.visibility='visible';">
As he spoke there was the sharp sound of horses'
hoofs and grating wheels against the curb, followed
by a sharp pull at the bell. Holmes whistled.
<P STYLE="visibility: hidden;" ID="holmes1">
"A pair, by the sound," said he. "Yes," he continued,
glancing out of the window. "A nice little brougham
and a pair of beauties. A hundred and fifty guineas
apiece. There's money in
this case, Watson, if there is nothing else."
</P>
<P>
"I think that I had better go, Holmes."
<P>
"Not a bit, Doctor. Stay where you are. I am lost
without my Boswell. And this promises to be interesting.
It would be a pity to miss it."
```

If you view this example in a Web browser, the hidden paragraph appears along with the other paragraphs of material, as you may expect.

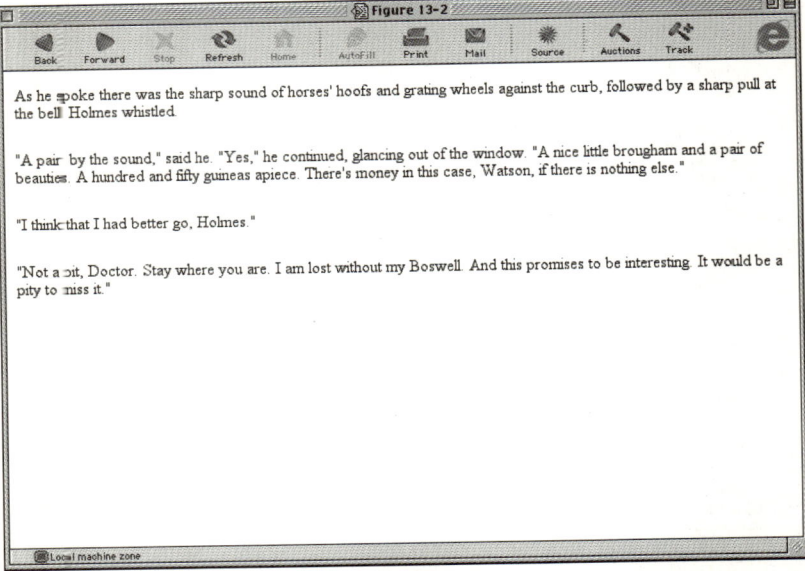

Figure 13-2 *JavaScript materializes the otherwise invisible paragraph.*

This example isn't too scintillating, but what if you add the following two hypertext reference links to this page? They both associate with the OnMouseOver event, which triggers whenever the user moves the cursor over the highlighted text.

```
<A HREF="#"
OnMouseOver="document.all.holmes1.style.visibility='visible';">
make it visible</A> |
<A HREF="#" OnMouseOver="document.all.holmes1.style.visibility='hidden';">
hide it</A>
```

Now you can start to see where CSS plus JavaScript can really give you a tremendous amount of power! In this example, moving your cursor over the link `hide it` sets the `visibility:` of the `holmes1` element to `hidden`, hiding the paragraph of text. Move your cursor over `make it visible` and the `visibility:` of `holmes1` sets to `visible`, revealing the paragraph again.

 **The** `HREF="#"` **is a common trick for a null hypertext reference that you tie to a JavaScript event. If you click it, you go to the same Web page, effectively making it an empty reference.**

Figure 13-3 shows how the page looks after I move the cursor over `hide it` to make the paragraph invisible again.

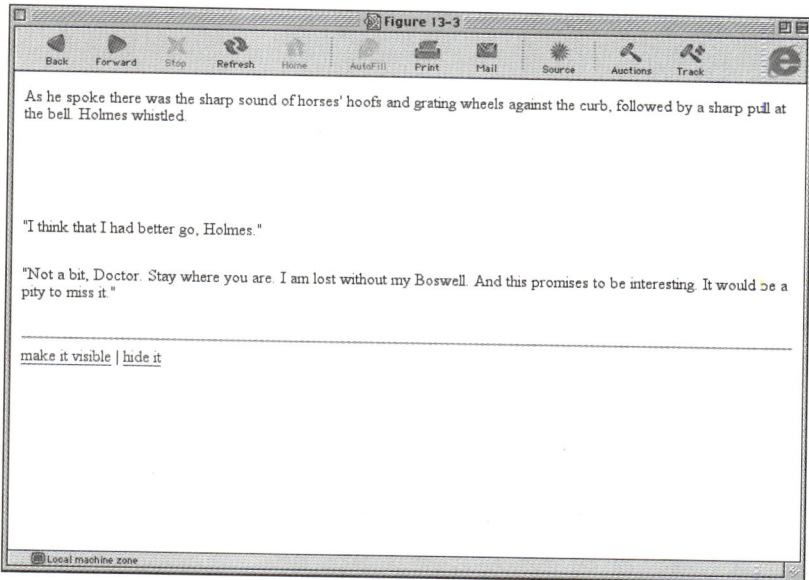

Figure 13-3 *JavaScript-enabled hypertext references enable you to control the visibility of a text passage.*

You can also use `<SPAN>` to tie a JavaScript event to a container, as in the following example:

```
"Not a bit, Doctor.
<SPAN OnMouseOver="document.all.holmes1.style.visibility='visible';">Stay
where you are.</SPAN>
I am lost without my
```

```
Boswell. And this promises to be interesting.
<SPAN OrMouseOver="document.all.holmes1.style.visibility='hidden';">
It would be a pity to miss it."</SPAN>
```

The interesting thing about using <SPAN> is that the enabled text appears completely identical to the surrounding text. Go back to Figure 13-3 and look closely at the two sentences shown in the preceding example: Stay where you are. and It would be a pity to miss it. You can see no visible indicator that they're turbocharged, capable of hiding or displaying a paragraph of the text on the user's whim!

Figure 13-3 is a great example to explore on your own computer!

10 Min.
To Go

Display Controls Visibility and Flow

Although the visibility: attribute is definitely valuable, it has one characteristic that makes it less than the ideal layout element: The browser allocates space for the invisible element even if it never appears on-screen. You can see that in Figure 13-1.

CSS offers a second style attribute that enables you to simultaneously control the visibility and whether the space for the element is allocated: display:.

According to the CSS 2.0 specification, the display: attribute offers a whole bunch of possible values, as in Table 13-1 enumerates.

Table 13-1   *Possible Values for* display, *According to CSS 2.0*

Value	Explanation
inline	A container with no break before or after.
block	A container with a forced line break above and below.
list-item	Creates both a box and list-item box (indented).
run-in	An element that you can insert into the subsequent container.
compact	An element that you can place adjacent to the subsequent container.
marker	Used for pseudocontainer references.
inline-table	An inline table container (which you can't do in regular HTML; regular tables are always block elements).
table	A table container.
table-cell	A table data-cell container.
table-row	A table data-row container.
table-row-group	A table data-row group container.

Value	Explanation
table-column	A table column container.
table-column-group	A table column group container.
table-header-group	A table header group container.
table-footer-group	A table footer group container.
table-caption	A table caption container.
none	An invisible container that gets no allocation for layout and flow.

The only values that need interest you are none, block, and inline. The attribute display: none sets the visibility: of the element to hidden and omits any allocated space for the container in the page layout. The other two possibilities, block and inline, share the same difference that differentiates <DIV> and <SPAN>: The former forces a blank line above and below, while the latter displays no break from the surrounding material.

Here's how you can use this new CSS attribute with the <SPAN> buttons of the last paragraph as our inspiration for this approach:

```
<BODY>
<P>
As he spoke there was the sharp sound of horses'
hoofs and grating wheels against the curb, followed
by a sharp pull at the bell. Holmes whistled.
<DIV ID="holmes1"
 STYLE="display: none; font-style: italic;">
"A pair, by the sound," said he. "Yes," he continued,
glancing out of the window. "A nice little brougham
and a pair of beauties. A hundred and fifty guineas
apiece. There's money in
this case, Watson, if there is nothing else."
</DIV>
<P>
"I think that I had better go, Holmes."
<P>
"Not a bit, Doctor.
<SPAN OnMouseOver="document.all.holmes1.style.display='block';">
Stay where you are.</SPAN>
I am lost without my
Boswell. And this promises to be interesting.
<SPAN
OnMouseOver="document.all.holmes1.style.display='none';">
It would be a pity to miss it."</SPAN>
</BODY>
```

This example is particularly interesting to experiment with on your own computer, but Figure 13-4 shows how the page initially loads and and Figure 13-5 shows how the page looks after I move my cursor over the sentence Stay where you are.

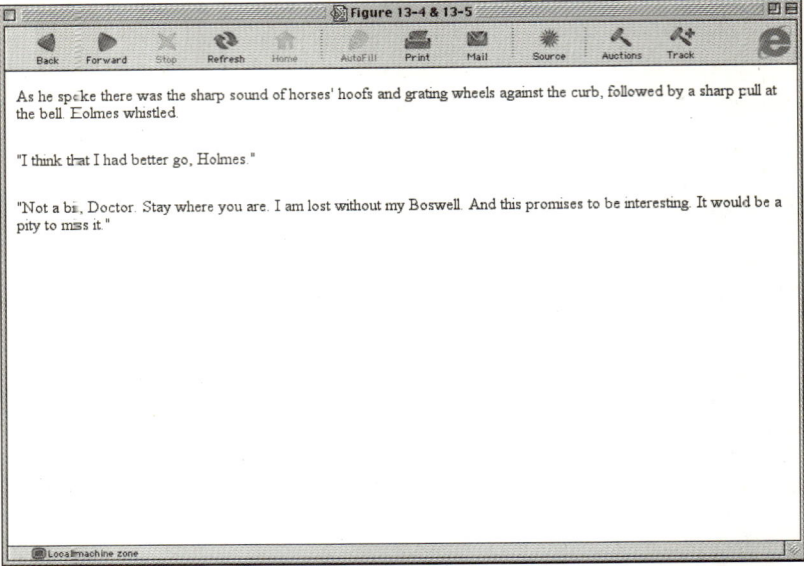

Figure 13-4 *The default layout with the* `<DIV>` *block hidden from view.*

Notice how no space or other indication in Figure 13-4 hints at anything lurking beneath the surface on this Web page.

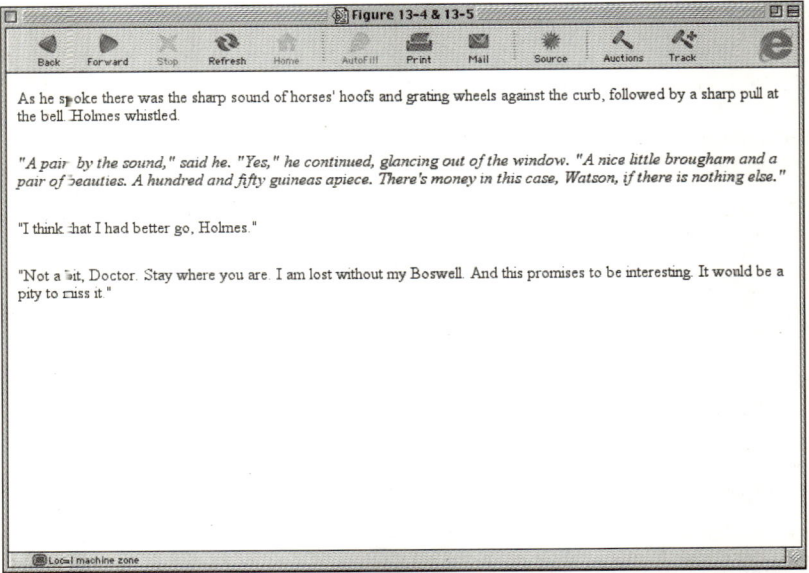

Figure 13-5 *The mouse is over the magic phrase, so the hidden paragraph emerges.*

In this case, I needed to change the JavaScript because I'm working with a different CSS attribute. Instead of `visibility: hidden` and `visibility: visible`, the settings are `display: none` and `display: block`. Inline elements use `display: inline` instead.

Here's how you can use `display: inline` to make acronyms automatically spell themselves out if someone puts the cursor over the acronym:

```
In this case I've had to change the JavaScript
Because we're working with a different
<SPAN
 OnMouseOver="document.all.css.style.display='inline';"
 OnMouseOut="document.all.css.style.display='none';">
CSS</SPAN>
<SPAN ID="css" STYLE="display: none;">
(Cascading Style Sheets)</SPAN>
attribute.
```

Type this small code snippet in and try it yourself; you're sure to like the results!

Notice the addition of a second JavaScript event: `OnMouseOut` triggers after the cursor moves out of the container. In essence, I set `display` to `inline` if the cursor is over the abbreviation CSS and reset it to none after the cursor moves on.

 **If you can't get these examples to work, have faith; after I really start to dig into JavaScript, I spend lots of time talking about compatibility across document object models and revisit these examples.**

Pop-up Elements

The combination of different CSS and JavaScript elements are what makes DHTML Dynamic, and now is a perfect time to whet your appetite with a simple example that combines display and positioning attributes with some JavaScript coding to tie actions to events.

Ready?

First off, the following example produces a fancy pop-up text box, with the initial state of display set to none so that it doesn't appear on-screen:

```
<SPAN ID="holmes1" STYLE="position: absolute; left: 30px;
 display: none; background: #EEE; width: 50%;
 padding: 2px; border: 2px solid black;">
"A pair, by the sound," said he. "Yes," he continued, glancing
out of the window. "A nice little brougham and a pair of
beauties. A hundred and fifty guineas apiece. There's money in
this case, Watson, if there is nothing else."
</SPAN>
```

Most important to notice is that I add a `position: absolute` specification to the STYLE attribute of this element and that I switch from a `<DIV>` to a `<SPAN>`. The forced blank lines above and below a `<DIV>` make it inappropriate for pop-up containers.

The activation links in the following block are identical to those in the earlier example:

```
"Not a bit, Doctor.
<SPAN OnMouseOver="document.all.holmes1.style.display='block';">
Stay where you are.</SPAN>
I am lost without my
Boswell  And this promises to be interesting.
<SPAN
OnMouseOver="document.all.holmes1.style.display='none';">
It would be a pity to miss it."</SPAN>
```

Figures 13-6 and 13-7 show the results as this example first loads and then after you drag the cursor across Stay where you are.

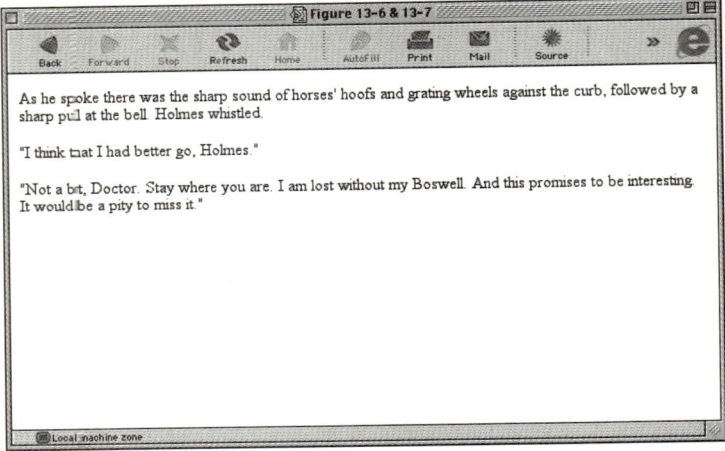

Figure 13-6   *The default page, with no hint of the hidden paragraph.*

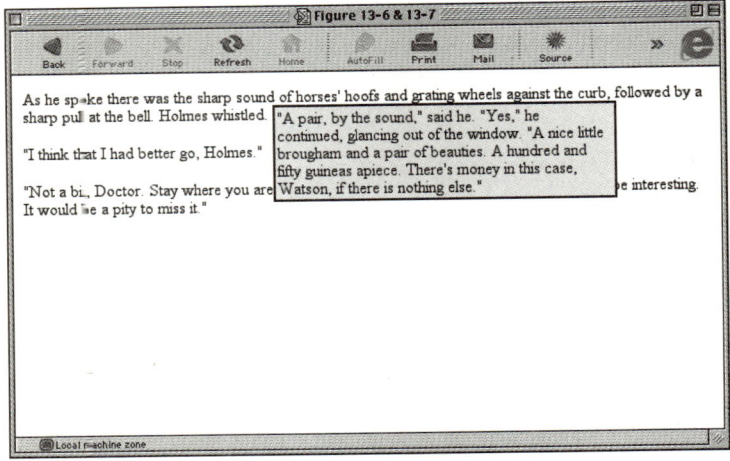

Figure 13-7   *A pop-up paragraph appears!*

You can do quite a bit more with these pop-up containers, as you see in the subsequent sessions.

For now, good job! This session marks a milestone in your *Weekend Crash Course* — the first one that ties CSS and JavaScript together.

Done!

REVIEW

This session covers two CSS attributes — visibility: and display:, exploring their differences and similarities. It then jumps into JavaScript to tie changes in attribute values to specific user events on the Web browser. The event triggers that the session explores are OnLoad (which, after the page fully loads, shows up in the <BODY> tag) and OnMouseOver (which, if the cursor is in that container, can function for any container on the page). It further explores the combination of event triggers and hidden containers in a variety of different examples, from simple to sophisticated.

QUIZ YOURSELF

1. Why do you need to add JavaScript to get pop-ups to work? (See "Controlling visibility by using JavaScript.")

2. What's wrong with the following style specification?
   ```
   <DIV STYLE="background-color: #FEE; visibility: 50%;">
   ```
   (See "Display Controls Visibility and Flow.")

3. The preceding <DIV> presents a more subtle problem regarding its suitability for pop-ups. What's the problem? (See "Display Controls Visibility and Flow.")

4. The following snippet contains a logical mistake involving its operation. What is it?
   ```
   <BODY OnLoad="document.all.bigview.style.visibility='visible';">
   This is critical information for the user to read before
   seeing 'bigview'.
   <SPAN ID="bigview" STYLE="position: absolute; width: 100%; height:
   100%; top: 0px; left: 0px; text-align: center;">
   This is the big view! </SPAN>
   </BODY>
   ```
   (See "Visibility Enables You to Hide Containers.")

5. What are the advantages and disadvantages of using <A HREF="#"> versus <SPAN> for a JavaScript trigger link? (See "Controlling visibility by using JavaScript.")

6. Using CSS styles, how can you make a <SPAN> link appear identical to a blank hypertext reference?

Layering Content: 3D Web Pages

Session Checklist

✔ Stacking: z-indexes

✔ Layering

✔ Changing z-values by using JavaScript

*30 Min.
To Go*

If one thing's come to characterize the Web, it's the two-dimensional nature of Web pages. Try as you may, drop shadows by themselves don't add the missing third dimension, *depth*, to the width and height of each page.

If you've been thinking about the combination of absolute positioning and visibility as a way to layer things atop each other, however, you've probably already realized that, suddenly, you've moved into a space where you can actually begin to manipulate that third dimension through the order and presentation of these layers.

This session explores the *z-index*, a concept that appears in both CSS and JavaScript. In addition, I show you how to add some simple scripting that enables you to click a layer to bring it to the top and then click it again to make it drop down to the bottom.

Stacking: Z-Indexes

I know it may have been years ago, but do you remember your high school geometry class? In the class, you undoubtedly learned about the three primary *axes* or *dimensions* of our physical space, as shown in Figure 14-1.

Other dimensions exist, notably time (duration), that also affect physical space, but fortunately (if geometry isn't a favorite of yours), I'm going to just look at the three core dimensions, which are known as *height*, *width*, and *depth*.

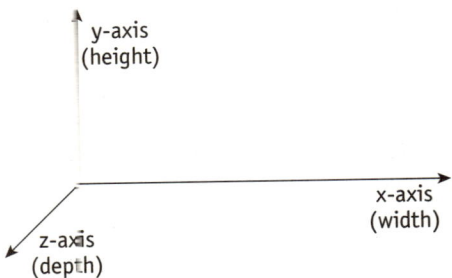

Figure 14-1   The three dimensions of physical space.

Imagine that each container on a Web page has its own depth value and that, the deeper the element, the lower is that depth value. A depth of zero is on the "bottom," and a depth of 100 is on the very topmost layer. If you have three layers, the depth values (which are known as *z-index values* in DHTML) may be z=0 for the bottom, z=1 for the middle, and z=2 for the topmost layer, as shown in Figure 14-2.

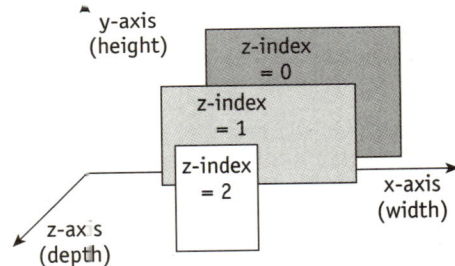

Figure 14-2   Three layers with different z-index values.

To translate this concept into CSS nomenclature is quite simple by using the attribute z-index. The z-index attribute accepts a single integer value from zero to 100, with higher values positioned above lower values.

Here's an example:

```
<SPAN STYLE="position: absolute; z-index: 0;
 background-color: blue; width: 250; height: 100;
 top: 105px; left: 14px;"></SPAN>

<SPAN STYLE="position: absolute; z-index: 1;
 background-color: red; width: 200; height: 150;
 top: 80px; left: 40px;"></SPAN>

<SPAN STYLE="position: absolute; z-index: 2;
 background-color: green; width: 100; height: 325;
 top: 10px; left: 90px;"></SPAN>
```

Figure 14-3 shows the result, which is quite attractive, particularly if you remember that each colored box is actually a full DHTML container and can hold graphics, hypertext links, or whatever else you want.

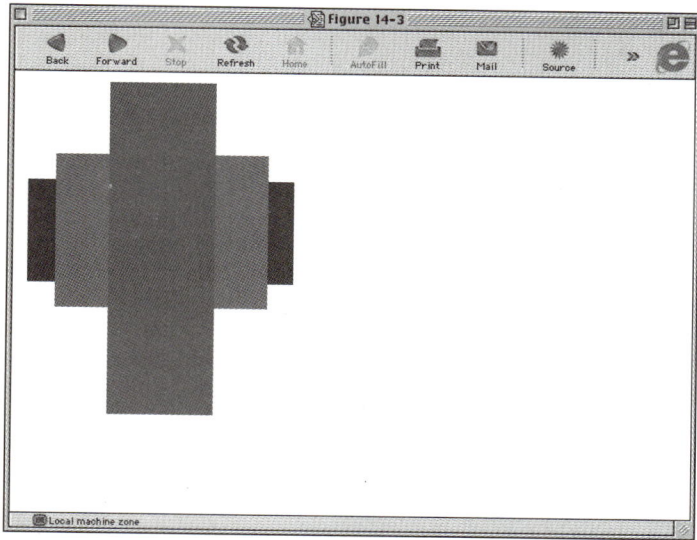

Figure 14-3   *Three colorful boxes, neatly stacked atop each other.*

**20 Min.
To Go**

The Quirky Netscape Navigator

Netscape Navigator treats many of the elements of CSS layers incorrectly, so most of the examples that I present here don't work at all if that's your browser. In particular, for the example in the preceding section, you find that it ignores `width:` and `height:` unless you have sufficient content to force the dimensions that you specify.

To fix the example in the preceding section so that it works with Netscape Navigator, I can simply add some content — in this case, a one-pixel transparent GIF image — and stretch it to the dimensions that I want, as follows:

```
<SPAN
  STYLE="position: absolute; z-index: 2; background-color: blue;
       width: 250; height: 100; top: 105px; left: 14px;">
<IMG SRC="1dottrans.gif" HEIGHT="100" WIDTH="250">
</SPAN>
```

This adjustment does the trick, and after you actually put content in your layers, things work more easily. Sort of.

I must vent here for a minute and say that Netscape's lack of complete support for CSS 1.0, let alone CSS 2.0, is really frustrating. By comparison, Internet Explorer does a very good job of supporting the vast majority of the CSS 2.0 standard and, certainly, almost every element of CSS 1.0. As a result, if you're using Netscape Navigator as your primary browser, you need to either upgrade to the experimental 6.0 release or switch to IE if you want the fullest support available for CSS.

Most of the CSS that I cover in this book works in both browsers, but invariably, if it fails in one of the two, it's in Netscape and not IE. Furthermore, as of this writing, Internet Explorer is by far the most common browser in use on the Internet, and I expect it to completely eclipse Netscape Navigator within a few years.

 **You can find a lot of Internet usage statistics and metrics, all online at CyberAtlas, at** `http://cyberatlas.internet.com/`.

Layering

Layering elements atop each other on your Web page through CSS isn't too hard; you can do so by using the combination of absolute positioning and z-index values.

To truly appreciate the power of the z index, I'm going to change the z-index values of the HTML example in the preceding section to see what happens, as follows:

```
<SPAN STYLE="position: absolute; z-index: 2;
 background-color: blue; width: 250; height: 100;
 top: 105px; left: 14px;"></SPAN>

<SPAN STYLE="position: absolute; z-index: 1;
 background-color: red; width: 200; height: 150;
 top: 80px; left: 40px;"></SPAN>

<SPAN STYLE="position: absolute; z-index: 0;
 background-color: green; width: 100; height: 325;
 top: 10px; left: 90px;"></SPAN>
```

All that the preceding example does is put the blue box on top, while the red box stays in the middle and the green box goes on the bottom. Figure 14-4 shows the results.

Although you're unlikely to build pages of colorful containers, I hope that you can appreciate the additional important third-dimensional control that the z-index offers on design and layout.

Furthermore, if you consider that some of the layers may appear on-screen only to explain other content on the page, offer a navigational shortcut (a pop-up menu), or otherwise appear only temporarily, the capability to control which lie atop which other elements is a critical one.

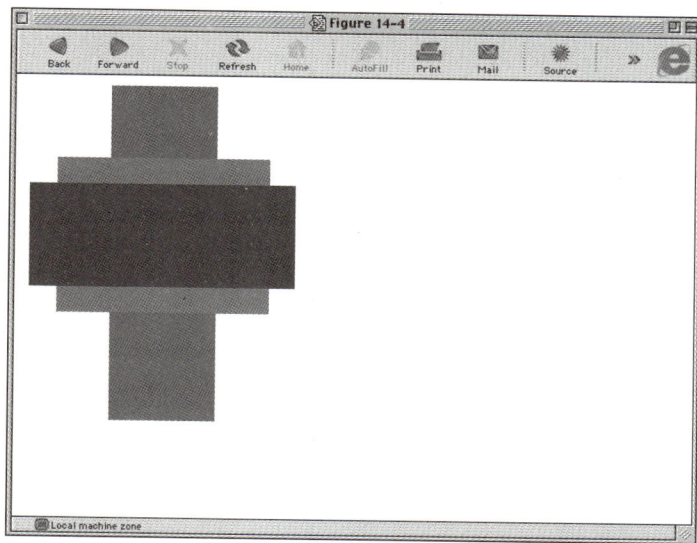

Figure 14-4   *The same three colorful boxes, with their stacking order reversed.*

**10 Min.
To Go**

Changing Z-Values by Using JavaScript

You can initially set z-index values within the CSS, but to dynamically change them requires you to jump into JavaScript again. The JavaScript event that you use for this task is the OnClick, which triggers the associated script after the cursor moves into the element and the user clicks the mouse button, as the follow example demonstrates:

```
<SPAN ID="blue"
 STYLE="position: absolute; z-index: 2;
        background-color: blue; width: 250;
        height: 100; top: 105px; left: 14px;"
 OnClick="document.all.blue.style.zIndex=100;">
 </SPAN>

<SPAN ID="red"
 STYLE="position: absolute; z-index: 1;
        background-color: red; width: 200;
height: 150; top: 80px; left: 40px;"
 OnClick="document.all.red.style.zIndex=100;"></SPAN>

<SPAN ID="green"
 STYLE="position: absolute; z-index: 0;
background-color: green; width: 100;
height: 325; top: 10px; left: 90px;"
 OnClick="document.all.green.style.zIndex=100;"></SPAN>
```

Figure 14-5 shows how this screen looks after clicking the red element to bring it to the top.

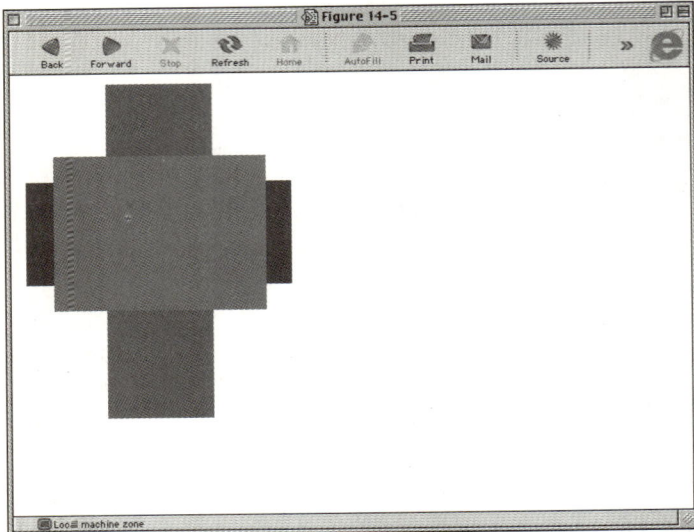

Figure 14-5   *Clickable layers enable you to bring the red box to the top with just a mouse click.*

This example is definitely one to explore off the CD-ROM!

This change appears to achieve the result that you want of creating layers that you can click to bring to the foreground. If you actually try changing the z-index of the different layers in your browser, however, you quickly find that, after you move all three to the z-index of 100, they can't move farther towards the top — so nothing changes.

This example definitely doesn't work in Netscape Navigator, because Navigator doesn't support JavaScript events within <SPAN> tags, or even <IMG> tags if you're using the stretched-image trick that I show you earlier. If you *must* stick with Navigator, try wrapping your image with a hypertext reference, as follows: <A HREF="#" OnClick="document.green.zIndex=100;">.

One solution to this problem is to make each layer move the other layers back to their original settings as it moves, so that each OnClick looks more like the following example:

```
OnClick="document.all.green.style.zIndex=100;
         document.all.blue.style.zIndex=2;
         document.all.red.style.zIndex=1;"
```

This solution works (sort of), but although each layer that you click does indeed jump to the front after you click it, your browser loses the relative z-index values of the other two layers after they automatically reset to their original values.

A more sophisticated approach to this situation makes the requested layer's z-index increment by one while those of the others decrement by one, as follows:

```
OnClick="document.all.green.style.zIndex += 1;
         document.all.blue.style.zIndex -= 1;
         document.all.red.style.zIndex -= 1;"
```

Here I'm using a convenient JavaScript shorthand: The += is an increment, so a+=1 is exactly the same as a = a + 1; it's just more succinct.

This solution kind of solves the problem, but now a new problem appears: You don't want any layers to ever get a z-index of less than zero, because that's an illegal value, and if you blindly subtract from a z-Index, you could easily end up with this problem.

Another level of JavaScript sophistication can bound the decrement statements so that the script checks for a zero value before deciding to subtract one, as in the following examples:

```
OnClick="document.all.blue.style.zIndex += 1;
         if (document.all.green.style.zIndex > 0) {
           document.all.green.style.zIndex -= 1; }
         if (document.all.red.style.zIndex > 0) {
           document.all.red.style.zIndex -= 1; }"
```

Of course, if you want to ensure that nothing is ever less than zero, you also need to check to ensure that nothing is ever greater than 100, the maximum z-index value that you can have, as the following example shows:

```
OnClick="if (document.all.blue.style.zIndex < 100 {
           document.all.blue.style.zIndex += 1;  }
         if (document.all.green.style.zIndex > 0) {
           document.all.green.style.zIndex -= 1; }
         if (document.all.red.style.zIndex > 0) {
           document.all.red.style.zIndex -= 1; }
```

To understand what's wrong with this seemingly reasonable solution, open this example from the CD-ROM in Internet Explorer and click the red layer for a half-dozen times; then click the blue layer. Figure 14-6 shows the result.

The result that you want is for the blue layer to move to the front after you click, but it doesn't work now. Clicking the red layer a half-dozen times increments its z-index each time, resulting in a red z-index of 7 (after starting out at z-index: 1, remember). Clicking blue then sets its z-index to 1 (after starting at 2 but decrementing to zero because of the clicks on red) and decrements the red layer from 7 to 6. Four more clicks on the blue region are necessary before the blue layer correctly moves to the top.

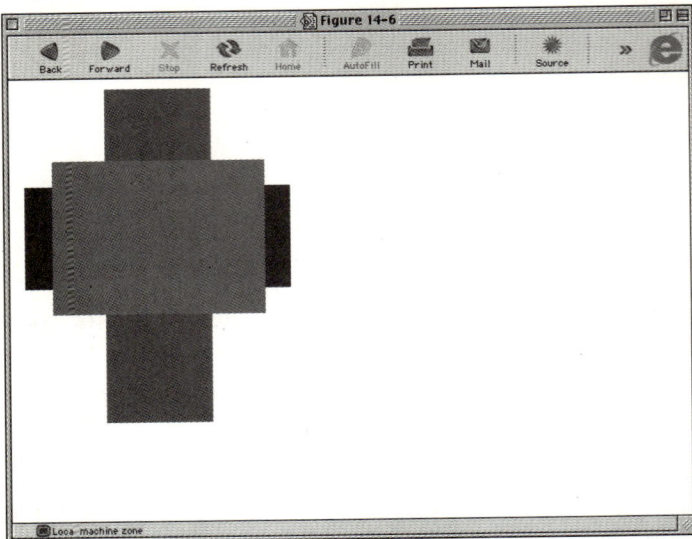

Figure 14-6 *I click blue, but it's too far behind now to pop forward.*

The complete solution is to actually write a sophisticated JavaScript function that checks the value of the other layers and ensures that the layer that you want increments sufficiently to move to the front. Subsequently clicking that layer doesn't result in any change to z-index values.

Netscape Navigator includes a built-in method (a fancy name for a subroutine) to accomplish what you want – moveAbove(id) – but it requires that you use the Netscape <LAYER> approach to layers rather than the more standard CSS <SPAN> tags, as shown in this session.

Taking inspiration from this problem, however, a JavaScript function implementing the moveAbove concept may look as follows:

```
<SCRIPT LANG="JavaScript">

function moveAboveIt(id1, id2) {
  id1o = eval("document.all."+id1+".style");
  id2o = eval("document.all."+id2+".style");

  if (id1o.zIndex > id2o.zIndex) {
    return 1;        // already above, nothing to do
  }

  if (id2o.zIndex == 100) { id2o.zIndex -= 1; }

  id1o.zIndex = id2o.zIndex + 1;

  return 1;
}
</SCRIPT>
```

This example represents quite a lot of JavaScript to present here just now, but it's really rather straightforward: If id1 already has a higher z-index value than id2, the function has nothing to do, and exits directly. If id2 is already at 100, id1 can't be one higher, so id2 must decrement by one, which you do by using the -=1 shortcut. Finally, id1's z-index is set so that it's one higher than id2's z-index.

One Final Note on Netscape Compatibility

Ironically, almost every line of the moveAboveIt function works fine in Netscape Navigator, even with its buggy CSS implementation. The only difference relates to the different document object model, and it changes the first two lines from what appears in the last example in the preceding section to the following:

```
id1o = eval("document."+id1);
id2o = eval("document."+id2);
```

The logical way to deal with this variation is to add a test for browser identification to the subroutine and both types of eval statements to the function. The result may look as follows:

```
if (browsertype == "Netscape") {
  id1o = eval("document."+id1);
  id2o = eval("document."+id2);
} else {
  id1o = eval("document."+id1);
  id2o = eval("document."+id2);
}
```

[handwritten annotations:]
id1o = eval ("document.all"+id1);
id2o = " (" " .all" + id2);
id1o = eval(" document.all' + id1);
id2o = "(' ————— .all' + id2);

The good news: I cover this type of sophisticated browser test and conditional object reference, which enable you to sidestep differences in document object models, in Sessions 19 and 20.

Done!

REVIEW

This session discusses the z-index and enables you to see it in action. In addition, I spend considerable time exploring a more sophisticated Dynamic HTML example that combines JavaScript and CSS layers. I also describe why Netscape Navigator isn't the best of Web browsers for CSS development or deployment, although I also discuss and demonstrate herein specific workarounds for its problems.

QUIZ YOURSELF

1. Name the four dimensions that I discuss in this session. (See "Stacking: Z-Indexes.")

2. The lowest z-index value is _____ and the highest is _____. (See "Stacking: Z-Indexes.")

3. What do you think happens with the following CSS snippet?

```
<SPAN STYLE="position: relative; z-index: 1;
 background-color: red; width: 200; height: 150;
 top: 80px; left: 40px;"></SPAN>
```

(See "Stacking: Z-Indexes.")

4. The following JavaScript approach to bringing a layer to the top incorporates a fundamental problem. What is it?

```
<SPAN ID="red"
 STYLE="position: absolute; z-index: 1;
        background-color: red; width: 200;
height: 150; top: 80px; left: 40px;"
 OnClick="document.all.red.style.zIndex=100;"></SPAN>
```

(See "Changing Z-Values by Using JavaScript.")

5. What's a *method*, in Netscape DHTML nomenclature? (See "Changing Z-Values by Using JavaScript.")

Putting It All Together: Drop-Down Menus

Session Checklist

✔ Building individual menu layers

✔ Cross-browser compatibility

✔ Positioning the menu

✔ Fine-tuning the menu events

**30 Min.
To Go**

The last few sessions explored the nuances of working with layers in the world of CSS. In this session, I pull together a number of different concepts that I've discussed so far to create a demonstration drop-down menu system.

This session also gives you a substantial preview of some of the ways that you can create cross-platform JavaScript, which is necessary because Netscape Navigator uses a different document-object model than Internet Explorer does. In fact, Netscape Navigator 4 uses a different document-object model than Navigator 6.0, so considerable nuances abound, as you soon see.

Note

> **Why three models? Netscape Navigator 4 was released with its DOM prior to any standardization efforts; then IE 4 was used by the W3C standards organization as the basis for the standardized DOM. Navigator 6 includes a hybrid DOM of its own.**

Building Individual Menu Layers

The easiest part of a menu system is to build the individual menus themselves in different layers. Here's how you may code a simple menu of Sherlock Holmes story titles:

Web Sites;

```
<DIV ID="menu1" STYLE="position: absolute;
        background-color: #EFE; visibility: hidden;
        width: 250px; border: 1px solid black;
        margin: 1em; padding: 3px;">
<B>Other Cool Web Sites</B>
<HR HEIGHT=1 NOSHADE>
```

```
<A HREF="http://www.bakerstreet221b.de/main.htm">Camden House</A>
<HR NOSHADE SIZE=1>
<A HREF="http://www.sherlockian.net">Sherlockian Net</A>
<HR NOSHADE SIZE=1>
<A HREF="http://www.evo.org/sherlock/international/">Sherlock Holmes
International</A>
<HR NOSHADE SIZE=1>
<A HREF="http://www.sherlock-holmes.co.uk/">The Sherlock Holmes Museum</A>
<HR NOSHADE SIZE=1>
<A HREF="http://holmes-sherlock.com/">Yoxley Old Place</A>
</DIV>
```

This creates an invisible layer that displays a useful list of Holmes-related Web sites, using an explicit width of 250 pixels, a one-em margin, and three pixels of padding inside the menu from the thin one-pixel solid-black border.

Unlike in the preceding session, I'm going to switch to using visibility **for pop-ups rather than the** display **CSS attribute. Netscape Navigator 4 doesn't support dynamic changes to the** display **element, so you can't show a hidden** display **element in NN4. You may recall that the major advantage of** display **over** visibility **is that a browser ignores** display: none **element for page layout, but because the menus use absolute positioning, browsers automatically ignore them for page layout anyway. One key, however: Make sure you use** DIV **not** SPAN **containers to ensure that the flow of the overall page isn't affected.**

For you to see it, you must activate a word or element on the page with some JavaScript. As you saw in the last session, using onMouseOver with a <SPAN> tag is the easiest way to proceed, as the following examples demonstrates:

```
<SPAN STYLE="color: yellow; font-weight: bold;"
 onMouseOver="document.all.menu1.style.visibility='visible';"
  onMouseOut="document.all.menu1.style.visibility='hidden';">
stories</SPAN>
```

To make things more interesting, I'm going to put the preceding menu activation link into a slightly more complex zero-border table, as follows:

```
<TABLE BORDER="0" CELLPADDING="5" WIDTH="100%"
 CELLSPACING="0">
<TR BGCOLOR="#000099">
<TD STYLE="color: white; font: 24pt arial bold;">
 The Adventures of Sherlock Holmes</TD>
<TD><SPAN STYLE="color: yellow; font-weight: bold;">
stories</SPAN></TD>
<TD>
<SPAN STYLE="color: yellow; font-weight: bold;"
  OnMouseOver="document.all.menu1.style.visibility='visible';"
  OnMouseOut="document.all.menu1.style.visibility='hidden';">
sites</TD>
</TR>
</TABLE>
```

The results are as shown in Figure 15-1 and then in Figure 15-2 after I move the cursor over the word sites in the menu bar on the page.

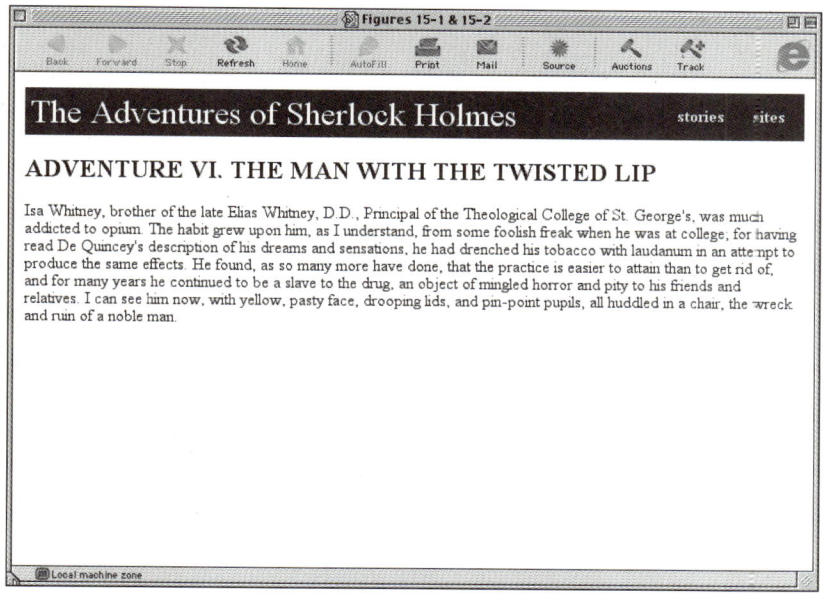

Figure 15-1   A simple menu bar in HTML.

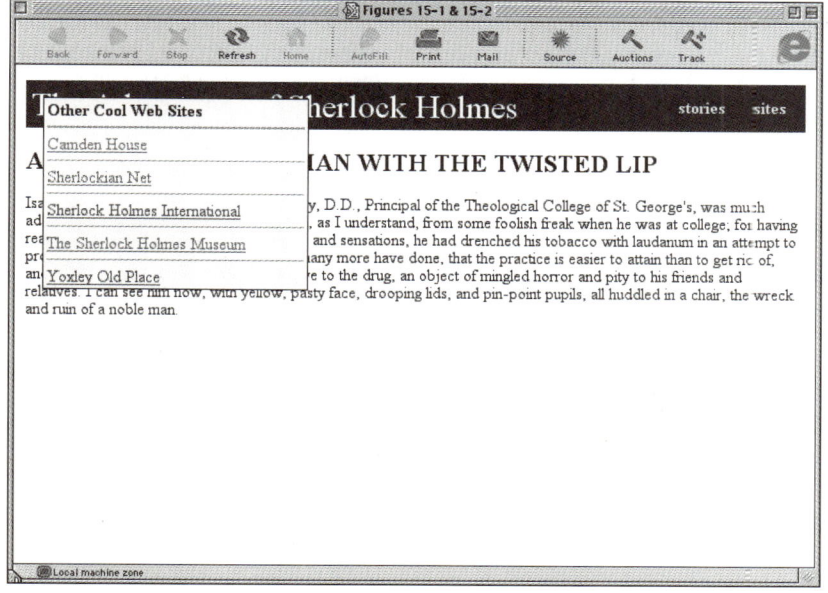

Figure 15-2   The menu appears on-screen, but in the wrong location.

This code presents a bunch of problems, not the least of which is that, if you're using Netscape Navigator, nothing about the page is at all dynamic.

Cross-Browser Compatibility

**20 Min.
To Go**

The problem is that the different browsers use different document-object models (DOMs), which means that they reference the same document attributes but use different notation to do so. In Internet Explorer, you turn visibility: from hidden to visible with the following code:

```
document.all.menu1.style.visibility = "visible";
```

But in Netscape Navigator 4, you perform the exact same task with the following code:

```
document.layers["menu1"].visibility = "show";
```

In Netscape Navigator 6, you accomplish the same task in an even more complex manner that's a hybrid of the two, as the following example shows:

```
obj = window.document.getElementById("menu1");
obj.style.visibility = "visible";
```

One solution is to make sure that all these statements appear in the code, trusting that, if the wrong one executes, the error is benign and the browser continues to interpret the script.

Not a great solution, however, and it probably doesn't work: Many browsers stop executing JavaScript as soon as they encounter any malformed statement.

The solution is to give the JavaScript the capability to detect which browser is in use and then make intelligent decisions in regard to referencing the document-object model, basing its decisions on its knowledge of DOM differences. To accomplish this task, you first need the capability to detect which browser is which, as shown in the following example:

```
var IE4 = (document.all && !document.getElementById) ?
  true : false;
var NS4 = (document.layers) ? true : false;
var IE5 = (document.all && document.getElementById) ?
  true : false;
var NS6 = (document.getElementById && !document.all) ?
  true : false;

var IE = (IE4 || IE5) ? true : false;
var NS = (NS4 || NS6) ? true : false;
```

In a nutshell, if the reference to the DOM element in parentheses returns a nonnull value (that is, it doesn't fail), the variable is set to true. (I'm using some shorthand here: The notation of test ? a : b should read as if (test) then a else b.) You can set only one of these possibilities for a given browser because they can't understand both document-object models at the same time.

Here's a test script to try that can detect the four major browsers for you:

```
<SCRIPT LANG="JavaScript">
var IE4 = (document.all && !document.getElementById) ?
  true : false;
var NS4 = (document.layers) ? true : false;
var IE5 = (document.all && document.getElementById) ?
  true : false;
var NS6 = (document.getElementById && !document.all) ?
  true : false;

var IE = (IE4 || IE5) ? true : false;
var NS = (NS4 || NS6) ? true : false;

if (NS6)        { alert("You're using Netscape 6"); }
else if (NS4) { alert("You're using Netscape 4"); }
else if (IE5) { alert("You're using Internet Explorer 5"); }
else          { alert("You're using Internet Explorer 4"); }
</SCRIPT>
```

Most of the JavaScript code that you see in the `<SCRIPT>` ~~tag~~ block is within explicit functions, but any top-level JavaScript executes immediately, so one nice side-effect of this style of coding is that the NS and IE variables are set as soon as the page loads. If I'm sufficiently eager, therefore, I can revise the earlier OnMouseOver and OnMouseOut lines from the following simple example:

```
ONMOUSEOVER="document.all.menu1.style.display='block';"
  ONMOUSEOUT="document.all.menu1.style.display='none';"
```

And make them more sophisticated — as well as cross-browser in nature — as the following example shows:

```
onMouseOver="if (IE) {          visibility='visible';
  document.all.menu1.style.display='block';}
  else { document.menu1.display='block' }"   visible
onMouseOut="if (IE) {   style.visibility='hidden'
  document.all.menu1.style.display='none'; }   menu1.style.visibility='hidden'
  else { document.menu1.display='none';}"   menu1.display visibility='hidden'
```

Don't type that code in just yet, however; the preceding snippet doesn't work with all browsers because of what's known as the *lexical scoping of variables* in JavaScript: The inline JavaScript element can't see the variables that you set in the `<SCRIPT>` block, so the visibility changes must shift into a couple JavaScript functions.

This problem forces me to change the code, but it also adds the delightful benefit of making the actual HTML section considerably more readable. Following are the two functions as written to work with the three major DOMs at the same time:

```
function menu1on() {
  if (IE) {
    document.all.menu1.style.visibility="visible";
  } else if (NS6) {
    obj = window.document.getElementById("menu1");
```

```
      obj.style.visibility = "visible";
    } else {
      document.layers["menu1"].visibility="show";
    }
  }

  function menu1off() {
    if (IE) {
      document.all.menu1.style.visibility="hidden";
    } else if (NS6) {
      var obj = window.document.getElementById("menu1");
      obj.style.visibility="hidden";
    } else {
      document.layers["menu1"].visibility="hide";
    }
  }
```

That's looking quite a bit better and is more understandable JavaScript code too. I'd hope that you can simply tweak the <SPAN> to look as follows:

```
<TD>
<SPAN STYLE="color: yellow; font-weight: bold;"
 OnMouseOver="menu1on();"  OnMouseOut="menu1off();">
stories
</SPAN>
</TD>
```

But Netscape Navigator 4 doesn't permit event handlers in <SPAN> elements. Instead, to make this example as compatible with different browsers as possible, I switch the SPAN to an empty hypertext reference, as I show in an earlier session, in the following example:

```
<TD>
<A HREF="#" STYLE="color: yellow; font-weight: bold;"
 onMouseOver="menu1on();"  OnMouseOut="menu1off();">
stories
</A>
</TD>
```

Now, finally, you get a pop-up menu that works for any of the major browsers.

You can try out this cross-browser example code on the CD-ROM. You find it there as Figure 15-2a.

Positioning the Menu

**10 Min.
To Go**

Now that you have a menu that pops up in any of the major browsers, you can go back to the problem that appeared earlier: The menu is popping up in the wrong place on-screen.

You can approach this problem in either of two ways. One has you explicitly positioning all the elements on the page by using WIDTH attributes. This method may look as follows:

```
<TABLE BORDER="0" CELLPADDING="5" WIDTH="700"
 CELLSPACING="0">
<TR BGCOLOR="#000099" HEIGHT="100">
<TD WIDTH="550" STYLE="color: white; font: 24pt arial bold;">
 The Adventures of Sherlock Holmes</TD>
<TD WIDTH="75">
<SPAN STYLE="color: yellow; font-weight: bold;">
stories
</SPAN>
</TD>
<TD WIDTH="75">
<A HREF="#"
   STYLE="color: yellow; font-weight: bold;"
 onMouseOver="menu1on();"  onMouseOut="menu1off();">
sites
</A></TD>
</TR>
</TABLE>
```

Now you can safely predict the location of the menu word sites to within a few pixels of 630,5 for the top-left corner of the box and 630+75,5+100 for the bottom-right corner.

width of cell ↘ *height of cell*

Most browsers automatically implement a 3- to 5-pixel padding within the main window, hence the 5-pixel offset in the preceding calculations.

The smarter way to make the menu pop up is to ascertain the location of the cursor as the OnMouseOver event occurs, but the code you need to write to do so is quite a bit more complex than even the cross-browser visibility code earlier in this session, so I'm going to defer that solution for a later session.

For now, I'm going to use the forced-table width and set the top and left attributes of the menu so that it appears in a reasonably compatible spot. The new <DIV> statement for the menu is as follows:

```
<DIV ID="menu1" STYLE="position: absolute;
 background-color: #EFE; visibility: hidden;
 width: 350px; border: 1px solid black;
 top: 25px; left: 255px; margin: 25px; padding: 5px;">
```
1em

Figure 15-3 shows how this example appears in Netscape Navigator 6 as the cursor lies over the sites link.

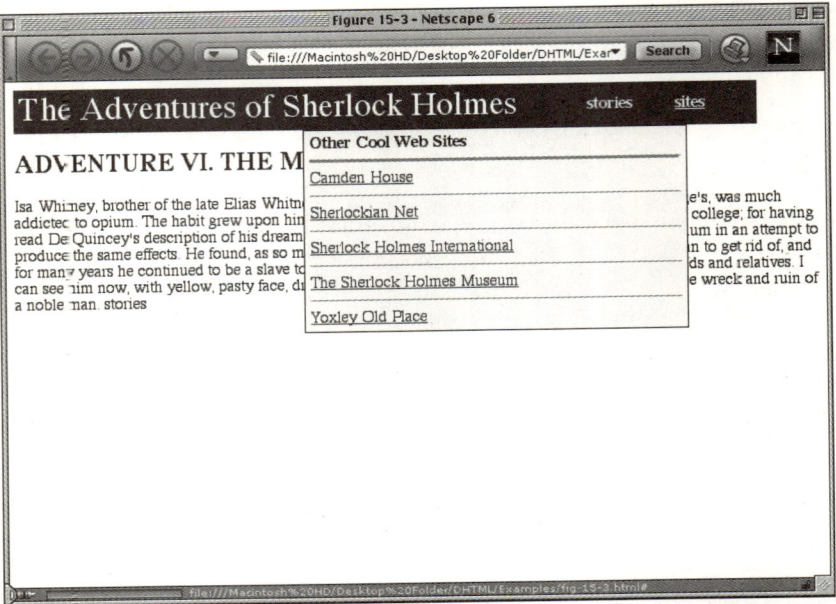

Figure 15-3 *Now the menu pops up in the right place, even in Netscape Navigator 6.*

A wee problem still remains: Every time that you try to move the cursor over the menu, it vanishes, because the OnMouseOut ties to the menu display word and not to the menu itself.

Fine-Tuning the Menu Events

To solve the problem of the disappearing menu is pleasantly straightforward: The OnMouseOut event simply needs to move from the activation word to the menu itself. The code then changes as follows:

```
<DIV ID="menu1" STYLE="position: absolute;
 background-color: #EFE; visibility: hidden;
 width: 350px; border: 1px solid black;
 top: 25px; left: 255px; margin: 25px; padding: 5px;"
 OnMouseOut="menu1off();">
```

Ah, but this example doesn't quite work either, and its failure is all because of the nested containers that make up the foundation of the document-object model. Frustratingly, the actual text in the menu is a different child container, so OnMouseOut is true whenever the cursor moves over a menu element — even the horizontal rule!

A simple solution is to change the JavaScript event from OnMouseOut to OnClick: Users then must click the menu itself (anywhere) to make it go away, as in the following example:

```
<DIV ID="menu1" STYLE="position: absolute;
 background-color: #EFE; visibility: hidden;
```

```
width: 350px; border: 1px solid black;
top: 25px; left: 255px; margin: 25px; padding: 5px;"
OnClick="menuloff();">
```

Leave the example here for now, but do try Figure 15-3a on the CDROM: It's the one where the menuloff() ties to the OnClick event.

Done!

REVIEWS

This session jumps head-first into the world of JavaScript as it applies to cross-platform compatibility. You simply can't avoid it. Furthermore, you must deal with greater complexities than simply those resulting from Internet Explorer versus Netscape Navigator; in this session, I touch on the three major document-object models, those of Navigator 4, Internet Explorer, and Navigator 6 (which is its own weird hybrid). You also learn about the subtleties of JavaScript events and their relationship to containers and subcontainers.

QUIZ YOURSELF

1. Why do you need to switch from display to visibility for the menus? (See "Building Individual Menu Layers.")

2. What's the story behind the three DOMs? (See "Cross-Browser Compatibility.")

3. Why do you switch from <DIV> to <A> for the menu activation? (See "Building Individual Menu Layers.")

4. What's the JavaScript shorthand for the following statement?
   ```
   If (condition) {
      statementA
   } else {
      statementB
   }
   ```
   (See "Cross-Browser Compatibility.")

5. What problem causes you to move to JavaScript functions from inline script code? (See "Cross-Browser Compatibility.")

6. What's the typical default padding within a Web browser's main page? (See "Positioning the Menu.")

Cool CSS Tricks

Session Checklist

✔ Floating identification bugs

✔ Floating text

✔ Drop caps

✔ Cool anchor link tricks

**30 Min.
To Go**

If you're going through these sessions in order and on schedule, take heart; you're at the end of Saturday's sessions, and you've learned a *ton* about Cascading Style Sheets — and even dabbled in some hardcore JavaScript along the way, to boot (particularly in that last session, eh?).

This session is a bit easier as you slide into your Saturday-night groove, providing a compendium of some wicked cool CSS tricks to inspire and amaze you. Some important elements lie herein, however — most notably, the pseudo-elements that I discuss in the anchor-link tricks section.

Well, I can hear you cranking up "Saturday Night Fever" and warning your dog that you're going out all night dancing . . . if you can just finish up this one session. So shake it, okay?

Floating Identification Bugs

I can remember the old days of television, where you could watch a channel without seeing its logo park on the bottom-right corner of the program the entire time. Then MTV and a couple of small cable stations tucked their logos into the corner, and today, channels use that space for all sorts of things, from the annoyingly large Fox Movie Channel logo that seems to take up about 20 percent of the screen to that of the Turner Broadcast Station, WTBS, a logo that spins, jumps, and morphs into ads for coming programs.

Industry jargon for you: These little logos are known as *bugs*.

Web sites joined the fun after GeoCities slapped its logo on the bottom right of every page that its servers hosted. Then the folks at GeoCities realized that they could charge you money to remove it if you used their server, which is eerily reminiscent of a Mafia protection scheme, but I don't think I'd better go there, okay? I'd hate to see something happen to your kneecaps!

With the power of CSS, you, too, can add a floating bug to your page, one that positions itself in the bottom-right corner and stays there, even as visitors scroll around to read the material. And I'm going to show you how you can do so.

My first approach is the direct one, as the following example demonstrates:

```
<STYLE TYPE="text/css">
body {  background-image:url("mybug.gif");
     background-attachment:fixed;
     background-repeat:no-repeat;
     background-position:bottom right;
     }
</STYLE>
```

This approach takes advantage of a number of specific background attributes that enable you to control the behavior of the element to position it in the bottom-right corner by using `background-position`, disable tiling (by using the `background-repeat: no-repeat`), and fix its location so that it doesn't scroll (by using `background-attachment: fixed`).

Figure 16-1 shows the results, which are slick.

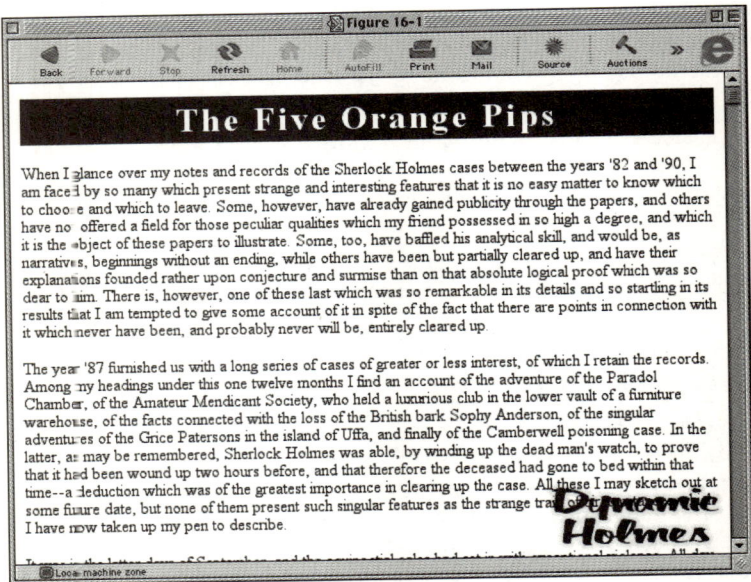

Figure 16-1 *Our Holmes bug floats in the bottom-right corner.*

The technique works well in both Internet Explorer and Netscape 6, but as I mentioned in the last session, Netscape Navigator 4 is the problem child of the CSS world, and the fact that the preceding CSS isn't sufficient to make this image appear in NN4 browsers, too, probably comes as no surprise, alas.

To solve this problem in a more universal fashion involves a fair bit of JavaScript, so I'd better take you through things one step at a time. Ready?

Cross-browser floating bug in JavaScript

The first step is to recognize that the graphic now must appear on the page itself within a `<DIV>` or `<SPAN>` tag. That's easily done, as the following example shows:

```
<DIV ID="floatingBug" STYLE="position:absolute">
<A HREF="#"><IMG SRC="mybug.gif" WIDTH="180"
   HEIGHT="77" BORDER="0"></A>
</DIV>
```

I choose to drop the bug on the very bottom of the page in case an ancient browser that can't support any of this code reads it: The bug just appears at the bottom of the page without any errors or other problems.

 **I set the bug so that it's pointing to its own page (HREF="#"), but you can just as easily make it point to an informational page, the index page, or whatever.**

The next step is to build a function that the browser calls every few milliseconds to reposition the bug in the right spot, as follows:

```
function refreshBug() {
   theBug.left = posX + (isNav?
      pageXOffset : document.body.scrollLeft);
   theBug.top  = posY + (isNav?
      pageYOffset : document.body.scrollTop);
}
```

As you can see, you need to define a lot of variables in this function elsewhere. Remember also the notation of x? a : b, which you want to read as "if x, then a, else b."

The main function in this JavaScript solution is the initialization routine that figures out what kind of browser is in use and sets the theBug object to enable cross-browser references without much fuss, as follows:

```
function initBug() {
  if (document.getElementById) {
    theBug = document.getElementById("floatingBug");
  } else if (document.all) {
    theBug = document.all["floatingBug"];
  } else {
    theBug = document.floatingBug;
  }

  if (theBug.style) theBug=theBug.style;
```

```
theBug.width = bugWidth;
theBug.height = bugHeight;

if (! isNav) {
   innerWidth = document.body.clientWidth;
   innerHeight = document.body.clientHeight;
}
posX = (innerWidth - bugWidth) - offsetWidth;
posY = (innerHeight - bugHeight) - offsetHeight;
}
```

The first set of conditional statements set theBug to match the document-object model of the current browser. After that occurs, a second check determines whether the ".style" reference is necessary and, if it is, modifies theBug to append it. Then the JavaScript interpreter assigns the dimensions of the graphical element, bugWidth and bugHeight, to the width and height attributes of theBug.

20 Min. To Go

The last few lines of the function set innerWidth and innerHeight, if necessary (in Navigator, they're already set and reflect the dimensions of the current window), and then compute a starting x,y position for the logo by calculating window width minus bug width and window height minus bug height. There are two additional offset values that'll be set elsewhere to help avoid scroll bar overlap.

You initialize many of these variables at the very top of the <SCRIPT> block, as follows:

```
var theBug, bugWidth = 180, bugHeight = 77;
var isNav = window.innerHeight; // using Netscape Navigator
var offsetWidth = isNav? 15 : 0, offsetHeight = isNav? 10 : 0;
```

Notice here that only Navigator needs the width and height offsets; IE correctly tucks the graphic into the corner without any additional tweaking of numeric values. The 180 x 77 dimensions are the width and height, respectively, of the graphic I'm using. You need to change them to match your graphic if it's different.

Almost done.

You now have all the code that you need to initialize and refresh the bug, but you don't yet have any way to turn this entire feature on after you load the Web page. To do so, one more function is necessary, as the following example shows:

```
function startBug() {
   initBug();
   window.onresize=initBug;
   bugID = setInterval("refreshBug()",25);
}
```

Note

The last line of this function is particularly interesting: It says to *invoke the subroutine* refreshBug() *every 25 milliseconds*.

And, finally, a single line of JavaScript in the <SCRIPT> block — but outside any function — starts everything going, as follows:

```
window.onload=startBug;
```

You can start the float function by adding the `OnLoad` attribute to the `<BODY>` tag, too, as follows:

```
<BODY OnLoad="startBug();">
```

I prefer the former approach, however, because it makes the solution a bit more self-contained.

Oh! If you're thinking, "This is great — I can drop this code snippet into its own file and include it on any page that I want," you're doing great . . . except that Netscape Navigator 4.0 — the cause of all this confusing coding in the first place — doesn't process the includes correctly, so it doesn't work. Frustrating, eh?

View the source of Figure 16-2 from the CD-ROM, and you see the complete JavaScript solution.

Now, with all this code put together in Figure 16-2, you can see the results in an old version of Netscape Navigator 4 on my Mac.

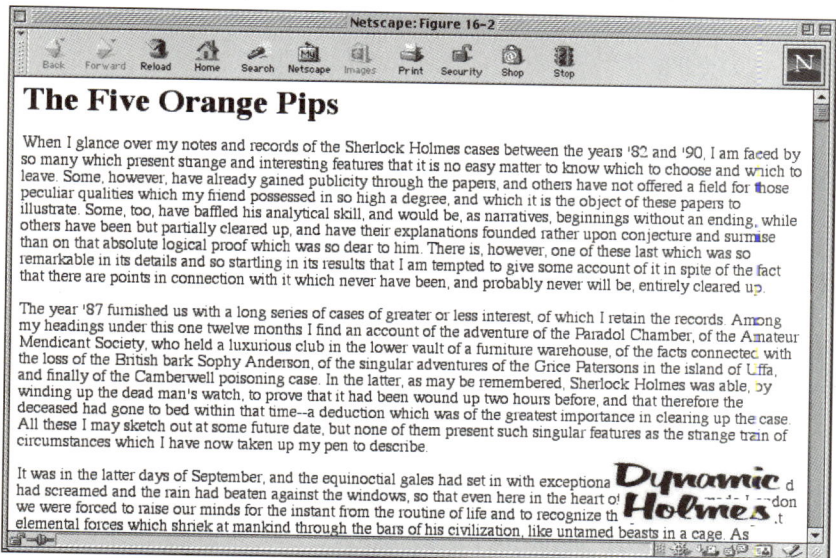

Figure 16-2   *The bug floats now, even in Netscape Navigator 4.*

Drop Caps

The final JavaScript floating bug is undoubtedly a complex solution to what's essentially a simple problem. The next few CSS tricks that I'm going to explore are simpler because they don't work *at all* in earlier browsers, short of engaging in ugly solutions such as turning text into GIF images.

One nice effect that I like on Web pages — something that mimics the beautiful work done by scribes hundreds of years ago — are ornate *drop capitals*. If you haven't seen these before, they're a way of sprucing up the appearance of text by making the first letter of the first word in a paragraph more decorative and set off from the rest of the prose.

I'm going to start with right off with an example, as shown in Figure 16-3. Then I look at the necessary CSS.

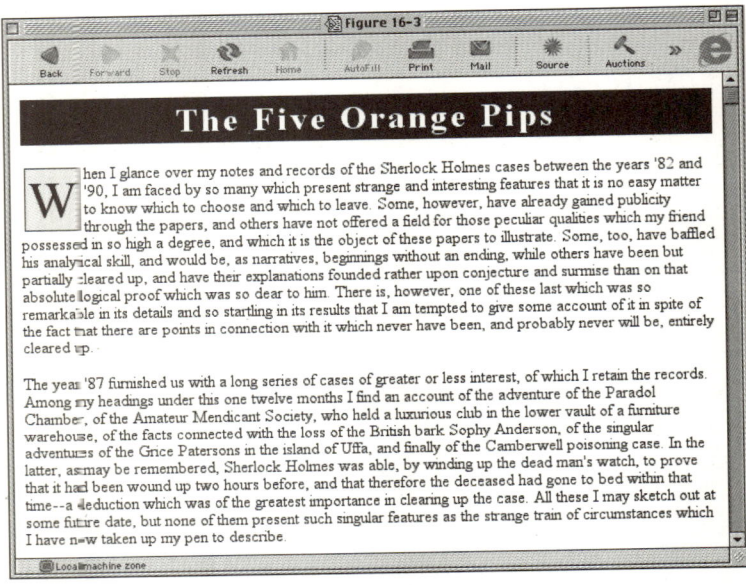

Figure 16-3   *Fancy drop caps look really nice on a Web page.*

Here's the simple CSS that produces this delightful effect:

```
<STYLE TYPE="text/css">
H1 { background-color: #006; color: white;
     font: 24pt arial bold; text-align: center;
     letter-spacing: 3px; padding: 4px; }
.dc { float: left; font-size: 300%;  color: #006;
      background-color: #EEF; padding: 3px;
      border: 1px solid black; margin: 3px; }
</STYLE>
```

Any time that you want a drop cap within the text, simply wrap it in a <SPAN> element, as in the following example:

```
<SPAN CLASS="dc">W</SPAN>hen I glance over my notes
and records of the Sherlock Holmes cases between the
years '82 and '90, I am faced by so many which present
strange and interesting features that it is no easy
matter to know which to choose and which to leave...
```

You undoubtedly want to fine-tune things for your own color scheme and type treatments, but a drop cap's one of the easiest visual effects to achieve in CSS.

Cool Anchor Link Tricks

Session 6 presents all the major selectors for CSS, with one notable exception: It omits so-called pseudo-classes. Recall that the structure of all CSS statements is as follows:

```
selector    { declaration block }
```

The CSS standard defines a number of different pseudo-classes, as shown in Table 16-1.

Table 16-1 *Pseudo-class Declaration Possibilities in CSS 2.0*

Pseudo-class	Description
:active	Any element as it's currently clicked (mousedown).
:after	Places generating content after the current element.
:before	Places generating content before the current element.
:first-child	An element that's the first child of another element.
:first-letter	The first letter of an element.
:first-line	First displayed line of an element.
:focus	Any element that currently has focus.
:hover	Any specified element as the cursor's on it.
:link	Any unvisited hypertext reference.
:visited	Any visited hypertext reference.

The very latest browsers support many of these elements but ignore :active, :before, :after, and :focus.

Now I'm going to take a look at what you can do with these elements to make your page considerably more interesting.

10 Min. To Go

Drop caps the easy way

First off, the following example offers an easier way to accomplish drop caps than by using the <SPAN> element (which I show earlier in this session, in "Drop Caps"):

```
P:first-letter {
        font-size: 300%;   color: #006;
        background-color: #EEF; padding: 25px;
        border: 1px solid black; margin: 2px; }
```

Looks good, but unfortunately it doesn't work quite right: Internet Explorer 5.5 ignores the padding, and Netscape 6.0 ignores the entire `:first-letter`. Ah well. Stay tuned to this pseudo-class attribute; it eventually works correctly.

Cool hypertext links

What browsers support more reliably are the set of pseudo-class elements that associate with hypertext references. `A:link`, `A:visited`, and `A:active` map directly to the `<BODY>` attributes `LINK`, `VLINK`, and `ALINK`. There's a new element, too: `A:hover` enables you to specify style changes while the cursor is over the link itself.

Add all these together, and you may use them as follows:

```
A:link    { font-weight: 900; font-size: 125%;
            color: #009; }
A:visited { font-style: italic; font-size: 100%;
            color: #090; }
A:hover   { background: #CCF; }
A:active  { color: red; }
```

This code sets unvisited links in dark blue, bold, and a little larger than the adjacent text, while visited links appear italicized and in dark green, the same size as the adjacent text, with a light blue background hover color, and the link text turns red as you press and hold the mouse button.

Here's some simple HTML that enables you to see what happens:

```
<DIV STYLE="font-align: center;">
Holmsian Links: <A
  HREF="http://www.bakerstreet221b.de/main.htm">Camden
  House</A> |
<A HREF="http://www.sherlockian.net">Sherlockian
  Net</A> |
<A HREF="http://www.sherlock-holmes.co.uk/">The
  Sherlock Holmes Museum</A> |
<A HREF="http://www.dontvisitme.com/">Live chat
  with Holmes</A>
</DIV>
```

In addition, I'm going to drop the first-letter style into the `<STYLE>` block, as follows:

```
P:first-letter {
  font-size: 300%; color: #006;
  background-color: #EEF; padding: 5px;
  border: 1px solid black; margin: 3px;
}
```

And, to make things more interesting, I'm also going to use the first-line pseudo-class attribute to make the first line of each paragraph change its appearance, as follows:

```
P:first-line { background-color: yellow; padding: 4px; }
```

Now you can see how this code all renders in both Internet Explorer and Netscape Navigator, as shown in Figures 16-4 and 16-5, respectively.

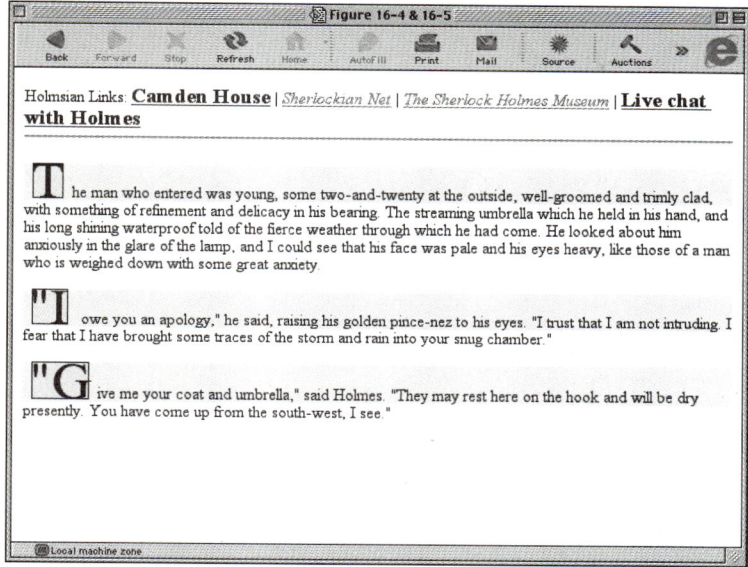

Figure 16-4   *Internet Explorer 5.5 renders pseudo-class elements one way.*

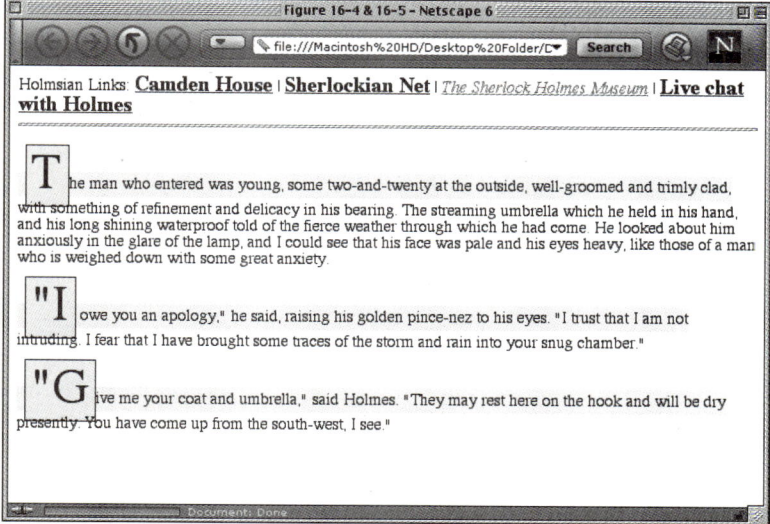

Figure 16-5   *Netscape 6 renders pseudo-class elements a second way.*

In these examples, I've visited the Sherlockian.net and Sherlock Holmes Museum Web sites prior to the screen capture. Notice that Netscape 6 fails to correctly change the styles of the Sherlockian.net link, although IE did just fine.

You can also see the (different) error in N6 in rendering the first-letter box in each paragraph and the visually interesting yellow background that each browser applies to the first line of each paragraph of text on the page.

Focus and first-child relationships

Two more pseudo-classes are worth exploring before I leave this topic completely — styles that can make your pages (particularly your forms) much more visually interesting.

The first is :focus, and if you apply it to elements that a user can tab between (for example, hypertext links and input fields), it can help them instantly see what's currently active. A common use of this element is to change the background color of the element subtly, as the following example shows:

```
A:focus { background-color: red; }
INPUT:focus { background-color: red; }
```

This code specifies that anchor (hypertext) focus is to change the background color from its current setting to red. It overrides the :hover pseudo-class, and Netscape 6 ignores it. The INPUT: focus affects text input elements in a similar way. For a complete solution for complex forms, you also want to add :focus changes for SELECT and TEXTAREA elements.

The second nifty pseudo-class is :first-child, which, if you associate it with a parent and child tag, enables the first occurrence of the child tag in the parent tag context to apply the specified style, as follows:

```
P B:first-child { color: white; background: black; }
```

This line specifies that the first bold element in each paragraph appears as white text against a black background, although subsequent bold tags appear as usual.

The entire <STYLE> block for Figure 16-6 is worth showing here, as follows:

```
<STYLE TYPE="text/css">
  A:hover   {background: #CCFFCC; }
  A:link    { color: #009900; }
  A:visited { color: #006600; }
  H2 { background: yellow; padding: 4px;
      border: 1px solid black; margin: 2px; }
  TD { font: 14pt arial; }
  INPUT,SELECT,TEXTAREA { font: 10pt courier; }
  INPUT:focus,SELECT:focus,TEXTAREA:focus
      { background: #CCF; }
  P B:first-child { color: white; background: black; }
</STYLE>
```

A declaration of the form A,B,C { style } **causes the specified style to apply to all three tags, A, B, and C.**

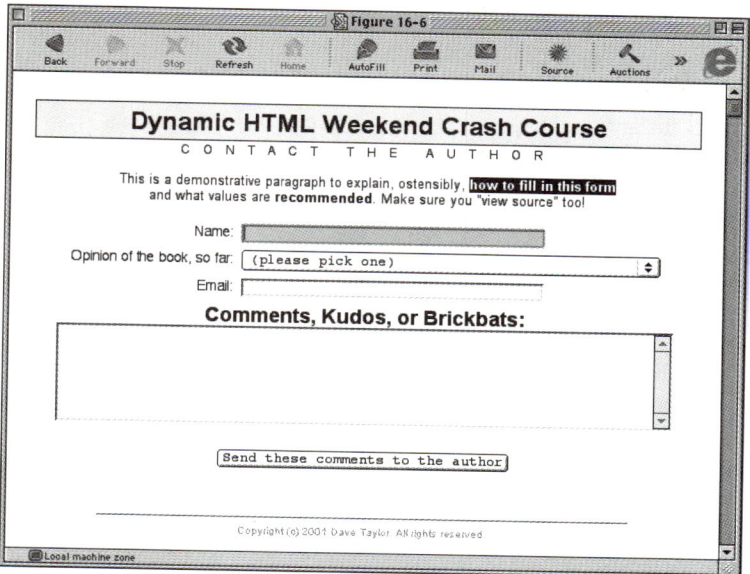

Figure 16-6   *An attractive form, with the focus on the first text area.*

Notice in Figure 16-6 that the first emphasized element in the descriptive paragraph is white text against a black background, while the second emphasized element appears in bold.

Done!

REVIEW

This session pulls together all the CSS you've learned so far and demonstrates a number of fun and interesting new styles that you can immediately add to your Web pages. Hassles still crop up in association with older browser compatibility issues, particularly the nuances of the annoying Netscape Navigator 4 and its unique document-object model. I also spend a lot of time exploring the pseudo-class elements and how they can perk up a simple Web site.

And now, the good news: You're ready to go and enjoy your Saturday night! See you tomorrow morning.

QUIZ YOURSELF

1. You can employ some very useful elements as a "bug" on your page. Name a couple of them. (See "Floating Identification Bugs.")
2. What problematic browser causes all the trouble with the CSS floating-bug solution? (See "Floating Identification Bugs.")
3. As a refresher question, what's the difference between a <DIV> and a <SPAN>? (See "Cross-browser floating bug in JavaScript.")

4. Describe what the following line of code does:

```
window.onload=startBug;
```

(See "Cross-browser floating bug in JavaScript.")

5. What problem prevents you from using an external JavaScript file for the code to implement the non-CSS floating-bug feature? (See "Cross-browser floating bug in JavaScript.")

6. What four pseudo-class elements don't the current generation of Web browsers support? (See "Cool Anchor Link Tricks.")

7. What does the :focus element enable you to control? (See "Focus and first-child relationships.")

P A R T

III

Saturday Afternoon

1. Padding is to margin in CSS as _____ is to _____ in an HTML `<TABLE>` tag.

2. True/False: You can't specify a negative padding.

3. What's likely to happen if you specify `padding: 49%` in your CSS?

4. What's wrong with the following CSS sequence?

```
BODY { background-color: blue;          }
P    { font-weight: bold; color: #00F }
```

5. Which is correct: `margin-left` or `left-margin`?

6. Which one is bigger: `0px`, `0em`, or `0mm`?

7. What's the CSS equivalent to the HTML `<P ALIGN="right">`?

8. If you want a container to float above others on a page but still scroll with the page, do you use `relative`, `absolute`, or `fixed` positioning?

9. True/False: The following is a valid CSS specification:

```
visibility: 50%
```

10. True/False: The following is a valid way to specify the location of a fixed object:

```
top: 100px; right: -14px;
```

11. What's likely to happen with the following CSS?

```
<DIV ID="advert" STYLE="position: absolute; width: 100%;
height: 100%; top: 0px; left: 0px">ad goes here</DIV>
```

12. True/False: Using the `onClick` event handler enables you to omit all your anchor tags while still having hyperlinked text.

13. What special value for the HREF attribute can you use with an anchor tag if you don't want it to take people off the page?

14. What CSS styles do you need to specify to make a <SPAN> look visually identical to a hypertext reference?

15. The three dimensions on a Web page are width, height, and
_____.

16. True/False: A *method* is essentially a function that you tie to a specific object.

17. If you compare the three DOMs to the three little pigs, which one builds its house out of bricks?

18. What's the long-winded way to write out the following JavaScript expression?

    a?b:c;

19. What's the name of the event handler that enables you to start JavaScript functions as soon as the page finishes rendering in the user's browser?

20. What's the purpose of focus and blur?

IV

Saturday Evening

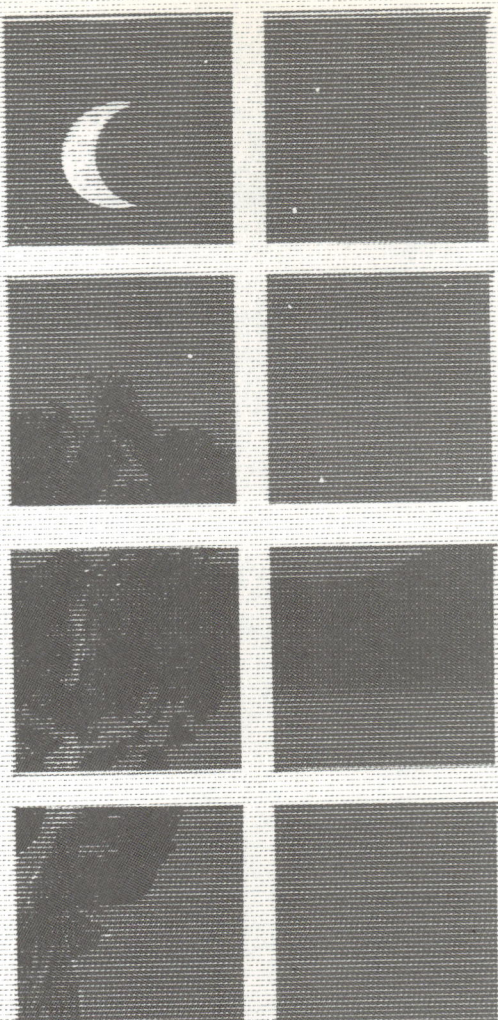

The Document Object Model

Session Checklist

✔ What's a document object model?

✔ Netscape's DOM

✔ Microsoft's DOM

✔ Events and event handlers

**30 Min.
To Go**

As I explain in earlier sessions of this *Dynamic HTML Weekend Crash Course,* Cascading Style Sheets offer considerable improvements in the formatting and presentation of information on a Web page. They don't enable you to access the *D* in DHTML, however. Unless you really stretch the definition, nothing much is dynamic about a CSS-enabled Web site.

Injecting dynamic behaviors into the Web is primarily the task of JavaScript and other scripting languages. That's why I talk about DHTML as the partnership of CSS and JavaScript: Either of them alone is useful, but together, they really enable you to move your Web development to the next level of appearance and sophistication.

This session explores the common ground between CSS and JavaScript: the document object model. And, to whet your appetite, the standard DOM is also the foundation of XML and XHTML future development, too. It's well worth understanding.

What's a Document Object Model?

The JavaScript that I present in the last few sessions gives you a taste of the rather vast level of complexity hiding behind the simplicity of the CSS style adjustments. Think about it: For every container, child, or parent, a site must track at least 50 different variables, from visibility and display to font, spacing, padding, colors, and more. An average Web page includes at least 30 or 40 different containers, so I'm talking about an extremely complex underlying structure with hundreds or even thousands of variables.

Unto itself, the level of complexity doesn't really matter to most people. (After all, I'm typing this chapter within Microsoft Word, which probably boasts an equally complex underlying infrastructure, but I ignore it.) If you want to start accessing and changing values through event-driven scripting, however, suddenly you need a standard mechanism for addressing all the different elements that may appear on the page.

That's the job of the Document Object Model.

Or, to be more accurate, that's the job of *a* document object model, because I need to address three major DOMs for a reasonable level of compatibility across Web browsers.

Worth noting is that the ugliness of multiple DOM support is relevant only if you care about cross-browser compatibility. If you're happy with a Web site that works only for, say, Netscape 6.0 and later or is dynamic only for Internet Explorer 5.5 users, you can blissfully ignore all these issues.

The problem with the preponderance of DOMs is that it involved an evolutionary process. In the mid 1990s, Netscape released the first Web browser with meaningful scripting support, and it included a new Navigator 4.0 document object model to enable scripts to access many of the elements that define the appearance of the page.

If you recall, the mid '90s was when Microsoft and Netscape were heating up the network wires with an aggressive competition to see who could produce the better Web browser and "win" the browser wars.

Unsurprisingly, then, after Microsoft released its Internet Explorer version 5.0 a few months after the release of Navigator 4, it put its own incompatible document object model in place.

As had happened many times in the history of Web-browser development, site developers were left with an ugly situation: write for one DOM or the other. Getting code to work for both object models was achievable but tricky. Worse, neither had received the blessing of the W3C committee as "the standard DOM."

Javascript is ECMA

The *W3C* is the World Wide Web Consortium, and it's an international standards body that's responsible for the evolution of HTML and associated technologies, including XML (eXtensible Markup Language), CSS, JavaScript, and more. I highly recommend a visit to its Web site to see what's new: www.w3c.org.

Eventually, the W3C decided that the Microsoft approach to the document object model was superior, and the Microsoft DOM became the basis of the official standard DOM associated by the group with CSS2.0.

Meanwhile, Netscape imploded as a company, was purchased by America Online, lost most of its brightest developers, and reinvented its browser-development project as an open-source community development project. Netscape skipped the version-5 number completely and released beta after beta of Netscape 6.0, built around its slick Gecko rendering engine (the underlying page rendering software that powers the Netscape 6 browser).

Microsoft also jumped browsers from 5.0 to 5.5 (a major improvement in CSS support coming as one of the cornerstones of this upgrade) and added complete support for the level-1 W3C DOM, the first generation of document object model standard. It also retained compatibility with their early *document-all* reference method that IE 5 introduced but *wasn't* compatible with the level-1 standard DOM.

The Gecko development group claims complete CSS2.0 compatibility as of this writing, but as you've already seen in my examples herein, Navigator 6 uses a slightly different document object model than either Navigator 4 or Internet Explorer. All I can say, as a developer, is "Ugh!"

Because working with different DOMs is an established fact of life and because imagining a future date where everyone uses a single, uniform Web browser is impossible, the next few sessions explore the different DOMs and how to minimize the effect of their differences on your own Dynamic HTML development.

Netscape's DOM

**20 Min.
To Go**

The first published document object model was from Netscape, and the company created it to support another of its inventions: JavaScript. Microsoft had the competing scripting language of Visual Basic Script (VBScript), but thankfully, JavaScript won and users ended up with the weird situation of Netscape's JavaScript molded over Microsoft's DOM.

As I say a few paragraphs ago, Netscape uses two different DOMs: the one in Navigator 4 and the new standards-based DOM incorporated into Netscape 6's Gecko rendering engine.

> **Netscape 6 has been in perpetual beta for quite a long time. By the time you read this section, you can hopefully go to the Netscape Web site — www.netscape.com — and download a nonbeta release.**

The document object model that Navigator 4 includes lit the path for future DOMs. In a nutshell, it codifies a hierarchical data structure, where elements in a document, as well as their attributes, are accessible through a straightforward addressing scheme.

Imagine that the data structure of your document is a tree, similar to a modern file system on a computer. It may look as follows:

```
document
    element1
        attribute1
    element2
    element3
        attribute1
        attribute2
```

To access the value of attribute2 in element3, the Navigator 4 DOM requires you write it as follows:

```
document.element3.attribute2
```

That's exactly how CSS attributes change in the Netscape DOM after you recognize that the unique ID that you assign to containers works as the element-level reference and that the attribute is a unique CSS style attribute name.

In the Navigator 4 DOM, images is an element that contains an array of all graphical elements on the page, so you reference an image by using the weird notation of the following example:

```
document.images['mybug']
```

You use this notation rather than the more straightforward example that follows:

```
document.mybug
```

If you want to change the actual image to implement, say, a rollover, where the graphic changes if the cursor is over it, you may write it as follows:

```
<A HREF="index.html"
   OnMouseOver="document.images['mybug'].src = 'overbug.gif';"
   OnMouseOut="document.images['mybug'].src='mybug.gif'>
<IMG SRC="mybug.gif" NAME="mybug" BORDER="0"></A>
```

Worse, the biggest limitation with the Netscape Navigator 4 DOM is that it's built around an assumption that you can specify style elements only before the page loads, with the exception of swapping same-size graphics on rollovers and a few other special cases. If you try to create a dynamic page that keeps reassigning the background color or font based on user interaction, you fail.

Even more frustrating, Navigator 4 introduced two new HTML tags, LAYER and ILAYER, that at the time were the recommended way for designers to create multiple or embedded layers in their HTML. The standardized DOM excludes these two tags, and they're unsupported in modern browsers. This situation leaves designers in a pickle concerning Navigator 4 support, and many online DHTML reference sites explicitly state that they either *don't* support Navigator 4 or that the support is probably broken.

As an example, consider this charming note from a DHTML tutorial on Builder.com: "The CSS method has its limits, however. It doesn't work on rickety, old Navigator 4." Or this related comment from JavaScript.com: "The introduction of Netscape 6 has worsened the browser-independent scripting situation. . . ."

Suffice to say, if you're starting to suspect that I'd love to say "Ignore Nav4 and write your DHTML only for modern browsers" you're right. Fortunately, cross-browser, cross-DOM approaches that alleviate much of the problem are available, and I discuss them a bit later today.

Netscape 6

So you'd think that, by now, everyone's learned the lesson of incompatible browsers and how much of a pain getting everything to work correctly is if everyone does everything differently. But, if so, you're wrong. After the Netscape development team released the Gecko-based Netscape 6, designers were surprised to discover that, instead of matching the well-entrenched IE5.5 DOM, Netscape opted instead to stick very closely to the DOM that the W3C group detailed (see www.w3.org/DOM/).

Among the changes in this new browser technology, Netscape 6 now completely ignores LAYER and ILAYER tags. Furthermore, it no longer supports the layers element, among many other changes, so references such as document.layers.layerID fail, as does the earlier document.images["mybug"] reference.

 **To be completely accurate, Gecko is the rendering engine, developed by an open source group and integrated into a browser by Mozilla.org (another spin-off of Netscape). Netscape 6 is the Netscape browser built on technology from both Mozilla and Gecko. Confused yet? I am.**

Netscape 6 introduces a stack of methods — subroutines that return necessary values without needing to tie you to the specifics of the internal data structure (DOM).

Meanwhile Internet Explorer's DOM uses the following:

```
document.all.elementID
```

To reference an element with ID="elementID", the equivalent in Netscape 6/Gecko is as follows:

```
document.getElementByID("elementID")
```

The getElementByID() is a *method*, a function that returns a value given an argument or two.

If you talk with purists, they tell you that the method-based approach is, in fact, the best strategy to develop W3C DOM-compatible DHTML, and they're right. Furthermore, other than the document.all that IE (but not N6) supports, both are reasonably compatible with the standard DOM. I can't get too upset at the DOM support in N6, but I do wish that it just magically worked with all the IE5.5 code.

 **Oh, and if you read the W3C DOM specification, be aware that the standardized version of JavaScript is known as *ECMAScript*. (ECMA is the European Computer Manufacturers Association.)**

Tip

Microsoft's DOM

Microsoft did a much better job than Netscape did of creating a solid and usable DOM, and indeed, the document object model inside Internet Explorer 5.0 became the basis of the W3C standard DOM.

The folk at Redmond, however, had one major area of the IE DOM that the standards committee rejected: the document.all container. Worse, IE5.5 still supports the legacy element document.all, although the browser is otherwise level-1 DOM compatible.

The good news is that Internet Explorer does support the standard method getElementByID(), so you can actually simplify your JavaScript conditional code quite a bit.

In the preceding session, I show you the following JavaScript code:

```
if (document.getElementById) {
  theBug = document.getElementById("floatingBug");
} else if (document.all) {
  theBug = document.all["floatingBug"];
} else {
  theBug = document.floatingBug;
}
```

This example enables you to set the variable theBug to the appropriate value regardless of which browser you're using, essentially supporting the three DOMs.

What isn't stated is that the second condition is unnecessary and frankly redundant. The following simpler code works just fine in Navigator 4, Netscape 6, and IE5:

```
if (document.getElementById) {
  theBug = document.getElementById("floatingBug");
} else {
  theBug = document.floatingBug;
}
```

Addressing the `.style` reference is necessary for the modern browsers, but that's easily dealt with, too, as follows:

```
if (theBug.style) theBug=theBug.style;
```

If you're following the code, you end up with, in essence, the following for newer browsers:

```
document.getElementById("floatingBug").style
```

And you get the following for Netscape Navigator 4:

```
document.floatingBug
```

**10 Min.
To Go**

Changing On-Screen Styles Dynamically

I can't go through an entire session without giving you at least one example, so here's a nifty set of JavaScript functions that are part of the DHTML Weekend Crash Course CSS-o-matic and work with all W3C DOM-compatible browsers (which is a fancy way of saying that they don't work for Navigator 4):

```
<SCRIPT LANGUAGE="JavaScript">
function initialize()
{ myObj = document.getElementById("changeme").style; }

function changeColor(value)
{  myObj.color = value; }

function changeBackground(value)
{  myObj.backgroundColor = value; }

function changeFontFamily(value)
{  myObj.fontFamily = value; }

function changeFontSize(value)
{  myObj.fontSize = value; }

function changeAlignment(value)
{  myObj.textAlign = value; }

function changeLinespace(value)
{  myObj.lineHeight = value; }
</SCRIPT>
```

The initialize routine calls from an OnLoad event in the <BODY> tag, to initialize the myObj variable, as follows:

```
<BODY OnLoad="initialize()">
```

Armed with this example, you can offer users an easy way to customize the presentation of the material on the page with a control strip such as the following:

```
<DIV STYLE="text-align: center; background: #EEE; border: 1px solid
black;">
<B STYLE="font-size: 18pt">CSS-o-matic</B><BR>
<B>type color:</B>
<SPAN OnClick="changeColor('red');">red</SPAN>,
<SPAN OnClick="changeColor('blue');">blue</SPAN> or
<SPAN OnClick="changeColor('green');">green</SPAN>
 
<B>face:</B>
<SPAN OnClick="changeFontFamily('arial');">Arial</SPAN>,
<SPAN OnClick="changeFontFamily('courier');">Courier</SPAN> or
<SPAN OnClick="changeFontFamily('times');">Times</SPAN>
 
<B>size:</B>
<SPAN OnClick="changeFontSize('36pt');">36pt</SPAN>,
<SPAN OnClick="changeFontSize('24pt');">24pt</SPAN>,
<SPAN OnClick="changeFontSize('14pt');">14pt</SPAN>,
<SPAN OnClick="changeFontSize('8pt');">8pt</SPAN> or
<SPAN OnClick="changeFontSize('4pt');">4pt</SPAN>
<BR>
<B>background color:</B>
<SPAN OnClick="changeBackground('yellow');">yellow</SPAN>,
<SPAN OnClick="changeBackground('white');">white</SPAN> or
<SPAN OnClick="changeBackground('#EFE');">light green</SPAN>
 
<B>text alignment:</B>
<SPAN OnClick="changeAlignment('left');">left</SPAN>,
<SPAN OnClick="changeAlignment('center');">center</SPAN> or
<SPAN OnClick="changeAlignment('right');">right</SPAN>
 
<B>line spacing:</B>
<SPAN OnClick="changeLinespace('1');">1.0</SPAN>,
<SPAN OnClick="changeLinespace('1.25');">1.25</SPAN> or
<SPAN OnClick="changeLinespace('1.5');">1.5</SPAN>.
</DIV>
```

This example looks as though it's an overwhelming amount of CSS, but if you look at it, it's all quite simple and straightforward — consider, for example, the following:

```
<SPAN OnClick="changeLinespace('1.5');">1.5</SPAN>.
```

This line specifies that, each time the visitor clicks the 1.5 number, the JavaScript function changeLinespace calls with 1.5 as its parameter. A quick flip back to the JavaScript function definitions reveals the following:

```
function changeLinespace(value)
{ myObj.lineHeight = value; }
```

That is, the changeme container's line height is set to the given value (1.5).

More generally, this function can be written as:

```
function changeAttrib(attrib,value)
    {
     document.getElementById("changeme").style[attrib]=value;
    }
```

and completely generalized to:

```
function changeAttrib(id,attrib,value)
    {
     document.getElementById(id).style[attrib]=value;
    }
```

Figure 17-1 shows how you can use this ability to dynamically reassign style and layout attributes to experiment with style properties, but you really need to access it on your own system to see how much fun it is!

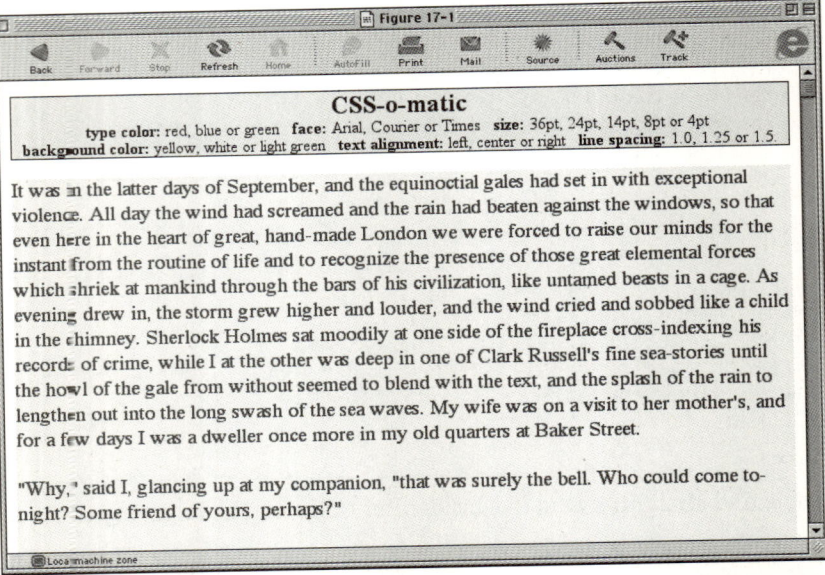

Figure 17-1 *CSS-o-matic enables you to tweak lots of style attributes in real-time.*

Events and Event Handlers

I touch on a couple of the JavaScript events that you can script — notably, OnClick, OnMouseOver, OnMouseOut, and OnLoad — but Table 17-1 lists all the defined events for your reference.

Table 17-1 *Scriptable Events in JavaScript*

Event name	Description
OnAbort	User cancels downloading of an image or element.
OnBlur	Input element loses focus. (User moves cursor elsewhere.)
OnChange	Similar to OnBlur, but the contents of the element change.
OnClick	A mouseclick event occurs.
OnDblClick	A double-click occurs.
OnFocus	User clicks into or tabs into a data element.
OnKeyDown	User presses a key on the keyboard.
OnKeyPress	User presses and releases a keyboard key.
OnKeyUp	User releases a key on the keyboard.
OnLoad	The page completely loads in the browser.
OnMouseDown	The user presses the mouse button.
OnMouseUp	The user releases the mouse button.
OnMouseOut	The mouse moves off the element.
OnMouseOver	The mouse moves over the element.
OnMove	The window moves.
OnReset	The Reset button is clicked.
OnResize	Window is resized.
OnSelect	User selects text in an INPUT or TEXTAREA element.
OnSubmit	User presses the Submit button.
OnUnload	Opposite of OnLoad: User leaves this page.

As you can see, most of these events aren't very useful for DHTML, with the exception of the four that I list earlier in the section "Events and Event Handlers." After I get to the FORM scripting, however, you see them in a whole new light.

Done!

REVIEW

You never knew that so much about DHTML revolves around the document object model, did you? This session explores the history of Web-browser development and how that affects the standardized document object model from the W3C. You also see how subtle browser incompatibilities and extensions can lurk and bite innocent DHTML developers. Fortunately, the session ends with a demonstration of the standard DOM and how to use it for a very nifty effect: real-time reformatting of text on a Web page.

QUIZ YOURSELF

1. The W3C is what? And it does what? (See "What's a Document Object Model?")

2. Which of the following isn't evolving to rely on the standardized DOM?

   HTML, XML, XHTML, JavaScript, ECMAScript

   (See "What's a Document Object Model?")

3. A typical Web page may have _____ variables or attributes associated with it. (See "What's a Document Object Model?")

4. What is the main reason that multiple document object models are still around? (See "What's a Document Object Model?")

5. What element does Internet Explorer 5.5 retain for compatibility with earlier versions of IE but isn't part of the blessed official DOM? (See "What's a Document Object Model?")

6. After the dust settles, you end up with _____'s scripting language superimposed over _____'s object model. (See "Netscape's DOM.")

7. One of the greatest weaknesses of the Netscape Navigator 4 DOM support is that the browser can't do what? (*Hint:* The example in this session highlights this same capability.) (See "Netscape's DOM.")

8. What are the most useful JavaScript event handlers for Web site development? (See "Events and Event Handlers.")

SESSION

18

Writing and Debugging JavaScript

Session Checklist

✔ Why JavaScript is hard to debug

✔ The JavaScript Console

✔ Smart JavaScript programming style

**30 Min.
To Go**

If you're following along with the examples in this book by checking them out off the CD-ROM, you've missed out on a potential source of fun: debugging JavaScript. Well, "fun" isn't exactly the best choice of words, but debugging's certainly interesting and challenging.

The problem with debugging JavaScript is that errors rarely, if ever, appear to the user, and because no cross-platform JavaScript development environment exists, the task is a guaranteed source of frustration.

So in this session, I spend a while looking at how bugs can occur, how to isolate them, and how to squash them to ensure that your JavaScript and resulting DHTML pages are clean and ready to publish on the World Wide Web.

Why JavaScript Is Hard to Debug

Imagine you're learning a foreign language and your tutor announces that a new rule's in place: As soon as you make a grammatical or word-choice error, she's going to ignore everything else that you say until you're done talking.

At first, you may say "Well, okay, just tell me if I get something wrong."

Then you realize the problem: If she doesn't tell you when the mistake occurs, you're doomed. You can never identify exactly where she stopped listening, and, indeed, you probably end up talking in shorter and shorter (and simpler and simpler) sentences until you end up talking. In very. Short. Sentences.

Debugging JavaScript is unfortunately very similar to this peculiar scenario. Some browsers flag certain code as an error, but much of the time, the browser simply stops interpreting the JavaScript after it encounters an error.

Consider the following fragment of a DHTML page:

language."javascript" ①

```
<SCRIPT LANG="JavaScript">
self.style.backgroundColor = "green";
window.style.backgroundColor = "blue";
document.getElementById("mybody").style.backgroundColor
    = "yellow";
alert("we've entered the JavaScript zone.");
</SCRIPT>
<BODY>
<DIV ID="mybody">
some text that should get a colored background?
```

What color do you think the current window receives as its background color assignment: green, blue, or yellow?

If you say, "None," you're right. In Internet Explorer, nothing happens after it reads this snippet of code. In Netscape 6, nothing happens either, unless you know how to launch the secret JavaScript Console, in which case you get the following confusing message Error: self.style has no properties. (See the following section to discover how to launch the JavaScript Console.)

If you puzzle through this example, you realize that the problem involves trying to change the background color of a container that isn't yet loaded. But instead, I'm just going to comment out the bad line and try again, as follows:

①
```
<SCRIPT LANG="JavaScript">
// self.style.backgroundColor = "green";
window.style.backgroundColor = "blue";
document.getElementById("mybody").style.backgroundColor
    = "yellow";
alert("we've entered the JavaScript zone.");
</SCRIPT>
<BODY>
<DIV ID="mybody">
some text that should get a colored background?
```

This time, you discover that window.style has no properties because the window object hasn't yet been created by the browser, so you should comment out that part, too. After all, the last statement should work; it's identical to the JavaScript that I use in the example in Session 17, right? Well, check out the following:

①
```
<SCRIPT LANG="JavaScript">
// self style.backgroundColor = "green";
// window.style.backgroundColor = "blue";
document.getElementById("mybody").style.backgroundColor
    = "yellow";
alert("we've entered the JavaScript zone.");
</SCRIP>
```

```
<BODY>
<DIV ID="mybody">
some text that should get a colored background?
```

Nope. It doesn't work. In fact, it results in a very similar error message:

```
document.getElementById("mybody") has no properties.
```

Why the error message again? Because you're trying to set a property to a container that you haven't yet defined. Worse, the browser simply ignores the `alert()` statement immediately below the failing line instead of providing a helpful dialog box with an OK button to confirm that you made it to that point.

The solution to this dilemma is to tie the background change to an `onLoad` event, which ensures that all the containers are defined. The fourth, and final version, then, appears as follows:

```
function yellowBack() {
   document.getElementById("mybody").style.backgroundColor
     = "yellow";
}
```

You hook it into the Web page with the following line:

```
<BODY OnLoad="yellowBack();">
```

By the way, after you comment out the erroneous `backgroundColor` lines and wrap the correct one into a function for later interpretation by the browser, the `we've entered the JavaScript zone` alert finally shows up.

In total, then, here's the DHTML listing that you need to explore:

```
<SCRIPT LANG="JavaScript">

function yellowBack() {
   document.getElementById("mybody").style.backgroundColor = "yellow";
}

alert("we've entered the JavaScript zone.");

</SCRIPT>
<BODY OnLoad="yellowBack();" BGCOLOR="white">

<H2 STYLE="text-align: center; font: 18pt Arial bold;
    background: #EEF; padding: 3px;
    border: 1px solid black; width: 100%">
 The Adventure of the Speckled Band</H2>

<DIV ID="mybody"
 STYLE="font-size: 14pt; background: #FFE;">
On glancing over my notes of the seventy odd cases
in which I have during the last eight years studied
the methods of my friend Sherlock Holmes...
```

**20 Min.
To Go**

The JavaScript Console

Because Netscape introduced JavaScript, the fact that the Netscape browsers have included a JavaScript debugging environment for a long time is really no surprise. The part that comes with Navigator 4, for example, is the *JavaScript Console*, a separate window where (some) error messages appear and you can type debugging JavaScript statements.

> **You can launch the JavaScript Console by typing** `javascript:` **into the Location text box in Navigator 4.**

You can see the JavaScript Console and its report on the snippet in the preceding section in Figure 18-1.

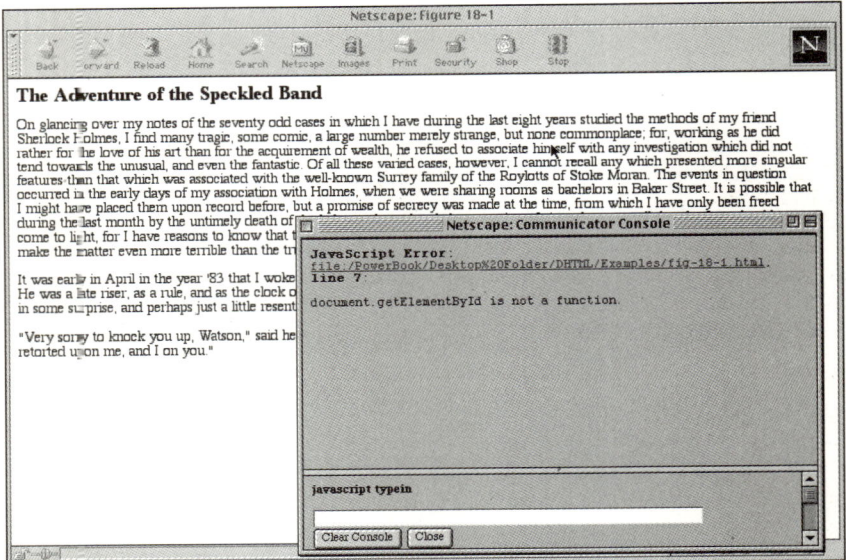

Figure 18-1   *The Navigator 4 JavaScript Console.*

More interestingly, Netscape also made available a JavaScript debugger for developers to download from its site. Unfortunately, the debugger vanished from the Netscape 6 distribution, although the JavaScript Console is still available. To get to it, however, you can't simply type `javascript:` in the Location text box of the browser anymore. Instead, choose Tasks or Communicator ⇨ Tools from the menu bar; you see JavaScript Console as the last choice. The console window should then pop up on your screen.

> **You'd think that perhaps the Netscape JavaScript debugger is useful even with Netscape 6, but the reality is — with some irony — that the code Netscape embedded in the license agreement to start the "SmartDownload" fails in Netscape 6, resulting in an** `object is not a function` **error. Try it — just check the following URL:** `http://developer.netscape.com/ software/jsdebug.html.`

To make this situation more interesting, I'm going to introduce some errors into the JavaScript section, as follows:

```
<SCRIPT LANG="JavaScript">
var num = 11, denom = 0;
var divByZero = num / denom;
document.badElement = "3";
function function() {
  alert("divByZero = " + divByZero);
}
function yellowBack() {
  document.getElementById("mybody").style.backgroundColor = "yellow";
}
alert("we've entered the JavaScript zone.");
</SCRIPT>
```

Launch the JavaScript Console, and you see some errors appear, as shown in Figure 18-2.

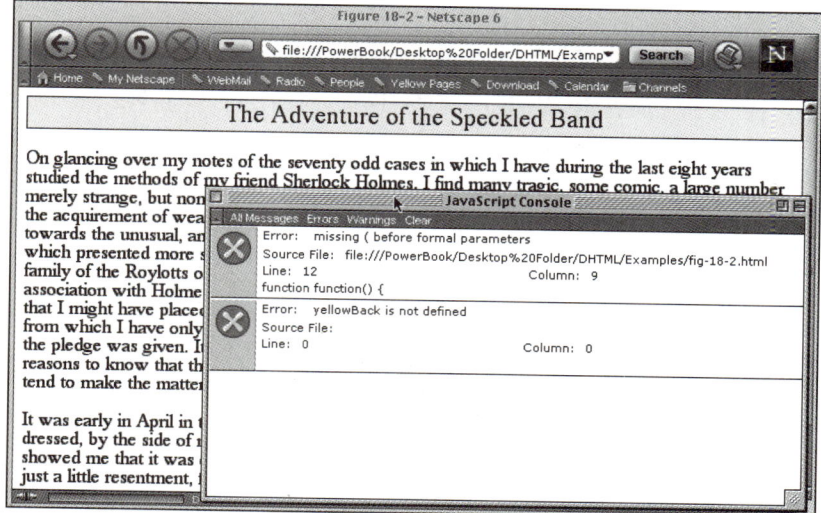

Figure 18-2 *Errors appear in the JavaScript Console, but are they the right errors?*

In just about any programming language, the division by zero produces an error. In fact, the value of 11/0 is undefined in mathematics. Try it in C or Perl, and bad things unquestionably happen. Try it in JavaScript, however, and it works!

Furthermore, you have a bad element reference (document.badElement) in an assignment statement, but no complaint about this illegal assignment appears in the Console window, as you can see.

What the Console does flag as an error is the attempt to redefine the word *function* as an explicit function: It's a reserved keyword in JavaScript and should generate an illegal function name error or similar. Instead, the error is the baffling missing (before formal parameters on that line.

As a result of the bad function error, the browser doesn't interpret the yellowBack() JavaScript function (remember that the interpreter ignores everything after it sees an error), the alert() doesn't tell you that you've entered the JavaScript zone, and after you finally do get to the OnLoad event that invokes yellowBack(). it fails, flagging the error in the Console but with an unknown line number rather than the line number of the OnLoad call. (The unknown line number is, of course, shown as 'line 0'.)

Basically, what you get is a mess of incorrect error messages and ignored problems, coupled with the browser then silently skipping valid and legal JavaScript. "Ugh!" indeed. Can you imagine a worse possible result?

Actually, a worse result *is* possible: Internet Explorer experiences all the same problems with the code, but it doesn't include any sort of JavaScript Console, so you don't even get those two quasi-helpful error messages in IE!

Microsoft does provide a generic Windows-only script debugger that's available on the Microsoft Developer Network site — http://msdn.microsoft.com/scripting/debugger/dbdocs.htm **— but it's aimed primarily at ASP and ActiveX scripting.**

Smart JavaScript Programming Style

The conclusion that you want to draw from this discussion is that you need to be a careful programmer if you're working with JavaScript. A little bit of extra time and thought can do wonders for your sanity.

To help minimize your frustration while developing your own JavaScript functions and functionality, the rest of this session presents a list of smart JavaScript development strategies.

Just remember: Code thoughtfully.

Phase in your code

I think that the most fundamental strategy for developing any software, whether in the error-message-free world of JavaScript or a 50-thousand-line Java application, is to phase in your code in slow, careful steps as you test each one.

As I develop software, I always try to break the functionality down into functions as much as possible and then stub-out (comment out) the functions until the main code sequence is working correctly. I'd start a complex JavaScript application, for example, as follows:

```
function mainFunc()
{
    var looper = true;
```

```
    initialize();
    while ( looper ) {
        read_information();
        looper = processInformation();
    }
}
function initialize()
{
    // variable and array initializations will go here
}
function read_information()
{
    // read the information to be processed
}
function processInformation()
{
    // process information. Return 'true' if all went well.
    return true;
}
```

Now I can expand each of the functions in simple, incremental steps and immediately know if things break. More important, if the JavaScript ceases to work in my DHTML page during testing, I can immediately conclude that the problem is isolated to the very latest code I added.

Explain your logic by using comments

In the example in the preceding section, you can see that I define and rough out the three subroutines that implement the main routine. Not only that, but I also add some explanatory comments that serve to remind me later what the purpose and characteristics of the function are.

Indeed, notice in my comment for processInformation() that I detail the return value of the routine and how to interpret it.

Good comments for a function include the purpose of the function, any input variables, changes made to global data structures, and the return value, if any. Within routines, add comments explaining conditions you're testing, algorithms you're using, and so on.

In general, ask yourself what you need to explain in your comments so that, if you return to modify the script six months later, it still makes sense.

As a reminder, you can add comments to your JavaScript two ways: A double-slash indicates that all text until the end of line is a comment (//), and a /* and */ sequence specifies that everything between the two sequences is a comment, even if it goes on for dozens of lines.

**10 Min.
To Go**

Use dialog boxes for debugging

You can display information from within JavaScript three ways — through the prompt(), alert(), and confirm() functions. For debugging, the alert() is unquestionably the champion, because it opens a simple dialog box that enables you to see what's going on at any point in your script.

Take another look at the following script, from earlier in this session, to see how alerts can help with debugging:

```
<SCRIPT LANG="JavaScript">
var num = 11, denom = 0;
var divByZero = num / denom;
document.badElement = "3";
function function() {
  alert("divByZero = " + divByZero);
}
function yellowBack() {
  document.getElementById("mybody").style.backgroundColor = "yellow";
}
alert("we've entered the JavaScript zone.");
</SCRIPT>
```

You can see in the preceding example that I've already started to work on debugging this script by adding two alerts: The first shows the value of the divByZero variable, as follows:

```
alert("divByZero = " + divByZero);
```

The second confirms that the JavaScript interpreter's read and interpreted every line, as follows:

```
alert("we've entered the JavaScript zone.");
```

You can also add alerts that you tie to specific scriptable events, as in the following example:

```
<INPUT TYPE=text OnChange="alert('things have changed');"
 NAME=fullname>
```

This particular alert pops up after you move into the input box and change the value from what it is before you move. Be aware, however, that not all the browsers support onChange.

The + notation enables you to concatenate (put together) strings and variables, so a sequence such as the following is quite common:

```
var locper = 3;
retvalue = myRoutine();
alert('looper = " + looper + ", and retvalue = " + retValue);
```

I encourage you to sprinkle these debugging alerts throughout your scripts liberally: A few spare dialog boxes are a small price to pay for knowing what's really happening in your code.

Use the Console if you're stumped

It's not glamorous and it lacks functionality, but if you're working in Netscape 6, you can access the JavaScript Console, and it does occasionally flag errors and give you a clue regarding what's wrong with your script. If you're developing code, therefore, leave it open!

Validate user input

If you accept input from the user, validating that input before you use it is very important to ensure that it's within an acceptable range. If you're asking the user for an e-mail address, for example, making sure that it's well formatted before you try to send it to a mailer function is the smart thing to do.

Another example: If you have a product order form, before using the quantity value to calculate total price, double-check to ensure that the listed quantity is a sensible value and then alert the user if you detect a problem. (I spend a lot of time talking about input validation later in the book, too.)

Catch errors with your own onerror function

Here's a cool function that you can drop into your DHTML pages while you're developing them! The following script feeds any errors to your own routine by associating errors with the onerror function:

```
<SCRIPT>
function catchError(errorMsg,url,line)
{
  // Catch the error by showing the error arguments
  alert("Error: " + errorMsg + "\n" +
    "URL: " + url + "\n" +
    "line number: " + line);
  return(true);
}
onerror = catchError;
  </SCRIPT>
```

One particularly interesting feature of this example is worth noting: The onerror event automatically feeds three variables to the event handler (the error message, the URL of the failing page, and the line number where the error occurs). The \n sequence also forces a line break within the text of the alert in a manner similar to how <BR> works within HTML code.

 **Make sure that you specify onerror as all lowercase. A bug in some versions of IE causes it to ignore the change otherwise.**

To trigger this function, simply put a problem in your code, as follows:

```
<BODY OnLoad="badFunctionCall();">
```

The results are as shown in Figure 18-3.

If you try this trick in Netscape 6, I must warn you that the output is less useful than in Internet Explorer. IE fails to define either the URL or the line number, and the entire error message is [objectKeyEvent].

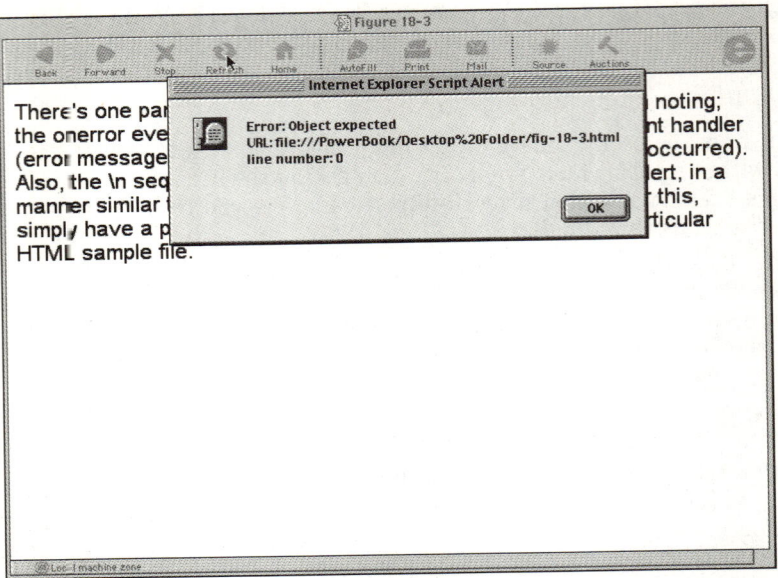

Figure 18-3 An error message that my own error handler is fielding.

Accept the inevitable: browser bugs

If everyone had the very latest version of the coolest browser, life would probably seem at least relatively straightforward for developers, but that ain't how it works. Instead, you see different browsers, different versions of JavaScript, different operating system platforms, and, frankly, different phases of the moon, too!

As an example, what do you think is the result of the following conditional statement in JavaScript?

```
if ("5' == 5)
```

The answer is "It depends."

In JavaScript 1.1, this test evaluates as true, because the string automatically converts into an integer value. In JavaScript 1.2, however, the result of the test is false, and version 1.3 "fixes" it so that it returns true again.

Whether you think this situation represents a bug or a reflection of the gradual evolution of the JavaScript language, stumbling over these problems now and then is hard to avoid. That's why testing the capabilities of the browsers in your code is so important, as you read in depth in Session 19.

Ask for help

You can send me e-mail if you're stumped, but your best bet is unquestionably to pop over to one of the developer Web sites, read through the online materials, and join in the discussion groups.

One good reference spot for JavaScript is Netscape itself. Within the Netscape DevEdge developers area is an area just for JavaScript (at `http://developer.netscape.com/js/`) and another area for the Netscape 6 DOM (http://developer.netscape.com/dom/).

I really like builder.com and find its discussion area a valuable resource myself if I'm stumped. You can start at the builder.com home page or jump directly to the discussions area at http://buzz.builder.com/. Look for the JavaScript/DHTML area!

If you want to keep up on Microsoft IE developments and so on, your best bet is to check `http://msdn.microsoft.com/msdnmag/` sporadically. A better choice, which focuses just on IE, is `http://msdn.microsoft.com/ie/`. I must warn you, however, that the discussion forums there aren't quite as useful. Check out Members Helping Members on the site to see what I mean.

Two more sites to check out, too, are `www.geckonnection.com/` and `www.mozillazine.org`.

Done!

REVIEW

This session focuses on the woolly world of working with JavaScript, explaining some of the many reasons that JavaScript is difficult to debug and develop — particularly if you're used to the more sophisticated development environments of other programming languages. All isn't lost, however, because you can combine a variety of different approaches to minimize problems while you code. Chief among them are using the JavaScript Console while working in Netscape 6 and coding thoughtfully. Specific debugging tips also include developing your code in slow, thoughtful steps, extensively commenting your code, adding your own error handler, and using alerts to show variable values and flow of control. The next session explores how to write browser-neutral JavaScript.

QUIZ YOURSELF

1. What's the main reason that JavaScript is difficult to debug? (See "Why JavaScript Is Hard to Debug.")

2. Why does the following snippet fail?

```
<SCRIPT LANG="JavaScript">
document.getElementById("shademe").style.backgroundColor ="#EEE";
</SCRIPT>
<BODY>
<DIV ID="shademe"> ...
```

   (See "Why JavaScript Is Hard to Debug.")

3. Why do many JavaScript errors end up associated with input line 0? (See "The JavaScript Console.")

4. Just remember: _____ (See "Smart JavaScript Programming Style.")

5. What are the two different styles of comment available in JavaScript? As a bonus, what's the format for comments in HTML? (See "Explain your logic by using comments.")

6. Which of the following is correct?

```
alert("looper = " looper);
alert("looper = %d", looper);
alert("looper = ", looper);
alert("looper = " + looper);
alert("looper = $looper");
```

(See "Use dialog boxes for debugging.")

7. Is ("5" == 5) true or false in JavaScript? (See "Accept the inevitable: browser bugs.")

Testing Browser Compatibility

Session Checklist

✔ The navigator object and its attributes

✔ Identifying the exact browser

✔ Browser tests by capability

✔ The window object and its attributes

**30 Min.
To Go**

The challenges of last session are probably enough to convince you that the capability to conditionally execute the JavaScript on your DHTML Web pages is an important one. This session, you start to explore different ways to test for compatibility and capability prior to asking the Web browser to execute a particular statement that may fail.

Much of this material you saw previewed in earlier sessions, from testing browser capabilities to using global variables to avoiding worries about whether the browser wants .style embedded in object references and similar. I explain it all in further detail in this session, and, in fact, this session serves as the foundation for the platform-neutral library that you develop in Session 20, coming up next.

The Navigator Object and Its Attributes

You find three types of tests useful in JavaScript: testing for the type of browser (for example, Internet Explorer versus Netscape Navigator), testing for the version of browser (4.7? 6?), and testing for specific capabilities (whether the browser knows the method getElementByID?). Let's start with the first of these tests.

The navigator object contains within it all attributes of the Web browser, as in Table 19-1 highlights.

Yes, even within Internet Explorer, this object is known as navigator. **Netscape got there first!**

Table 19-1 *Attribute Values of the* navigator *Object*

Attribute Name	Explanation
appCodeName	The code name of the browser.
appName	The name of the browser.
appVersion	The version number.
language	The language that this browser supports ("en" for English) – more recent browsers refer to browserLanguage, systemLanguage and userLanguage.
platform	The hardware platform/OS (JavaScript 1.2 and newer).
userAgent	The HTTP_USERAGENT value (also sent as part of the http environment).

To see how you can use these attributes in a simple script, consider the following example:

```
<SCRIPT LANG="JavaScript">
function showInfo()
{
  document.write("<BR>Information about your browser
     is as follows:<BR>");
  document.write("<UL><LI>appName = " + navigator.appName);
  document.write("<LI>appVersion = " + navigator.appVersion);
  document.write("<LI>userAgent = " + navigator.userAgent);
  document.write("<LI>appCodeName = " + navigator.appCodeName);
  document.write("<LI>platform = " + navigator.platform);
  document.write("<LI>language = " + navigator.language);
  document.write("</UL><HR>\n");
}
showInfo();
</SCRIPT>
```

(handwritten annotation: language='javascript')

Running this JavaScript code shows a number of interesting characteristics about Netscape 6, as shown in Figure 19-1.

Note

One of the most helpful methods associated with the document **object is** write, **which enables you to dynamically add content to the Web page from within your JavaScript. Also available is the kissing cousin** writeln, **which is completely identical except that it appends a carriage return after each line of output.**

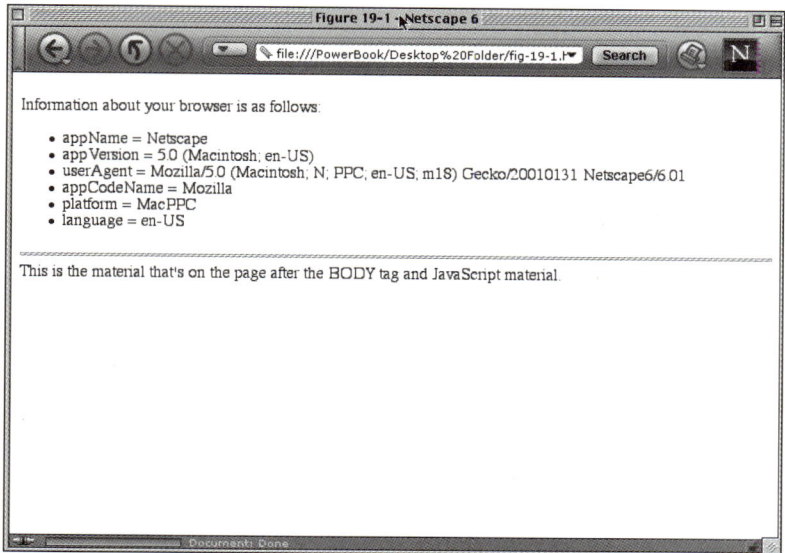

Figure 19-1   *The* navigator *object's property values in Netscape 6.*

This output is useful and interesting, but it's limited because it requires that you already know the names of all the attributes. Instead, a more sophisticated JavaScript function uses a for loop, as follows:

```
function showItAll()
{
  document.write("<BR>Information about your browser
      is as follows:<UL>");
  for (propertyName in navigator) {
    document.write("<LI>", propertyName, " = ",
      navigator[propertyName]);
  }
 document.write("</UL><HR>\n");
}
showItAll();
```

Not only is this method shorter and easier to understand, but it actually shows that the navigator object has quite a few more attributes, as shown in Figures 19-2 and 19-3, which show the results that you get in Netscape 6 and Internet Explorer 5.5, respectively.

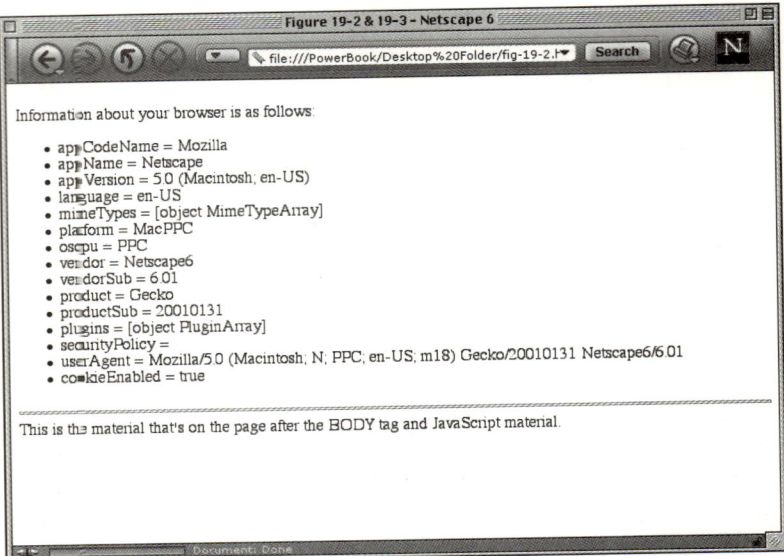

Figure 19-2 *All* navigator *object attributes in Netscape 6.*

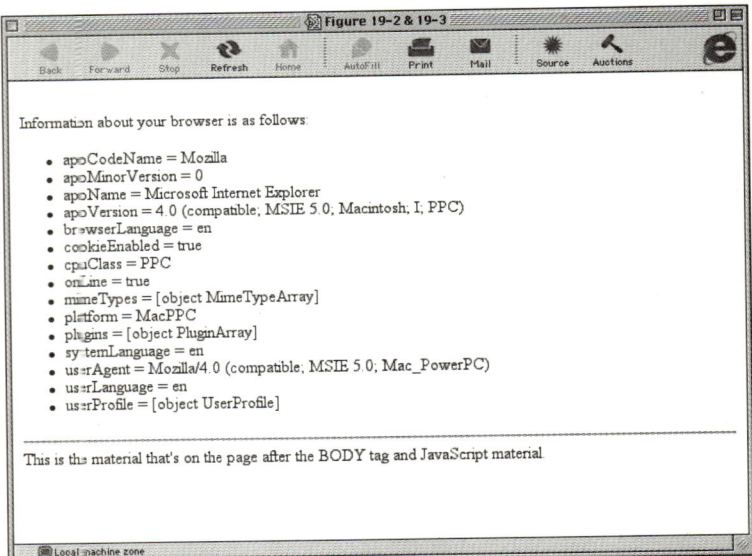

Figure 19-3 *All* navigator *object attributes in Internet Explorer 5.5.*

Very interesting output, I'd say. What's most interesting is the plugins array, which you can examine with the following example:

```
function showPlugIns()
{
  document.write("<HR>Browser Plugins Installed: -- " +
      navigator.plugins.length + "<UL>\n");
  for (propname in navigator.plugins) {
    document.write("<LI>" + navigator.plugins[propname].name);
  }
  document.write("</UL><HR>\n");
}

showPlugIns();
```

This example neatly demonstrates the ease with that you can work with arrays in JavaScript and is a distinct pleasure to read if you compare it to the complexity of accomplishing a similar array reference in the C programming language.

 **An *array* is a list of components that masquerades as a single variable. Arrays can be any size, and you can reference them by numeric slot value or a unique key. To define a variable, simply list its values:** var myArray = ["cat","dog","squirrel","aardvark"];.

Figure 19-4 shows the list of plug-ins installed by default with Internet Explorer 5.5 on the Macintosh. Try this code on your browser to see what you've installed.

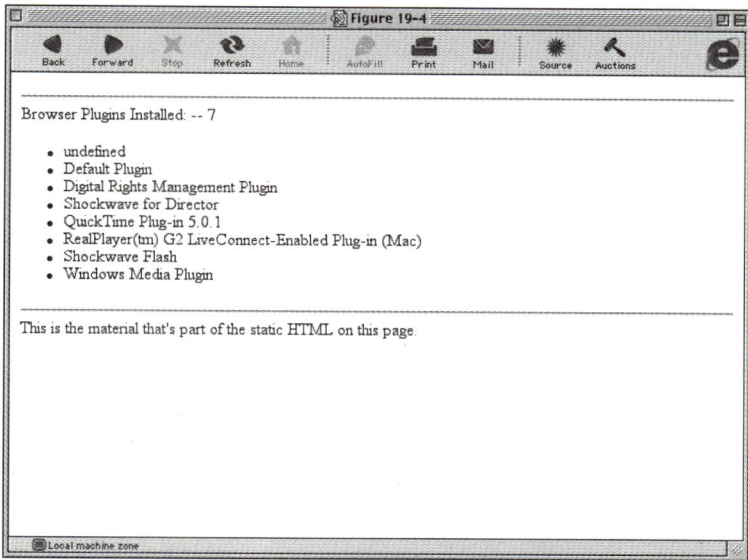

Figure 19-4　*Plug-ins included and installed with Internet Explorer 5.5.*

Identifying the Exact Browser

With all this new information about the navigator object, writing some code that figures out the browser, browser version, and OS platform is a breeze. Here's a first try:

```
var browser = navigator.appName;
var versionNumber = navigator.appVersion;
var OS = navigator.platform;
```

You shouldn't be surprised that this example doesn't quite work as you want. Slipping it into some JavaScript in IE5.5 and following it with an alert() produces the following values:

- browser = Microsoft Internet Explorer
- versionNumber = 4.0 (compatible; MSIE 5.0; Macintosh; I; PPC)
- platform = MacPPC

Not quite what the doctor ordered . . . way too much information.

The trick is to test and set the value based on a subset of the information that the navigator object values give. You can most easily do so by using the indexOf method, which enables you to easily test whether a substring appears in a given object.

If, for example, test = "dynamic HTML", what do you think that the following statement returns?

```
test.indexOf("HTML")
```

It returns 7 (the starting point of the first match with the pattern). What about the following statement?

```
test.indexOf("CSS")
```

It returns –1, an error condition.

Therefore, testing for Windows, for example, is straightforward with the following statement:

```
navigator.appName.indexOf("Win")
```

This object enables you to simplify the code a bit, as follows:

```
var browser = navigator.appName;
var versionNumber = parseInt(navigator.appVersion);
var OS = navigator.platform;

if (browser == "Microsoft Internet Explorer") browser = "IE";
if (OS.indexOf("Mac") != -1) OS = "Mac";
if (OS.indexOf("Win") != -1) OS = "Windows";
```

Therefore, with that additional snippet of code as the initial test, you can have the following:

```
if (browser == "IE" && versionNumber >= 3) {
    statements appropriate for IE3 and above
```

```
} else if (browser == "Netscape" && versionNumber > 4) {
  statements appropriate for Netscape 5 and above
}
```

Because anticipating all possible values is remarkably difficult, however, testing by capabilities is much smarter, as you see in a moment.

Operating System Tests

I don't mean to say that the capability to detect platform and OS isn't useful. You may want use the following code to create a page that offers a <u>Learn more about your operating system</u> link that automatically points to the appropriate Web site, as follows:

```
function OSsite()
{
  if (OS == "Win") page = "http://www.microsoft.com/";
  if (OS == "Mac") page = "http://www.apple.com/";
  document.write("<A HREF=\"" + page + "\">");
}
```

A more succinct style, however, is to use the x?a:b notation, if you're only going to test for Win and Mac values, as follows:

```
page = (OS == "WIN" ? "http://www.microsoft.com/" :
"http://www.apple.com/");
```

Frankly, you can make it even shorter by integrating the condition into the write() method's call itself, as follows:

```
document.write("<A HREF=\"" +
  OS == "WIN"? "http://www.microsoft.com/" : "http://www.apple.com/" +
  "\">");
```

In the same way, you can test to see what version of Windows the user is running and offer a FAQ based on that, too, which is a nice addition to the home page.

Browser Tests by Capability

The first generation of our example JavaScript code tested by version and browser information, but a better and more popular way to write conditional code, as I also demonstrate in Session 18, is as follows:

```
if (document.getElementById) {
    theBug = document.getElementById("floatingBug");
  } else {
    theBug = document.floatingBug;
  }
```

This example takes advantage of a characteristic of JavaScript: You can check for the existence of a defined method by slipping it into a conditional statement, as shown.

You can reverse the logic of the test – testing for a method that isn't defined — by using the JavaScript ! (not) operator as follows:

```
if (! document.getElementById) {
    alert("getElementById not supported in this browser.");
}
```

Now you can also see the logic of testing for the .style attribute with the following line:

```
if (theBug.style) theBug=theBug.style;
```

If no .style attribute for the variable is defined, you can ignore it. But if it has one, you redefine the variable to include that attribute.

In the next session, I push farther with this concept to write a portable JavaScript library for further DHTML development.

The Window Object and Its Attributes

Before I wrap this session up, I'm going to examine one more object.

All Web pages are built around an overarching object known as the window object. In fact, in the last session, in assigning onerror to your own error handling function, what you were really doing was redefining a method for the window object. You can accomplished the same task with the following:

```
window.onerror = catchError;
```

A large number of different attributes associate with the window object, the most interesting of which I summarize in Table 19-2.

Table 19-2   *Useful Attributes of the* window *Object*

Attribute	Explanation
defaultStatus	Default value appearing in the status line.
status	The status line in the Web browser.
document	A reference to the document object.
history	The history of sites that this browser visited (not accessible directly for security reasons).
location	The current URL loaded.
name	The name of the window.
opener	The object that opened this window (if a subwindow) or null.

Attribute	Explanation
parent	The parent window if this window is a framed element.
self	Identical to window.
top	If it's a framed element, the topmost window.

Again, you can use some simple JavaScript to reveal the properties and their values in the browser, as follows:

```
<SCRIPT LANGUAGE="JavaScript">
function showPlugIns()
{
    document.write("<HR>Window properties:<UL>\n");
    for (propname in window) {
        document.write("<LI>" + propname + " = "
            + window[propname]);
    }
document.write("</UL><HR>\n");
}
showPlugIns();
</SCRIPT>
```

The results for Internet Explorer 5.5 are as follows:

- closed = false
- defaultStatus =
- document = [object Document]
- event = [object Event]
- frame = [object Window]
- history = [object History]
- length = 0
- location = file:///PowerBook/Desktop%20Folder/fig-19-6.html
- name =
- navigator = [object Navigator]
- offscreenBuffering = auto
- opener = null
- parent = [object Window]
- screen = [object Screen]
- self = [object Window]
- status =
- top = [object Window]
- window = [object Window]

and there are even more attributes to the Window object in Netscape 6:

- parent = [object Window]
- scrollbars = [object BarProp]
- frames = [object WindowCollection]
- name =
- scrollX = 0
- scrollY = 0
- window = [object Window]
- self = [object Window]
- navigator = [object Navigator]
- screen = [object Screen]
- history = [object History]
- statusbar = [object BarProp]
- directories = [object BarProp]
- closed = false
- crypto = [object Crypto]
- pkcs11 = [object Pkcs11]
- opener = null
- status =
- defaultStatus =
- location = file:///PowerBook/Desktop%20Folder/fig-19-6.html
- title =
- innerWidth = 752
- innerHeight = 388
- outerWidth = 752
- outerHeight = 466
- screenX = 232
- screenY = 145
- pageXOffset = 0
- pageYOffset = 0
- length = 0
- document = [object HTMLDocument]
- components = [xpconnect wrapped nsIXPCComponents]
- top = [object Window]
- _content = [object Window]
- sidebar = [xpconnect wrapped nsISidebar]

- prompter = [xpconnect wrapped nsIPrompt]
- menubar = [object BarProp]
- toolbar = [object BarProp]
- locationbar = [object BarProp]
- personalbar = [object BarProp]
- controllers = [xpconnect wrapped nsIControllers]

In addition, Netscape 6 makes the complete list of error handlers available through the window object, too: onmousedown, onmouseup, onclick, onmouseover, onmouseout, onkeydown, onkeyup, onkeypress, onmousemove, onfocus, onblur, onsubmit, onreset, onchange, onselect, onload, onunload, onclose, onabort, onerror, onpaint, ondragdrop, onresize, and onscroll.

You can do a lot with the window object and its many attributes, as you see throughout the rest of the book. To whet your appetite, however, try running the following script to see what your JavaScript can access as your programming gets more sophisticated:

```
document.write("</UL>Your screen data:<UL>\n");
    for (value in window.screen) {
        document.write("<LI>" + value + " = "
            + window.screen[value]);
    }
    document.write("</UL><HR>\n");
```

I promise that you're going to be enthused about the results.

This JavaScript code and the OS testing code shown earlier are also available on the CD-ROM as fig-19-5.html

Done!

REVIEW

This session started out talking about the necessity of writing cross-browser and cross-operating-system code, and examining the navigator object and its many useful attributes. In particular, appName, appVersion and platform offer considerable information for script writers. However, tests by capability prove to be a much smarter and flexible coding style than explicitly testing for browsers and versions. There are situations where knowing the OS or browser can be helpful, however, as discussed. Finally, the session wrapped up with a discussion of the window object and its huge list of possible values.

QUIZ YOURSELF

1. Why do you call it the navigator object rather than the browser object or, for that matter, the explorer object? (See "The Navigator Object and Its Attributes.")

2. Which of the following lines are valid JavaScript?

```
document.writeout("hello<br>");
document.write("hello<br>");
document.print("hello<br>");
document.echo("hello<br>");
```

(See "The Navigator Object and Its Attributes.")

3. What's an array, and why is it useful? (See "The Navigator Object and Its Attributes.")

4. How does the method indexOf() work? (See "Identifying the Exact Browser.")

Creating a Cross-Platform JavaScript Library

Session Checklist

✔ Ascertaining capabilities

✔ Positioning functions

✔ Window and screen dimensions

✔ Object dimensions

✔ Putting it all together

**30 Min.
To Go**

The last few sessions should have convinced you that Dynamic HTML is considerably easier to develop if you can write a reusable library of basic JavaScript functions and link to it as necessary. That's what this session presents: It's a synthesis of the last few sessions.

Ascertaining Capabilities

The first step for a portable JavaScript library is to create the capability to reference objects without needing to worry about which of the document object models are understood. You can accomplish this task in two ways; the first involves setting some document object model descriptive variables for later use in the program, as follows:

```
var useID = 0, useLayers = 0, useAll = 0, N6 = 0, MSIE = 0;

if (document.getElementById) useID = 1;
if (document.layers) useLayers = 1;
if (document.all) useAll = 1;
```

This example is helpful, but sporadically, because JavaScript code requires knowing exactly which browser is in use. You can determine this information by looking at the `navigator.appName` and `navigator.appVersion`, or you can do so by checking what type of references are understood, as in the following example:

```
var MSIE = (useID && useAll);
var N6   = (useID && (! useAll) );
```

The combination of these statements details exactly what object model is in use and, therefore, how to reference the elements therein. In fact, the getElementById method is the official mechanism for accessing objects according to the World Wide Web Consortium (W3C) document object model specification, so you could also name useID w3cCompatible as a reminder.

 **The library that I present herein I'm primarily aiming at the latest generation of Web browsers. I've tested it on Internet Explorer 5.5 and Netscape 6. More portable libraries are available on the Net, as I discuss at the end of this session.**

Portable Object References

Armed with a set of variables that describe the document object model accurately, you can now create a function that correctly maps ID names to object references. That is, if you have an ID of floater, getObj maps it to document.getElementById('floater').style or the equivalent, based on the DOM, as follows:

```
function getObj(obj)
{
  // cross platform tool for accessing the object style
  var myObj;
  if (useID) myObj = document.getElementById(obj).style;
  else if (useAll) myObj = document.all[obj].style;
  else if (useLayers) myObj = document.layers[obj];
  return myObj;
}
```

Now things are cooking! Instead of worrying about the exact syntax of the object reference, you can use something more akin to the following:

```
OnClick="var mine=getObj('floater');mine.width=200px"
```

This line resizes the floater object to 200 pixels wide in a portable fashion (that is, a manner that works for all browsers).

Even better, here's a simple function that makes creating this code even easier:

```
function setWidth(obj, width)
{
  // set the width for the specified object
  var myObj = getObj(obj);
  myObj.width = width;
}
```

The following example simplifies the preceding line even more:

```
onClick="setWidth('floater',200)"
```

In addition to accessing the `.style` subcontainer, occasionally you need to get to the main object itself, so you need one more function in the library essentials, as follows:

```
function getObjCore(obj)
{
  // same as getObj() except it lets you access the core object
  var myObj;
  if (useID) myObj = document.getElementById(obj);
  else if (useAll) myObj = document.all[obj];
  else if (useLayers) myObj = document.layers[obj];
  return myObj;
}
```

Two more functions demonstrate how easily you can tweak object attributes with these portable object references, as follows:

```
function showObj(obj)
{
  // turn on visibility for the object
  var myObj = getObj(obj);

  myObj.visibility = "visible";
}

function hideObj(obj)
{
  // turn off visibility, hiding the object
  var myObj = getObj(obj);

  myObj.visibility = "hidden";
}
```

Positioning Functions

The first set of functions that you want to create enable you to position objects wherever you want in the window and nudge them a bit in the desired direction.

First off, here's a portable function that positions objects:

```
function moveObj(obj, x, y)
{
  // move the specified object to the x,y coordinates
  var myObj = getObj(obj);

  if (document.moveTo) {
    myObj.moveTo(x,y);
  } else {
    myObj.left = x;
    myObj.top = y;
  }
}
```

Earlier versions of Netscape use the method moveTo, which I use if it's available. Otherwise, the left and top attributes of the object specify its location relative to its parent container.

The moveObj() function is sufficient to write a simple menu stub with a layer element if you think about it. Imagine that you have a menu in its own container that's 100 pixels wide, of which the rightmost 20 pixels are a vertical label. You can hide the menu (other than the vertical label) by specifying moveObj('menu', -80,0) and then activating it by using moveObj('menu', 0,0).

 **I explore this sliding menu later on in Session 25 — stay tuned!**

Given that function, to using relative rather than absolute motion isn't much of a leap. That is, instead of saying "move the object to 100,136," the nudgeObj function enables you to move it up 3 and across 11 by using, say, nudgeObj(obj, 3, 11). Here it is:

```
function nudgeObj(obj, x, y)
{
  // move the object (x,y) pixels from its current loc
  var myObj = getObj(obj);

  if (myObj.moveBy) {
    myObj.moveBy(x, y);
  } else if (MSIE) {
    myObj.pixelLeft += x;
    myObj.pixelTop  += y;
  } else {
    myObj.left = parseInt(myObj.left) + x;
    myObj.top = parseInt(myObj.top) + y;
  }
}
```

In this case, notice that IE requires that you access pixelLeft and pixelTop rather than the W3C DOM elements left and top. Fortunately, doing so is easy to accomplish, as you can see in the listing.

The following pair of functions give you access to the top-left corner coordinates of any object, visible or hidden:

```
function getX(obj)
{
  // return the x coordinate of the object
  var myObj = getObj(obj);

  if (MSIE) {
    x = myObj.pixelLeft;
  } else {
    x = myObj.left;
  }
  return(parseInt(x));
```

```
  }

  function getY(obj)
  {
    // return the y coordinate of the object
    var myObj = getObj(obj);

    if (MSIE) {
      y = myObj.pixelTop;
    } else {
      y = myObj.top;
    }
    return(parseInt(y));
  }
```

Again, you must use `pixelTop` for Internet Explorer, as is shown in this listing.

Before you go bug-eyed typing all this code, please remember that the entire library is on the book's accompanying CD-ROM, and you can also get a copy online at the official Web site for this book at www.intuitive.com/dhtml.

If you're not sure that the routines are working, you can easily test them with the following sequence:

```
moveObj('floater', 100,135);
alert("Floater is now at " + getX('floater') + ", "
      + getY('floater'));
```

In theory, the alert box should show that the `floater` object is at 100,135.

Window and Screen Dimensions

**20 Min.
To Go**

While you're creating functions that provide access to useful characteristics of the browser, following are functions that return the `width` and `height` both of the browser window and of the user's screen:

```
function windowWidth()
{
  // return the width of the browser window
  if (MSIE) {
    width = document.body.clientWidth;
  } else {
    width = window.innerWidth;
  }
  return(parseInt(width));
}

function windowHeight()
{
  // return the width of the browser window
```

```
if (MSIE) {
  height = document.body.clientHeight;
} else {
  height = window.innerHeight;
}
return(parseInt(height));
}
```

The W3C document object model specifies that the dimensions of the window are in units of pixels, so the `window.innerHeight` value is 530px rather than just 530. That's where the `parseInt()` function is useful, because it turns the pixel notation into an integer value. It's not really necessary for the MSIE code, but an integer given to `parseInt` returns itself, so no harm's done.

The other half of this set of functions enables you to determine the user's screen size, again in pixels, as follows:

```
function screenWidth()
{
  // return the width of the users screen
  return(parseInt(window.screen.width));
}

function screenHeight()
{
  // return the height of the users screen
  return(parseInt(window.screen.height));
}
```

The `window.screen` object has a number of interesting values, as listed in Table 20-1.

Table 20-1   *Common Attributes of the* `window.screen` *Object*

Value	Exemplary Value	Description
availHeight	843	Height of screen minus space reserved for OS.
availWidth	1139	Width of screen minus space reserved for OS.
colorDepth	16	Number of colors available (in bits, so 16 bits = 2^{16} colors, or 65,536 colors).
height	870	Absolute screen height, in pixels.
width	1152	Absolute screen width, in pixels.

My main computer — a Macintosh — is set to 870 x 1152 resolution, but the Macintosh operating system eats up a bit of that with its menu bar on the top, so the `availHeight` and `availWidth` attributes show the *useable* dimensions, 843 x 1139.

Curious about your own values? Use the following convenient shortcut to list them:

```
<SCRIPT LANG="JavaScript">
for (value in window.screen) {
```

[handwritten annotation: Language = "javascript"]

```
        document.write(value + " = " + window.screen[value] + "<BR>");
    }
</SCRIPT>
```

Object Dimensions

Another pair of useful functions gets the dimensions of a given object, as follows:

```
function objHeight(obj)
{
  // return the height of the specified object
  var myObj = getObjCore(obj);

  if (myObj.offsetHeight) {
    ht = myObj.offsetHeight;
  } else {
    ht = myObj.clip.height;
  }
  return(parseInt(ht));
}
```

Notice that these functions use the getObjCore function, because the offsetHeight is an attribute of the overall object and not the style subobject.

The objWidth function is a simple mirror of the preceding objHeight function, as follows:

```
function objWidth(obj)
{
  // return the height of the specified object
  var myObj = getObjCore(obj);

  if (myObj.offsetWidth) {
    wd = myObj.offsetWidth;
  } else {
    wd = myObj.clip.width;
  }
  return(parseInt(wd));
}
```

**10 Min.
To Go**

Putting It All Together

Now you have enough functions to create a simple routine that centers an object in the window by calculating its width and the width of the window, as in the following example:

```
function centerObj(obj)
{
  // center the object in the window (horizontally only)
  var y = getY(obj), width = windowWidth();
```

```
    var owidth = objWidth(obj);
    var newX = Math.floor((width - owidth) / 2);
    moveObj(obj, newX, y);
}
```

Another example of a useful function is as follows:

```
function narrow(obj)
{
    var myObj = getObj(obj);
    myObj.width = parseInt(myObj.width) - 10;
}
```

Given an object, the preceding function narrows it by 10 pixels each time it's called. Generalizing it to make the change in width, a parameter sent to the function is quite easy, too.

For Figure 20-1, you must define the `floater` object, as follows:

```
<DIV ID="floater" STYLE="position: absolute;
 border: 1px solid black; padding: 10px; background: #EEF;
 top: 150; left: 200; font: 16pt arial bold; width: 300;">
When you've eliminated the impossible, whatever remains, however
improbable, must be the truth"
<DIV STYLE="font: 9pt arial; font-style: italic;
 text-align:right;">
Sherlock Holmes</DIV>
</DIV>
```

Then a series of onClick elements that you wrap in <SPAN> tags provide easy and entertaining access to all these functions. Ready? It's a lot of HTML, but it's quite straightforward, as follows:

```
<DIV STYLE="text-align: center">

<SPAN orMouseOver="setBgColor('floater', 'red')"
      orClick="setBgColor('floater', 'yellow');moveObj('floater',
300,200)"
      orMouseOut="setBgColor('floater', 'green')">
  click to change floater appearance</SPAN>
or change width:
<SPAN OrClick="narrow('floater')">narrow</SPAN> or
<SPAN OrClick="widen('floater')">widen</SPAN>
<BR>
Nudge floater:
<SPAN OnClick="nudgeObj('floater', 0,-5)">up</SPAN> |
<SPAN OnClick="nudgeObj('floater', 0,5)">down</SPAN> |
<SPAN OnClick="nudgeObj('floater', -5,0)">left</SPAN> |
<SPAN OnClick="nudgeObj('floater', 5,0)">right</SPAN> --
<SPAN OnClick="centerObj('floater')">center</SPAN> --
<SPAN OnClick="alert('floater is at ' + getX('floater') +
  ', ' + getY('floater'))">
where's the floater?</SPAN> and
```

```
<SPAN OnClick="alert('floater is ' + objHeight('floater') +
  ' x ' + objWidth('floater'))">
how big is it?</SPAN>
<BR>
<SPAN OnClick="alert('window itself is ' + windowWidth() +
  ' x ' + windowHeight())">window size</SPAN> and
<SPAN OnClick="alert('screen is ' + screenWidth() + ' x '
  + screenHeight())">screen size</SPAN>
<BR>
Random changes:
<SPAN OnClick="bigWeird('floater')">weird</SPAN> or
<SPAN OnClick="backToNormal('floater')">
not so weird</SPAN>
<BR>
Visibility control:
<SPAN OnClick="showObj('floater')">show</SPAN> |
<SPAN OnClick="hideObj('floater')">hide</SPAN>

</DIV>
```

Instead of my explaining this example further, you should try this one yourself. Figure 20-1 shows how it all looks after the page first loads.

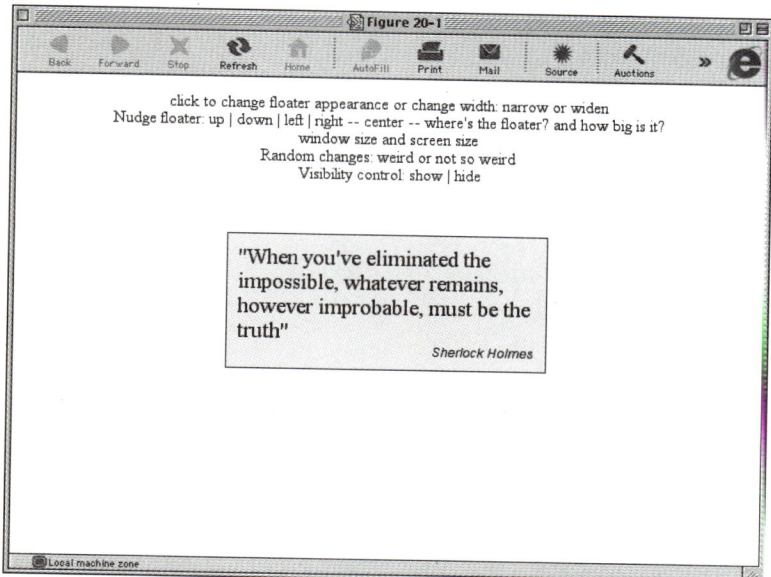

Figure 20-1   *The portable JavaScript library test suite.*

As I mention at the beginning of this session, some very sophisticated cross-browser JavaScript libraries are well worth exploring if you want maximal support for older browsers. They're quite a bit longer than the succinct code that I show here, but the underlying concepts are identical. The one that I suggest you explore to get a sense of how complex a JavaScript library can grow is DynAPI from SourceForge.

DynAPI is online at `http://dynapi.sourceforge.net/`.

Done!

REVIEW

This session develops a cross-platform library that provides the foundation for future examples in this book. Using it helps you develop your own DHTML pages quickly, reliably, and portably.

QUIZ YOURSELF

---

1. Why do you need to write both getObj and getObjCore? (See "Portable Object References.")

2. Given all the functions that I define, write a function that does absolute centering, both vertically and horizontally. (See "Positioning Functions.")

3. Modify the example DHTML listing to enable you to dynamically increase or decrease the padding within the floater container. What do you think happens if your padding is greater than half the width of the object? (See "Putting it all Together.")

4. Which of the site characteristic variables indicates that the browser is W3C DOM-standard compatible? (See "Ascertaining Capabilities.")

5. Why do you need to use parseInt with these functions? (See "Window and Screen Dimensions.")

6. One difference between browsers is the reported width of a similar object. How wide is the floater object in your browser? Why do you think it may vary from the explicit width in the <DIV> statement? (See "Object Dimensions.")

7. Write a function that automatically tucks an object in the top-right corner of the browser. (See "Positioning Functions.")

PART

IV

Saturday Evening

1. True/False: Java is a compiled version of the JavaScript language.
2. True/False: JavaScript and ECMAScript are essentially the same.
3. If you consider the DOM, a typical Web page has how many variables, attributes, or properties associated with it?
4. What popular older browser uses a completely different DOM than even the newest version of the same browser?
5. True/False: One of the major accomplishments of the World Wide Web Consortium is its standardization of JavaScript.
6. Name two of the most helpful JavaScript event handlers for DHTML developers.
7. What's the difference between onMouseDown and onClick?
8. Why are so many JavaScript errors associated with input line zero?
9. You can use two types of comments in JavaScript. List them.
10. For that matter, what's the sequence necessary for comments in HTML?
11. Good coding style hides SCRIPT blocks in HTML comments. Demonstrate how to include a SCRIPT block on an HTML page.
12. Is the following correct? `alert("looper" = looper);`
13. Is the following correct? `alert("looper = " looper);`
14. Is the following correct? `alert("looper = %s", looper);`
15. Is the following correct? `alert("looper = " + looper);`
16. Is (`"53" == 53`) true or false in JavaScript?

17. Browser properties are accessible through the _____ object.

18. What built-in JavaScript function forces the browser to interpret a variable as an integer?

19. What trick do JavaScript programmers use to force the browser to interpret an integer as a string?

20. What method enables you to ascertain whether a @ is present in a variable that stores a possible e-mail address?

☑ Friday

☑ Saturday

☑ **Sunday**

PART

V

Sunday Morning

Graphical Rollovers

Session Checklist

✔ Image containers

✔ Including the JavaScript library

✔ Changing images on user events

✔ Tying events to other elements on the page

**30 Min.
To Go**

S tarting with this session, you're going to take an in-depth look at a wide variety of DHTML effects for your Web site. Invariably, they involve fancy formatting using the CSS you've learned in the last few days — it's Sunday afternoon now, so you've been diligently plugging away with me this entire weekend — and the JavaScript library that you created in the last session.

CD-ROM

Reminder: The library is on the CD-ROM as crashcourse.js; **you can also find it online at the book's Web site:** www.intuitive.com/dhtml/.

Because this book is about Dynamic HTML, the fact that everything appearing static on this book page is less than optimal is probably no surprise to you. Take this situation as a reminder to try out all the examples — and use the View Source capability of your browser — to better understand what's happening and why.

Image Containers

If you go to a Web site such as that of the New York Times online or ESPN.com, the stream of information that the site sends to your browser includes a significant number of different files: the core HTML file, a file for each graphical element, and perhaps external CSS and JavaScript files, too. What may not be apparent is that each element pours into its own container in the document object, essentially building a larger and larger tree of data within the browser memory space. That's what the document object model is — a way to access all the elements of this data tree.

Each image has its own internal object, which is what this chapter concerns. Load a simple page and have a peek by using the following script:

```
<SCRIPT LANG="JavaScript">          language= "javascript"

function showImgInfo(name)
{
  if (document.images) {
    var imgObj = document.getElementById(name);
    for (value in imgObj) {
      document.writeln(value +" = "+ imgObj[value] + "<BR>");
    }
  }
}
</SCRIPT>
<BODY BGCOLOR="white">
<DIV STYLE="border: 6px groove #CCC; padding: 0px;
  font: 14pt arial bold;
  color: #666; text-align: center; width: 500;">
<IMG ID="walrus" NAME="walrus" SRC="Pics/walrus.jpg"
 STYLE="margin-top: 7px;">
<BR>
Large walrus on ice contemplating
the photographer<BR>
- Odobenus rosmarus divergens -
</DIV>
<DIV STYLE="font: 12pt arial">
Location: Bering Sea, Alaska<BR>
Photo Date: 1978 June<BR>
Photographer: Captain Budd Christman, NOAA Corps
</DIV>
<HR>
<SPAN OnClick="showImgInfo('walrus');">info
  about this image</SPAN>
```

The basic page is as shown in Figure 21-1. Notice how the CSS styles (border, type treatment, and alignment) turn this page into a very attractive image-presentation format.

Clicking the info about this image link in the browser reveals a remarkable amount of information about the image — information that is different in the different browsers, alas. In Internet Explorer, for example, the image dimensions and URL are accessible through height, width, and src, respectively. Netscape 6 shows the height and width attributes, but they're set to zeros because they aren't specified in the <IMG> tag itself. You see no trace of the source URL.

The particular attribute of the image object that you tweak for image rollovers is the src attribute.

Figure 21-1   *Walrus on the ice.*

Creating a New Image Container

As images stream in from the server, the Web browser automatically allocates space for the image object, but you need to allocate space manually for rollovers, because you don't retrieve the images until you need them.

Allocation of a new object is conveniently done by using the sensibly named new command. In use, it looks as follows:

```
var myImgObj = new Image();
```

Image() is a built-in function that returns an image container.

After you have the new image, you can set specific attributes of it as with any container, as the following example shows:

```
myImgObj.name = "walrus";
myImgObj.height = 279;
myImgObj.width = 467;
myImgObj.src = "Pics/walrus.jpg";
```

Most JavaScript programmers are lazy, however, and set only the src attribute for rollovers.

Before I go farther, I want to incorporate the JavaScript library from the last session into the example.

Including the JavaScript Library

Earlier in the book, you learn how to include external CSS files by using the LINK instruction. JavaScript is a wee bit trickier to include because not every browser uses the same inclusion format. The simple way to include the external JavaScript file is as follows:

```
<SCRIPT LANGUAGE="JavaScript" SRC="crashcourse.js"></SCRIPT>
```

This method works fine for most browsers.

The problem arises if you're writing to a specific version of JavaScript and want to qualify the inclusion as only for browsers that support that version.

In theory specifying the exact version within the <SCRIPT> tag automatically causes browsers that don't support that version of JavaScript to skip it, as in the following example:

```
<SCRIPT LANGUAGE="JavaScript1.3">
  stuff for JS1.3 compatible browsers only
</SCRIPT>
```

The problem arises with the SRC attribute: Some browsers ignore the LANGUAGE specification in this circumstance and automatically include the separate JavaScript file regardless of what version you specify.

If you're having problems with this example because you're writing super-advanced JavaScript, try the following sneaky solution:

```
<SCRIPT LANGUAGE="JavaScript1.2">
 document.write("<SCRIPT SRC='crashcourse.js'><\/SCRIPT>");
</SCRIPT>
```

This addition specifies that, if the browser supports JavaScript 1.2, it must include the crashcourse.js JavaScript source file.

Although I'm talking about how to frame your <SCRIPT> tags, I need to mention that good form and backward compatibility dictates that you wrap your JavaScript with HTML comment tags so that ancient browsers don't toss their digital cookies.

This task, too, is easily accomplished, as follows:

```
<SCRIPT LANGUAGE="JavaScript">
<!--
  your fancy JavaScript
// -->
</SCRIPT>
```

Recall that the HTML comment sequence is <!-- comment --> and that a double slash // denotes JavaScript comments.

Changing Images on User Events

The first step is to define the new image containers for the rollover. I'm using three different images so that you can get an image on onMouseOver and a different image for onMouseDown. The third image is the default that onMouseOut restores.

Just as the new Image() call creates an image object, an array is a JavaScript object, so it requires you to create a new object, as follows:

```
<SCRIPT LANGUAGE="JavaScript" SRC="crashcourse.js"></SCRIPT>

<SCRIPT LANGUAGE="JavaScript">

walrus = new Array();

walrus[0] = new Image();
walrus[1] = new Image();
walrus[2] = new Image();
```

The first line adds the JavaScript library; then you create a new array that you call walrus and substantiate each of the first three elements with an empty image object.

Now you can assign the critical src value to each element, as follows:

```
walrus[0].src = "Pics/walrus.jpg";
walrus[1].src = "Pics/walrus-caption.jpg";
walrus[2].src = "Pics/walrus-negative.jpg";
```

The following simple function reassigns the src attribute of the image object to the appropriate image:

```
function switchImage(num)
{
  // switch the walrus image to image[num]
  imgObj = document.getElementById("walrus");
  if (document.images) {
    imgObj.src = walrus[num].src;
  }
}
```

10 Min. To Go

The final step is to hook in some code that activates this rollover effect. This step is easy, fortunately, and just requires a few simple modifications to the IMG tag:

```
<IMG ID="walrus" NAME="walrus" SRC="Pics/walrus.jpg"
  STYLE="margin-top: 7px;"
  onMouseOver="switchImage(1);"
  onMouseDown="switchImage(2);"
  onMouseOut="switchImage(0);">
```

Figure 21-2 shows the result of moving the cursor over the graphic, and Figure 21-3 shows the result of clicking and holding the mouse button.

Figure 21-2   `onMouseOver` *adds the caption.*

Figure 21-3   `onMouseDown` *switches the image to a color-inverted "negative" version.*

Nifty, eh? Obviously, you can use this same effect with navigational buttons or any other element. You want a more generic `switchImage` function for such purposes, however, which may look as follows:

```
function switchImage(id, switchTo)
{
  // switch the ID image to switchTo
  imgObj = document.getElementById(id);
  if (document.images) {
    imgObj.src = switchTo.src;
  }
}
```

If you're having problems getting your own rollovers to work, double-check to make sure that you specify both a NAME and ID for the <IMG> tag.

A nice approach to rollovers is to create an array but make the index of the array the same as the element ID. It looks a lot more complicated, but if you're going to put a lot of rollovers on a page, this method is a nice, portable way to do so, as the following example shows:

```
rollovers = new Array();

rollovers["walrus"] = new Array();
rollovers["walrus"]["Over"] = new Image();
rollovers["walrus"]["Out"] = new Image();
rollovers["walrus"]["Down"] = new Image();

rollovers["walrus"]["Over"].src = "Pics/walrus-caption.jpg";
rollovers["walrus"]["Out"].src = "Pics/walrus.jpg";
rollovers["walrus"]["Down"].src = "Pics/walrus-negative.jpg";
```

This sequence takes advantage of what's known as *an array of arrays,* which is a fairly complicated data structure. Notice, too, how this approach exploits the array indexing by name rather than by numeric value to make everything remarkably readable.

The new switcher routine that follows is almost identical to the old, just a *lot* more general purpose:

```
function fancySwitch(id, eventName)
{
  imgObj = document.getElementById(id);
  if (document.images) {
    imgObj.src = rollovers[id][eventName].src;
  }
}
```

Finally, here's how you rewrite the activated image:

```
<IMG ID="walrus" NAME="walrus" SRC="Pics/walrus.jpg"
STYLE="margin-top: 7px;"

onMouseOver="fancySwitch('walrus', 'Over');"
onMouseDown="fancySwitch('walrus', 'Down');"
onMouseOut="fancySwitch('walrus', 'Out');">
```

It requires a bit more typing, but this version is much easier to understand than the earlier one shown in this session.

Tying Events to Other Elements on the Page

You can tie the events to the image itself by putting the onEvent attributes in the HTML, as you've seen earlier in this session. Now I'm going to demonstrate how you can tie these image events to any other element on the page. In this case, I'm replacing the info about this image link with a new one that I call snorff?

```
<SPAN OnMouseOver="switchImage(1);"
      OnMouseDown="switchImage(2);"
      onMouseOut="switchImage(0);">snorff?</SPAN>
```

The screen shots shown here as Figures 21-2 and 21-3 are identical if the cursor is over the snorff? link now, which is pretty nifty.

Done!

REVIEW

This session introduces you to the image object and shows how to use new in JavaScript to create new objects for your own use, whether they're images or arrays. Building on that, I explore a variety of ways to create an array of rollover images and access them through a JavaScript function. Finally, I tie them all together with event handlers that I plug into an <IMG> tag for a true rollover and then into a SPAN element to demonstrate how rollovers can affect other elements on a page.

QUIZ YOURSELF

1. Why do you need the new command in JavaScript? (See "Creating a New Image Container.")
2. Why does the <IMG> object contain different attributes in different browsers? (See "Image Containers.")
3. Write out the necessary characters to hide the following script from older browsers:
   ```
   <SCRIPT LANGUAGE="JavaScript">
   alert("greetings from planet website");
   </SCRIPT>
   ```
   (See "Including the JavaScript Library.")

CHALLENGING

4. Modify the example so that, in addition to the onMouseOver and onMouseDown events, it also opens a hidden layer that contains the information about the picture rather than the picture itself appearing. This task requires synthesizing information from a few previous sessions, too. (See "Changing Images on User Events.")

DHTML Scrolling Text

Session Checklist

✔ Working with frames

✔ Moving the scroller

✔ Repeating commands by using `setInterval`

✔ Adding text frames

✔ Implementing scroll up and scroll down

**30 Min.
To Go**

This session shows you some nifty tricks, including how to use the very helpful `setInterval` function to force timed iteration of events from within JavaScript. After you finish the session, you're going to have a mechanism whereby you can set scroll controls in one frame to move the contents of another frame, a very nice effect if you need to present lots of information.

"Frames? I thought those things were passé?"

Well, in the latest edition of my book *Creating Cool HTML 4 Web Pages*, I talk about frames but comment that they've fallen out of favor because of legacy issues. The reality now, however, is that just about everyone on the Web uses a browser that supports frames, can bookmark frame-based sites correctly (for the most part), and can even print a multi-frame page correctly.

Find out more about my HTML book at www.intuitive.com/coolweb/.

More important, some effects are relatively easy to accomplish in frames – such as the scrolling text example in this session – but are considerably more difficult to accomplish without frames.

You have `ILAYER` and `IFRAME` HTML tags, but the former is Netscape 4 only, and Netscape Navigator 4 doesn't support the latter at all. In the interest of keeping your code to less than the size of a small novel, using regular frames is easier. You can definitely expect to revisit this question in 6–12 months, however, I'm sure.

If you've a good memory, you recall that the Netscape engineers promised that they'd always support ILAYER **when they included it in Navigator 4. Well, times change, alas.**

To get to the end goal of scrolling text, I need to take you on a few sidetracks along the way, but just stay with me. It's worth it. Fair warning: This session may prove a 35- to 40-minute marathon!

Working with Frames

A quick refresher: You create frames by using a FRAMESET tag that specifies how to break the window into individual elements (by row or column) and individual FRAME tags that assign a URL to each of the elements.

To break a Web page into two pieces, one for your site navigation, and one for the main page, the code for the index.html page may look as follows:

```
<FRAMESET ROWS="100,*">
  <FRAME SRC="navigation.html">
  <FRAME SRC="mainpage.html" NAME="main">
</FRAMESET>
```

This code splits the window into a 100-pixel-high frame with navigation.html therein and assigns the remainder of the window as mainpage.html, giving it the mnemonic name of main for later reference.

In the world of the document object model, you run into a bit of a sticky wicket in that the window object for navigation.html no longer includes the contents of either the other frame or of the top-level parent. To make navigation.html's JavaScript access an element in the main frame, therefore, requires a different object reference method, as the following example shows:

```
function getFrameObj(fname, id)
{
  // get the object of the ID in the specified frame name
  var myObj;

  if (useID) {
    myObj = top[fname].document.getElementById(id).style;
  } else if (useAll) {
    myObj = top[fname].document.all[id].style;
  } else if (useLayers) {
    myObj = top[fname].document.layers[id];
  }
  return ( myObj );
}
```

This code is an exact mirror of the earlier getObj function that enables you to access attributes in the current window in a browser-neutral fashion. The difference is that it doesn't use a line like the following to access the specified object:

```
document.getElementById(id).style
```

to jump one level up the DOM hierarchical tree and access the top object, which is the *root* of the DOM tree. There you can use the frame name itself as an array index. After you add this prefix, the rest is identical to an in-window reference.

If you have a function that returns the style subobject, you also need a function that returns the core object, for portability. Again, it's a mirror of the getObjCore function with the top[fname] prefix added to each reference, as follows:

```
function getFrameObjCore(fname, id)
{
  // get the core object of the ID in the specified frame
  var myObj;

  if (useID) {
    myObj = top[fname].document.getElementById(id);
  } else if (useAll) {
    myObj = top[fname].document.all[id];
  } else if (useLayers) {
    myObj = top[fname].document.layers[id];
  }
  return ( myObj );
}
```

By using the sample <FRAMESET> tag that I show you earlier, changing the background color of the DIV element 'changeme' is something that you can accomplish in a W3C-compatible browser with the following line:

```
top[main].document.getElementById('changeme').style.backgroundColor="blue"
;
```

Or, more generally, you can use the following:

```
var myObj = getFrameObj('main', 'changeme');
myObj.backgroundColor = "blue";
```

Make sense?

To make life easier, I slipped the getFrameObj and getFrameObjCore functions into the crashcourse.js file, so if you've already looked at it from your CD-ROM, you had a sneak preview.

Moving the Scroller

If you're okay with seeing scroll bars in individual frames, you discover that scrolling is quite easy. (More so than the cloyingly obvious "Well, yeah, use the scroll bar, dude!" answer, that is!)

The W3C document object method specifies three scrolling methods that you can apply to a window object: `scroll`, `scrollBy` and `scrollTo`. They enable you to scroll to a specified x,y position or a +x,+y change from the current position. Confusingly, `scroll` and `scrollBy` offer the same functionality.

Within the same window these methods are a breeze to use, even without frames. To create a quick jump-to-top link, for example, just add the following anywhere on your page:

```
<A HREF="#" OnClick="window.scrollTo(0,0)">jump to top</A>
```

To scroll down one line, the following tag does the trick:

```
<A HREF="#" OnClick="window.scroll(0,1)">down one line</A>
```

You can now logically conclude that you can place on your page a floating, absolutely positioned object that offers scroll controls, as does the following example:

```
<DIV STYLE="position: fixed; top: 0px; left: 0px;
  background-color: black; padding: 3px; color: white">
<A HREF="#" OnClick="window.scrollBy(0,1)"
  STYLE="color: white">down</A> |
 <A HREF="#" OnClick="window.scrollBy(0,-1)"
  STYLE="color: white">up</A> |
  <A HREF="#" OnClick="window.scrollTo(0,0)"
  STYLE="color: white">top</A> |
  <A HREF="#" OnClick="window.scrollTo(0,99999)"
  STYLE="color: white">bottom</A>
</DIV>
```

Well, the first problem with this code is that `position: fixed` doesn't work in Netscape 6, and Internet Explorer 5.5 has the following bug: If you have hypertext links within a fixed layer, the scrolling controls themselves scroll with the underlying content, so although you can still *see* the link names, the actual clickable part of it scrolls off-screen. Not too useful!

You face another problem, too: Netscape 6 has a very buggy implementation of the `scroll` methods — sometimes they don't work at all and other times they work but immediately snap back to the original scroll position. Sporadically, they work just fine.

This change isn't sufficient for our needs, particularly if you couple it with the fact that in-window scrolling is disabled if you specify SCROLLING="no" in the <FRAME> tag to disable the display of the scroll bar in Netscape Navigator 4 and Netscape 6.

So you need to find a different solution!

Repeating Commands by Using setInterval

You now know how to access frame elements, and I detoured you slightly to see the scroll methods, but even after you finally achieve your own scrolling solution, a characteristic of it is going to be new: It needs to repeat until an event stops. Specifically, if you click an up or down arrow to scroll, what you're really doing is starting the following loop:

```
while mouse button is down { incrementally scroll(direction) }
```

So to make sure that your solution meets this logical functionality, you need to learn about a very cool function built in to JavaScript: setInterval.

Given a function and a delay in milliseconds, setInterval waits the specified time and then automatically invokes the function. Sounds simple, but it's the magic behind all sorts of cool DHTML features. You find a MoveTo function in the crashcourse.js library, for example, but what if, instead of just zipping the element to its new location, you could visibly slide it there?

The following section describes how to accomplish that trick.

Building slideObj

The first step in our solution is to define some shared variables that both define the default behavior and enable the two functions that you need to share some values conveniently, as follows:

```
var delayTime = 5;    // milliseconds. Smaller = faster
var skipFactor = 2;   // smaller = more steps

var deltaX=0, deltaY=0, x, y;   // shared across both functions
```

As you can see, the delayTime is a millisecond timer. If you want things to move incredibly slowly, therefore, at one step per second, you can use delayTime = 1000 — but I'm sure that looks really bizarre. The skipFactor is the number of pixels to move on each step, in whatever direction is necessary. Then deltaX and deltaY are going to hold the skipFactor value that moves the object one step in the desired direction, and x, y are the current location of the object.

Now take a look at the wrapper function, in its first, basic form:

```
function slideObj(obj, newX, newY)
{
  // move the object to the new coordinates, skipFactor pixels
  // at a time

  x = getX(obj), y = getY(obj); // identify the current spot

  if (x < newX) deltaX = skipFactor;
  if (x > newX) deltaX = -skipFactor;
  if (y < newY) deltaY = skipFactor;
  if (y > newY) deltaY = -skipFactor;

  doSlide(obj, newX, newY);
}
```

This is straightforward JavaScript: It identifies the current location of the object and then computes the deltaX and deltaY values based on whether the newly requested position is greater than or less than the current x,y position. Finally, it invokes the looper routine doSlide, passing along the given parameters.

 Notice how good variable names and extensive comments help make the JavaScript quite easily understood. This discipline is a critical skill to develop as you learn more about DHTML and JavaScript scripting.

The doSlide function is a little bit more tricky, as the following example shows:

```
function doSlide(obj, newX, newY)
{
  // do the actual slide. Apps should call slideObj.

  if (x == newX) deltaX = 0; // reached spot on x axis
  if (y == newY) deltaY = 0; // reached spot on y axis

  if (deltaX + deltaY == 0) return; // done!

  x += deltaX; // increment element
  y += deltaY; // by delta values

  moveObj(obj, x, y); // and do the actual move

  cmd = "doSlide('" + obj + "'," + newX + ", " + newY + ")";
  setTimeout(cmd, delayTime); // loop again after delayTime
}
```

The heart of doSlide is the increment of the x,y coordinates, based on the deltaX and deltaY values, and then the call to moveObj in the crashcourse.js library.

After this function completes the current step, it uses the setTimeout function to schedule another call to doSlide in delayTime milliseconds. Because setTimeout expects a regular JavaScript command, you build it into the cmd string variable.

Suppose that slideObj is called as follows:

```
slideObj('floater', 100,30)
```

If so, the calls to setTimeout look like as follows:

```
setTimeout(doSlide('floater',100,30), delayTime)
```

Another timing function, setInterval, requests that a recurring event is invoked every *delay* milliseconds. I explore that function in the next session. The difference between the two is that setTimeout makes the requested JavaScript call once, while setInterval does it over and over, until you tell it to stop.

Here's how you can use slideObj with some DHTML:

```
<SCRIPT LANGUAGE="JavaScript" SRC="crashcourse.js"></SCRIPT>
```

First, include your JavaScript library in the HTML source with an external link and then add the following:

```
<BODY STYLE="background-color: #EEE">
```

```
<DIV STYLE="position: absolute; background-color: #060;
  font: 11pt Times, Times Roman, serif;
  padding: 9px; width: 300px; height: 180px; overflow: hidden;
  color: #FFF; top: 0; left: 0" ID="floater">
And then, just as they were sure that all was safe, the
dog leapt from the bushes. Holmes immediately noticed
that its jowls were flecked with foam, but with startling rapidity
the hound was upon them, snarling and whipping its head wildly
from side to side.<P>"Methinks it's time to begone, Watson"
Holmes said with less than his usual calm tone, and they ran
across the moors, fending off the rabid cur with every step.
<P>The dog chased them, got tired, and collapsed on the peat
to have a rather peaceful nap.
</DIV>
```

This code creates a moveable object for experimentation. Notice the overflow: hidden attribute, which ensures that, if the box is too small for the text, the overflow vanishes rather than spilling over onto the page.

 **Possible values for** overflow **are** auto, hidden, scroll, **and** visible, **which automatically manages the overflow, hides it, pops up scroll bars if needed, or lets it spill out onto the page, respectively.**

Now you need to add a couple calls to slideObj, after an admittedly lazy HTML way to push the content down below the floater workspace, as follows:

```
<BR><BR><BR><BR><BR><BR><BR><BR><BR><BR><BR><BR><BR><BR>
  <!-- don't get covered up! -->

The floating excerpt is not exactly from the Hound of the
Baskervilles, but it's inspired by the story!
<P>

<SPAN OnClick="slideObj('floater', 200, 0)">slide right</SPAN>
or
<SPAN OnClick="slideObj('floater', 0,0)">slide left</SPAN>
```

Figure 22-1 shows the end result of clicking the slide right link after the text box completes its smooth, tranquil glide across the screen.

One necessary improvement to slideObj

This code does have one problem: What happens if you specify an odd endpoint, and the object is currently on an even-numbered spot on the relevant axis? In other words, say that the 'floater' object is at 0,0, and you request slideObj('floater', 1,1). Do you know what's going to happen? The text window dutifully slides off to the right and downward until the browser crashes, because x + deltaX never equals newX. (Remember that the skipInterval is 2.)

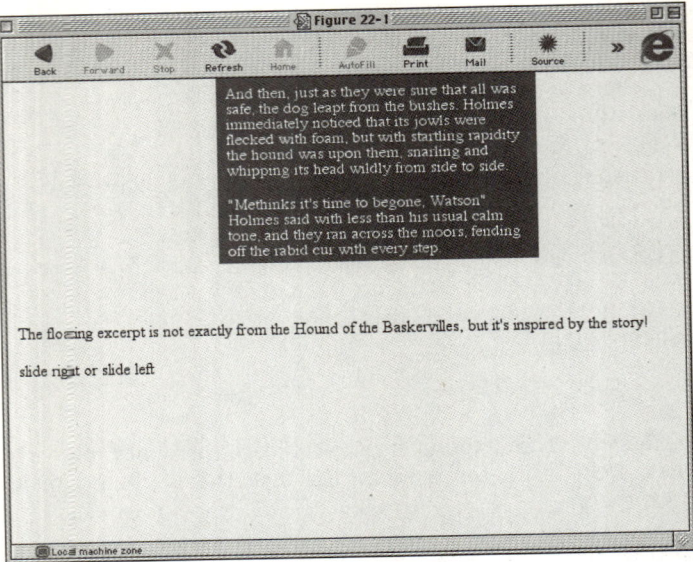

Figure 22-1   *The text box glides smoothly across the screen.*

You have two ways to solve this problem. One way is to always set the `skipInterval` to 1, but adding the following test to `slideObj` is a more sophisticated solution and enables the function to support any skip value:

```
if (skipFactor > 1) {
  if ((newX % skipFactor != 0) || (newY % skipFactor != 0)) {
    alert("slideObj can't move object to a spot that " +
    isn't\nan even multiple of the skipFactor (" +
    skipFactor + ").\nMove cancelled.");
    return;
  }
}
```

If you specify a bad parameter, the function gives you an error message, as shown in Figure 22-2. (The % in the code is the remainder symbol. It's the value remaining after you divide the numerator into the denominator, so 5 % 2 = 1 and 14 % 6 = 2.)

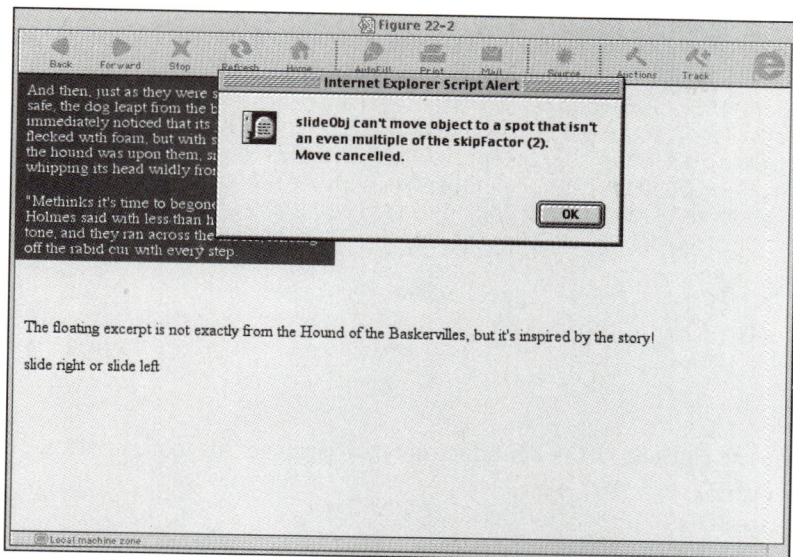

Figure 22-2 *Specify an incompatible endpoint and* slideObj *complains.*

Implementing Scroll Up and Scroll Down

10 Min.
To Go

The problem that I describe in the preceding section is quite a sidetrack, but it demonstrates how setInterval is a great tool in your JavaScript toolkit. Time, however, to get back to the frame-scrolling problem!

By using the <FRAMESET> HTML, you can create a document that displays multiple frames, and by using the top[fname] reference (which is part of getFrameObj), you can access specific characteristics of a different framed element than the one you're in.

Now I'm going to put it all together.

First off, here's the top-level frame definition:

```
<FRAMESET ROWS="90,*,35" BORDER=0
 FRAMEBORDER="NO" FRAMEMARGIN=0>
  <FRAME SRC=top-banner.html SCROLLING="no">
  <FRAME SRC=main-section.html NAME="main" SCROLLING="no">
  <FRAME SRC=scroll-controls.html>
</FRAMESET>
```

Notice that I assign the main frame the name main. That point proves important in the next code snippet, as you'll see!

The top-banner is straightforward HTML with some CSS sprinkled in, so I invite you to check it out on the CD-ROM rather than take the space to show it here.

The `main-section.html` file is also simple, as the following code shows:

```
<DIV ID="scrollregion"
 STYLE="border-left: 5px double #99F;
    border-right: 5px double #99F; padding: 4px;
    position: absolute; top: 5px; font-family: arial;
    width: 500; left: 100; background-color: white;">
I had called upon my friend Sherlock Holmes upon the second
morning after Christmas, with the intention of wishing him

lots of stuff omitted to save space and a few trees

<I>... continues ...</I>
</DIV>
<BR><BR><BR><BR><BR>
```

Notice here that the content `<DIV>` container gets an assigned ID, too: `scrollregion`. Now for the fun part!

Defining the scroll universe

To start, I add a wave of global variables, as follows:

```
var currentLoc = 4, topLoc = 4, maxScrollValue = 0;
var scrollIncrement = N6 ? 7 : 4;
var scrollIt = 0, goUp = 1, goDown = 0;
var otherFrameHeight = (90 + 35), navBarHeight = 75;
var myObj, myObjCore;
```

To keep track of where you are with scrolling, you use `currentLoc` as your y offset (`currentLoc = 0` means that you're at the very top of the document), set the topmost point just a few pixels below the top edge of the frame, and then define a variable called `maxScrollValue`, which holds the y value for when you scroll to the very bottom of the content.

The `scrollIncrement` is conditionally set to sidestep a problem with Netscape 6's slower rewrites of content than IE's: You just make the increment a bit bigger to help things scroll faster. The other variables of interest here help you deal with another N6 problem: You have no easy way to ascertain the exact height of an individual frame in a multiframe design. Instead, you must calculate the height of the browser, subtract the height of the other frames (90 for the title bar and 35 for the scroll elements on the bottom), and then subtract another small amount for the height of the navigational elements.

Next, the wrapper routine that calls from within the DHTML to enable the scrolling regions is as follows:

```
function scroll(fname, id, dir)
{
  myObj=getFrameObj(fname, id);
  myObjCore=getFrameObjCore(fname, id);

  scrollIt = 1;
```

```
    currentLoc = parseInt(myObj.top);

    // first let's get height of the scrollable contents
    if (myObjCore.offsetHeight != null) {
      maxScrollValue = myObjCore.offsetHeight;
    } else {
      maxScrollValue = myObjCore.clip.height;
    }

    // now factor out the visible portion
    if (useAll) {       // MSIE
      maxScrollValue -= parent.document.all[fname].height;
    }
    else { // NS6 and/or W3C DOM, doesn't have visible height, so
           // we'll have to calculate it as shown.
      var visiblePixels = (window.outerHeight -
      otherFrameHeight - navBarHeight);
      maxScrollValue -= visiblePixels;
    }

    // finally, switch it to a negative value for later tests
    maxScrollValue = - maxScrollValue;

    doScroll(dir);

    return false;
}
```

Extensive comments helps this code remain at least semi-understandable . . . I hope! In essence, the `maxScrollValue` gets calculated each time that a scrolling event starts — in case the window is resized in the interim — and the formula is as follows:

scrollable contents - window size - other frames - navbar height

You can see most of that formula in the line that computes `visiblePixels`. The good news is that IE uses a nonstandard height value that correctly instantiates to the height of the specified frame, enabling you to sidestep this calculation and simply use the following formula to calculate the bottom point:

scrollable contents - viewable contents height

The final step is to invoke `doScroll` to loop and do the actual scrolling of the frame on-screen, as the following section describes.

The core function: doScroll

The heart of the frame scrolling solution is doScroll, as the following example shows:

```
function doScroll(dir)
{
  if (scrollIt == 1) {
    if ((dir == goUp) && (currentLoc <= topLoc)) {
```

```
    currentLoc += scrollIncrement;
    if (currentLoc > topLoc) {
      currentLoc = topLoc;
      scrolling = 0;
    }
    myObj.top = currentLoc;
  }
  else if ((dir == goDown)&&(currentLoc >= maxScrollValue)) {
    currentLoc -= scrollIncrement;
    if (currentLoc < maxScrollValue) {
      currentLoc = maxScrollValue;
      scrolling = 0;
    }
    myObj.top = currentLoc;
  }

  nextcmd = 'doScroll(' + dir + ')';
  setTimeout(nextcmd, 0);
  }
}
```

This function checks what direction to scroll and then ensures that the user hasn't already scrolled to the limit in that direction by comparing the currentLoc against either topLoc or maxScrollValue. If scrolling is necessary, myObj.top gets a new value, which the browser implements by actually moving the visible portion of the scrolling region.

After that process ends, the function invokes itself again with setTimeout until it finishes scrolling.

One of the two final pieces is a stopScroll function to ensure scrolling ends after you release the mouse button and the DHTML to actually enables you to scroll up and down, as follows:

```
function endScroll()
{
  scrollIt = 0;
}
```

The other is the DHTML, which the following example shows:

```
<SPAN STYLE="color: #999"
 onMouseDown="scroll('main', 'scrollregion', goUp)"
 onMouseUp="endScroll()">scroll up</SPAN> |

<SPAN STYLE="color: #999"
 onMouseDown="scroll('main', 'scrollregion', goDown)"
 onMouseUp="endScroll()">scroll down</SPAN>
```

Figure 22-3 shows the result after the window scrolls up just a wee bit. I encourage you to try this example yourself. It's quite nifty!

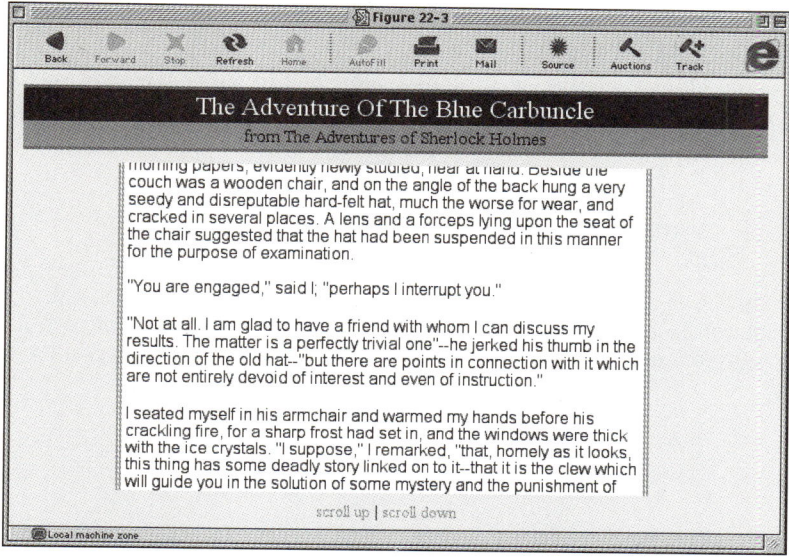

Figure 22-3 *Clicking the* `scroll` *down link moves the text down just a bit.*

The JavaScript is also saved as `scroller.js` on the CD-ROM. Make sure that you set the `otherFrameHeight` as necessary before you apply it to your own DHTML.

Done!

REVIEW

This super-long session enables you to really dig into the cool parts of the DHTML/JavaScript teaming, explaining the `setInterval` timer and showing how to use it to animate objects on-screen. Building on that, I explore how to store frames-based layouts in the document object model and how to access their attributes through JavaScript. It all fits together in the complex off-frame scrolling example that I present — an example that demonstrates a variety of sophisticated JavaScript coding techniques and solves a tricky problem, too. I had fun with this chapter I hope that you did, too!

QUIZ YOURSELF

1. What's the story with `<ILAYER>` and why isn't it a viable solution for scrolling a region of information within a DHTML page? (See introductory paragraphs.)
2. What's the most important attribute to remember in the `<FRAME>` tag if you're going to use the scrolling tool? (See "Working with Frames.")
3. Why can't you use `getObj` and `getObjCore` with frames? (See "Working with Frames.")

4. What's the difference between `setInterval` and `setTimeOut`? (See "Repeating Commands by Using setInterval.")

5. What situation do you sidestep by wrapping an alert box in multiple conditionals in `slideObj`? (See "Building slideObj.")

6. What's the purpose of `otherFrameHeight` and `navBarHeight`? (See "The core function: doScroll.")

CHALLENGING

7. Build a page that uses columns of data rather than rows and then hook scroll controls in one column to the content frame in another. Think carefully about what settings to assign `otherFrameHeight` and `navBarHeight`. (See "The core function: doScroll.")

Clocks and Calendars

Session Checklist

✔ Getting the time and date

✔ Floating clocks and other date tricks

✔ Building a calendar

**30 Min.
To Go**

The last session was the toughest so far in the book, but I'm hoping that you haven't taken the "crash" in crash course literally! This session not only is a little bit easier, but it's also fun and full of neat ideas to make your Web site more fun. I show you a very easy way to enable people to specify their birthday, for example, and then to find out — in one JavaScript statement — what day of the week they were born.

The time's about ripe, so go to it!

Getting the Time and Date

Your computer's been hiding a secret from you for a long time. That secret is that it keeps track of time in milliseconds, the same time unit that the JavaScript `setInterval` function (which I discussed last session) uses.

Splitting a second into 1,000 units, a millisecond proves a nice value for a variety of operating system functions, but its use also means that you need to take some extra steps to make the date easily readable to your visitors.

Getting the time and date in JavaScript couldn't be easier: Simply substantiate a variable with a call to `Date()`, as follows:

```
var rightNow = new Date();
```

The output may not turn out exactly as you want, however. Take, for example the following simple function:

```
function showTime()
{
    var rightNow = new Date();
```

```
document.write("It's " + rightNow);
}
```

This function results in the following output:

```
It's Tue Jun 19 06:52:27 PST 2001
```

The good news is that a number of different methods associate with a date object that enable you to very easily extract individual elements to produce a more attractive date or split out just the current time.

Check out, for example, the following code:

```
hours   = rightNow.getHours();
minutes = rightNow.getMinutes();
seconds = rightNow.getSeconds();

function getTime() {
  var myTime = hours + ":" + minutes + ":" + seconds;
  document.write("It's " + myTime);
}
```

This time, the output consists only of the fields that you want, but you still see a bit of a problem in the format, as the following line shows:

```
It's 7:2:3
```

You probably normally see times appear as a one- or two-digit hours value, followed by two-digit minute and second values — 7:02:03 rather than 7:2:3.

The capability for variables to easily switch from numeric to string values proves a real blessing in this situation, as the following example shows:

```
hours = "" + ((hours > 12)? hours-12 : hours);
minutes = ((minutes < 10)? "0" : "") + minutes;
seconds = ((seconds < 10)? "0" : "") + seconds;
```

This code fixes the 24-hour clock to go from 1 to 12 and then 1 to 12 again; then it ensures that you get a leading zero for both the minutes and seconds values.

One more line, as follows, and you get the a.m./p.m. value, too:

```
amPm = (hours >= 12)? "pm" : "am";
```

Now take one more pass at the getTime function, as follows:

```
function getTime() {
  var myTime = hours + ":" + minutes + ":" + seconds +
    " " + amPm;
  document.write("It's " + myTime);
}
```

This code produces the following output:

```
It's 7 02:06 pm.
```

Great!

Extracting the Current Date

20 Min. To Go

The date is a bit trickier because the Date methods return numeric values for the month and weekday, starting with zero (that is, January is month 0, according to JavaScript). Here's a solution that uses an external array to store month names and day names and then access them directly:

```
var monthNames = new Array("January","February","March",
    "April","May","June","July","August","September",
    "October","November","December");

var dayNames = new Array("Sunday","Monday","Tuesday",
    "Wednesday","Thursday","Friday","Saturday","Sunday");

function getDate() {
  // return date in Dayname, DD Month, Year format
  var myDate = dayNames[rightNow.getDay()] + ", " +
      rightNow.getDate() + " " +
      monthNames[rightNow.getMonth()] + ", " +
      rightNow.getYear();
  return myDate;
}
```

You can see that starting the array indexing at zero neatly enables us to ignore the problem of month values and day-of-week values starting at zero, too. This function actually returns a date string that the following exemplifies:

```
Monday, 24 June, 2001
```

To make things more portable, however, I'd make one tweak to the preceding getDate function to ensure no problems with Y2K (e.g., the four-digit year being 101 instead of 2001, 102 instead of 2002, etc), as follows:

```
function getYear() {
  var yr = today.getYear();
  if (yr < 1900) yr += 1900;
  return yr;
}
```

Add the preceding example and replace rightNow.getYear() with getYear() in the getDate function, and you're fine.

Notice that you can load values into an array as part of the object-creation process with the new statement. This shortcut is an important one to remember.

Before I go further, take a look at the most useful of the many, many different Date() methods that JavaScript defines, as shown in Table 23-1.

Table 23-1   *Some of the Most Useful Date-Related Methods*

Method	Description
getDate	The day of month (range 1-31).
getDay	The day of week (range 0-6).
getFullYear	Return four-digit year value.
getHours	Hours unit (0-23).
getMinutes	Minutes unit (0-59).
getMonth	Month of year (range 0-11).
getSeconds	Seconds unit (0-59).
getTime	Number of milliseconds since reference date (1 January, 1970).
getYear	Years unit (may return year as 1900 on older systems).
setDate	Specify new month in date object (range 0-11).
setFullYear	Specify new year (4-digit) in date object.
setHours	Specify new hours value in date object (range 0-23).
setMinutes	Specify new minutes value in date object (range 0-59).
setMonth	Specify new month in date object (same as setDate).
setSeconds	Specify new seconds in date object.
setTime	Specify time for date object in milliseconds (see getTime).
setYear	Specify new year in date object. (See note in getYear.)
toLocaleString	Return locale-based date/time string (most useful for switching date format strings to local conventions and languages, as the individual user specifies).

Figure 23-1 shows a sample page with some of the different date functions that the preceding table demonstrates. The following DHTML generates the bottom bar (and I'm also showing a few lines from the end of the file just before the <DIV>, too):

```
lots of stuff omitted

We heard the door open, a few hurried words, and
then quick steps upon the linoleum. Our own door flew
open, and a lady, clad in some dark-colored stuff,
with a black veil, entered the room.
<P>
<I>continues...</I>
<DIV STYLE="position: relative; top: 0; left: 0;
```

```
background: #600; text-align: center;
font: 9pt sans-serif;padding: 3px; width: 99%;
color: #C99;margin-top: 25px;">
<SCRIPT LANGUAGE="JavaScript">
document.write("Site last updated on " + getDate() +
" at " + getTime());
</SCRIPT>
</DIV>
```

Did you notice the `sans-serif` type-family specification rather than a specific typeface name? This example also demonstrates that you can embed `<SCRIPT>` elements in your Web pages to place JavaScript-based results where you need them on the page.

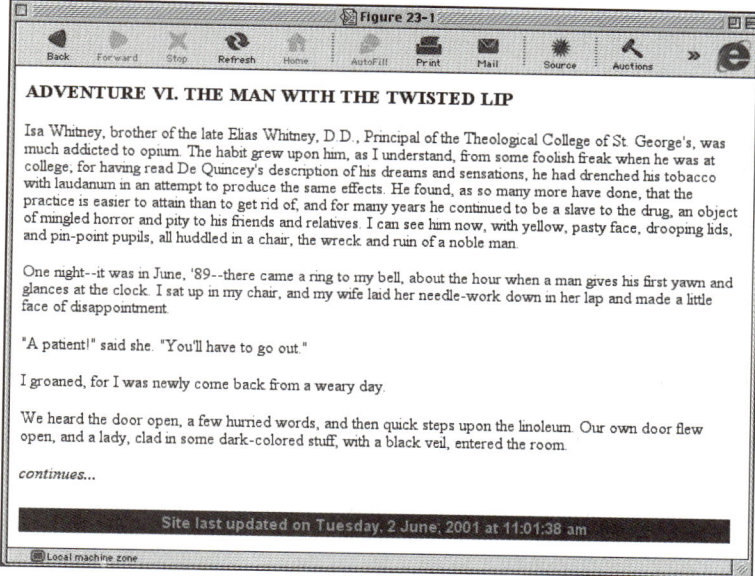

Figure 23-1 *Adding date and time values to your Web page.*

This stuff is pretty sneaky; the page displays a last-updated value that's always, by coincidence, the current date and time!

To make things a bit subtler, you can subtract a day from the current date by using the following JavaScript sequence:

```
var oneDay = 1000 * 60 * 60 * 24;

function backUpADay() {
  // changes the rightNow time to subtract 24 hours
  // remember, time is computed in milliseconds...
  rightNow.setTime(rightNow.getTime() - oneDay);
}
```

As a result, the embedded JavaScript block changes to the following:

```
<SCRIPT LANGUAGE="JavaScript">
 backUpADay();
 document.write("Site last updated on " + getDate() +
 " at " + getTime());
</SCRIP>
```

This example offers a straightforward solution — and one that foreshadows some of our other date tricks.

Floating Clocks and Other Date Tricks

Before I talk about creating a clock that keeps track of the time, I need to talk about a few more date functions.

First off, are you curious about what day of the week you were born? The following function returns the dayname of any date that you specify. Conveniently, you can take advantage of the fact that you can specify a date as you instantiate a date object here, too, as follows:

```
function whatDayWasIt(dateString)
{
   // given a date string, return the day name
   var myDate = new Date(dateString);
   return( dayNames[myDate.getDay()] );
}
```

Now I'm going to take you on a quick side trip into interacting with FORM elements on a Web page so that you can create a page that enables you to type a date, click tell me, and see the result appear on the page, okay?

Tying the whatDayWasIt function into a FORM

I'm jumping ahead a little bit, but all elements of a form are accessible through the document object model. Start with your input form, as follows:

```
<FORM NAME="f1">
Enter date here:
<INPUT TYPE=text NAME="yourDate" ID="yourDate">
<INPUT TYPE=button VALUE="What day was that?"
 onClick="figureDay()">
<HR>
That was a:
<INPUT TYPE=text NAME="dayname" ID="dayname" WIDTH=20
 STYLE="font-weight: bold; background-color: #EEF;"><BR>
</CENTER>
</FORM>
```

Notice what's missing here? The *Submit* button. Because you're scripting everything, instead of a Submit, you can tie the date calculation to the onClick event of a generic button that you specify by using TYPE=button. Each field also needs an ID, as you can see.

To access a particular field value, use the following line:

```
document.form[formnum].fieldname.value
```

As shown here specifically for this code example:

```
var userDate = document.forms[0].yourDate.value;
```

You have a lot of other ways to access `form` **objects, as I explore in Session 24, coming up next.**

You can assign this value attribute a specific value, too, so that the `figureDay()` function proves incredibly short, as the following example shows:

```
function figureDay()
{
  var userDate = document.forms[0].yourDate.value;
  document.forms[0].dayname.value = whatDayWasIt(userDate);
}
```

Figure 23-2 shows on what day of the week my daughter was born. I enter her birthday in a standard date format and then click the What Day Was That button, and the dayname automatically appears in the bottom field of the form.

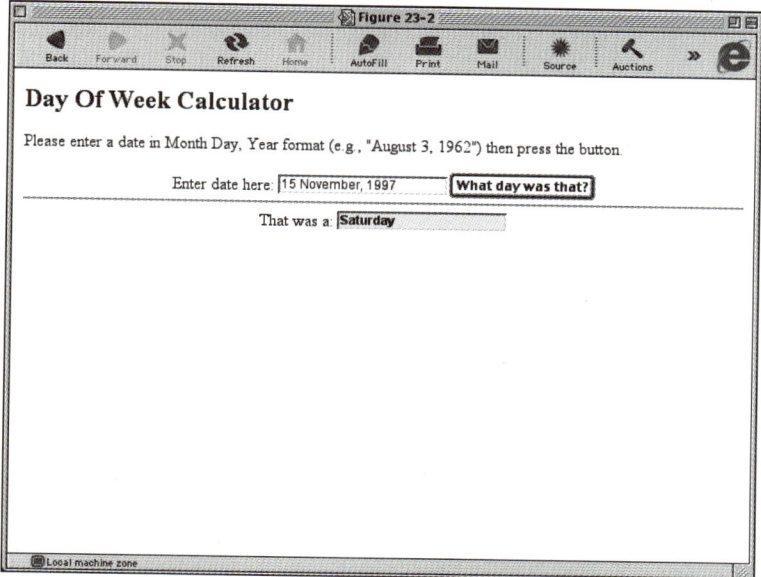

Figure 23-2 *JavaScript automatically fills in a field on this form after you enter information and click the button.*

I want to show you one more fun function to play with before I jump into calendars.

Days between dates

Whether you're using a countdown timer or a simple calculation of how many days you've been alive, computing the number of days between two dates is interesting and useful, and the following example shows you how:

```
function daysBetweenDates(d1, d2)
{
  var date1 = new Date(d1);
  var date2 = new Date(d2);
  var msecsBetween = Math.abs(date1.getTime() -
      date2.getTime());
  return ( msecsBetween / oneDay );
}
```

The Math.abs() method returns the absolute value of a calculation, enabling you to specify a date in the past or future: It's still the same number of days between the two dates, after all.

File fig-23-2a.html **on the CD-ROM contains a simple form that enables you to explore the preceding** daysBetweenDates **function. By the way, in using the preceding code, I find out that I've been alive 14,183 days, as of today.**

Floating clocks

**10 Min.
To Go**

I want to return to the clock example one more time to show you how setTimeout can enable you to create a clock that continually updates itself on a DHTML page.

First off, you need to use a completely self-contained clock function, as in the following example:

```
function clock(withSeconds) {
  var now = new Date();

  var hours = now.getHours();
  hours = (hours > 12) ? hours - 12 : hours;

  var minutes = now.getMinutes();
  minutes = (minutes < 10) ? "0" + minutes : minutes;

  var seconds = now.getSeconds();
  seconds = (seconds < 10) ? "0" + seconds : seconds;

  var amPm = (hours > 11) ? "pm" : "am";

  if (withSeconds)
    dispTime = hours + ":" + minutes + ":" + seconds +
```

```
        " " + amPm;
    else
      dispTime = hours + ":" + minutes + " " + amPm;

    if (document.getElementById) {
      document.getElementById("clockspace").innerHTML
        = dispTime;
    }
    setTimeout("clock("+withSeconds+")",
      withSeconds ? 1000 : 60000);
}
```

You see a lot going on in the preceding example, but the first dozen lines or so should look familiar when compared to earlier examples in this session. The `withSeconds` variable enables you to control whether to include seconds in the display, and the `getElementById` reference to the element gives you a very portable solution that enables you to assign the clock to a `<DIV>` or `<SPAN>`. Finally, `setTimeout` calls the `clock` function over and over again, with a delay of the milliseconds that you specify: either every one second (1,000 milliseconds) or every 60 seconds (60,000 milliseconds).

You must invoke the `clock` function so that it starts keeping track of time. You can do so within the initial JavaScript block, but more traditionally, you tie this function to the `onLoad` event in the `<BODY>` tag, as follows:

```
<BODY onLoad="clock(1)">
```

Finally, here's a line of text in the Web page that just happens to mention the current time:

```
The current time is
<SPAN ID="clockspace"></SPAN>
and it magically stays up-to-date. Amazing, eh?
```

Figure 23-3 shows this line as it appears in a Web browser. Every second, it updates to the correct time, as if by magic.

Change the `<SPAN>` to give it absolute positioning and you can stick a floating clock on the page, which remains in view even as the user scrolls to read the material thereon.

Building a Calendar

Building a calendar is straightforward, because you can now ascertain the current day of the week and the current month. So jump right in with the following code:

```
var dayCounts = new Array(31, 28, 31, 30, 31, 30, 31,
    31, 30, 31, 30, 31);
var monthNames = new Array("January","February","March",
    "April","May","June","July","August","September",
    "October","November","December");
```

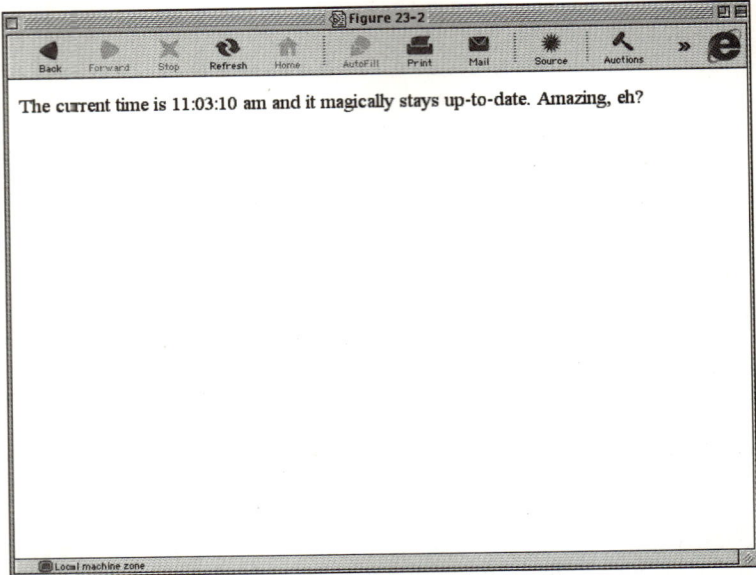

Figure 23-3 *Your inline clock keeps track of the time!*

First off, I present a couple arrays to help make calculations easy (in the preceding example) and then I get right into the function itself, as follows:

```
function showMonth()
{
  // show the month in a compact table view
  var day, firstDay, theDay = 1, daysInMonth, now = new Date();

   // now let's figure out what day of week the first day of the month was
  firstDayObj = new Date(now.getYear(), now.getMonth(), 1);
  firstDay    = firstDayObj.getDay(); // day of week of first day of month
  today       = now.getDate();
  daysInMonth = dayCounts[now.getMonth()];

  document.writeln("<TABLE BORDER=1 CELLPADDING=2 " +
    "CELLSPACING=1 STYLE='font: 18pt Arial Bold'><TR>");
  document.writeln("<TH COLSPAN=7 BGCOLOR='yellow'>" +
    monthNames[now.getMonth()] + " " +
    now.getFullYear() + "</TH></TR>");

  document.writeln("<TR>");

  // first week is special: it might have blank days

  for (day=0; day < firstDay; day++) {
    document.writeln("<TD BGCOLOR='#DDD'> </TD>");
  }
```

```
  for (day = firstDay; day < 7; day++, theDay++) {
    if (theDay == today)
      document.writeln("<TD ALIGN=right BGCOLOR='#FCC'>" +
        theDay + "</TD>");
    else
      document.writeln("<TD ALIGN=right>" + theDay +
"</TD>");
  }

  // now let's do the rest of the calendar weeks

  while (theDay <= daysInMonth) {

    document.writeln("</TR><TR>");

    for (day = 0; day < 7; day++, theDay++) {
      if (theDay > daysInMonth)
        document.writeln("<TD BGCOLOR='#DDD'> </TD>");
      else if (theDay == today)
        document.writeln("<TD ALIGN=right BGCOLOR='#FCC'>" +
      theDay + "</TD>");
      else
        document.writeln("<TD ALIGN=right>" + theDay +
              "</TD>");
    }
  }
  document.writeln("</TR></TABLE>");
}
```

The variable daysInMonth keeps track of how many days are in the current month, while theDay is the current day appearing on-screen. As the day outputs, the function compares it to today, and if the values match, assigns that data cell a light-red background color (#FCC) to highlight on-screen it. All empty cells get a light-gray background to differentiate them from the days of this month (color #DDD).

Figure 23-4 shows the results for this month.

This example is a fairly involved, but by using the code in the <SCRIPT> block of your page, you can drop the calendar anywhere by adding a few simple lines. Here's the HTML body of the page, as shown as Figure 23-4:

```
The calendar for today is:
<HR><CENTER>
<SCRIPT LANGUAGE="JavaScript">
showMonth();
</SCRIPT>
</CENTER><HR>
```

This example isn't a complete calendar solution by any means. One glaring bug is evident, and you can enhanced this code in a number of ways — for example, put it on its own layer and offer next and prev links to enable people to step through dates.

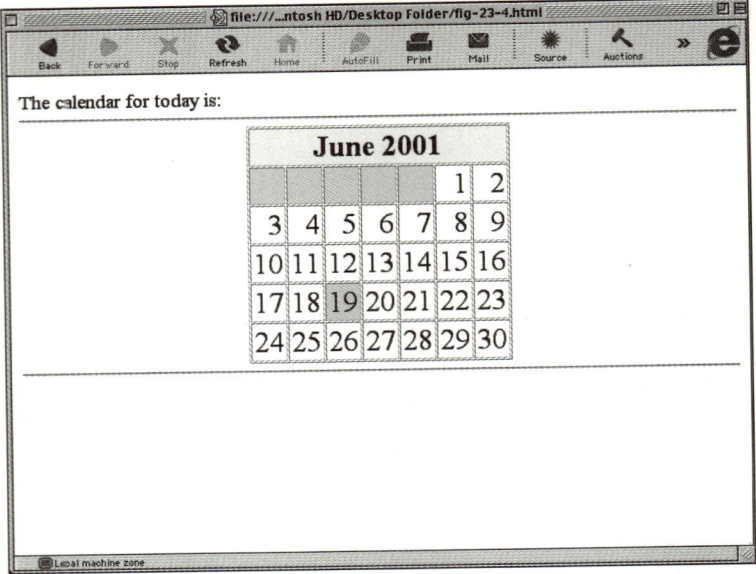

Figure 23-4   *The current month, as shown in a nice calendar view.*

Some terrific JavaScript calendar objects are available online if you want to get into something more sophisticated. I suggest that you check out the following URLs to get a taste of this sort of thing:

- `www.softricks.com/js/Calendar/Calendar.html`
- `http://cnet.com/webbuilding/0-7690-8-5680015-1.html`

REVIEW

Done!

This session explores the many facets of the `Date()` object and its many methods, including demonstrations of how to code a constantly updating clock and two calculators that produce the number of days between two dates and the day of the week of a specific date. In addition, you get a sneak preview of how to access form elements from within JavaScript and see more sophisticated JavaScript programming techniques at work, too.

QUIZ YOURSELF

1. What *is* that glaring bug in the calendar program? (See "Building a Calendar.")
2. Why does `getFullYear()` exist? (See "Extracting the Current Date.")
3. Because you know the date that I ran these examples, and that it's 14,183 days since I was born, you can write a JavaScript `date` function that calculates the day of my birth (well, generally, the date *X* days in the past). (See "Floating Clocks and Other Date Tricks.")

4. If you want the showDay function to run once every 24 hours, how do you write the setTimeout call? (See "Floating Clocks and Other Date Tricks.")

5. How many <SCRIPT> blocks can you have on a DHTML Web page? (See "Extracting the Current Date.")

CHALLENGING

6. Integrate the updating clock and the floating bug from Session 16 to create a clock that floats in the lower-right corner of the page. (See "Floating Clocks and Other Date Tricks" and Session 16.)

7. Enhance the calendar function to include a next and a prev link. (See "Building a Calendar.")

Forms and Testing Values

Session Checklist

✔ Form-related event handlers

✔ Testing values for appropriate content

✔ Grabbing values to test

✔ Hooking tests in by using OnFocus or OnBlur

✔ In-place forms

✔ Dynamic form values

30 Min. To Go

One of the most useful and important capabilities of JavaScript is its capability to turn dumb, passive forms into sophisticated user-interaction areas on your Web site. From making simple checks to ensure that fields aren't left blank to cross-validating data, to popping up fields based on user input, JavaScript and Cascading Style Sheets make your forms remarkably sophisticated.

One important caveat before I start, however. Because not every Web browser on the Net includes software that supports the entire range of tests and validation steps that I discuss herein, you need to realize that incorrectly formatted data can still transmit to your back-end Common Gateway Interface (CGI) scripts. If you're expecting a well-formed e-mail address, for example, what happens if your backend program gets something completely different? If you're testing to ensure that a user's last name is no longer than 25 characters, what happens if the CGI script receives a last-name field that's actually 300 characters long?

I talk more about this data validation issue as I go, but keep in mind that the most sophisticated form on the Web still needs some fail-safe code that double-checks all the fields — and can flag errors — on receipt of the form data.

Form-Related Event Handlers

In earlier sessions, the main JavaScript event handlers that I mention are onMouseOver, onMouseOut, onClick, and onLoad. More events are defined, however, and moving into the world of HTML forms requires that you start by exploring the following events: onBlur, onFocus, onChange, and onSubmit.

To understand the blur and focus concepts, imagine that you're filling in a form and you either tab or use your mouse to move to and then click a phone text field. You can define such a field as follows:

```
<INPUT TYPE="text" NAME="phone" SIZE="20">
```

This line produces a 20-character-wide single-line text-input field with the mnemonic name of phone. Clicking the field produces an onFocus event (you're now focusing your attention on this field) and then tabbing or clicking outside the field — even clicking the Submit button — produces an onBlur.

As an experiment, try the following:

```
<FORM>
<INPUT TYPE="text" NAME="phone" SIZE="20"
 onFocus="alert('focus!');" onBlur="alert('blur!')">
</FORM>
```

See what happens as you click in and out of the text field. Beware if you're using Netscape 4.7, though; it might trap you in a loop because of its peculiar way of returning focus to the element after the dialog box has completed!

To test the values, you need to associate your test routine with the onBlur event: After the user enters data, you can test its contents to see whether it's what you seek.

Even better, however, is to harness the onChange event, which triggers only if the user focuses on that particular form field *and changes the value therein* (whereas onBlur is true regardless of whether the user changes the information).

The following refinement on the preceding script can demonstrate what I mean:

```
<FORM>
<INPUT TYPE="text" NAME="phone" SIZE="20"
 onFocus="alert('focus!');" onChange="alert('change!')">
</FORM>
```

You don't want to keep the onBlur **event handler, too, in this case, because both events trigger if the user changes the field value and removes focus. That's why we've switched to** onChange **instead.**

Forcing Events

In addition to capturing events, you can also force events to occur with some built-in methods. The following example creates a field that you can't fill out:

```
<INPUT TYPE="text" NAME="blank" OnFocus="blur()">
```

The built-in method `blur()` automatically defocuses the element, and because it ties to the onFocus event, you can never fill in that field. Similarly, you can use the `focus()` event that ties to onBlur to create a field that, after you enter it, you can never leave. (Why? Because trying to leave the field creates an onBlur event, which forces you back into the field with the `focus()` method. A nasty trick, for sure!)

Silly as these examples sound, the `focus()` event in particular is quite useful, because by using it, you can capture the user as he's leaving a field, test the field's new value, and force the user back into the field if any errors result. You see a demonstration of this process in just a few minutes.

Grabbing Values to Test

**20 Min.
To Go**

To progress further, I'm going to show you how to access a form's data from within JavaScript. Confusingly, the `getElementById()` method isn't the best strategy for this task. Instead, the recommended method of referencing forms is either of the following:

```
document.formname
document.forms[i]
```

You specify the form's actual name or the numeric index (starting at zero) of the form on the page — for example, a simple page with a single form as follows:

```
<FORM METHOD="get" ACTION="search.cgi" NAME="searchbox">
<INPUT TYPE="text" NAME="pattern">
</FORM>
```

The object reference for the form can be either of the following:

```
document.searchbox
document.forms[0]
```

Most commonly, JavaScript uses the latter reference method, but I intend to develop a version of `getObj` that enables you to specify either of these methods, enabling you to more easily put multiple forms on a page.

To get to individual elements, you can again use either a named reference or an index into an array, as follows:

```
document.searchbox.pattern
document.forms[0].elements[0];
```

You can see how this approach works with the following example, which demonstrates the named reference approach:

```
<FORM METHOD="get" ACTION="search.cgi" NAME="searchbox">
<INPUT TYPE="text" NAME="pattern"
 onBlur="alert('searching for ' +
         document.searchbox.pattern.value)">
</FORM>
```

Figure 24-1 shows the results of my entering a search pattern and then using the Tab key to remove focus from the element, triggering the alert() box that appears.

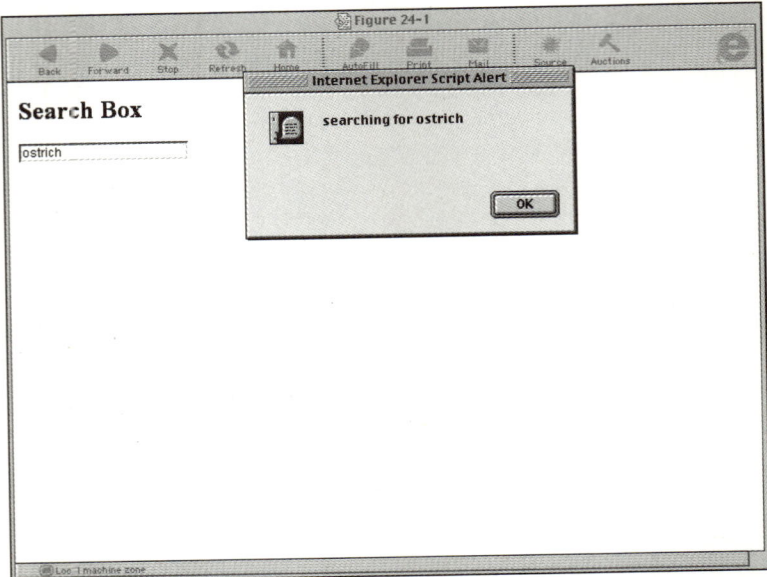

Figure 24-1 *Blurring the text field produces an alert confirming the input value.*

The getFormObj function

You can see in the preceding sections how to reference form elements, so I'm going to create a version of getObj for forms. The easiest version assumes that you have only one form on the page, as follows:

```
function getFormObj(elementName) {
   // cross platform tool for accessing a form object
   return( eval("document.forms[0]." + elementName) );
}
```

By using the preceding code, you can check the value of a form element with the following:

```
var myObj = getFormObj("pattern");
alert("pattern is " + myObj.value);
```

This method is nice and portable.

A more sophisticated way to access form objects is to specify the name of the form. But needing to specify the form name on every getFormObj call is awkward, so instead I break it into the following two functions:

```
<SCRIPT LANGUAGE="JavaScript">
```

```
var formName = "forms[0]";            // default value

function setFormName(fName)
{
  // easy shortcut for setting form name. Used with getFormObj
  formName = fName;
}

function getFormObj(elementName) {
  // cross platform tool for accessing a form object
  return( eval("document." + formName + "." + elementName) );
}
</SCRIPT>
```

This pair of functions enables you to ignore the formName variable for pages that display only a single form (because the default is "forms[0]") but enables you to specify the name of a form before a series of getFormObj calls, if you need it.

If you want your version of the function to require you to always call setFormName, simply replace the preceding simple version of getFormObj with the following:

```
function getFormObj(elementName) {
  // cross platform tool for accessing a form object
  if (formName == "forms[0]")
    return(alert("Call setFormName before getFormObj"));
  return( eval("document." + formName + "." + elementName) );
}
```

A nifty check-box improvement

A simple effect that shows off some of the capabilities that you can add to your forms is one that enables users to click the words adjacent to a check box to select it, instead of needing to click the box graphic itself. Check boxes are peculiar beasts in the world of HTML forms because they only go off to the backend CGI script if someone selects them. All other form elements are sent regardless of value.

Here's some example code:

```
function toggleCheckBox(fieldName)
{
  // given the name of a checkbox, toggle its value
  var myObj = getFormObj(fieldName);
  myObj.checked = (myObj.checked? false : true);
  return false;
}
```

Notice that, instead of worrying about the .value attribute, you simply examine the .checked attribute, which can have either of two values: true or false.

You can use this code in your HTML as follows:

```
<INPUT TYPE="checkbox" NAME="pepperoni">
<SPAN OnClick="toggleCheckBox('pepperoni')">pepperoni</SPAN>
```

Now the user can click the word pepperoni in the pizza order form shown in Figure 24-2 to select the individual elements instead of needing to click the box itself.

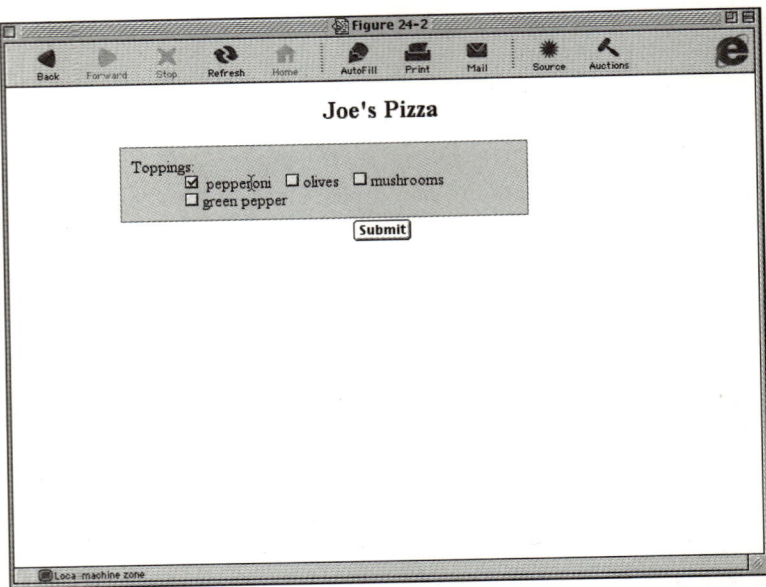

Figure 24-2 *JavaScript activates the words adjacent to the check boxes so that you can click the word in addition to the box itself.*

Testing Values for Appropriate Content

Sticking with the pizza-order page from the preceding section, I first want to make it a bit more sophisticated in layout and then add a second field: pizza size. This example also shows you how I'm creating the shaded box that you see around the check boxes in Figure 24-2.

First, here's the HTML that produces the slightly more sophisticated form shown in Figure 24-3

```
<FORM METHOD="post" ACTION="not-a-real.cgi">
<DIV STYLE="margin-left: 1in; width: 4in; border: 1px solid red;
          padding: 10px; background-color: #FCC">
Size:
<SELECT NAME="size"><OPTION VALUE="12">12" (small)
<OPTION VALUE="15">15" (medium)<OPTION VALUE="18">18" (large)
<OPTION VALUE="24">24" (monster)</SELECT><BR>
```

```
Toppings:
<DIV STYLE="margin-left: 3em">
<INPUT TYPE="checkbox" NAME="pepperoni">
<SPAN OnClick="toggleCheckBox('pepperoni')">
pepperoni</SPAN>  
<INPUT TYPE="checkbox" NAME="olives">
<SPAN OnClick="toggleCheckBox('olives')">olives</SPAN>  
<INPUT TYPE="checkbox" NAME="mushrooms">
<SPAN OnClick="toggleCheckBox('mushrooms')">mushrooms</SPAN><BR>
<INPUT TYPE="checkbox" NAME="extrasauce" onClick="checkOrder()">
<SPAN OnClick="toggleCheckBox('extrasauce');checkOrder()">
extra sauce (monster size only)</SPAN>
</DIV>
</DIV>
</FORM>
```

Notice that I'm adding the `toggleCheckBox` hook to each of the `checkbox` text fields, including the long `extra sauce (monster size only)` label at the end. Taking a closer look at that form field is worthwhile, too: The checkbox itself has an `OnClick` validation test that checks the size of the pizza to see whether it's legit for the user to request extra sauce. The `<SPAN>` element that enables users to click the associated words simply appends the call to the existing `onClick` element.

Now to add the interesting part, `checkOrder()`, as follows:

```
function checkOrder()
{
  // check: users can only order extra sauce on a monster pizza
  // this is only called when the extrasauce checkbox is changed

  var sauceObj = getFormObj("extrasauce");
  var sizeObj  = getFormObj("size");
  if ((sauceObj.checked == true) && sizeObj.value != "24") {
    alert("Sorry, but we can't add extra sauce to " +
      sizeObj.value + "\" pizza pies,\n" +
      "only 'monster' size pizzas. Time to super-size it?");
    sauceObj.checked = false;        // force it back to unselected
  }
}
```

Notice that everything boils down to the following simple test in the middle of the code:

```
if (extra sauce is checked  and  size != 24-inch pie) ...
```

Notice, too, the last code line, which removes the ~~removal of the~~ check mark from the box.

One really nice improvement to this DHTML is for the SELECT object to force the removal of the check mark from the extra-sauce box if you resize the pizza to a size other than monster; currently, you can pick a 24-inch pizza, choose extra sauce, and then pick the size that you really want. Of course, you can accomplish this with an exit-validation test of variables, too. Either approach offers a good solution to this problem.

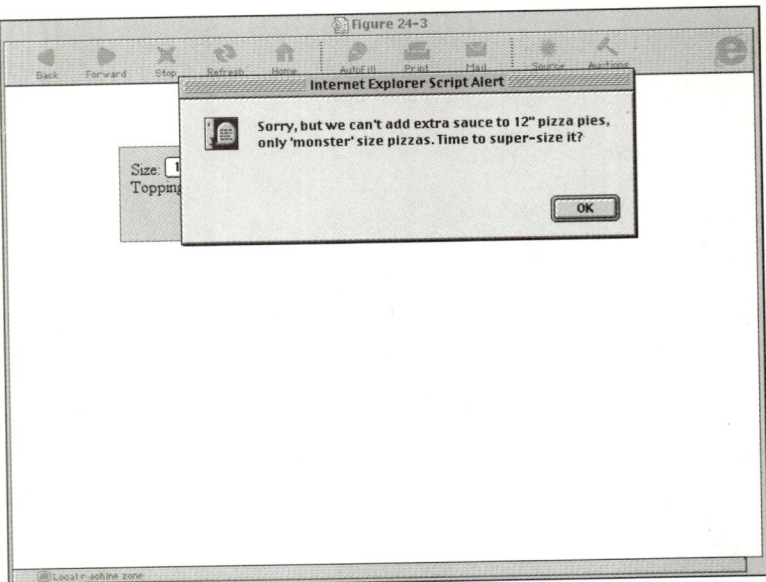

Figure 24-3   *I selected a small pizza and then requested extra sauce, but. . . .*

In-Place Forms

As you saw in the preceding session, one trick you that can do is to tie events to an INPUT TYPE=button and avoid the SUBMIT element completely, instead embedding the script into the page by using JavaScript. One nice example appears on The Weather Channel Web site, with its in-place Fahrenheit/Celsius conversion function. That feature is easy to duplicate, as the following example demonstrates:

```
function convertTemp(direction)
{
  // if we have a Fahrenheit temp, compute Celsius, or vice-versa
  var fObj = getFormObj("ftemp"), cObj = getFormObj("ctemp");
  if (direction == "ftoc") {
    cObj.value = Math.round((fObj.value - 32) * (5/9));
  } else {
    fObj.value = Math.round((parseInt(cObj.value) * (9/5)) + 32);
  }
}
```

The basic formula here is that Celsius = Fahrenheit * (9/5) + 32 and Fahrenheit = (Celsius + 32) * (5/9), as you can see. The direction variable enables you to use the same function to calculate in either direction.

The associated HTML is as follows:

```
<FORM STYLE="border: 1px double blue; background-color: #DDF; padding:
4px;">
```

```
Fahrenheit:
<INPUT TYPE="text" NAME="ftemp" SIZE="7"
 OnChange="convertTemp('ftoc')"> is the
same as Celsius:
<INPUT TYPE="text" NAME="ctemp" SIZE="7"
 OnChange="convertTemp('ctof')">
</FORM>
```

It's pleasantly short and sweet. You can see in Figure 24-4 that I added one more capability: The Clear button calls the following JavaScript function:

```
function clearvalues()
{
  // clear both values to blank
  var fObj = getFormObj("ftemp"), cObj = getFormObj("ctemp");
  fObj.value = "";
  cObj.value = "";
}
```

Before I present the form, however, I'm going to drop a second in-line form into it, too, to make things more interesting.

A Mortgage Payment Calculator

The temperature calculator that I show you how to create in the preceding section is simple and demonstrates the basic steps necessary to add live calculators to your Web page. Another helpful calculator is to compute monthly payment amounts given the number of payments, initial principle, and fixed interest rate of a mortgage. The formula is more complex than it initially seems, because you must divide the interest rate by 12 to get the monthly interest and then compute the compound value on a gradually decreasing principal. Don't worry, however, as I don't fully understand it either. I just know that the formula that I'm embedding in the following function works:

```
function myPaymentCalc(form)
{
  // calculate the monthly and total payments for a simple
  // loan given the interest, duration and principal of the loan.

  setFormName("form2"); // make sure we're referencing the form

  var interestRate = getValue("interest"),
      numberOfPayments = getValue("payments"),
      principal = getValue("principal"), accumulatingInterest = 1;

  interestRate = (interestRate > 1)?
      interestRate / 100.0 : interestRate;

  monthlyInterestRate = interestRate / 12;

  for (i=0; i < numberOfPayments; i++)
    accumulatingInterest *= (1 + monthlyInterestRate);
```

```
monthlyPayment = 0.01 * Math.round(100*(accumulatingInterest *
        principal * monthlyInterestRate) /
        (accumulatingInterest - 1));

totalPayment = monthlyPayment * numberOfPayments;

// clean up the display format to make it attractive...

monthlyPayment = centNotation(monthlyPayment);
totalPayment   = centNotation(totalPayment);

var tp = getFormObj("totalpayment"),
    mp = getFormObj("monthlypayment");
tp.value = totalPayment;
mp.value = monthlyPayment;
}
```

You'll need to ensure that you've included setFormName **in the JavaScript code section for this to work.**

Most of this code is straightforward, if somewhat complex. Temporarily ignore the mathematics here and just look at the function that gets the value of a field value (getValue) and the last few lines that set the post-computed values. Here's getValue, which is a simple shorthand:

```
function getValue(fname)
{
  // return the value of the given field in a form
  var myObj = getFormObj(fname);
  return( myObj.value );
}
```

Another function that I added is centNotation, which ensures that the dollar amounts appear with a two-digit cents value, as follows:

```
function centNotation(value)
{
  // return the value in normalized dollars.cents notation

  dollars = Math.floor(value);    // chop floating point portion
  cents   = Math.floor((value % 1) * 100); // and everything else
  if (cents < 10) cents = "" + cents + "0";

  return(dollars + "." + cents);
}
```

 The mathematical *floor* of a value is simply the value with any decimal portion removed, so 11.9 and 11.01 both have a *floor* of 11.

Finally, here's the HTML code that all this JavaScript enables:

```
<FORM NAME="form2">
<TABLE BORDER="0" CELLPADDING="2">
<TR><TH COLSPAN="2" ALIGN="center" BGCOLOR='#CCFFCC'>Mortgage
Calculator</TH></TR>
<TR><TD ALIGN="right">Number of Payments</TD>
<TD><INPUT TYPE="TEXT" NAME="payments" SIZE="5"></TD></TR>
<TR><TD ALIGN="right">Interest Rate</TD>
<TD><INPUT TYPE="TEXT" NAME="interest" SIZE="6"></TD></TR>
<TR><TD ALIGN="right">Amount of Loan (principal)</TD>
<TD><INPUT TYPE="TEXT" NAME="principal" SIZE="9"></TD></TR>
<TR BGCOLOR="#CCCCCC"><TD ALIGN="right">Monthly Payments</TD>
<TD><INPUT TYPE="TEXT" NAME="monthlypayment"
 onFocus="blur()"></TD></TR>
<TR BGCOLOR="#CCCCCC"><TD ALIGN="right">Total Payments</TD>
<TD><INPUT TYPE="text" NAME="totalpayment"
 onFocus="blur()"></TD></TR>
</TABLE>
<INPUT TYPE="button" VALUE=" Figure Payments "
 onClick="myPaymentCalc()" STYLE="font-size: 80%;
 background-color: #CFC">
</FORM>
```

Most of the HTML here involves placing the elements in an attractive table-based design. Notice the onFocus="blur() statements added to the two computed values in the table to prevent users trying to enter their own values, and the little trick with the STYLE attribute to change the appearance of the Figure Payments button. Figure 24-4 shows both forms calculating values.

This example is probably more complex than any on-screen calculator you ever create for yourself, but it does demonstrate the range of capabilities available and gives you a very good idea how to make your forms considerably more sophisticated.

Dynamic Form Values

Before I wrap up this session, I need to insert a quick note to tell you that you can combine all the elements that I present herein to create forms with values that appear or disappear based on specific user input. If someone specifies that he lives outside of the United States of America, for example, you may want to prompt the person for a postal code rather than a Zip code, because *Zip code* is an Americanism and annoyingly ethnocentric to overseas surfers.

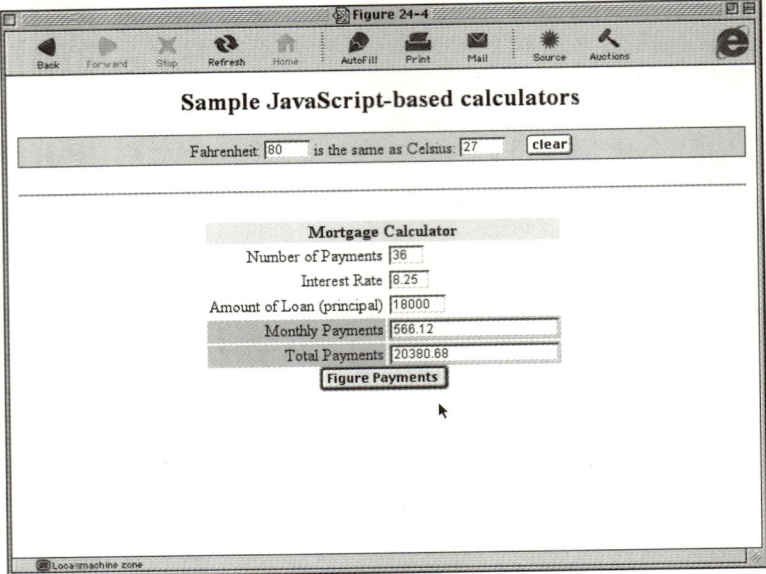

Figure 24-4   *Temperature and mortgage payment calculators combining on a Web site — what a pair!*

You can accomplish this task in either of two ways: One way is to name containers and pump new values into them based on user input (which is particularly straightforward with menus and other dynamically labeled elements), and the other way is to actually use more than one relatively positioned element on the page, all but one of which you set to display=none. Change the settings, test the value, and flip display=block to turn on the correct container of fields and display=none to turn off the wrong one.

Because dynamic menus are commonly seen on JavaScript-enabled pages, the following section provides a very brief example of how to add pop-up menu items to your page that populate form values based on other settings in the form.

Dynamic Menus

The first step is to create an object that contains a list of all values for all possible settings of the control element. Because this example deals with toppings available for specific pizza styles, here's how the code for it looks:

```
toppings = new Object();
toppings.thincrust = new Array("Tofu","Sprouts","Brie");
toppings.deepdish = new Array("Extra Cheese","Sausage","Beef");
toppings.ny = new Array("Oil","Mozzarella","Pepperoni");
toppings.none = new Array("-- none yet --");
```

With that defined, the function to update the toppings SELECT element values is straightforward, as the following example shows:

```
function updateMenus()
{
  var sObj = getFormObj("pieStyle"),
      aObj = getFormObj("toppings");

  switch (sObj.selectedIndex) {
    case 1: tp = toppings.thincrust;        break;
    case 2: tp = toppings.deepdish;            break;
    case 3: tp = toppings.ny;                break;
   default: tp = toppings.none;
  }
  aObj.length = tp.length; // resize object to array length
  for (i=0; i < tp.length; i++)
    aObj.options[i].text = tp[i];
}
```

As you can glean here, a SELECT element stores its values in the array options, the text value of which is actually what appears in the Web browser.

The associated HTML, again, is straightforward, as follows:

```
<TABLE BORDER="0" CELLPADDING="2">
<TR><TD VALIGN="top" ALIGN="right">What kind<BR>of pizza<BR>
 do you want?
</TD><TD VALIGN="top">
<SELECT NAME="pieStyle" SIZE="5" onChange="updateMenus()">
  <OPTION>(choose one)<OPTION>thin crust<OPTION>deep dish<OPTION>New York
</SELECT>
</TD><TD VALIGN="top" ALIGN="right">
Available<BR>Toppings:</TD><TD>
<SELECT NAME="toppings" SIZE="5">
  <OPTION>-- none yet --
</SELECT></TD></TR>
</TABLE>
```

Probably the weirdest thing about this kind of menu approach is that the menu changes width each time that you make a new selection, which can cause changes to ripple throughout the layout of the page. Quite disturbing to an unsuspecting viewer!

This example is on the CD-ROM as Figure 24-5.html if you want to explore it and see how it works. Indeed, check out all the examples from this session on your own computer because I intend them all to represent dynamic examples of live, active forms.

Done!

REVIEW

This session is a long one, but it shows you a ton of different cool things that you can do to forms after you really understand JavaScript and how to work with event handlers. In this session, I explore specific event handlers for form-based interaction, including those that force events to occur and those that enable you to access – and change – individual elements on a form. I extend the helpful `crashcourse.js` library to include some form-based functions and spend considerable time on in-place JavaScript-powered forms that can turn your Web pages into super-helpful calculators.

QUIZ YOURSELF

1. What's the difference between `onChange` and `onBlur`? (See "Form-Related Event Handlers.")

2. Why do I use an empty `<FORM>` element and an `INPUT TYPE="button"`? (See "Form-Related Event Handlers.")

3. What's the difference between `Math.round()` and `Math.floor()`? (See "In-Place Forms.")

4. Using `convertTemp` as a model, write a function that enables you to enter a typographic point size and make it display the equivalent in inches . . . or vice versa. (Recall that 72 points = 1 inch.) (See "In-Place Forms.")

FAIRLY CHALLENGING

5. Fix the bug in the extra sauce enhanced form shown earlier so that if the user selects extra sauce while specifying the monster pizza size and then selects a different-sized pizza, the extra sauce option automatically deselects. (See "Testing Values for Appropriate Content.")

VERY CHALLENGING

6. A nice enhancement to the same pizza-ordering form is one that enables it to show a running total as you select different toppings and sizes. Add the code to accomplish this enhancement, using the following prices: small = $10, medium = $12.50, large = $15, monster = $25, and each topping is one-tenth the price of the pizza. (A monster pizza with extra sauce and pepperoni, for example, costs $25 + $2.50 + $2.50 = $30.)

SESSION

Navigation with Menus

Session Checklist

✔ Better pop-up menus

✔ Sliding menus

✔ Cascading menu refinements

✔ Automatically closing menus by using hide-me timers

**30 Min.
To Go**

Way back in Session 15, I began an explanation of pop-up menus, with a simple layer of hypertext references that appears after a user places the cursor over a specific SPAN element on a page. In this session, I'm going to take that simple device and step it up to the next level, making an attractive, general purpose pop-up menu. Building on that core, I then show you how to make simple sliding menus. Then you get to create the Holy Grail of DHTML programmers: cascading menus.

This session is a long, complex one full of way-cool information, so get started!

Better Pop-Up Menus

If you flip back to Session 15, you may remember that you used layers to make a menu pop up but had lots of problems with its placement on the page. In a nutshell, because you let the top navigational bar stretch to the entire width of the window, ascertaining exactly where to position the menu after it became visible was difficult. You also had a problem knowing how to turn *off* the menu, but I get to that topic a bit later in this session.

The easiest way to remember the state of your pop-up menus from Session 15 is to view `fig-15-3a.html` **on the CD-ROM.**

To start, I'm going to take the boring pop-up menu and apply some CSS style to it to produce a design that really looks great, as the following example demonstrates:

```
.menu { position: absolute;
        background-color: #009;
        display: block; width: 200px;
        border-bottom: 1px solid #000;
        border-right: 1px solid #000;
        border-left: 1px solid #666;
        border-top: 1px solid #666;
        margin: 3px; cursor: nw-resize;
      }

.mi   { padding: 1px; color: white;
        border-bottom: 1px solid #003;
        border-right: 1px solid #003;
        border-left: 1px solid #00C;
        border-top: 1px solid #00C;
        background-color: #009;
        font-family: sans-serif; font-size: 75%;
      }
```

Pay attention to the colors in both styles: The bottom and right edges are darker than the background color, while the top and left edges are lighter than the background color. This color scheme produces the familiar quasi-3D look that you've seen for years on your computer interface, and this approach makes our menus really look smart.

Also notice that I'm introducing a new style element, cursor:, that enables you to specify what shape you want the cursor to become while over that particular element.

SIDEBAR: changing the mouse pointer

The cursor: element, which only CSS2-compliant browsers support, offers a surprising number of possible values and even enables you to easily load your own value by using the url(value) format, (although none of the current browsers yet support it). What does work are any of the values in Table 25-1.

Table 25-1 *Mouse Pointer Values in CSS 2*

Appearance (in IE)	cursor: value
+	crosshair
✛	pointer
🖑	move
▲	n-resize
◥	ne-resize
▸	e-resize

Appearance (in IE)	cursor: value
⬊	se-resize
⬍	s-resize
⬋	sw-resize
◀	w-resize
⬉	nw-resize
I	text
⏱	wait
?	help

In this example, I'm using the handy "northwest" arrow to help users see when they're over, and selecting, from a menu. (It's really only for use in resizing, but it's visually interesting, so I subvert it to this task.)

Back to the menu

The next step is to define the menu object itself, which I do by using a sequence of nesting `<DIV>` elements. You also immediately notice that I'm using the onClick event handler to change page location rather than a hypertext reference. The main reason: I can format the link exactly as I want without worrying about underlines and so on, as you see in the following example:

```
<SPAN CLASS="menu" ID="menu2" onClick="menuOff('menu2');">

<DIV CLASS="mi" ID="m1"
 onMouseOver="setBgColor('m1','#069')"
 onClick="location.href='http://www.bakerstreet221b.de/main.htm'"
 onMouseOut="setBgColor('m1','#009')">
Camden House
</DIV>
<DIV CLASS="mi" ID="m2"
 onMouseOver="setBgColor('m2','#069')"
 onClick="location.href='http://www.sherlockian.net/'"
 onMouseOut="setBgColor('m2','#009')">
Sherlockian Net
</DIV>
<DIV CLASS="mi" ID="m3"
 OnMouseOver="setBgColor('m3','#069')"
onClick="location.href='http://www.evo.org/sherlock/international/'"
 onMouseOut="setBgColor('m3','#009')">
Sherlock Holmes Intn'l
</DIV>
<DIV CLASS="mi" ID="m4"
 onMouseOver="setBgColor('m4','#069')"
```

```
onClick="location.href='http://www.sherlock-holmes.co.uk/'"
onMouseOut="setBgColor('m4','#009')">
The Sherlock Holmes Museum
</DIV>
<DIV CLASS="mi" ID="m5"
 onMouseOver="setBgColor('m5','#069')"
 onClick="location.href='http://holmes-sherlock.com/'"
 onMouseOut="setBgColor('m5','#009')">
Yoxley Old Place
</DIV>
</SPAN>
```

You can see all the key elements here: the overall CLASS="menu" container and the individual menu item entry with CLASS="mi", a unique ID (m1 for the first, m2 for the second), and calls to set the background color to a dark aqua (#069) if the mouse is over the element and back to a dark blue (#009) after it moves off.

The repeated five lines for each element of the menu suggest that you can create a simple function to produce this effect, and so you can, taking advantage of the document.writeln method, as follows:

```
var menuItemId = 1;

function addMenuItem(url, label)
{
  var id = "menuItem" + menuItemId;
  menuItemId++;

  document.writeln("<DIV CLASS=\"mi\" ID='" + id + "'");
  document.writeln(" onMouseOver=\"setBgColor('" + id +
    "', '#069')\"");
  document.writeln(" onClick=\"location.href=\'" + url + "'\"");
  document.writeln(" onMouseOut=\"setBgColor('" + id +
    "', '#009')\">");
  document.writeln(label + "\n</DIV>");
}
```

With this function in the <SCRIPT> block at the top of the DHTML page source, creating a menu is as straightforward as the following example demonstrates:

```
<SPAN CLASS="menu" ID="menu2">
<SCRIPT LANGUAGE="JavaScript">
addMenuItem("http://www.bakerstreet221b.de/main.htm",
   "Camden House");
addMenuItem("http://www.sherlockian.net/", "Sherlockian Net");
addMenuItem("http://www.evo.org/sherlock/international",
   "Sherlock Holmes Int'l");
addMenuItem("http://www.sherlock-holmes.co.uk/",
   "The Sherlock Holmes Museum");
addMenuItem("http://www.holmes-sherlock.com/",
   "Yoxley Old Place");
</SCRIPT>
</SPAN>
```

This approach is more elegant and considerably easier to maintain than dozens upon dozens of lines of redundant code, too.

Notice that I don't require specific ID tags in the call to addMenuItem. Because the JavaScript uses them only internally, I have the function automatically produce its own ID tags by using the variable menuItemId. The first menu item has menuItem1 as its ID, for example.

While I'm at it, adding one more function that enables you to add a static title to a pop-up menu is easy, too, as the following example shows:

```
function addMenuTitle(label)
{
  var id = "menuTitle" + menuItemId;
  menuItemId++;

  document.writeln("<DIV CLASS=\"mt\" ID='" + id + "'>");
  document.writeln(label + "\n</DIV>");
}
```

The associated style .mt (menu title) is almost identical to the menu item style (.mi), but you get a different background color and the text appears in bold, as in the following example:

```
.mt    { padding: 1px;
         border-bottom: 1px solid #003;
         border-right: 1px solid #003;
         border-left: 1px solid #00C;
         border-top: 1px solid #00C;
         background-color: #669;
         color: white; font-family: sans-serif;
         font-size: 75%; font-weight: bold;
       }
```

You can invoke the menu title simply by adding a single call before all the addMenuItem calls, as follows:

```
addMenuTitle("Holmsian Web Sites");
```

Placing the menu

**20 Min.
To Go**

For this first menu example in this session, I'm going to be lazy and make the menu appear on the top-left corner, just below the link "sites," which I position to ensure that the menu is placed exactly where I want. Before you think that this setup isn't realistic, check out how many Web sites take exactly this approach with their pull-down or pop-up menus.

Here's the rewritten <SPAN> that wraps the entire menu:

```
<SPAN CLASS="menu" ID="menu2" STYLE="left:25px;top:50px;">
```

Notice here that I'm absolutely positioning the menu (if visible) to sit at 25,50 relative to the top-left corner of the page. The next step is to position the link that makes the menu pop up on demand; to do that, I'm going to force the overall contents of my page to extend to exactly 650 pixels wide. I'm going to do so in the following example by using a nifty trick that you can particularly appreciate if you've suffered through wrapping entire pages in <TABLE> tags:

```
<BODY STYLE="width: 650px">
```

Now, finally, I add the beginning of the Web page contents — the title bar that includes the menu pop-up activation link — as follows:

```
<TABLE BORDER="0" CELLPADDING="5" WIDTH="100%" CELLSPACING="0">
<TR BGCOLOR="#000099">
<TD><SPAN STYLE="color: yellow; font-weight: bold;
 top:10px;left: 10px"
 onMouseOver="menuOn('menu2');">sites</SPAN></TD>
<TD STYLE="color: white; font: 24pt arial bold;">
 The Adventures of Sherlock Holmes</TD>
</TR>
</TABLE>
```

A final few lines of code for the simple menuOn() function:

```
function menuOn(id)
{
  // turn on the specified menu
  var myMenu = getObj(id);
  myMenu.display="block";
}
```

Ironically, after putting so much effort into the appearance of the menu, the page itself appears rather dull and pedestrian. Figure 25-1 shows what I mean (and shows off the pop-up menu, too).

Oh! A gaping bug crops up in this example, too: The menu pops up, but it never goes away again after you finish with it. One way to solve this problem that's cheesy but effective is to write a simple closeMenu function, as follows:

```
function closeMenu(id)
{
  obj = getObj(id);
  obj.display='none';
}
```

Then add an onClick="closeMenu('menu2')" attribute to the <BODY> tag. Then the user can click anywhere on the page to close the menu. That fix works for now.

You need to stay tuned for just a few minutes before I show you how to solve that problem in a more friendly and graceful manner by using timers, in "Automatically Closing Menus by Using Hide-Me Timers."

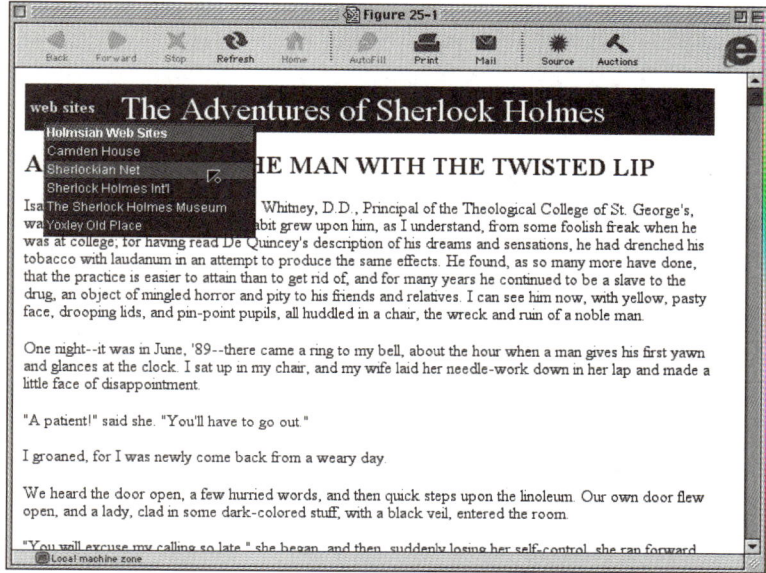

Figure 25-1   *An unexciting page, but with a way-cool pop-up menu appearing.*

Sliding Menus

Pop-up menus that drop down from links are unquestionably nice, but before you finish your construction project, I need to take you on a detour for a moment to look at a different kind of menu: a *sliding menu*. The basic idea is simple: Create a menu that displays an edge tab and then have only the tab appear. If the user clicks it, the menu slides into view, and if the user then clicks the tab again, the menu hides again.

This task is remarkably easy to accomplish, given all the functions and JavaScript you've seen so far, including most notably the slideObj() function in crashcourse.js. To build the tab, I resort to creating it as a simple graphical element and then drop it into the current menu layer by turning the list of <DIV>s into a two column table: the Web-links menu built earlier as the first column, and the tab graphic itself as the second column.

This time, I'm placing a set of predefined constants at the top of the JavaScript section that enables me to fine-tune parameters later, an approach that makes the code particularly reusable, as the following example shows:

```
var smenuName = "slide";        // name of the sliding menu
var topPos    = 14;             // pixels down from top
var leftOn    = 0;              // left position, menu visible
var leftOff   = -208;           // left position, slid off
var currPos   = leftOff;        // current position
```

The next step is to write a function that can toggle the menu state between hidden (off screen) and fully visible. (Notice that the `leftOff` position is 208 pixels to the *left* of the browser window, effectively hiding all but the rightmost 15 pixels or so.) The following example shows how:

```
function toggleMenu()
{
  var menuObj = getObj(smenuName);

  newPos = (currPos == leftOff? leftOn : leftOff);
  slideObj(smenuName, newPos, topPos);
  currPos = newPos;
}
```

Not much more to it. The biggest decision is how to structure the newly improved menu itself. The following example shows how to do so:

```
<SCRIPT LANGUAGE="JavaScript">
document.writeln("<SPAN CLASS='menu' ID='" + smenuName +
  "' STYLE='top:" + topPos + "px; left:" + leftOff + "px;'>");
document.writeln("<TABLE BORDER=\"0\" CELLSPACING=\"0\"
  CELLPADDING=\"0\">");
document.writeln("<TR><TD WIDTH=\"205\">");

addMenuTitle("Holmsian Web Sites");
addMenuItem("http://www.bakerstreet221b.de/main.htm",
  "Camden House");
addMenuItem("http://www.sherlockian.net/", "Sherlockian Net");
addMenuItem("http://www.evo.org/sherlock/international",
  "Sherlock Holmes Int'l");
addMenuItem("http://www.sherlock-holmes.co.uk/",
  "The Sherlock Holmes Museum");
addMenuItem("http://www.holmes-sherlock.com/",
  "Yoxley Old Place");
</SCRIPT>
</TD><TD VALIGN="top" BGCOLOR="white"><SPAN
  onClick="toggleMenu()">
  <IMG SRC="sliding-menu-tab.gif" BORDER="0"
    HEIGHT="51" WIDTH="20">
</SPAN>
</TD></TR>
</TABLE>
</SPAN>
```

You can see the results, with the menu just sliding into view, in Figure 25-2.

Getting the sliding menu to work required a few small additional changes: I removed the border elements in the "menu" CSS for aesthetic reasons, and I increased the width of the menu from 200 to 225 pixels. One more step adds a little space down the left edge so that the tab doesn't cover any of the contents, as follows:

```
<BODY BGCOLOR="white" STYLE="width: 650px;margin-left: 26px">
```

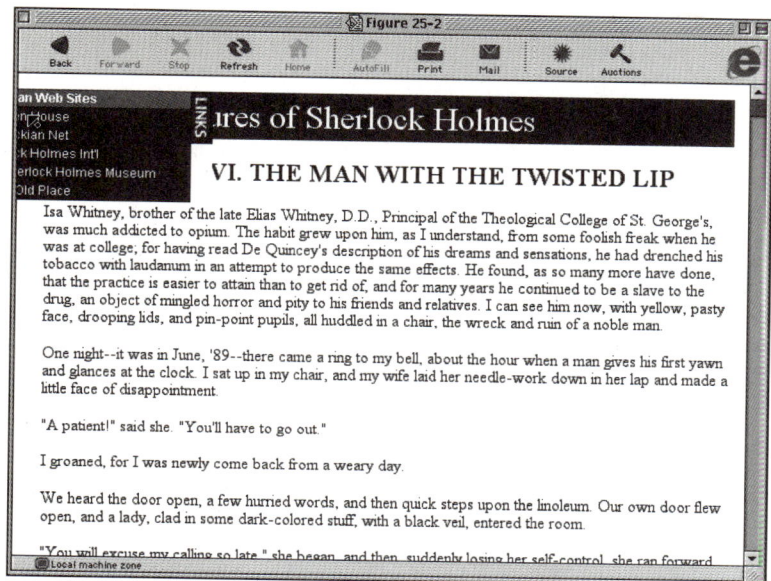

Figure 25-2 *A sliding menu, just sliding into view.*

If I were building this example as a general-purpose sliding menu, I'd pour all the initialization into a single function and put the name/URL data in an array. You see what I mean shortly.

Did you notice the refinement to the individual menu element display function? I'm reassigning `window.status` **to make the associated URL appear in the browser status display. Roll over the menu choices again and watch the very bottom left of the browser.**

**10 Min.
To Go**

Cascading Menu Refinements

The next step in menu design is to create submenus or cascading menus, where an individual menu element opens another menu of even further choices. You can see a number of different approaches to this feature on various Web sites. Fundamentally, cascading menus are a great navigational device for Web sites, because they enable you to offer shortcuts to dozens of different pages in a completely clutter-free manner. In fact, I'm sure that you're going to find this cascading menu package one of the most useful solutions in the entire book.

This process is complex, however, because I'm writing it as a portable package, enabling you to create a menu with submenus as easily as the following example shows:

```
newMenu(1, "mainMenu", 25, 50);
addMenuTitle("Holmsian Web Sites");
addMenuItem("http://www.bakerstreet221b.de/main.htm",
  "Camden House");
addMenuItem("http://www.sherlockian.net/", "Sherlockian Net");
```

```
addSubmenu("submenu2", "publications...");
addMenuItem("http://www.evo.org/sherlock/international",
  "Sherlock Holmes Intl");
addMenuItem("http://www.sherlock-holmes.co.uk/",
  "The Sherlock Holmes Museum");
addMenuItem("http://www.holmes-sherlock.com/", "Yoxley Old Place");
addSubmenu("submenu1", "more web sites...");
endMenu();
```

Instead of using the embedded SPAN elements, I push the entire menu-creation task into individual functions. Indeed, endMenu simply outputs a </SPAN> tag and nothing else.

Remember you'll also need to include crashcourse.js **in your DHTML page!**

newMenu, however, is the interesting function to examine, because it not only starts the menu definition sequence, but it also stores the menu name (and hierarchy level) in an array for later tracking purposes, as the following example demonstrates:

```
function newMenu(level, id, xVal, yVal)
{
if (level > maxDepth)
    return( alert(
      "Too deep: newMenu("+id+") called with level > max depth") );

  menunames[level][ menucounts[level]++ ] = id; // remember new ID
  currentLevel = level+1;                        //  counter + 1
  document.write  ("<SPAN CLASS=\"menu\" ID=\"" + id + "\" ");
  document.writeln("STYLE=\"top:"+yVal+"px; left:"+xVal+"px\">");
}
```

You can see that a global variable, maxDepth, defines how many levels of cascading menus you can use (I leave it at four), against which it compares the level of the new menu. Level 0 is the topmost level (the page itself), level 1 is the topmost set of menus, level 2 is the first set of submenus, and level 3 is the sub-submenus.

I also use two arrays to keep track of the IDs of all defined menus, by level, to later manage the opening and closing of the menu elements, as shown in the following function:

```
function closeMenus(level)
{
  // closes all menus at any level higher than that specified
  for (var lvls = level; lvls < maxDepth; lvls++) {
    for (var i=0; i < menucounts[lvls]; i++) {
      menuOff(menunames[lvls][i]);
    }
  }
}
```

This function enables you to easily close all menus at the current or a higher level. In the main menu level, for example, after you move the cursor onto a nonsubmenu link (a regular menu item), it automatically requests that all submenus close, as shown in the following line from the newly rewritten addMenuItem:

```
document.writeln(" closeMenus(" + currentLevel + ");\"");
```

This way, you can link multiple submenus to a single menu and make them appear and vanish as the user moves his cursor over the menu items. The behavior is exactly analogous to cascading menu behavior on your computer.

Unfortunately, the entire listing is rather lengthy, and because these sessions are set at 30 minutes, I'm going to ask that you go to the listing for Figure 25-3 on the CD-ROM and use View Source to see exactly what I'm doing for the spiffo cascading menus. Pay particular attention to addSubmenu() and notice how the definition of the menus themselves are now within the top <SCRIPT> block.

If you don't have the CD-ROM, visit the *DHTML Weekend Crash Course* Web site to see the code instead, at www.intuitive.com/dhtml/.

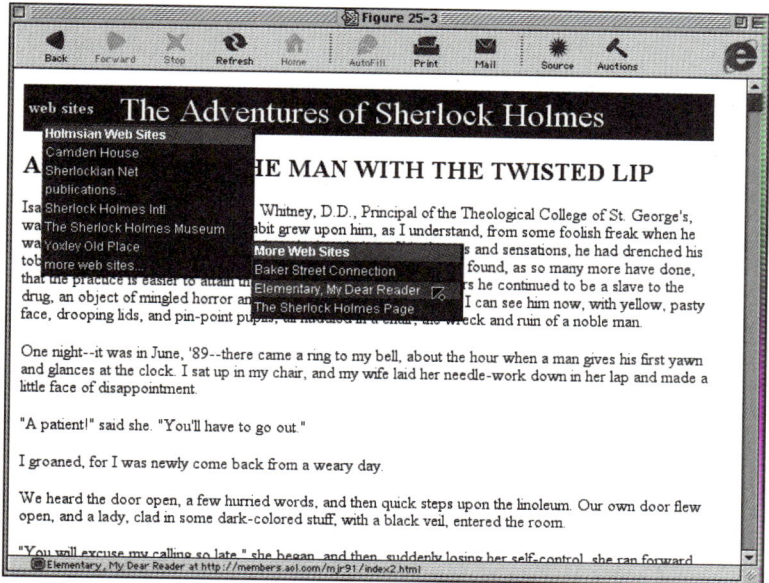

Figure 25-3   Cascading menus: Two levels appear.

Automatically Closing Menus by Using Hide-Me Timers

I want to squeeze one more topic into this important session before I wrap up: using
JavaScript timers to automatically close menus after the user is through using them. Sound
easy? Well, some nuances make this task a bit tricky to implement. The most important
consideration is that you never want a timer to close a menu while the user's cursor is over
any of its elements. You also don't want to close a menu if the user moves the cursor off the
menu and then slides it back on just before the timer runs out. To accomplish these tasks,
you need to use a *state variable* that indicates whether the timer can close a menu if it's
counting down.

If the mouse is over any menu element, the timer can't launch, so I call that the state
canCloseMenu = 0. After an onMouseOut event, you want the timer to launch and begin
counting down, so that's canCloseMenu = 1. After the timer runs out, you need to do a
last-second check of the canCloseMenu to ensure that it doesn't switch in the interim, as
follows:

```
function timedClose(lvl)
{
  canCloseMenu = 1; // we got here, so it must start out okay
  setTimeout("smartClose(" + lvl + ")", menuDelay);
}

function smartClose(lvl)
{
  if (canCloseMenu == 1) closeMenus(lvl);
  canCloseMenu = 0;
}
```

The scripted events on the page call timedClose, which then sets a countdown timer to
invoke smartClose after menuDelay milliseconds. Then smartClose simply ensures that it
can still close the menu before it requests a closeMenus event.

Above that sequence lie some global variables that start the canCloseMenu status variable in a known state and enable you to fine-tune the delay on closing menus, as follows:

```
var canCloseMenu = 0;    // 0 = don't close menu, 1 = close ok
var delayFactor = 1000;         // multiplier to get seconds
var menuDelay   = 3 * delayFactor; // autoclose delay (try 3-4)
```

Changes trickle through the various functions for the cascading menus, starting with the
following two lines adding to newMenu:

```
document.write  ("onMouseOver=\"canCloseMenu = 0\" ");
document.writeln("onMouseOut=\"timedClose('" + level + "');\">");
```

Then the change to addNewItem parallels the addition of the flag switch on onMouseOver
earlier in this section, as follows:

```
document.writeln("canCloseMenu=0");
```

In a nutshell, by making canCloseMenu a global variable, you can directly change its setting in any event handler or function. Every time that the user moves the cursor over any menu element and triggers an onMouseOver, the canCloseMenu status variable is set to 0 (that is, don't close the menu if a timer's counting down).

I can't display this example here in the book, because you must actually experiment with it to see what happens. So I encourage you to explore Figure 25-4.html on the CD-ROM to see how it works.

> You can expand and enhance the cascading menu package in many, many ways, and I encourage you to experiment. If you come up with a novel use or even just a nice example of this menu code in action, please let me know!

Done!

REVIEW

This session continues to push the envelope of your JavaScript and CSS knowledge, exploring different ways to create and incorporate pop-up and slide-on menus into your Web pages. As the session progresses, I generalize individual JavaScript elements into functions such as addMenuItem, which I then enhance with additional capabilities. You also learn about the fun mouse-pointer changes possible in CSS 2 and see how to use a timer tied to a global status variable to delay events a few seconds into the future without losing control of their subsequent execution.

QUIZ YOURSELF

1. Why do I specify four different border settings in the CSS for menu elements? (See "Better pop-up menus.")

2. Write this same four-line border specification in CSS using different CSS elements. Is it easier to understand? (See "Better pop-up menus.")

3. When do you use the cursor: wait style? (See "changing the mouse pointer" sidebar.)

4. What's the difference between document.write and document.writeln? (See "Back to the menu.")

5. Why do most site designers tie their menu-activation links to specific spots on the page? (See "Placing the menu.")

6. With adding the delayed close timer feature to the cascading menus, a slight bug in the code (although it's really more of a logic error) now slips into the onClick event handler in the <BODY> tag. What is it? (See "Automatically Closing Menus by Using Hide-Me Timers.")

BONUS FOR MAD SCIENTISTS:

1. What happens if you create a menu where you define all the elements by using `<SPAN>` rather than `<DIV>` tags? (Pay particular attention to Netscape 6.)

2. Create a drop-shadow for the menus that's dark gray and three pixels wide.

3. Arguably, you want to tie the delayed menu close feature to specific menu IDs instead of just closing all menus at that level. Make the changes necessary for that to work, and see whether you think it's better or worse than the solution that I present in this session.

4. Because you can tie events to the `onClick` of the entire window contents, try writing a function that completely hides a menu until the user clicks, after which the menu appears in context. You can try `getX` and `getY` from the `crashcourse.js` library to identify the mouse-click location.

Working with Windows

Session Checklist

✔ Tweaking the browser window

✔ Pop-up browser windows

✔ How interstitials work

✔ Nifty navigational bars

**30 Min.
To Go**

The last few sessions have been rather intense, long, and jammed full of information, some of which I can't even get to in the book. This session also covers a lot of material, but I think you can get through it without reaching for your local headache remedy (particularly if you played mad scientist after Session 25!).

In this session, I'm going to look at windows, from the browser itself to nifty pop-up windows and floating navigational elements. You see how some of the pop-up ad-based Web sites perform their dirty tricks and find out how to exploit onBlur and onFocus to control how the user interacts with the window.

Tweaking the Browser Window

A couple different objects have associated attributes and methods that enable you to exert a remarkable level of control over the user's browser experience. Chief among them is the window object. To make JavaScript references easy, browsers define the self object as a shortcut for the current browser's window object.

Before I look at it, however, I want to show you how easily you can set the page title within the document object. Following are a few lines that always include the current month and year in the title of the document (great for an online newsletter):

```
var monthNames = new Array("January","February","March",
  "April","May","June","July","August","September",
  "October","November","December");
```

```
var now = new Date();
var monthName = monthNames[now.getMonth()];

document.title = "The Acme Times (edition of " +
    monthName + ", " + now.getFullYear() + ")";
```

Moving the browser window on-screen

The self object offers a variety of methods that enable you to move and resize the browser window on-screen. The key methods for moving the browser are moveTo and moveBy. To move the browser to the top-left corner, for example, the following line does the trick:

```
self.moveTo(0,0)
```

MoveTo enables you to move to a specific spot, whereas moveBy is a relative change: To move the browser window 10 pixels to the right, for example, you can use the following line:

```
self.moveBy(10,0)
```

You can't move windows off-screen so a call such as moveTo(-10,-10) either fails or acts exactly as moveTo(0,0) does.

Because you can figure out the size of the window and the size of the screen, you can also create a function that automatically centers the window on-screen, too. You do face a couple of nuances, however, including the fact that the window size elements return the size of the displayable area of the browser window rather than the outside-edge. To compensate, I'm adding two variables, heightPadding and widthPadding, as you can see in the following example:

```
var heightPadding = 100; // factor for nav bars, etc...
var widthPadding = -12;
```

In addition, a problem in Internet Explorer prevents it from computing the window dimensions unless you write something to the window. To compensate, you can output a single nonbreaking space element *before* you test the size (with routines in crashcourse.js), as follows:

```
document.write(" ");

var bwidth = windowWidth();
var bheight = windowHeight();

var swidth = screenWidth();
var sheight = screenHeight();
```

Now you can calculate the correct location and use the moveTo method to reposition the window on demand, as follows:

```
function centerMe()
{
    // center the browser window on the screen
```

```
    var x = Math.round( (swidth - bwidth) / 2);
    var y = Math.round( (sheight - (bheight+heightPadding)) / 2);
    self.moveTo(x, y);
}
```

Dropping a link on your page that enables the user to center his browser on demand is easy, too, as the following line shows:

```
<SPAN onClick="centerMe()">[center]</SPAN>
```

Resizing the window

Another nifty trick that you can perform is to resize the browser window. Do you really want to design your page for a 600-pixel-wide display? And you're okay forcing the user to that size? Then use the `resizeTo` method, as follows:

```
self.resizeTo(600,450)
```

For slightly more sophistication, you can change just the width and leave the height alone by referencing the earlier size information, as follows:

```
self.resizeTo(600, sheight)
```

Even better, resize only if the window isn't already at least 600 pixels wide, as follows:

```
if (swidth < 600) self.resizeTo(600, sheight)
```

 **You need to recognize that your users may consider automatic changes in the window size quite annoying, so a better course, perhaps, is to use a link similar to the following example:**

```
<SPAN onClick="if (swidth<600)
    self.resizeTo(600,sheight)">optimize width</SPAN>
```

Here the user can initiate the action and, therefore, not get caught by surprise as it occurs.

To force the window to expand to the full size of the screen, use `resizeTo` and feed it the width and height of the screen itself, with adjustments for navigational toolbars and so on, as follows:

```
<SPAN onClick="self.moveTo(0,0);
self.resizeTo(swidth+widthPadding, sheight+heightPadding)">
zoom to full screen</SPAN>
```

Notice that I'm politely moving the browser to the top-left corner, too, to ensure that the resize doesn't result in some of the window running off-screen.

Figure 26-1 shows a window that offers you one-button access to most of these resize and reposition elements in a simple toolbar. I resized the window and clicked the center link to center it on-screen.

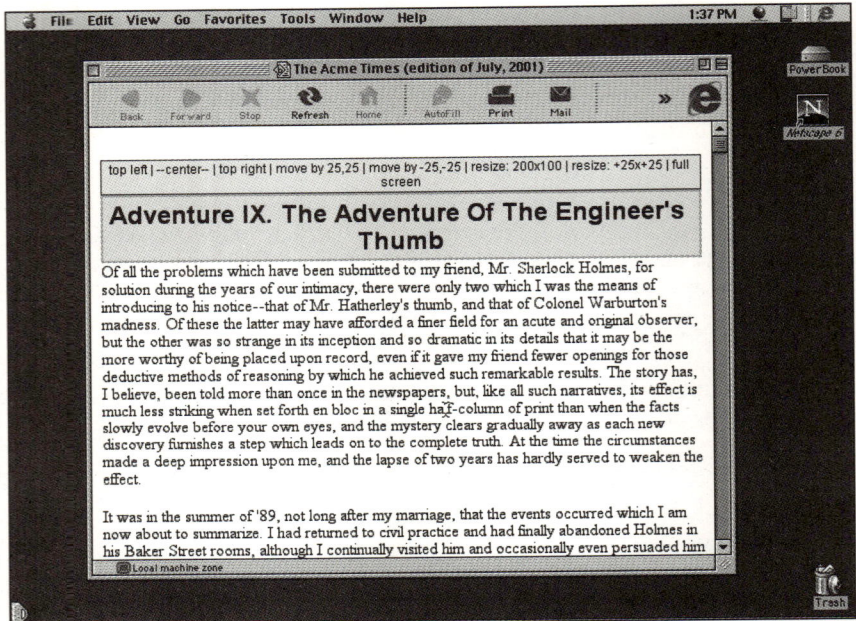

Figure 26-1   *Resizing and repositioning the browser by using appearance methods and the self object.*

Check out the title of the page as you look at Figure 26-1 on CD-ROM, too. You see that it magically becomes the current month and year rather than a static value.

 You also have a `resizeBy(x,y)` **method, but frankly, I can't imagine any situation where you'd use it. But if you come up with one, I'd like to hear about it!**

Pop-Up Browser Windows

A helpful method that you're sure to want to add to your toolkit is `window.open()`, which enables you to create new browser windows wherever and however you want. At its simplest, you can use it to open a new window that duplicates the navigational bars, size, and so on of the current window by using the following formula:

```
window.open(url, windowname)
```

To create a new window that enables you to explore the Hungry Minds Web site, for example, try the following:

```
hmi = window.open("http://www.hungryminds.com/", "hungryminds")
```

You use the name element with the TARGET attribute of the anchor tag (as in <A HREF=*url* TARGET="hungryminds"> link pointed to the new window </A>), whereas JavaScript references use the object that the open call returns (hmi, in this case). As an example, to ensure that the new window is at the top, immediately follow the preceding open() call with the following line:

```
hmi.focus();
```

Alternatively, to immediately drop the window behind the current window (which is how interstitials work, as you see shortly), use the following:

```
hmi.blur();
```

Window creation offers you considerable control over the layout of the new window through a constructed string value that's an optional third parameter. Table 26-1 shows its primary values.

Table 26-1   *Window Features with* window.open *Method*

Value	Description
copyhistory	New window gets same history list as current window.
favorites	Displays favorite sites bar (IE only).
height	Window height, in pixels
menubar	Displays menu bar with window. (PC only; Macs always have a visible menu bar.)
resizable	Enables the user to resize the window.
scrollbars	Includes scroll bars if content is larger than window.
status	Displays status bar.
toolbar	Displays toolbar (back, forward, home, and so on).
width	Window width, in pixels.

You can make Windows open as the page is loading by placing window.open calls in the JavaScript or tying them to an onLoad event handler in the <BODY> tag, as follows:

```
<BODY onLoad="window.open('sale-info.html','sale',
'height=100,width=200')">
```

The behavior of the feature list that you specify as the third parameter is actually rather interesting, because if you leave it blank, the new window opens with all the same charac-teristics as the existing window, including size, displayed toolbars, and so on. If you specify *any* parameter, however, everything defaults to off, so the preceding call produces a small window containing the contents of the sale-info.html file without any scroll bars, toolbars, status line, and so on.

To make a toolbar or similar item appear, specify toolbar=1 in the parameter list; to ensure that it correctly defaults to hidden, specify toolbar=0. Writing a simple routine that enables you to control the characteristics of an opening window, therefore, is quite easy, as the following example shows:

```
function myOpener(toolbar, scrollbar, menubar,
                  status, url, name)
{
  return(window.open(url, name,
    "'toolbar=" + (toolbar?"1":"0") +
    ",scrollbars=" + (scrollbar?"1":"0") +
    ",menubar=" + (menubar?"1": "0")+
    ",status=" + (status?"1": "0"));
}
```

Here's a very typical use of this function that you might find on a Web page:

```
<SPAN OnClick="myOpener(0,0,0,0,'http://www.hungryminds.com/',
    'hungryminds')">explore the Hungry Minds web site</SPAN>
```

Or you can skip the myOpener() function and drop the call into a button so that you can specify the dimensions of the window, too, as follows:

```
<INPUT TYPE="button" VALUE="Explore the Hungry Minds web site"
  OnClick="window.open('http://www.hungryminds.com/',
  'hungryminds','noscroll,noresize,favorites=1,'+
  'height=300,width=550');">
```

The inclusion of the favorites **bar works only in Internet Explorer because it's not one of the toolbars available in Netscape Navigator or Netscape 6.**

A more likely use for your pop-up window is to load a graphic or simple HTML page, tying it to a specific event occurring on the main Web page.

20 Min. To Go

Floating Pictures

The following example creates a button on a page that, after a user clicks it, opens a new floating window displaying the associated JPEG image:

```
<INPUT TYPE="button" VALUE="open picture"
  onClick="window.open('little-gareth.jpg','picture',
  'noscroll,noresize')">
```

This code is straightforward, but it exhibits different behavior in different browsers: In Netscape 6, the new window is a little bit smaller than the image (for which N6 ignores the noscroll). Internet Explorer, by contrast, opens a new window that's the same size as the parent window, so it's large with a small picture tucked into the top-left corner. Not a good result at all.

Instead, a quick check of the image itself reveals that it's 175×196 pixels, suggesting that an improved call should do the trick, as the following attempts to demonstrates:

```
<INPUT TYPE="button" VALUE="open picture"
  onClick="window.open('little-gareth.jpg','picture',
  'noscroll,noresize,width=175,height=196')">
```

But, surprisingly, the image ends up too small and displays forced horizontal and vertical scroll bars in Netscape 6 — while it's off center and *big* in Internet Explorer, as you can see from the comparisons of the two in Figure 26-2.

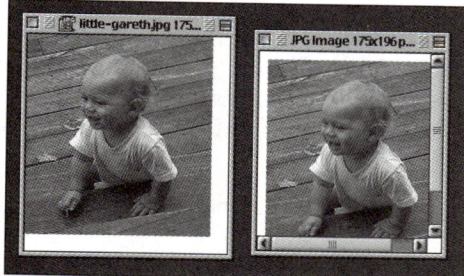

Figure 26-2 *Can't quite get the image size right in either Internet Explorer 5.5, on the left, or Navigator 6, on the right.*

This situation is super-frustrating, as you may expect. Tweaking and fine-tuning can produce dimensions that give you just the image with no edge in both browsers, but each browser requires different numbers to get the result that you want.

Figure 26-2 on the CD-ROM offers you buttons with various dimensional settings for this picture, so experiment in your browser and see what results you get.

The best strategy is simply to create a page that contains the graphic. This approach gives you a much greater level of control over the end product. Because you can use the object that the window.open() call feeds back to you with document.write and similar statements, seeing how this function works is quite cool, as the following example shows:

```
function picWindow(url, title, wd, ht)
{
  var height=ht + 30; // space for title & close link

  w3 = window.open("", 'pic','noresize,noscroll,height='+
        height+',width='+wd);
  w3.document.write("<BODY STYLE=\"margin:0px;padding:0px;
background-color:#669\">");
```

```
    w3.document.write("<CENTER><SPAN STYLE='color:#CCF;font-family:sans-
serif;font-size:90%;font-weight: bold;'>" +
title + "</SPAN><BR><IMG SRC=" + url + "ALT='" + title + "'><BR>");
    w3.document.write("<A HREF='#' STYLE='color: #69C;font-family:sans-
serif;font-size: 50%'
onClick=\"self.close()\">close</A></CENTER></BODY>");
    w3.document.close();
    w3.document.title=title;
}
```

Notice that the function assigns the w3 object the result of the window.open(); as a result, you can easily use various methods with the new, open window, such as w3.document.write() to add material and w3.document.close() to close the window. Notice, too, that I set the title of the pop-up window by using JavaScript, too, instead of adding a <TITLE> tag in the HTML sequence.

Be careful with the document.write() **function: If you write to a window that already contains material — in particular, a Web page — you blank out and replace the contents with the new material you're writing. That's why this example creates a window with no initial content: Notice the first parameter to the** window.open() **call in** picWindow()**.**

The Web page calls this function from the same Figure 26-2 listing, as the following example shows:

```
<INPUT TYPE="button"
   VALUE="open picture with picWindow function"
   OnClick="picWindow('little-gareth.jpg',
   'Gareth Samuel',175,196)" >
```

Figure 26-3 shows the results for both browsers. They're not quite the same, but because I'm producing a dark background and centering the material with a title and a tiny close link on the bottom, the viewer can easily ignore the differences in size.

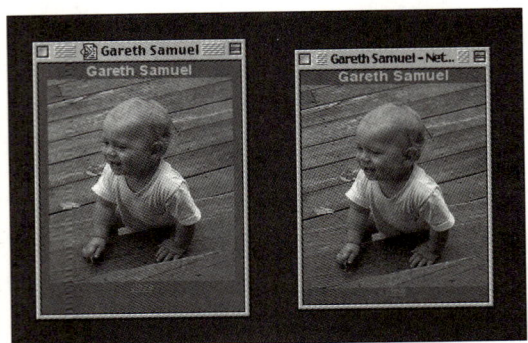

Figure 26-3   *A better picture presentation: Internet Explorer on the left and Navigator 6 on the right.*

How Interstitials Work

If you've surfed the Web recently, you're well aware of the latest trend in online advertising: pop-up advertisements — ads that pop up as you make the transition between pages and ads that pop *underneath* the current window, which you find after you leave the site and close your main browser window.

All these windows are simple variants on what you've learned already in this session, so take a look! Before we do, however, a quick warning: Many people find interstitials quite annoying, so use them sparingly, and at your own risk.

Pop-up ads

The most common use of pop-up windows is to slap up an advertisement as the user first arrives at a Web site. This window may highlight a special promotion on the site or it may hold an unrelated advertisement for a third-party site. Either way, it all ties to the onLoad event in the <BODY> tag, and it's most likely a simple HTML page that appears.

The <BODY> tag ends up looking as follows:

```
<BODY onLoad="window.open('promo.html','promo',
  'noresize,noscroll,height=140,width=225')">
```

And the promo.html file can look as follows:

```
<HTML>
<TITLE>S. Holmes, Detective</TITLE>
<BODY BGCOLOR="AADDFF">
<CENTER>
<DIV STYLE="font: 22pt bold Arial; color: #030;
 padding: 6px; border: 3px double green;width: 100%">
 New Client Special</DIV>
<DIV STYLE="font: 14pt Arial; color: #090; padding: 4px">
first consultation free</DIV>
<DIV STYLE="font: 7pt sans-serif; color: #696;
 margin-top: 4px">
 restrictions apply</DIV></CENTER>
</BODY></HTML>
```

Figure 26-4 shows how this page looks in its own small 225×140 window.

Pop-up between pages

This pop-up is super-easy to do after you figure out how to make the advertisement pop up. In fact, you need to add only *two additional characters* to the example in the preceding section. The gist of what you need to do is that you tie the open window event to onUnload rather than onLoad, which causes the window to pop up after visitors leave the page.

It looks as follows:

```
<BODY onUnload="window.open('promo.html','promo',
  'noresize,noscroll,height=140,width=225')">
```

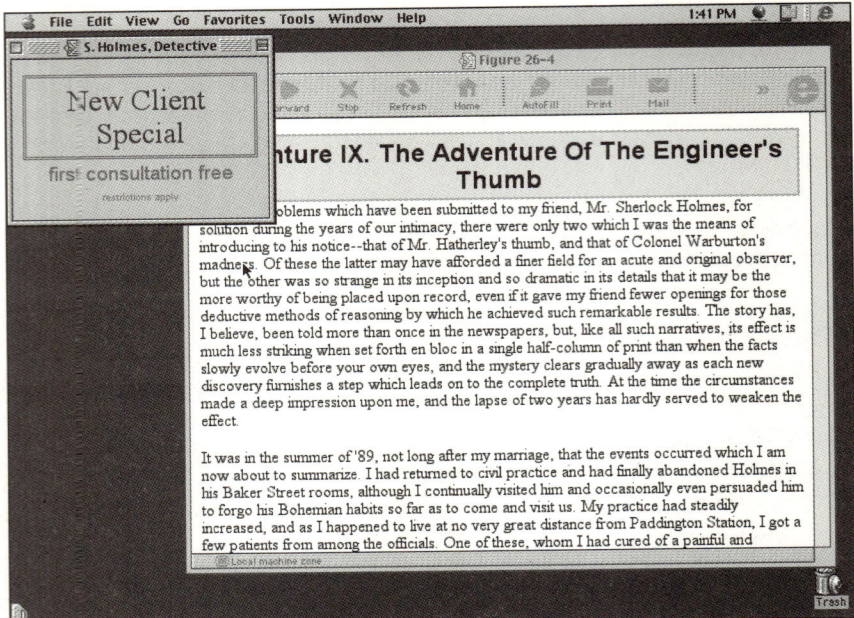

Figure 26-4   *A simple pop-up advertisement appears as the page loads.*

Pages underneath the current page

The final interstitial trick is to make a page pop up and automatically go behind the current page so that the user can continue to focus on the existing content. You accomplish this effect through a combination of `blur()` and `focus()` events and can drop them all into the `onLoad` or `onUnload` event handler.

Here's an example of how to modify the free consultation advertisement in Figure 26-4 to ensure that the advert pops up but that the main window remains the top-most active window for the user:

```
<BODY BGCOLOR='#FFFFFF'
onLoad='x=window.open('promo.html','promo','noresize,noscroll,
height=140,width=225');x.moveTo(0,0);x.blur();self.focus();">
```

Notice that I'm moving the pop-up window to the top-left corner of the screen by using the `moveTo()` method, using `blur()` to remove focus from that window, and ensuring that it does what I want by turning `focus` to the current `self` (main) window.

**10 Min.
To Go**

Nifty Navigational Bars

Only two more topics remain to discuss here: How do you push new pages out to the pop-up window, and how do you make events in the pop-up window affect the main window?

You can start by recognizing that you can make the HTML in the pop-up window as sophisticated as you want, so you can create a timer that reloads the page with new content every 60 seconds. It looks as follows (and remember that this example is in the promo.html file):

```
<SCRIPT LANGUAGE="JavaScript">
function showNext()
{
  self.location.href="promo2.html";
}
</SCRIPT>
```

Then you tie it into the page and start it by using the following line:

```
<BODY onLoad="setTimeout('showNext()',6000)">
```

One thing to realize is that this code needs to appear in *each* of the promo pages, because after you load in the new page, the JavaScript vanishes from the old. The other ways to solve this problem are to tie the JavaScript timeout loop to the main page or to make a tiny controller window pop up behind the pop-up window.

The parent window can push new pages out to the promo window by referencing the window object that returns as the window is created. This approach involves a slightly cleaner invocation of the pop-up window and kicks off the timed-page changes, too, as follows:

```
function makePopUp()
{
  popup = window.open('promo.html','promo',
    'noresize,noscroll,height=140,width=225');
  popup.moveTo(0,0);
  popup.blur();
  self.focus();
  setTimeout("changePopUp()", 6000);
}
```

Now you can define an array of URLs and access the popup object in a loop, as follows:

```
var mylist = new
      Array("promo1.html","promo2.html","promo3.html");
mylist.count = 3;
mycount = 0;

function changePopUp()
{
  if (popup == null || popup.closed) {
    alert("You've closed my lovely popup window!");
    return;
  }
  if (mycount == mylist.count) mycount = 0;
  popup.location.href = mylist[mycount];
  mycount++;
  setTimeout("changePopUp()", 6000);
}
```

Notice that, because the user can close the window, you need a simple test at the top of changePopUp to confirm that the window still exists before you actually change its attributes. Whether you *want* the pop-up alert, well, that's up to you!

This autocycling pop-up window is on the CD-ROM as fig26-4a.html.

You can use this sort of timed loop for quite a different number of tricks. You can change an image with a reassignment of an image object's .src attribute, for example, or you can change the color of the background by using popup.style.backgroundColor, and so on.

Sending Changes Back to the Parent Window

The only piece of the puzzle left is to demonstrate how to make events in the pop-up window (more properly the child window) affect the parent window. This task proves surprisingly easy because of the opener object, which points to the window object of the parent window.

Within the navigational pop-up window, then, you simply change URLs by using the following formula:

```
opener.location.href = "new-url.html";
```

To make that line of code a bit more readable, you can create a succinct function, as follows:

```
function go(url)
{
  opener.location.href = url;
}
```

Then all the references in the pop-up window can look as follows:

```
<SPAN onClick="go('page2.html')">page 2</SPAN>
```

An alternative strategy for this functionality is to actually name the main window with a line at the top, as follows:

```
<SCRIPT LANGUAGE="JavaScript">
window.name = "contents";
</SCRIPT>
```

Then the navigational pop-up window can redirect things by using the TARGET attribute of hypertext references and (more important) FORM elements, too, as in the following example:

```
<FORM METHOD="get" ACTION="search.cgi" TARGET="contents">
```

I prefer the former method because it requires no change on the parent page, but you're likely to find both useful at different times.

Done!

REVIEW

This session gives you a whirlwind tour of many of the different capabilities of the window object, including in particular how to open new windows and control them through various methods. You also learn how to resize and move the main browser window, how to create external navigational controllers (which some people call *remote controls*), and how to replace the contents of a window on a mouse click, load event, unload event, or even just after a certain amount of time elapses.

QUIZ YOURSELF

1. Why do you need to use heightPadding in computing how to center the browser window? (See "Moving the browser window on-screen.")

2. What's the fastest way to ascertain the dimensions of a Web graphic? (See "Floating Pictures.")

3. Go find a Web site with a pop-up window and use View Source to see how the site does it. Does it use the same methods as I show you in this session? (See "pop-up ads.")

4. When would you want to use the copyhistory option in the window.open() method? (See "Pop-up Browser Windows.")

5. Modify the conditional resize line (where the user can resize the browser window to 600 pixels wide) so that you also center the browser window automatically by using the moveTo method. (See "Resizing the window.")

PART

V

Sunday Morning

1. The `img` object has different attributes in different browsers because the browsers _____.

2. What are the two main event handlers that you use for rollovers?

3. To change the text on the status line, you need to assign a value to what property?

4. If you want to script your FRAME-based design, what's the most important thing to remember?

5. What's the difference between `setInterval` and `setTimeOut`?

6. What simple condition enables you to use `getYear()` instead of `getFullYear()`?

7. True/False: JavaScript includes the method `isLeapYear()`.

8. What are the units of the delay-interval parameter to `setInterval`?

9. True/False: You're limited to six `<SCRIPT>` blocks on a page of HTML, according to the W3C standard.

10. What's the difference between `onBlur` and `onChange`?

11. Why do you often need to use an empty `<FORM>` tag with a JavaScript-enabled form?

12. What's the result of `Math.floor(4.25)`?

13. What's the result of `Math.ceil(4.25)`?

14. True/False: In the world of typefaces, 1 point = ¹/₇₂ inch.

15. Which is correct: `border-bottom` or `bottom-border`?

16. What CSS statements are necessary to make a <SPAN> element behave exactly like a hypertext anchor? Include the necessary cursor change, too.

17. True/False: document.write automatically appends a carriage return after each line of output.

18. Refresher: What's the basic difference between <DIV> and <SPAN>?

19. What's the lazy shortcut for ascertaining the dimensions of a Web-ready graphic?

20. You should use the _____ method to create a separate pop-up window in JavaScript and probably tie it to the _____ method, too.

PART

VI

Sunday
Afternoon

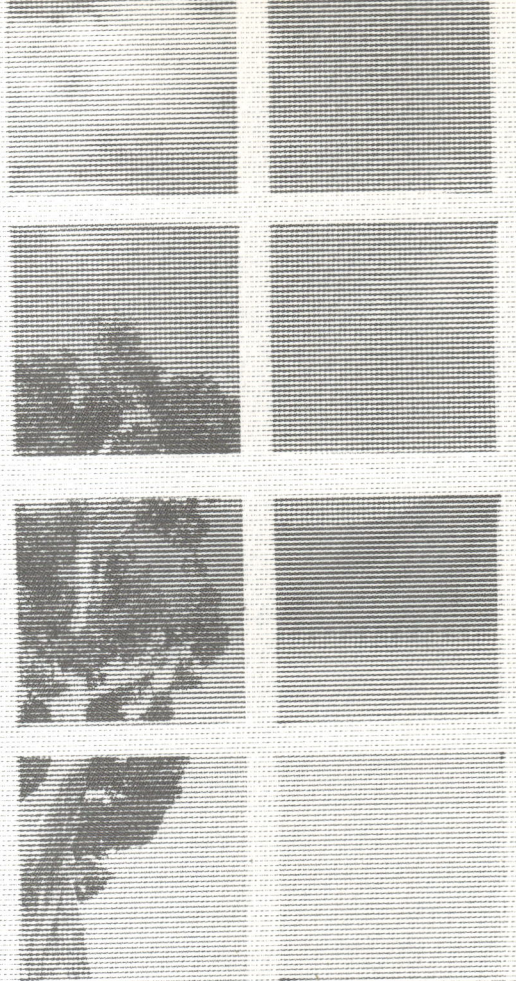

27

Web Site Memory with Cookies

30 Min. To Go

Y ou're coming into the home stretch now, and these last few sessions continue our trend of neat gadgets and gizmos for your Web site. In this session, I'm going to focus on one of the most controversial capabilities of Web browsers: *magic cookies*.

The original idea of magic cookies (or just *cookies*) was to solve the *stateless* problem of Web browsers. In a nutshell, every time that you visit a Web site or even just ask for graphics, subsequent pages, and so on, you're essentially a new visitor with no history whatsoever. Not bad for privacy but not good for a site that tries to offer you a customized experience.

The designers of the early Web browsers came up with a spiffy solution with cookies: Web sites could leave a persistent *state* variable on a user's browser that would then feed back to the server each time that browser communicated. It was a useful solution while you're busy surfing a site, but it proved extremely useful if you wanted to come back to the site a few days later and have it remember your identity.

The problem with cookies is that some sites make very bad decisions about what information to store therein, saving credit card numbers, social security numbers, passwords, and other highly personal and confidential information. Because the cookie data file on any computer is unencrypted plain text, easy to open and examine, before long, people were finding their private information becoming all too public.

Then some smart JavaScript programs began to exploit bugs in these same browsers that enabled them to reap all the cookies that the user had from any site, even though the browser is supposed to enforce an if-you-didn't-send-it-you-can't-see-it rule. Whether anecdotal or true, cookies became Public Enemy #1 in the late '90s, and for a while, they looked as if they'd soon vanish completely from the Web user's experience.

What kept cookies around is that they're just so darn useful. You can see what I mean by going to your favorite Web browser and selecting Cookies from your Preferences dialog box (accessed through the Edit ⇨ Preferences menu option). The amount of cookies that your system saves may astonish, especially as some come from sites that you don't even remember visiting!

I participate in a number of different Web discussion groups, including ones at BusinessWeek.com, About.com, and Builder.com, and every one of these sites helps me jump into the conversation quickly by remembering my account information in a cookie. If I go to Amazon.com, it welcomes me back. Whenever I visit the *San Jose Mercury News* online, it already knows my preferences and geographic location.

 **So why do people call them magic cookies? I believe it's because of an old Unix joke associated with the Cookie Monster in Sesame Street. Early Unix had a program "cookie" that, if run, prompted "Cookie?" over and over until you typed "COOKIE!". The point? Persistence.**

The Nuts and Bolts of Cookies

In their essence, cookies are quite straightforward. They're a name=value pair with some additional information, as shown in Table 27-1.

Table 27-1   *Cookie Field Values*

Field Name	Value	Explanation
domain	domain qualifier	Specific subdomain that's to receive the cookie. (It must lie at least two-levels deep — for example, hungryminds.com. rather than just .com)
expires	GMT time	Point in time that the cookie expires.
path	pathname	Area of Web site that to which cookie reflects. *applies.*
secure	*no value, just present or absent*	Indicates whether you can consider the cookie secure. (Not used, in my experience.)

As an example, a cookie that keeps track of how many times you visit a Web site is one that you may decide to call count, and it may look as follows:

```
count=1; path=/; domain=intuitive.com
```

Or, if it includes an expiration date, it may appear as follows:

```
count=1; path=/; domain=intuitive.com;
    expires=Sat Jul 7 18:18:57 CST 2001
```

First generation browsers that supported cookies required that you specify the path, and some even insisted on domain settings, too. Nowadays, however, you can get away with just a little information — even providing only the name=value pair, if you want. I still recommend that you always include an expiration date, if nothing else, so that you know how long the cookie should hang around.

In fact, creating a JavaScript function that you can use to compute the expiration date for a cookie is pretty straightforward, as the following example shows:

```
function expiresIn(days)
{
  // return a string that has an appropriately formatted date for
  // a cookie expiration value 'days' in the future

  var expireDate = new Date();   // starts out as the current time

  expireDate.setTime(expireDate.getTime() + (days*24*60*60*1000));

  return(expireDate);
}
```

To get an expiration date that's two weeks in the future, for example, just use `expiresIn(14)`. A day in the past? Using `expiresIn(-1)` does the trick.

Setting and Reading Cookies

**20 Min.
To Go**

I'm going to jump into the world of cookies head first now, okay?

Here's a JavaScript routine for extracting the cookie value from the document object:

```
function getCookie(name)
{
  // return the value of the specified cookie, if available
  // cookies are always in the form NAME=value; NAME=value

  var lhs = name + "=", i=0;

  while (i < document.cookie.length) {
    var j = i + lhs.length;
    if (document.cookie.substring(i, j) == lhs)
      return(getCookieValue(j));
    i = document.cookie.indexOf(" ", i) + 1;
    if (i == 0) break;
  }
  return null;
}
```

The preceding example's a bit complicated, because I need to do some fancy string manipulation to separate out the name=value from the rest of the cookie. (And remember that you can have more than one name=value pair in the cookie string.) In the preceding function, lhs is the left-hand side that I'm trying to match. You may notice a helper function that getCookie() needs, which I call getCookieValue(). Check out the following example:

```
function getCookieValue(offset)
{
  // return cookie value starting at offset until a
```

```
// semicolon or the end of string

if ((endstr = document.cookie.indexOf (";", offset)) == -1)
  endstr = document.cookie.length;

return(unescape(document.cookie.substring(offset, endstr)));
}
```

The preceding example's basically a *copy until ';' or end of line, starting at offset* function using the indexOf method to see whether it finds a semicolon.

Actually, I'm using a common C programmer trick here, which is worth noting: The if expression is assigning endstr the result of the indexOf call and then comparing it to the value -1. If it matches, it means no semicolon is in the segment of the string that starts at offset, so the condition is true and endstr is reassigned the .length value of the cookie. Neat, eh?

The escape() and unescape() functions are part of the built-in capabilities of JavaScript. They wrap up a string so that the browser can safely send it as a URL to a server (with spaces becoming %20, for example) and restore the string, respectively.

Setting a cookie

Setting a cookie is super-easy, particularly if you use the expiresIn() function that I show you in the previous section, as follows:

```
function setCookie(name, value, expires)
{
  // given a name=value pair and an expiration, save as a cookie

  document.cookie = name + "=" + escape(value) + "; path=/" +
    ((expires != null) ? "; expires="+expires.toGMTString() : "");
}
```

You can now test this function by using a Web page that includes the following:

```
<BODY onLoad="setCookie('count', 1, expiresIn(14))">
```

The preceding line sets a cookie that I call count that expires in 14 days.

Before I try this code, I'm going to change the preferences of my Web browser so that it asks me before accepting cookies. Interestingly, the latest crop of browsers show very little information about the incoming cookie, so I'm going to resort to Netscape 4.7, which outputs the dialog box shown as Figure 27-1.

The page underneath isn't worth showing yet, so I'm actually going to take this simple counter and turn it into a per-visitor visit counter.

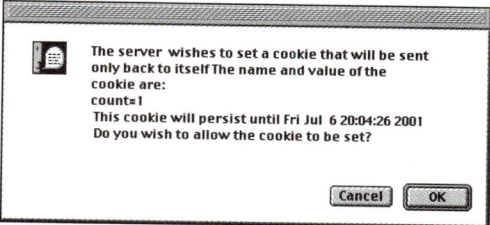

Figure 27-1   Warning: Do you want to accept this cookie?

Deleting cookies

Before I work with the counter from the preceding section, however, I need one more function. To delete a cookie from the user's cookie file (cookie jar?), you need to send the same name=value pair and an expiration date that's in the past. You can accomplish this task with the following example:

```
function deleteCookie (name)
{
  // Expire the specified cookie by setting its
  // expires= date to now - 1

  expireDate = expiresIn(-1);
  document.cookie = name + "=" + getCookie (name) +
    "; expires=" + expireDate.toGMTString();
}
```

Notice the call to expiresIn(), which returns an expiration date of 24 hours in the past.

Cookies in Action!

With the cookie toolkit that I show you how to use in this session, writing a Web-page counter that tracks visits per user (rather than a collective count) is easy. If the user already has a count cookie from the page, just increment its value and send it back. If not, start the count at 1 and send the user his first cookie. The following example shows you how to do so:

```
function visitCounter()
{
  if ((count = getCookie('count')) == null) {
    setCookie('count', 1, expiresIn(30)); // new counter
    return(1);
  } else {
    deleteCookie('count'); // delete old cookie value
    setCookie('count', parseInt(count)+1, expiresIn(30));
    return(count);
  }
}
```

The key thing to notice here is that you need to delete the old name=value pair before you set the new one. Otherwise, you end up saving count=1, count=2, count=3, and so on in the user's cookie file.

Now you can drop a visit counter just about anywhere on your Web page, as you can see in the following example:

```
<DIV STYLE="text-align:center;font-family:sans-serif;
    color: #339;font-size: 75%">
<SCRIPT LANGUAGE="JavaScript">
  document.write("You've been here " + visitCounter() +
   " times, and it's " + expiresIn(0))
</SCRIPT>
</DIV>
```

I demonstrate the results of this example in Figure 27-2.

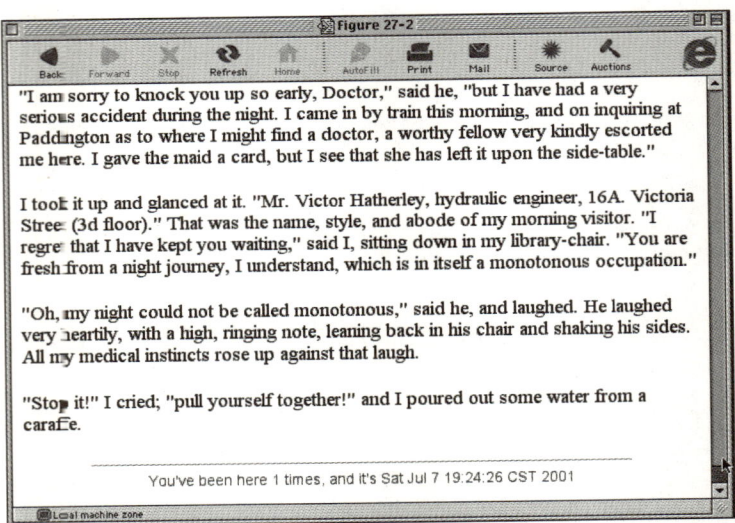

Figure 27-2   *Notice the counter at the bottom of the page.*

You can also drop the following into the <BODY> tag to see in a pop-up alert box how many times you've visited the site:

```
<BODY onLoad="alert('count set to ' + getCookie('count'));">
```

I hope that you realize that, if you can do this much, you can also change the appearance of a page based on the frequency of a surfer visiting your site. If a visitor's popped by dozens of times, you may present an abbreviated navigation mechanism, but on that user's first visit, perhaps you present a new tutorial window that pops up to offer a tour.

In fact, you can do dozens of different things with cookies now that you have a handy library of cookie functions, as I present you with in this session.

Show a pop up only once

Here's an example of what you can do with these pop ups. Say that you want a `Welcome—please take our survey` window to pop up the first time that the user visits your site, but never again, regardless of whether the person actually answers the survey. Here's an easy solution:

```
function popupIf()
{
  // pop up a survey window if this is your first visit

  if (getCookie('visits') == null) {
    setCookie('visits', 1, expiresIn(365));
    openSurvey();
  }
}
```

Notice that I set a one-year expiration date. Ideally that date enables you to collect lots of survey information and, a year later, ask these same users survey questions again.

To-do lists

**10 Min.
To Go**

Because you can place any information into a cookie, how about adding a simple to-do list that magically returns each time that the visitor comes to the Web site? You can accomplish this feat completely in JavaScript with a cookie remembering the to-do items, as shown in Figure 27-3.

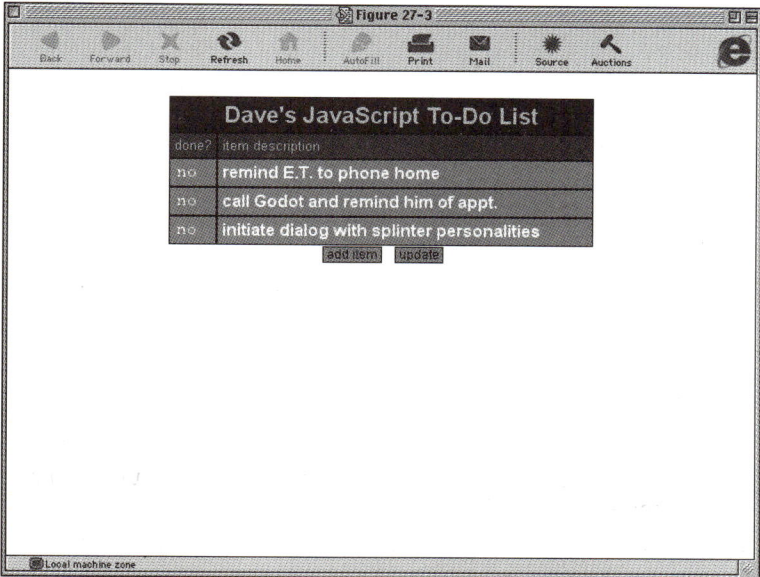

Figure 27-3   *A slick to-do management system, all in JavaScript.*

The code that implements the to-do list is worth studying, as it's a nice blend of CSS styles for presentation and layout and JavaScript for the actual functionality. It's quite long, however, so I'm going to present only a couple highlights here and encourage you to access the figure on your computer and then use View Source on it yourself.

The basic design revolves around two parallel arrays of information: todoList contains the text associated with each to-do item, and keepToDo has a value of 1 if you want to keep the item, and 0 if it's complete and you can delete it.

You can examine both by using a JavaScript for loop, as I demonstrate in the following routine, which I tie to the onUnload event in the <BODY> tag:

```
function saveToDo()
{
  // We're leaving the page, so it's time to write out the
  // current status of the to-do list.

  var yourToDo = "", added = 0;
  for (var i=0; i < todoCount; i++) {
    if (keepToDo[i] == 1) {
      if (added > 0) yourToDo += "|";
      yourToDo += todoList[i];
      added++;
    }
  }

  deleteCookie('todo'); // clear the old one...
  setCookie('todo', yourToDo, expiresIn(14));
}
```

The to-do's accumulate in yourToDo, separated by the | symbol, but they add onto the list only if their keepToDo value is 1. The global variable todoCount remembers how many to-dos the user is saving at the current time.

The other interesting routine is the following surprisingly succinct function that enables you to add a new to-do item to the list or update the list after you mark an event or two as done:

```
function todoControls()
{
  // Smart add event and update todo list buttons that exploit the
  // history list to force a refresh of the current page.

  document.write  ("<SPAN CLASS='add' onClick=\"x=prompt(New ");
  document.write  (" item:'); if (x) { todoList[todoCount] = x;");
  document.write  ("keepToDo[todoCount++] = 1; history.go(0);");
  document.write  (" }\">add item</SPAN>   ");
  document.write  ("<SPAN CLASS='add' onClick=\"history.go(0)\");
  document.writeln("'>update</SPAN>");
}
```

You can see one of the nifty JavaScript tricks in the to-do list here, too: The history object offers a method go() that enables you to force the page to reload with an entry in the user's history list. If it displays an offset of zero, it reloads the current page.

The other technique to look out for as you view the source is the swapping containers that implement the yes/no toggle on the to-do list itself. As implemented, if you click yes, it flips to no and vice versa. It functions much like a FORM check box, but using only text!

Window and Document Object Redux

Rather than list more JavaScript code in the remainder of this section, I think that a more useful course is to list for you some of the most valuable methods and properties of two objects that are quite important to sophisticated scripting: the window object and document object.

The window object

This object you use as the container for the entire browser window or each of the frames in a frames-based layout. It uses more than 40 properties and almost as many methods, but I'm just focusing here on the most important ones, as shown in Tables 27-2 and 27-3.

Table 27-2	*The Most Useful* window *Object Properties*
Property	**Explanation**
closed	Determines whether the window is closed. It's most useful for pop ups, as I show in Session 26.
history	The history object shows where the user's already visited.
location	The URL of the current location. Use location.href, however, to redirect the browser.
name	The name of the window, as you use it with TARGET attributes.
opener	The window object of the window that opened this window (useful for pop-ups).
parent	The window object of the parent that defines this frameset element.
self	A shortcut reference to the current window object.
status	The text of the status bar (at the bottom edge of the browser window).

Table 27-3	*The Most Useful* window *Methods*
Method	**Explanation**
alert()	Displays an alert dialog box. Displays only one button: OK.
blur()	Removes focus from the current window.

(continued)

Table 27-3 *Continued*

Method	Explanation
close()	Closes the current window.
confirm()	Displays a message including two buttons: OK or Cancel. Clicking the former results in the method returning true; clicking Cancel returns false.
focus()	Brings the window to the front. Other windows receive an onBlur event.
moveBy()	Moves the window the specified x,y increment on-screen.
moveTo()	Moves the window to the specified x,y coordinates on-screen.
open()	Opens a new window. Returns a new window object.
prompt()	Displays a dialog box enabling the user to enter text. It displays two buttons: OK and Cancel, and returns true or false, respectively, based on which button the user clicks.
resizeBy()	Changes size of browser window by specified x,y increment.
resizeTo()	Change size of browser window to x,y.
scroll()	Scrolls window to x,y point (using 0,0 to jump to top).
scrollBy()	Scrolls window by x,y increment.

The document object

The other object that's worth listing properties and methods for, as a reference, is the document object. In this session, I focus on the cookie property, but quite a few more are available, as show in Table 27-4.

Table 27-4 *The Most Useful document Object Properties*

Property	Explanation
alinkColor	Active link color (A:active).
bgColor	Background color of the document.
cookie	The magic cookies associated with this document. (See earlier in this session.)
domain	The hostname of the server from which this document comes.
fgColor	Foreground color of the document.
linkColor	Color of nonvisited hyperlinks (A:link).

Property	Explanation
location	The URL of the current document.
referrer	The URL of the page from which this was accessed. Often blank.
title	The title of this document (as shown in the browser frame).
vlinkColor	Color of visited links (A:visited).

Various methods also associate with the document object are worth listing. (I use document.write() extensively in this book, for example.) I list these methods in Table 27-5.

Table 27-5	*The Most Useful* document *Object Methods*

Method	Explanation
clear()	Clears the current document in preparation for new material.
close()	Closes the stream through which you've been writing to the document. Doesn't, however, close the window. (That's window.close().)
open()	Opens a stream through which you can write to the document. Doesn't open a new window. (That's window.open().)
write()	Writes the specified content to the document stream.
writeln()	Same as write() but appends a carriage return.

Every object in the document object model has its own set of properties and methods, a list that's frankly quite overwhelming. If you're burning to know them all, some terrific references are available online. But I want you to stay focused for now. I explain new properties and methods as you encounter them, and then, in Session 30, I point you to some of the best online resources. Okay?

REVIEW

Done!

This session explores in depth the many ways that cookies can help you make smarter Web pages, showing all the crucial functions necessary to build a general-purpose cookie library. I also explore some of the history and controversy surrounding cookies in the Web community and then built a useful JavaScript function by using cookies: a visitor counter. You also see how you can easily ensure that pop-up windows appear only once for each visitor and then get a tantalizing sample of the code necessary to build a JavaScript-based to-do manager. (Remember: The entire code — with extensive comments — is on the CD-ROM.) Finally, this session wraps up with a reference list of some of the most useful properties and methods associated with both the window and document objects.

Quiz Yourself

1. What original problem in the design of the Web did cookies solve? (See the session introduction.)
2. Go into your Web browser preferences and check how many cookies you have in file from different Web sites. (See the session introduction.)
3. True or false: Cookies are limited to one name=value pair per site that you visit. (See "The Nuts and Bolts of Cookies.")
4. What does the escape() function do and when is it most useful? (see "Setting and Reading Cookies")
5. What's your theory on why the most recent browsers display the least helpful messages if you want to monitor cookies coming in as you surf the Web? (See "Setting a cookie.")
6. How do you delete a cookie from within a JavaScript program? (See "Deleting cookies.")
7. Modify the visit counter to also track the name of the user. The first visit should prompt for a name, and subsequent visits should welcome that user back by name. (For extra credit, change the welcome based on how many times the person visits the site.) (See "Cookies in Action!")
8. While you're working with the visit counter, fix the annoying grammatical bug that produces You've been here 1 times to make it use time if the value is 1 and times otherwise. (See "Cookies in Action!")

Mad Scientist Playground

1. If you really want to get your hands dirty, how about creating Search Buddy, a pop-up window that enables users to search their favorite Web site, with the results appearing in the main window and not the pop up? Use a cookie to ask visitors which search engine is their favorite and then automatically make that one the preselected choice on their subsequent visits.

Poetry and Pictures

Session Checklist

✔ Drag and drop a picture puzzle
✔ A nifty embedded slide show

**30 Min.
To Go**

This session is a grab-bag of cool DHTML solutions that you can drop directly onto your own Web site or modify for your particular needs. Whether you really need a bunch of objects that you can drag around to solve a puzzle or an on-screen slide show, you still do well to read through the examples in detail and learn more of these advanced DHTML techniques.

In particular, most of the DHTML cookbook recipes I've seen seem to use either CSS or JavaScript, but rarely are they tightly integrated as you saw with the to-do list manager in the last session — and as you see in this session, too. DHTML is the integration of style (CSS) and scripting (JavaScript) so understanding how they can work together is critical.

Drag and Drop a Picture Puzzle

Having two young children, I'm quite acquainted with modern children's toys and puzzles. I've also determined which of those playthings most engages my daughter. One of her favorites is a simple puzzle where you take a common photograph, cut it into strips, and then must sort them into the correct order to restore the image.

As you're becoming a DHTML expert — and you're at the tail-end of your weekend in this crash course — I'm going to show you how to duplicate one of these picture puzzles on a Web page!

Drag and drop

The core technology that you need to implement the picture puzzle is the capability to drag and drop objects onto the Web page. This capability ties to a couple new events: onMouseDown and onMouseMove. In essence, after the browser receives an onMouseDown event, it continually updates the location of the object to match the location of the mouse on onMouseMove events until onMouseUp triggers.

Programmatically, the first step is to tie the event-handler functions with their respective events on the page (wrapping it in `<SCRIPT>` block and including `crashcourse.js`), as the following example shows:

```
function initialize()
{
  document.onmousedown = mouseIsDown;
  document.onmousemove = mouseIsMoving;
  document.onmouseup   = mouseIsUp;
}
```

Now take a look at the easiest of the functions in the following example:

```
function mouseIsUp()
{
  obj = null;
}
```

After the user releases the mouse button, that action ~~simply~~ resets the global object `obj` to `null`. What happens if the `mouseIsDown` function is quite a bit more complex? Check out the following example:

```
function mouseIsDown()
{
  obj = event.srcElement.parentElement.style;
  clickX = event.offsetX;
  clickY = event.offsetY;
}
```

The new object here is the global event object, and its parameters are different in just about every different browser. These examples are all for Internet Explorer 5; Netscape 6 shows up shortly.

~~In fact,~~ The only properties that both IE and Netscape share for the event object are `screenX` and `screenY`, the location of the click relative to the entire screen, and `type`, which is the type of event that triggers. But in Netscape's model, it hands event objects to the event handlers as parameters, meaning that they're only accessible while within the event handler itself, whereas IE ~~expects them as global.~~ sets them as globally accessible variable.

In the preceding code, the `offsetX` and `offsetY` values are coordinates relative to the containing element (the browser window), ~~and clientX and clientY are the click locations relative to the viewable area.~~ I know — it's confusing!

The third function is called again and again by the browser while the user drags the object with the mouse, as follows:

```
function mouseIsMoving()
{
  if (obj) {
    obj.pixelLeft = event.clientX - clickX +
      document.body.scrollLeft;
    obj.pixelTop = event.clientY - clickY +
      document.body.scrollTop;
    return false;
  }
}
```

Each time that the mouse move event triggers, the new object location resets to the change in location from the mouseDown spot (that's the clientX – clickX value) plus the scrollLeft or scrollTop parameter to adjust it as necessary if the window scrolls down or horizontally.

The CSS style elements to make the puzzle attractive and the necessary HTML for each of the photo slices are as follows:

```
<STYLE TYPE = "text/css">
.pic { position: absolute; padding: 0px; cursor: move; }
.title { width: 90%; text-align: center; padding: 3px;
         background-color: #99F; font: 18pt bold Arial;
         cursor: pointer; }
</STYLE>

<BODY onLoad="initialize()">

<DIV CLASS="title" OnClick="fixit()">Fix the Picture, please!</DIV>

<DIV CLASS="pic" ID="slice1" STYLE="left:50;top:200;">
<IMG SRC="gslice1.jpg">
</DIV>

<DIV CLASS="pic" ID="slice2" STYLE="left:120;top:98;">
<IMG SRC="gslice2.jpg">
</DIV>

<DIV CLASS="pic" ID="slice3" STYLE="left:95;top:157;">
<IMG SRC="gslice3.jpg">
</DIV>

<DIV CLASS="pic" ID="slice4" STYLE="left:90;top:180;">
<IMG SRC="gslice4.jpg">
</DIV>
```

Notice the call to initialize() on loading the page. Notice, too, that although each of the <DIV>s that contains slices has a unique ID, they all share a single CLASS, enabling them to share ~~an easy CSS style~~. a single css style.

Figure 28-1 shows the resultant puzzle page, as loaded, in Internet Explorer.

If you try to view this puzzle in Netscape Communicator 4.7 or earlier, you find that almost nothing works: That version doesn't support <DIV> tags, has a completely different object model, and needs you to use the nonstandard <LAYER> tags for movable elements.

Click the title as you run this example yourself. Neat trick, eh? View the full source to see how it implements.

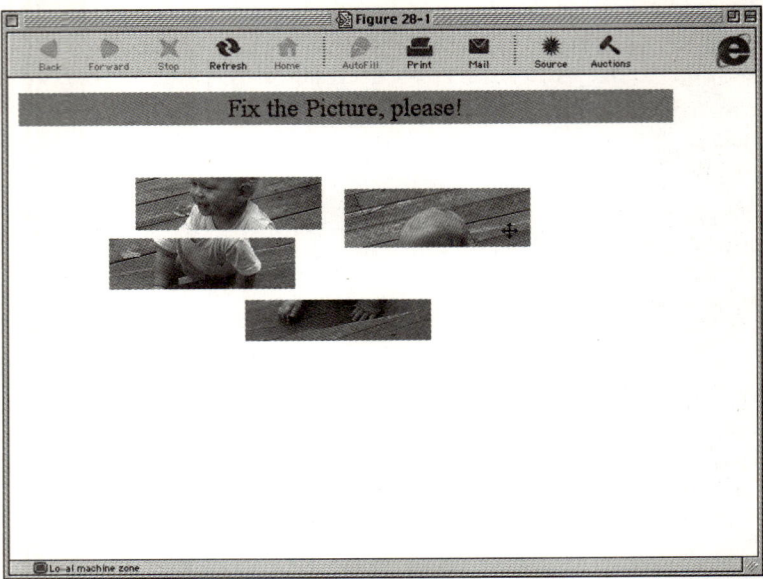

Figure 28-1   *A picture puzzle in Internet Explorer.*

20 Min.
To Go

Expanding to include Netscape 6

Fortunately, Netscape 6 has a document object model that represents the future of JavaScript, thanks to the efforts of the Mozilla team in implementing the CSS 2 specification. Don't get too cheered, however: It's completely different from what you need to code for Internet Explorer.

In fact, your code is going to explicitly test for Netscape 6 by accessing the N6 global variable set in crashcourse.js. To start, here's the new improved initialization function:

```
function initialize()
{
  if (N6) {  // Netscape 6 only, but the future of the DOM...
    document.getElementById("slice1").addEventListener("mousedown",
    mouseIsDown, false);
    document.getElementById("slice2").addEventListener("mousedown",
    mouseIsDown, false);
    document.getElementById("slice3").addEventListener("mousedown",
    mouseIsDown, false);
    document.getElementById("slice4").addEventListener("mousedown",
    mouseIsDown, false);
  }
  else {
    document.onmousedown = mouseIsDown;
    document.onmousemove = mouseIsMoving;
    document.onmouseup   = mouseIsUp;
  }
}
```

Notice that, with the Netscape 6 DOM, you must tie the event handler to each `<DIV>` rather than the easier connection to the document object. On the other hand, you need to tie only the mousedown event, not all three. You see why that's the case as soon as you look at the additions to the `mouseIsDown` function in the following example:

```
function mouseIsDown(evt)
{
  if (N6) {
    window.onmousemove = mouseIsMovingN6;
    window.onmouseup = mouseIsUp;

    clickX = evt.clientX;
    clickY = evt.clientY;
  }
  else {
    obj = event.srcElement.parentElement.style;
    clickX = event.offsetX;
    clickY = event.offsetY;
  }
}
```

The code here isn't much more complex than the IE code, but you can see that the N6 version doesn't use the global `obj` variable but does associate your functions with the necessary events at this juncture. Critical to observe also is that the `mouseIsDown` function now includes a parameter that enables the N6 code to access the event object for the trigger event.

Before you get into the big function, here's what `mouseIsUp` has become:

```
function mouseIsUp()
{
  if (N6)
    window.onmousemove = null;
  else
    obj = null;
}
```

The most significant difference between IE and N6, however, involves how the browsers handle the mousemove event. In fact, they're so different that I've just written a completely different `mouseIsMoving` function for Netscape 6 rather than trying to make them share a single function, as the following example shows:

```
function mouseIsMovingN6(evt)
{
  // Netscape 6 is so different, this is an N6 only
  // version of MouseMoving

  switch (evt.target.name) {
    case "s1" : obj = getObj("slice1");  break;
    case "s2" : obj = getObj("slice2");  break;
    case "s3" : obj = getObj("slice3");  break;
    case "s4" : obj = getObj("slice4");  break;
```

```
    }

    deltaX = evt.clientX - clickX;
    deltaY = evt.clientY - clickY;

    newX = parseInt(obj.left) + deltaX;
    newY = parseInt(obj.top)  + deltaY;

    obj.left = newX + "px";
    obj.top  = newY + "px";

    clickX = evt.clientX;
    clickY = evt.clientY;
    }
```

Most of this function is calculating relative changes and moves for the object, but the first switch maps target names with the associated <DIV> element. Events associate with the closest container, so clicking an image that's within a <DIV> results in the event object getting the information about the image, not the <DIV>, hence the first few lines.

The function then computes the difference between the event location and the original mousedown location; then stores the new location of the moving object in a temporary variable, newX or newY. The function then assigns these values to the object's left or top properties, appending a "px" to ensure that the system defaults to the correct unit of measure.

 **Don't fall for the trap of thinking that you can just slap + "px" on the end of the** newX **and** newY **statements and save a step:** *Integer + integer + string* **produces a string, but it skips the mathematical operation and just concatenates them. In other words,** 1 + 1 + "px" = "11px".

Some changes are also necessary to make to the <DIV> statements themselves, namely adding NAME attributes to the IMG tags, as follows:

```
<DIV CLASS="pic" ID="slice1" STYLE="left:50;top:200;">
<IMG SRC="gslice1.jpg" NAME="s1">
</DIV>

<DIV CLASS="pic" ID="slice2" STYLE="left:120;top:98;">
<IMG SRC="gslice2.jpg" NAME="s2">
</DIV>

<DIV CLASS="pic" ID="slice3" STYLE="left:95;top:157;">
<IMG SRC="gslice3.jpg" NAME="s3">
</DIV>

<DIV CLASS="pic" ID="slice4" STYLE="left:90;top:180;">
<IMG SRC="gslice4.jpg" NAME="s4">
</DIV>
```

That's it. Piece o' cake, isn't it?

Seriously, armed with this code, you can create cross-browser drag-and-drop solutions similar to the one that you see in Figure 28-2, which works just fine in both IE and N6.

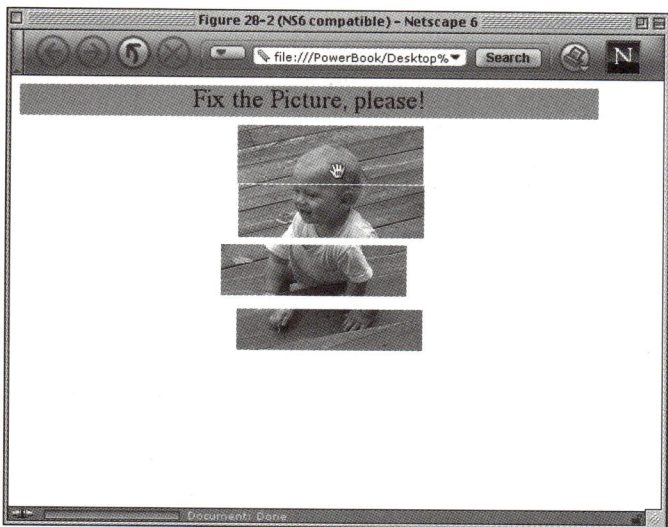

Figure 28-2   *The picture puzzle in Netscape 6.*

A Nifty Embedded Slide Show

**10 Min.
To Go**

Time to take a bit of a break from the complex JavaScript that's necessary to implement cross-browser drag and drop and to focus on a more pedestrian — but visually exciting — task: creating an in-place slide show.

Slide shows are really just a slight variation on the theme of image rollovers, because they involve much of the same basic ideas of creating image objects, assigning them to specific URLs, and then swapping .src properties on demand.

For this example, I'm going to use four beautiful pictures of the big island of Hawaii, one of my favorite relaxation spots. They're named hawaii1.jpg, hawaii2.jpg, hawaii3.jpg, and hawaii4.jpg, and they all live in a folder that I call slideshow.

The initialization of the four image objects occurs at the top of the <SCRIPT> section, as follows:

```
<SCRIPT LANGUAGE="JavaScript">

photo1 = new Image();
photo1.src = "slideshow/hawaii1.jpg";

photo2 = new Image();
photo2.src = " slideshow/hawaii2.jpg";

photo3 = new Image();
photo3.src = " slideshow/hawaii3.jpg";

photo4 = new Image();
photo4.src = " slideshow/hawaii4.jpg";
```

```
var totalSlides  = 4, currentSlide = 1;
```

Notice that I'm also setting two global variables, one that keeps track of the current slide and the other of which remembers the total number of slides in the show.

The easiest routine to understand is the one that increments the current slide counter and then shows the specified slide, as in the following example:

```
function nextSlide()
{
  if (++currentSlide > totalSlides) currentSlide = 1;
  document.slideshow.src = eval("photo" + currentSlide +".src");
}
```

The ++currentSlide notation is another lazy shortcut: It adds 1 to the current value of the variable before any further evaluation occurs. In this case, if currentSlide is 2, the test against totalSlides occurs with currentSlide as 3, because it's already incremented.

Going backward is very similar, but you subtract one and ensure that you aren't yet at currentSlide = 0, which is an undefined object, as follows:

```
function prevSlide()
{
  if (--currentSlide < 1) currentSlide = totalSlides;
  document.slideshow.src = eval("photo" + currentSlide + ".src");
}
```

The only other piece that you need for the slide show is the information for the first slide on the screen, the HTML portion, which the following example shows you:

```
<CENTER>
<h2>Visit The Beautiful Big Island of Hawai'i</h2>
<IMG HEIGHT=212 WIDTH=350 SRC="slideshow/hawaii1.jpg"
 NAME="slideshow" STYLE="border: 8px double #393;
 padding: 10px; background-color: #66C;">
</CENTER>
```

Notice the name that I specify with the image tag. That's what's I use with the document reference in the "next" and "previous" slide functions.

To add Next and Previous buttons is a simple matter of tying their functionality to buttons on the page, as follows:

```
<INPUT TYPE="button" VALUE="prev" onClick="prevSlide()">
<INPUT TYPE="button" VALUE="next" onClick="nextSlide()">
```

What's vastly cool is that you can also make the slide show run by itself by using the setInterval function to call nextSlide every few seconds. An associated clearInterval function stops the iterative timer, as you can see in the following example:

```
<INPUT TYPE="button" VALUE="loop"
 onClick="player = setInterval('nextSlide()', 2000);">
<INPUT TYPE="button" VALUE="stop"
 onClick="clearInterval(player)">
```

That's all that you need to do. And you get a nifty slide show, as shown in Figure 28-3.

Figure 28-3   *A Hawaiian slide show with controls.*

 **All the images that I use in this slide show come from the wonderful photo library of the U.S. Government National Oceanic and Atmospheric Administration. I highly encourage you to visit them online at**
`www.noaa.gov/.`

Done!

REVIEW

This session focuses on two different gizmos for your Web site, one of which demonstrates the basic code that you need for a drag-and-drop functionality within JavaScript. As you see, this particular edge of DHTML is very rough, with each Web browser demonstrating a rather different implementation of event handling. The second doohickey in this session is a simple JavaScript-based slide show that offers visitors a high level of control over the presentation.

QUIZ YOURSELF

1. What new events do you use with drag and drop? (See "Drag and drop.")
2. Why do you think you see such a divergence in event models in different browsers? (See "Drag and drop.")

3. Which of the browsers, Netscape 6 or Internet Explorer 5, sends the event object as a parameter to the event handler function? (See "Drag and drop.")

4. As a reminder, what's the rule regarding when to use an ID versus a CLASS with CSS?

CHALLENGING

5. One nice addition to the picture puzzle is a "Did I win?" button, which looks at the x y coordinates of all the puzzle slices and determines whether the user got them in the right order. Build it.

Putting It All Together

Session Checklist

✔ Magic Sticky Notes

✔ Link Reference Window

✔ Special Bonus

**30 Min.
To Go**

By my calculations, it's early Sunday evening, and your brain is just about completely full of DHTML information by this point. As a result, these last few sessions are much more about showing you some of the many great things that you can accomplish by using JavaScript + CSS than they are about teaching you new techniques or information per se.

Similar to the preceding session, this one describes two very different and very useful DHTML solutions that offer you easy ways to add a greater level of interactivity to your Web site with surprisingly little work.

Magic Sticky Notes

If you're like me, you've seen those ubiquitous sticky notes sticking on just about any surface imaginable. I've seen people layer them atop each other around all four sides of computer monitors and stick them on walls, chairs, books — even the occasional forehead!

A similar capability may prove useful on your Web pages, particularly if the notes can pop up and hide as necessary to keep the screen from getting cluttered. Discovering that implementing this capability in DHTML is straightforward and builds atop the development of the pop-up menus that I showed you a few sessions ago probably comes as no surprise to you by now.

I'm going to explain this one backward, if you don't mind, just to see whether you're still coherent after more than 14 hours of DHTML discussion.

To start, then, here's a new, lazy way to include some repeated HTML code on your page:

```
"And yet," said I, smiling, "I cannot quite hold myself
<SCRIPT>popup("absolved")</SCRIPT>
```

from the charge of sensationalism which has been
urged against my records."

I know, I know — I should specify the LANGUAGE **with the** <SCRIPT> **tag, but extensive testing shows that this method works just fine, though standards only work if everyone follows them!**

The popup function is responsible for the few lines of HTML that produce the linked text on the Web page, as the following example shows:

```
function popup(text)
{
  // simplify the task of in-line pop-up links
  document.write  ("<SPAN OnMouseOver=\"popUpWindow(event, '" +
      text + "');\"");
  document.write  ("OnMouseOut=\"popDownWindow('" + text +
  "');\" CLASS=\"link\">");
  document.writeln(text + "</SPAN>");
}
```

The advantage of this approach is that turning words in the HTML into active links, without any worry about needing to debug event handlers and so on, is quite a trivial task. By using this function, you can easily add a second pop-up by using the following line:

```
<SCRIPT>popup("disputatious")</SCRIPT>
```

The pop-up windows themselves you define by using a <DIV> tag with its visibility set to hidden by default, as in the following example:

```
<DIV CLASS="popup" ID="absolved">
<B>ab-solve</B>
<DIV STYLE="margin-left: 1em">
1 : to set free from an obligation or the consequences of guilt<BR>
2 : to remit (a sin) by absolution</DIV></DIV>

<DIV CLASS="popup" ID="disputatious">
<B>dis-pu-ta-tious</B>
<DIV STYLE="margin-left: 1em">
1 : inclined to dispute<BR>
2 : provoking debate, controversial</DIV></DIV>
```

The preceding code defines two definition windows, each with an ID that matches the word that you're defining.

Those are the easy parts of the solution — the activated link and the definition window. The next part is pure JavaScript.

Popping up the sticky note

The popUpWindow function needs to compute the location of the cursor after the onMouseOver event triggers, and then it needs to set the location of the appropriate pop-up window to match and flip its visibility setting so that it appear on-screen.

That simple solution doesn't work correctly, however, because you always want to position the pop-up window such that it's completely visible, and in this example, you're going to center the pop-up window below the cursor location. The result is that a bunch of calculations are necessary, including calculating the width of the browser window and the width of the pop-up window.

Here's how the code looks:

```
function popUpWindow(evt, id)
{
  // display a pop-up window immediately below the cursor,
  // adjusting to ensure that the pop-up isn't horizontally
  // offscreen
   var myObj = getObj(id);

   // now let's compute the width and centerpoint of the popup
   var popupWidth = objWidth(id);
   var halfPopupWidth = Math.round(popupWidth / 2);

   // and the acceptable boundaries of the left edge
   var rightEdge = windowWidth() - popupWidth - 5;
   var leftEdge = 5;

   // where did the user click their mouse?
   if (evt != null) event = evt;  // keeps Netscape happy
   x = getEventX(event);
   y = getEventY(event);

   // now let's tweak the location to ensure that the
 // popup isn't offscreen

   x -= halfPopupWidth;         // center pop-up below cursor

   if (x > rightEdge) x = rightEdge - 5;
   if (x < leftEdge)  x = leftEdge + 5;

   myObj.left = x ;
   myObj.top  = y + 5;
   myObj.visibility = "visible";
}
```

I think that example demonstrates reasonably straightforward JavaScript. Certainly, by this point in your Weekend Crash Course, you should understand this code. Notice how this code deals with the difference in event handlers differently than does the code in Session 28: Here, the function assumes that an event object is going to arrive as a parameter and compares it to the null value to see whether it should override the global event property.

If you're trailblazing with Internet Explorer 6 beta, you might find that the test evt != null generates an error. If so, just comment it out completely and you should be fine.

The value 5 that you can see in the code is a padding factor to move the edge of the pop-up window just a few pixels from the left or right edge of the browser window. It's purely aesthetic, but if you experiment by removing it, you find that the results are less attractive.

To turn off the pop-up window, `popDownWindow` does the job, as follows:

```
function popDownWindow(id)
{
    var myObj = getObj(id);
    myObj.visibility = "hidden";
}
```

Adding some style

Oh, I have one more thing to show you before you get to see the end result: the CSS block, as in the following example:

```
<STYLE TYPE="text/css">
.link   { color: #060; cursor: pointer;
          text-decoration: underline; }
.popup  { width: 200; background-color: #DFA; font-size: 80%;
          padding: 6px; border: 3px double black;
          position: absolute; visibility: hidden; }
.title  { width: 100%; background-color: #C9C;
          font: 18pt bold Arial; padding: 3px;
          border-bottom: 4px groove blue; text-align: center;
          margin-bottom: 10px; font-variant: small-caps }
</STYLE>
```

That the pop-up uses absolute positioning and its visibility is set to hidden by default should come as no surprise. What may surprise you, however, is the presentation style for the links themselves. To make them stand out from the adjacent text while still remaining subtle, I show them in dark green with an underline. In fact, switch green to blue and you get a set of CSS properties that exactly defines the appearance and behavior of a hypertext reference. Finally, I use the title style for the page title, as you can see in Figure 29-1.

This pop-up window is a great example of where the double-line border proves just what the doctor ordered in terms of making the sticky notes look attractive.

In terms of the big picture, notice how I put considerable effort into making the code sufficiently flexible that I can save it as separate JavaScript and CSS files and then add these magic sticky notes to dozens of pages with minimal effort.

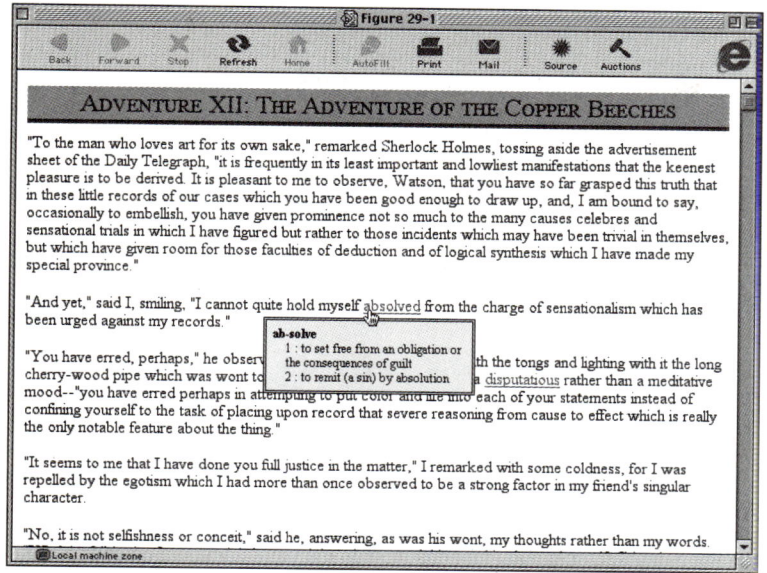

Figure 29-1 *Magic sticky notes on the page — notice the cursor location.*

Link Reference Window

Speaking of pop-ups, this next gadget is a great addition to your site if you have pages that contain lots of hypertext reference links buried in tons of prose. For this example, I'm using a page from my own Web site that lists some of my favorite spots on the Web. It's a nice page, but if you want a quick list of URLs, it's not the easiest design. Instead, what if a small link appeared at the bottom of the page that produces a separate pop-up window containing a summary of just the links?

This time, I'm moving all the JavaScript into a separate file to show how easily you can add a complex feature to an existing Web site. I'm adding the following two lines to the top of the favorites page:

```
<SCRIPT LANGUAGE="JavaScript" SRC="crashcourse.js"></SCRIPT>
<SCRIPT LANGUAGE="JavaScript" SRC="linktext.js"></SCRIPT>
```

The very last line prior to the </BODY> tag is also new, as follows:

```
<DIV STYLE="font: 75% sans-serif;color: #666;
text-align:center;cursor:pointer;text-decoration: overline;"
onClick="showLinks();">link reference</DIV>
```

That's all the code that's necessary to enable the user launch the pop-up window shown in Figure 29-2.

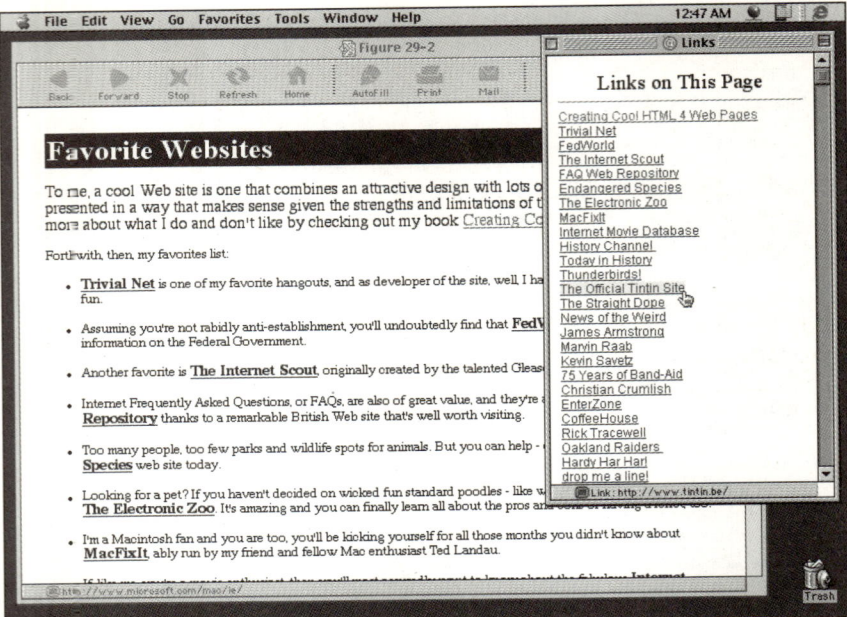

Figure 29-2   *A pop-up navigational window for any page.*

The `linktext.js` file contains the interesting portion of this page, and I'm sure that how short it is surprises you! Indeed, if you strip out all the formatting and style elements, the core function is as follows:

```
function showLinks()
{
  popupWindow = window.open("","linkref",
    "width=250,height=400,scrollbars=yes");

  with (popupWindow.document) {
    open();

    writeln("<H2>Links on This Page</H2><HR>");

    for (i=0; i < document.links.length; i++) {
      linktext = (useAll? document.links[i].innerText :
document.links[i].text);
      addlink(document.links[i], linktext, popupWindow);
    }

    writeln("<HR><DIV OnClick='window.close()'>close</DIV>");
    close();
  }
}
```

The actual function is more complex because of all the formatting and CSS style attributes that it specifies, but that's the gist of it. Notice the use of the `with` statement here: It automatically prefixes the specified object to all unspecified methods. Instead of typing `popupWindow.document.open()`, for example, I can just type `open()` and make the code considerably more readable.

This function demonstrates another general principle of the document object model; everything is somewhere in the DOM if you can just reference it correctly.

For the hypertext reference `<A HREF=url>linkable words</A>`, I store the URL in the `document.links` array, and the associated text resides either in the `text` or `innerText` property, depending on the browser type.

The `addLink` function controls the output of each individual link, as follows:

```
function addlink(url, text, winObj)
{
   winObj.document.writeln("<A HREF=\"" + url + "\" TARGET=\"_new\">");
   winObj.document.writeln(((text.length > 1) ? text : url) + "</A><BR>");
}
```

The complete version of `showLinks` is on the CD-ROM, or you can visit this book's Web site to see the CSS that I add to produce the attractive layout shown in Figure 29-2.

As a reminder, the book's Web site is at www.intuitive.com/dhtml/.

Special Bonus

I know of more cool DHTML solutions than I can fit in this book. In fact, this session originally had a third gizmo — a nifty hidden message that requires you solving a bit of a puzzle beforehand. I added it to the CD-ROM, so I encourage you to look for Figure 29-3 there. If you don't have the disk any more, the book's Web site displays this example, too.

To whet your appetite, I can tell you that you must click the title tab on the example page and then move your cursor around. A graphic lies in an invisible layer that tracks with the cursor and enables you to see text where it all looks like a pure black background fill. Quite nifty.

Done!

REVIEW

This session focuses on two useful functions for your Web development projects: one featuring a portable pop-up sticky note solution and the other offering a useful window that lists all the hypertext references in the parent page. Along the way, you see the value of writing general-purpose functions and trying to abstract as much of the specific code necessary in the Web pace as possible. The second function reduces the code necessary to three lines: two at the top and one at the bottom. Finally, I demonstrate the `with` function as a way to minimize typing.

QUIZ YOURSELF

1. In addition to laziness, you have another excellent reason for using the popup function instead of writing the few lines of HTML. What is it? (See "Magic Sticky Notes.")

2. Referencing the three-color technique that you use to produce 3D menus earlier in the book, modify the styles for the pop-up sticky notes to make them appear 3D, too. (See "Magic Sticky Notes.")

3. Modify the popupWindow function to make the sticky notes always appear centered vertically at the cursor location but at least 25 pixels to the right. Make sure that you test it so that the sticky notes can't end up off-screen! (See "Popping up the sticky note.")

4. Incorporate what you've learned to ensure that sticky notes never end up off-screen vertically because the current code doesn't check. (See "Popping up the sticky note.")

MAD SCIENTIST SANDBOX

5. Here's a bonus one for you: Without peeking at the actual `linktext.js` file on the CD-ROM, study Figure 29-2 and then try to duplicate the CSS styles to match what actually appears on-screen.

Stepping Stones to the Next Level

Session Checklist

✔ Reference Web Sites

✔ Places to Find Cool Solutions

✔ Other Cool Places to Explore

**30 Min.
To Go**

You've come a long way in this weekend crash course, and you should feel comfortable tomorrow morning telling your boss that, yes, indeed, you know DHTML pretty darn well and are ready and eager to revamp the Web site immediately! You're probably still going to need this book in your briefcase, but perhaps you can glue the cover from your favorite Tolstoy or Austen book to it to pretend that you're superliterate?

In any case, this last session is a directory of some of the best places that I know of online to dig up cool JavaScript and DHTML information, prebuilt solutions, and people to chat with and ask to help debug your own blossoming DHTML projects.

Reference Web Sites

The first category of online information to explore are sites that offer useful reference information, including exhaustive listings of all possible properties and methods for all objects, up-to-date comparisons showing the level of compatibility of the many different browsers, and more.

European Computer Manufacturers Association

`www.ecma.ch/`

The standards committees neatly sidestepped some political landmines when they endorsed EMCAScript as the official scripting language of the Web rather than the Netscape-invented JavaScript. The secret that everyone knows, however, is that EMCAScript is pretty much 1:1 with JavaScript. Knowing where to find solid references to the ECMA version is useful, however, and the specific URL that takes you right to the spot is `www.ecma.ch/ecma1/stand/ecma-262.htm`.

The EMCAScript specification is in Adobe's PDF format, and you need the Acrobat reader to read it. Fortunately, it's on the CD-ROM that I include with this book if you don't already have a copy on your computer.

Netscape's DevEdge

`http://developer.netscape.com/`

This address is the developer area on Netscape's enormous Web site, and it offers the definitive information on JavaScript (which Netscape invented) and lots of great information on Web technologies. This page is the best place to download a copy of the latest version of the Netscape browser, too (the Netscape 6.1 beta having just become available as I write this session), and you can also find some interesting code archives and online tutorials here.

The two areas that I find most helpful on this site are the conformance test suites (at `http://developer.netscape.com/evangelism/tools/testsuites/`) which, again, enable you to compare the performance of your browser against the official specification, and the busy DevEdge newsgroups (at `http://developer.netscape.com/support/newsgroups`). The newsgroups can prove contentious places to talk about problems and solutions, but a lot of very bright people are participating, so a little bit of patience can yield some gems of insight.

Oh, I recommend a third area, too: the Cascading Style Sheets area, which you find at `http://developer.netscape.com/tech/css/`, offers tons of great information and examples for using CSS in your development work.

Fair warning: You can all too easily drop into historical information on this site and find out that you're reading a tutorial about how to write a JavaScript application for Netscape 4.7 or similar — and that it doesn't work even on Netscape 6, let alone on other browsers. Keep an eye on the date of publication of these articles whenever you surf this site.

The Open Directory Project

`www.dmoz.org/`

The Open Directory Project is a very cool idea; it's an online directory of thousands upon thousands of different Web sites, all managed by a staff of volunteers dedicated to individual areas. If you have a passion for paleontology, philately, or even pandas, check it out; your area of interest may need a volunteer coordinator.

For Dynamic HTML-related information, either use the search feature to find specific information or start at `http://dmoz.org/Computers/Programming/Languages/` and click either HTML to learn more about HTML and CSS or JavaScript to explore that area.

The World Wide Web Consortium

www.w3.org/

If the Web's a bunch of alien spacecraft flying around the universe, the W3C is the home planet, without question. The definitive source for all specifications and standards, the site includes the exact definition of HTML 4.0, HTML 4.01, CSS 1, CSS 2, the document object models underlying JavaScript and Netscape 6, and much more.

Of special notice are the nifty CSS validator (at http://jigsaw.w3.org/css-validator/), which can help you debug peculiar problems in separate CSS files that you may be building for your site, and the under-construction DOM test suites (at www.w3.org/DOM/Test/), if you want to really understand what parts of the standard DOM your browser does and doesn't understand.

**20 Min.
To Go**

Places to Find Cool Solutions

Looking for actual scripts and CSS that'll get your creative juices flowing, rather than reading dry specifications? There are a number of different sites on the Internet offering libraries of cool solutions. These are some of the very best.

Builder.com

http://builder.cnet.com/

If I must pick a single favorite Web site — one that offered me assistance with the code I developed for this book and with lots of friendly folk, too — it's C|Net's Builder.com site. Although it doesn't offer a very large archive of JavaScript (the JavaScript Source being a much better library of these solutions), the featured articles on producing nifty effects and Stupid Web Tricks are excellent and well worth studying each week. Of particular note is the Builder Buzz discussion area.

While you're visiting this site, make sure that you check out the legal-resources area, too. And in the right column, the site's featured columns are universally very good, with particular kudos to Stupid Web Tricks and SuperScripter. And, as is true of Javascript.com, Builder.com offers a remarkable collection of newsletters that you can receive for free, ranging from e-commerce to Web building, auction news to online shopping guides, and much more. Just click all newsletters below the sign-up box for the builder newsletter.

Cut and Paste JavaScript

www.infohiway.com/javascript/indexf.htm

This site isn't the best of breed for JavaScript solutions, but the few hundred that it presents offer some great ideas for your own development. Look for the monthly online newsletter that offers well-written tutorial information about JavaScript. Unfortunately you must go to the site each month to read it — it's not available through e-mail. Worth exploring are some of the nice JavaScript-based games that the site features. For a shortcut, click the `JavaScript Archives` link in the top-left corner of the home page, and you go straight to the index of available scripts.

Dynamic Drive

`www.dynamicdrive.com/`

Another place to explore for an archive of useful solutions, this site seems to split evenly between IE-only solutions and all-browser solutions. It talks about DHTML, but it's basically all JavaScript. Worth particular notice: The games in the site's DHTML Games archive (at `www.dynamicdrive.com/dynamicindex12/`) offer some great ideas for advanced JavaScript interaction. Don't miss the Webmaster resources section either (at `www.dynamicdrive.com/resources/`).

Internet Related Technologies

`www.irt.org/`

This site offers a remarkable amount of information about different developer technologies, including good areas on DHTML, CSS, and JavaScript. (How the folks behind the site think that DHTML is different from CSS + JavaScript escapes me, but perhaps you can make sense of it if you visit the site.) Of particular notice is the JavaScript Programmers Reference, an online version of some of the material that Cliff Wootton's huge book of the same name exhaustively lists. You're likely to find that you've already learned just about all the good stuff in this *Weekend Crash Course*, but the online JavaScript object-reference information (at `www.irt.org/xref/index.htm`) is sure to prove a great adjunct.

The JavaScript Source

`http://javascript.internet.com/`

This site is one of my absolute favorite places to browse and poke around for good JavaScript solutions, and it boasts more than 800 different scripts in its archives. To get an idea of how many different solutions the site offers, just take a look at its calculator solutions. I count more than 50 different types of inline calculators alone (although why I'd want to add an Armor Penetration Calculator to my site escapes me).

 **Keep an eye on the submission dates of these scripts: Those that are pre-2001 probably don't work correctly with Netscape 6 and the very newest browsers.**

Sign up for the site's JavaScript daily newsletter. (The link is right on the home page.) It's a nice source of inspiration, but beware: Many of the scripts the site sends out are buggy, and you need to rewrite them or otherwise clean them up. Do check out some of the other newsletters that the parent site Internet.com offers, too, as they cover electronic commerce, Internet-related news, Internet-usage statistics, and Web-developer issues.

JavaScripts.com

www.javascripts.com/

Another of my favorite online archive sites, JavaScripts.com makes an incredible number of different scripts available and offers a sophisticated search engine that helps you zero in on the solution that you seek. As is true of the other archive sites, you need to remain alert to the submission date of these scripts; these dates give you a quick clue as to whether the scripts are likely to work in the latest browsers before you bother to download or cut and paste them. The site claims, by the way, to have thousands of JavaScript solutions. You save a lot of wandering if you scroll to the bottom and click JavaScript Archives. Doing so takes you directly to a listing of the featured scripts by month.

 **My only gripe with JavaScripts.com is that it has an annoying 145K advert pasted onto each page from jobs.internet.com, and it's just too darn big if you're surfing via modem connection. Consider yourself warned.**

**10 Min.
To Go**

The Microsoft Developer Network

http://msdn.microsoft.com/

I must be candid. I don't think that this site is particularly useful for DHTML developers, because the company is busy pushing its developer tools for a wide variety of different categories, and Web developers seem mostly left out in the cold. In fact, some sort of reality distortion field seems to surround Redmond; the code examples that you can find on the site are for IE only. I don't think that you can find even a mention of Netscape, Opera, or any other Web browser on the entire site.

The site's Dynamic HTML Developer Workshop, for example, is worth visiting, but don't be surprised to find that it's distinctly *not* cross-browser. The site does include a very good area on Cascading Style Sheets in the Developer Workshop, and the Filters and Transitions area is quite interesting if your target audience uses IE on Windows.

 **Start right out in the Developer Workshop area and save yourself some grief: Just go straight to** http://msdn.microsoft.com/workshop/entry.asp**.**

Website Abstraction

http://wsabstract.com/

Yes, you can find a ton of different sites online offering JavaScript archives and more Web developer resources than this one. Website Abstraction, however, is notable for its well-written tutorials and Java-applet archive in addition to a nicely organized JavaScript library and DHTML area. Check out the neat solutions in Random Stuff if you pop into the site's archive!

Other Cool Places to Explore

Enough serious stuff. Here are some other interesting Web sites that you'll want to bookmark!

Cross Browser.com

http://cross-browser.com/

Frankly you don't find too much of use here, but I just think that the solar system model built with DHTML (at http://cross-browser.com/ss/solar_system2.html) is too cool to pass up. Check it out and then view the source code. Beware, however, as it may make your scroll bars vanish on your main browser window. If that happens, close the window (File->Close Window) and launch a new one when you're done on their site.

Dynamic HTML Weekend Crash Course

www.intuitive.com/dhtml/

Don't forget to also check in with the official Web site for this book. I'm posting updates, errata notices, user comments, sample code, and much more, all online. If you're looking for an HTML book, you can also check out www.intuitive.com/coolweb/ to find out more about my book *Creating Cool HTML 4 Web Pages*, too.

Web Reference

www.webreference.com/

A great general-purpose site from the same group that's responsible for the JavaScript Source (see the section of that name, earlier in this session), you really want to make this site your first stop on any search for Web or developer-related information due to its vast store of information.

Webreview.com

www.webreview.com/

An okay site with a great hidden weapon: The browser compatibility chart is a great way to quickly figure out what browsers, on what platforms, work with what HTML, Java, JavaScript, and much more. If you're truly interested in ultimate compatibility, this site is a great place to do some research.

Web Site Garage

www.websitegarage.com/

Started by a couple friends of mine, Web Site Garage offers a raft of nifty online tools to help you check your HTML, optimize your graphics, check for broken links on your site, and verify your submission on various search engines. If you think that you're done coding, pop over to the Garage and ensure all is well.

Discussion Groups

I'm sure that you can find a number of different places where you can interact with other DHTML developers, ask questions, and get answers, but to me, the standout in this crowd is the wonderful Builder Buzz (at http://buzz.builder.com/), run by the folks at C|NET. After you get to the Builder Buzz home page, you see a lot of choices for discussion forums. The DHTML discussion is in the Programming & Scripting area, and it's called JavaScript/ DHTML. Well worth visiting.

The Netscape DevEdge site also has a good discussion forum (at http://developer. netscape.com/), but the folk there focus more on Netscape-specific issues, in my experience, rather than the world of cross-browser compatibility and solutions. Your mileage may, as people say, vary considerably!

Done!

REVIEW

This session gives you a map highlighting more than a dozen different Web sites that are worth adding to your bookmark list and exploring. In particular, I encourage you to explore these sites whenever you *aren't* buried under a project deadline and can enjoy the pleasure of just poking around and seeing what's available. After you get to some of the better script archive sites, I'm sure you're going to vanish therein for quite a while!

FINAL THOUGHTS

This session marks the end of this *Weekend Crash Course*. I've had a great time sharing this material — and learning a lot more about CSS and JavaScript as well — through the last 30 sessions, and I hope you've enjoyed our journey, too.

I want to end by sharing a story: In 1877, Leyland Stanford engaged an English photographer by the name of Eadweard Muybridge to take a series of high-speed photographs of his horse Occident to resolve a wager. The bet? Whether a running horse has all four hooves off the ground at any moment. Muybridge's high-speed sequence of 24 photographs of the horse not only demonstrated that, indeed, the horse does sometimes fly (winning Stanford a nice wager, according to the rumors), but also establishing an important milestone in the development of modern cinema.

The point? Writing a book about a dynamic, evolving topic such as the Web and DHTML is a fast-moving target, quite similar to the running horse of the Stanford bet. This book is like Muybridge's famous photographic sequence: It's the best, most up-to-the-minute information that I can jam into this book, but it's a snapshot of a moving animal.

Inevitably, you're going to find some gaffes, and things are sure to change between the time when the publisher "puts the pages to bed" and you read them in this bound book. As a result, I want to invite you to answer this very last set of questions in an e-mail message to me at dhtml@intuitive.com.

> **You can also use the shortcut of the convenient book feedback form on the CD-ROM, which you find as the material associated with Session 30.**

1. What do you think of this book? Is it helpful and informative?
2. What material do you find herein that's inaccurate or fails to work for you as expected?
3. What material do you find that you wish I'd covered in more depth? What has too much coverage?
4. If I could make one change to this book, what would it be?
5. Finally, what's your favorite part of this book, and are you comfortable recommending it to friends and colleagues?

Thanks a lot for your feedback and for learning Dynamic HTML the *Weekend Crash Course* way with me. Stay in touch — and good luck on your Web journeys.

Dave Taylor

taylor@intuitive.com

PART

VI

Sunday Afternoon

1. Most likely, magic cookies are associated with what well-known character from Sesame Street?

2. Cookies help solve a fundamental problem in the architecture of the Web. What is it?

3. True/False: Cookies can contain only a maximum of 24 bytes of information.

4. True/False: Cookies can have expiration dates set years in the future.

5. True/False: The JavaScript method getAllCookies() enables your script to examine the value of cookies that other Web sites give to the user.

6. What does the escape() and unescape() function pair accomplish?

7. What's the result of escape("Mary had a little lamb")?

8. How do most JavaScript programmers delete a cookie?

9. The following is/is not a valid cookie?

    ```
    font=Arial
    ```

10. You want a box to pop up and ask for the user's name so you use the _____ method of the window object.

11. You want to inform the user that an event is occurring but present him with only a single OK button. What method do you use?

12. If the user clicks Cancel to the prompt in the following sequence, what's the output?

    ```
    if (confirm("are you sure?"))
    document.write("yes");
    else
    document.write("no");
    ```

13. What cursor value is ideal for a drag-and-drop JavaScript solution?

14. Drag and drop functionality ties to what three event handlers?

15. Only the _____ browser sends the actual event object as a parameter to the event handler instead of as a global variable.

APPENDIX

Answers to Part Review Questions

This weekend crash course has included quite a lot of questions — and there are over a hundred more self-assessment questions on the CD-ROM — but I hope you have taken the time to try and answer these yourself before flipping back to this section. Either way, you've just said "open sesame" and here are all the answers to the Part Review questions.

Friday Evening

We started out slow, with a review. I hope you figured out the answers to all these questions without too much struggle!

Introduction to Dynamic HTML

1. Graceful degradation is very much a good thing
2. BIG is closer to the original intent of HTML.
3. Microsoft invented Web style sheets, while Netscape invented JavaScript.
4. False.
5. False: `</P>` is the closing tag for the `<P>` tag.
6. Anticipating the exact name for a typeface on every platform is difficult, hence the font-family attribute in CSS.
7. False. You can also use it to produce numbers in an ordered list.
8. Issued a variety of bug fixes and patches as HTML 4.01.
9. The World Wide Web Consortium (W3C).
10. False. The punctuation mark in question is a semicolon.
11. True.
12. `counter += 3` or `counter = counter + 3`
13. `hisQuote = '"it\'s exactly as you predicted, Dr. Frankenstein!"';`
14. Either use `//` or `/* comment */`

15. You write it as follows:
    ```
    i=0;
    while (i< 10) {
    write("another line is output");
    i++;
    }
    ```
16. You write it as follows: `if (status == 1) x = 4; else x = 5;`
17. DHTML has no standard specification. It's a trick question.
18. LAYER.
19. False. It's totally fine.
20. ActiveX instead of Java and VB Script instead of JavaScript.

Saturday Morning

Finally, we have some new material — the skinny on Cascading Style Sheets.

Cascading Style Sheets

1. False.
2. `<DIV>` tags are more like the `<P>` tag.
3. `<SPAN>` tags are more like the `<TT>` tag.
4. CLASS.
5. False. 1em is the width of the m character in the typeface at the specified size. Without a size specification, you have no way of knowing the exact width.
6. False. 1 point = $\frac{1}{72}$ inch and 1 inch = 2.5 centimeters; therefore, 12 points = 0.42 centimeters.
7. Typographical errors while entering HTML tags or attributes.
8. Frosch and aeroporto.
9. You need to correct both lines as follows because they both use comments incorrectly:
    ```
    .jane { font-family: cursive; /* jane always curses */ }
    .larry { color: green; } // larry's always been envious of jane
    ```
10. These two lines are correct already.
11. Yes.
12. The # character.
13. The . character.
14. Yes, but . . . it doesn't' actually make sense. A container selector says that if the second tag occurs within the range of the first tag, but putting a paragraph within another paragraph is incorrect nesting in HTML.
15. An attribute selector.

16. `<B>`, `<I>`, `<FONT>`, `<BLINK>`, `<U>`, `<TT>`, `<BIG>`, `<SMALL>`, `<BIGGER>`, `<SMALLER>`, and `<STRONG>` are some of the HTML tags that CSS makes obsolete.
17. An ID selector.
18. `<TT>` has the same function as `font-family: monospace`.
19. False. You should quote multiword typeface names.
20. You can use either `font-size: 20pt` or `font-size: 125%`, but the latter is more flexible.

Saturday Afternoon

Now we can start picking up some speed with sophisticated uses of CSS.

Advanced Cascading Style Sheets

1. `CELLPADDING` is to `CELLSPACING`
2. False.
3. You end up with a container that has no space for its contents because it has only 2 percent of its space *not* justified as padding.
4. The text ends up the same color as the background.
5. `margin-left`. It's all right; I make this mistake all the time.
6. They're all 0, so they're all the same size. Trick question!
7. The equivalent is `text-align: right;`.
8. Absolute — but not fixed — positioning works just fine.
9. False. Visibility has a true/false value only.
10. False. You have no right property.
11. The `<DIV>` layer completely covers any other content on the page.
12. True, although it may not prove a great idea for backward compatibility.
13. Use `HREF="#"` to use an anchor tag with an `onClick` event.
14. The correct sequence of CSS is as follows:
    ```
    text-decoration: underline
    color: blue;    // assuming default link colors on the page
    ```
15. Depth.
16. True.
17. Surely it's the most recent — the W3C DOM that Netscape 6 implements.
18. The equivalent is as follows:
    ```
    if (a) {
      b
    } else {
      c
    }
    ```

19. onLoac.

20. focus moves the browser attention point to the specified element or window, and blur moves it back away.

Saturday Evening

At this point in the weekend, we've finished Cascading Style Sheets and are now ready to dig into the fascinating subject of JavaScript programming.

JavaScript

1. False.

2. True.

3. Hundreds, if not thousands. Lots more than you think.

4. Netscape 4 uses a completely different DOM than any other.

5. False. They bailed on standardizing JavaScript, alas.

6. onClick is one, and onLoad is the other.

7. onMouseDown triggers after you click the mouse button and occurs immediately, whereas onClick occurs after you click and then release the mouse button, so it happens after the mouse-button click.

8. Much of JavaScript shows up as event handler code within an HTML tag, so no line associates with it within a <SCRIPT> block.

9. One is two slashes, //, and the other is a slash-star star-slash set: /* comment */.

10. You embed HTML comments in <!-- comment -->.

11. The correct style is as follows:
```
<SCRIPT>
<!--
your script material here
// -->
</SCRIPT>
```

12. No.

13. No.

14. No.

15. Yes.

16. It evaluates true in some versions of JavaScript and false in others, frustratingly.

17. The navigator object, even in Internet Explorer.

18. parseInt.

19. stringValue = "" + integerValue;.

20. indexOf.

Sunday Morning

A night of rest, a chance to have all the material of Saturday gel in your brain, and you're ready to get into some very advanced JavaScript applications.

Advanced JavaScript

1. The browsers use different document object models. Alas.
2. onMouseOver and onMouseOut.
3. window.status.
4. Name each of your frame panes by using the NAME attribute.
5. setInterval loops, repeat the command forever (or until a clearInterval event), whereas setTimeOut executes the event once.
6. You can use the following:
   ```
   year = (now.getYear() < 1900)? now.getYear() + 1900 :
   now.getYear();
   ```
7. False.
8. Milliseconds.
9. False. It has no limit.
10. onBlur triggers each time that you leave an element, but onChange triggers only if the user changes the event value.
11. Some browsers don't render form elements such as <INPUT> unless the tags are within a <FORM> tag range.
12. The floor function drops all the fractional part.
13. The ceiling function goes to the next possible value if any fractional part is there at all.
14. True.
15. border-bottom. I get confused, too.
16. You should use the following:
    ```
    text-decoration: underline;
    color: blue;        // assume standard link colors
    cursor: pointer;
    ```
17. False. That's what document.writeln does.
18. <DIV> forces a break above and below, while <SPAN> is an inline element.
19. Dragging and dropping the graphic onto an open Web-browser window.
20. Use window.open to create windows, and you probably tie it to onLoad in the <BODY> tag.

Sunday Afternoon

Now that you've learned all about JavaScript, it's time to see it in action with some sophisticated and visually exciting solutions to Web problems you probably didn't even know you had!

Advanced Gadgets and Widgets

1. Cookie Monster. Sadly, no technology terms are associated with Bert or Ernie!
2. The Web is stateless, which makes remembering visitors very difficult.
3. False. A limit exists, but it's quite a bit larger.
4. True.
5. False. It'd be a major security hole, wouldn't it?
6. The escape function translates its argument to ensure that you can safely send it as a URL, while unescape reverses the translation.
7. The result is Mary+had+a+little+lamb
8. Send a set-cookie line with an expiration date in the past.
9. It's perfectly valid.
10. Use prompt (correctly, window.prompt).
11. Use confirm (correctly, window.confirm).
12. The output is no.
13. Ideal is cursor: move;
14. onMouseDown, onMouseMove, and onMouseUp.
15. Netscape.

What's on the CD-ROM

The CD-ROM that accompanies this book contains the following programs and files:

- Every example file and JavaScript library file that I develop or discuss in the text.
- A self-assessment test to help you measure how much you've learned.
- Microsoft Internet Explorer 5.5, our reference browser for the book.
- Quick reference materials from DevGuru that offer valuable information on CSS, JavaScript, and HTML right on your computer as you work.
- A complete version of this book in PDF format, easily searchable, for quick reference and to keep on your computer for those times that you don't have the book available. (Of course, you can always buy a second copy of this book, but that's another story entirely!)
- A PDF version of the first nine chapters of my book *Creating Cool HTML 4 Web Pages*, to ensure that you're up-to-date with your core HTML knowledge.
- The complete text of a dozen stories from Project Gutenberg's *The Adventures of Sherlock Holmes* for your reading pleasure.
- The following specifications from the World Wide Web Consortium (www.w3c.org):
  - The HTML 4.01 specification
  - The Cascading Style Sheets, level 2, specification.
  - The CD-ROM is also jammed full of the following useful shareware and commercial software demos and applications to help you develop your DHTML skills:
    - ACD System's ACDSee 32
    - Adobe Acrobat Reader 5.0
    - Adobe Photoshop 6.0
    - Adobe Premiere 6
    - Bare Bones Software BBEdit 6.0 and BBEdit Lite 4.6
    - CoffeeCup Software's HTML Editor
    - Helios System Solutions TextPad 4

JASC Paint Shop Pro 7

Lemke Software GraphicConverter

Macromedia Dreamweaver 4.0

Macromedia Flash 5

Macromedia Home Site 4.5

Western Civilisation Style Master Pro

System Requirements

This CD-ROM should be compatible with any Windows or Macintosh system that has a CD-ROM drive installed. Individual software applications have their own system requirements, which you can boil down to the following: Have a lot of RAM and a nice monitor.

Installation Instructions

The recommended method for installing the files on the CD-ROM is to drag and drop all the examples and reference materials onto your own hard disk. Individual applications, commercial and shareware, have their own installation directions on the disk.

The Self-Assessment Test directory contains the installation program Setup.exe. With the book's CD-ROM in the drive, open the Self-Assessment Test directory and double-click the program icon for Setup to install the self-assessment software and to run the tests. The self-assessment software requires that the CD remain in the drive while the tests are running.

Index

Hungry Minds, Inc. End-User License Agreement

READ THIS. You should carefully read these terms and conditions before opening the software packet(s) included with this book ("Book"). This is a license agreement ("Agreement") between you and Hungry Minds, Inc. ("HMI"). By opening the accompanying software packet(s), you acknowledge that you have read and accept the following terms and conditions. If you do not agree and do not want to be bound by such terms and conditions, promptly return the Book and the unopened software packet(s) to the place you obtained them for a full refund.

1. **License Grant.** HMI grants to you (either an individual or entity) a nonexclusive license to use one copy of the enclosed software program(s) (collectively, the "Software") solely for your own personal or business purposes on a single computer (whether a standard computer or a workstation component of a multi-user network). The Software is in use on a computer when it is loaded into temporary memory (RAM) or installed into permanent memory (hard disk, CD-ROM, or other storage device). HMI reserves all rights not expressly granted herein.

2. **Ownership.** HMI is the owner of all right, title, and interest, including copyright, in and to the compilation of the Software recorded on the disk(s) or CD-ROM ("Software Media"). Copyright to the individual programs recorded on the Software Media is owned by the author or other authorized copyright owner of each program. Ownership of the Software and all proprietary rights relating thereto remain with HMI and its licensers.

3. **Restrictions On Use and Transfer.**

   (a) You may only (i) make one copy of the Software for backup or archival purposes, or (ii) transfer the Software to a single hard disk, provided that you keep the original for backup or archival purposes. You may not (i) rent or lease the Software, (ii) copy or reproduce the Software through a LAN or other network system or through any computer subscriber system or bulletin-board system, or (iii) modify, adapt, or create derivative works based on the Software.

   (b) You may not reverse engineer, decompile, or disassemble the Software. You may transfer the Software and user documentation on a permanent basis, provided that the transferee agrees to accept the terms and conditions of this Agreement and you retain no copies. If the Software is an update or has been updated, any transfer must include the most recent update and all prior versions.

4. **Restrictions on Use of Individual Programs.** You must follow the individual requirements and restrictions detailed for each individual program in Appendix B of this Book. These limitations are also contained in the individual license agreements recorded on the Software Media. These limitations may include a requirement that after using the program for a specified period of time, the user must pay a registration fee or discontinue use. By opening the Software packet(s), you will be agreeing to abide by the licenses and restrictions for these individual programs that are detailed in Appendix B and on the Software Media. None of the material on this Software Media or listed in this Book may ever be redistributed, in original or modified form, for commercial purposes.

5. **Limited Warranty.**

   (a) HMI warrants that the Software and Software Media are free from defects in materials and workmanship under normal use for a period of sixty (60) days from the date of purchase of this Book. If HMI receives notification within the warranty period of defects in materials or workmanship, HMI will replace the defective Software Media.

(b) HMI AND THE AUTHOR OF THE BOOK DISCLAIM ALL OTHER WARRANTIES, EXPRESS OR IMPLIED, INCLUDING WITHOUT LIMITATION IMPLIED WARRANTIES OF MERCHANTABILITY AND FITNESS FOR A PARTICULAR PURPOSE, WITH RESPECT TO THE SOFTWARE, THE PROGRAMS, THE SOURCE CODE CONTAINED THEREIN, AND/OR THE TECHNIQUES DESCRIBED IN THIS BOOK. HMI DOES NOT WARRANT THAT THE FUNCTIONS CONTAINED IN THE SOFTWARE WILL MEET YOUR REQUIREMENTS OR THAT THE OPERATION OF THE SOFTWARE WILL BE ERROR FREE.

(c) This limited warranty gives you specific legal rights, and you may have other rights that vary from jurisdiction to jurisdiction.

6. Remedies.

(a) HMI's entire liability and your exclusive remedy for defects in materials and workmanship shall be limited to replacement of the Software Media, which may be returned to HMI with a copy of your receipt at the following address: Software Media Fulfillment Department, Attn.: *Dynamic HTML Weekend Crash Course*™, Hungry Minds, Inc., 10475 Crosspoint Blvd., Indianapolis, IN 46256, or call 1-800-762-2974. Please allow four to six weeks for delivery. This Limited Warranty is void if failure of the Software Media has resulted from accident, abuse, or misapplication. Any replacement Software Media will be warranted for the remainder of the original warranty period or thirty (30) days, whichever is longer.

(b) In no event shall HMI or the author be liable for any damages whatsoever (including without limitation damages for loss of business profits, business interruption, loss of business information, or any other pecuniary loss) arising from the use of or inability to use the Book or the Software, even if HMI has been advised of the possibility of such damages.

(c) Because some jurisdictions do not allow the exclusion or limitation of liability for consequential or incidental damages, the above limitation or exclusion may not apply to you.

7. U.S. Government Restricted Rights. Use, duplication, or disclosure of the Software for or on behalf of the United States of America, its agencies and/or instrumentalities (the "U.S. Government") is subject to restrictions as stated in paragraph (c)(1)(ii) of the Rights in Technical Data and Computer Software clause of DFARS 252.227-7013, or subparagraphs (c) (1) and (2) of the Commercial Computer Software - Restricted Rights clause at FAR 52.227-19, and in similar clauses in the NASA FAR supplement, as applicable.

8. General. This Agreement constitutes the entire understanding of the parties and revokes and supersedes all prior agreements, oral or written, between them and may not be modified or amended except in a writing signed by both parties hereto that specifically refers to this Agreement. This Agreement shall take precedence over any other documents that may be in conflict herewith. If any one or more provisions contained in this Agreement are held by any court or tribunal to be invalid, illegal, or otherwise unenforceable, each and every other provision shall remain in full force and effect.

Get Up to Speed
in a Weekend!